Winston Churchill and the Art of Leadership

For Bob Grieco, a true leader and friend

Winston Churchill and the Art of Leadership

How Winston Changed the World

William R. Nester

FRONTLINE BOOKS

First published in Great Britain in 2020 by
Frontline Books
An imprint of
Pen & Sword Books Ltd
Yorkshire – Philadelphia

ISBN 978 1 52678 124 6

A CIP catalogue record for this book is
available from the British Library.

Typeset by Mac Style
Printed and bound in the UK by TJ International Ltd,
Padstow, Cornwall.

MIX
Paper from
responsible sources
FSC
www.fsc.org   FSC® C013056

Pen & Sword Books Limited incorporates the imprints of Atlas,
Archaeology, Aviation, Discovery, Family History, Fiction, History,
Maritime, Military, Military Classics, Politics, Select, Transport,
True Crime, Air World, Frontline Publishing, Leo Cooper, Remember
When, Seaforth Publishing, The Praetorian Press, Wharncliffe
Local History, Wharncliffe Transport, Wharncliffe True Crime
and White Owl.

For a complete list of Pen & Sword titles please contact

PEN & SWORD BOOKS LIMITED
47 Church Street, Barnsley, South Yorkshire, S70 2AS, England
E-mail: enquiries@pen-and-sword.co.uk
Website: www.pen-and-sword.co.uk

Or

PEN AND SWORD BOOKS
1950 Lawrence Rd, Havertown, PA 19083, USA
E-mail: Uspen-and-sword@casematepublishers.com
Website: www.penandswordbooks.com

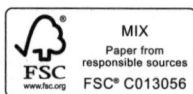

Contents

Acknowledgements

I want to express my deep gratitude and pleasure at having had the opportunity to work with the outstanding Frontline editorial team of Lisa Hoosan, Stephen Chumbley, John Grehan and Martin Mace, who were always as kind as they were professional. I am especially grateful to Martin for finding and captioning that wonderful array of Churchill photos.

List of Illustrations

Second Lieutenant Winston Churchill in 1895.

Churchill whilst being held as a prisoner of war in the Second Anglo-Boer War.

Churchill watching German Army exercises near Breslau, Germany in 1906.

Churchill at the Siege of Sidney Street in London's East End in January 1911.

Churchill in the uniform of the First Lord of the Admiralty.

Churchill, wearing his French helmet, at the headquarters of XXXIII Corps, French Army, at Camblain L'Abbé on 15 December 1915.

Lieutenant Colonel Winston Churchill pictured in uniform during the winter of 1915/16.

Churchill at his seat in the Cabinet Room at No.10 Downing Street, London, during the Second World War.

Churchill tours a section of the South Coast to see anti-invasion defences and preparations in the summer of 1940.

Churchill inspecting the damage caused by the first day of the Blitz.

Churchill seeing the work of the emergency services first-hand.

Churchill on the bridge of HMS *Kelvin* during his voyage across the English Channel en route to Normandy on 12 June 1944.

The 'Big Three', Churchill, Roosevelt and Stalin, during the Yalta Conference in February 1945.

The Royal Family and Winston Churchill waving at the crowds that have gathered in front of Buckingham Palace on VE Day.

Churchill at Chartwell.

Churchill during a visit to Denmark, 9 October 1950.

Introduction

'History with its flickering lamp stumbles along the trail of the past, trying to reconstruct its scenes, to revive its echoes and kindle with pale gleams the passion of former days.'

'For my part, I consider that it will be found much better by all parties to leave the past to history, especially as I propose to write that history myself.'

Winston Churchill is among history's most dazzling characters, renowned as the great statesman who led Britain through first the devastating defeats and then the exhilarating triumphs of the Second World War. King George VI asked him to become prime minister on 10 May 1940, the day that Nazi Germany's blitzkrieg erupted into France and the Low Countries. At the age of 65, Churchill had finally achieved his greatest ambition amidst the worst perils that ever confronted his nation: 'I felt as if I were walking with destiny and that all my past life had been but a preparation for this hour and for this trial.'[1]

It is not as well known that in Churchill's earlier decades he was a decorated soldier who fought in scores of battles, killed a dozen or so enemy soldiers and even spent a month as a prisoner of war before making a daring escape. His last round of combat was a half-year stint in the trenches of the First World War. He volunteered to serve there as atonement for disgrace. He had resigned as First Lord of the Admiralty after the Dardanelles campaign that he had advocated became a blood-drenched stalemate. On the front line he hoped either to retrieve his honour as a live or dead hero. He went as a major and was promoted to lieutenant colonel but Whitehall rejected his request to receive a brigadier general's star and command an infantry brigade. To that latest disappointment, he penned these words: 'I have fallen back reposefully into the arms of fate but with an underlying instinct that all will be well and that my greatest work is at hand.'[2] His fatalism was rewarded with redemption. Prime Minister David Lloyd George offered him the Ministry of Munitions in his government. And from there he resumed his seesaw political career, alternating between phases as an insider and as a pariah until 1940 when he finally became prime minister.

A handful of leaders in history personify their country during an especially challenging and tragic era. For the United States, one thinks of George Washington for the Revolution, Abraham Lincoln for the Civil War and Franklin Roosevelt for the Great Depression and the Second World War. There are others like Queen Elizabeth I, Louis XIV and Napoleon renowned for the ages named after them. Rarer still is the leader who becomes the enduring face for a nation that transformed itself over generations. Winston Churchill personified Great Britain during the Victorian Era, the First World War, the interwar era, the Second World War and the Cold War.

The Values

What did Winston Churchill believe in other than his own destiny? Above all he was a patriotic Briton who gloried in his nation's history, culture, triumphs and empire:

> In the British Empire we not only look out across the seas toward each other, but backwards to our own history, to the Magna Carta, to Habeas Corpus, to the Petition of Right, to Trial by Jury, to English Common Law and to Parliamentary democracy. These are the milestones and monuments that mark the path along which the British race has marched to leadership and freedom.[3]

As for Britain's lack of a political blueprint, he would retort: 'Why the British Constitution is mainly British common sense.'[4] One institution above all was the jewel in the political crown: 'The House of Commons ... is the citadel of British liberty; it is the foundation of our laws; its traditions and privileges are as lively today as when it broke the arbitrary power of the Crown and substituted that Constitutional Monarchy under which we have enjoyed so many blessings.'[5]

From a young age Churchill was obsessed with becoming one of Britain's greatest heroes and leaders. He consciously lived in history and history subconsciously lived in him. Clement Atlee found at least half a millennium in him: 'One layer was certainly the seventeenth century. The eighteenth century in him is obvious. There was the nineteenth century and a large slice, of course, of the twentieth century; and another curious layer which may possibly have been the twenty-first.'[6] Most vitally, Churchill was born and bred a Victorian who lived, often uncomfortably, through most of the twentieth century. These words best reveal his most cherished values: 'But what is the purpose which has brought us all together? It is the conviction that the life of Britain, her glories and message to the world, can only be achieved by national unity and national unity can only be preserved upon a cause which is larger than the nation itself.'[7]

Yet Churchill also cherished the American side of his heritage from his mother. During speaking tours in the United States, he enjoyed telling audiences that he was 'fifty per cent American and one hundred per cent British'.[8] He revelled in the glory that Britain had given birth to America along with other English-speaking nations, best expressed with his four-volume *History of the English Speaking Peoples*.[9] In a 1943 speech at Harvard University, he explained what bound them: 'Law, language, literature … Common conceptions of what is right and decent, a marked regard for fair play, especially to the weak and poor, a stern sentiment of impartial justice and above all the love of personal freedom.' He then made a stunning proposal to reverse the history that drove Americans and Britons apart two centuries earlier: 'This gift of a common tongue is a priceless inheritance and it may well some day become the foundation of a common citizenship.'[10]

History rather than ideology was Churchill's guiding light: 'No greater calamity can happen to a people than to break utterly with its past. It is only by studying the past that we can see, however dimly or partially, the future. It may well be that it is only by respecting the past that we can be worthy of the future.'[11] He was at once a man of action, thought, ambition and ethics, proceeding consciously through time:

> History with its flickering lamp stumbles along the trail of the past, trying to reconstruct its scenes, to revive its echoes and kindle with pale gleams the passion of former day. What is the worth of this? The only guide to a man is his conscience. The only shield to his memory is the rectitude and sincerity of his actions. It is very imprudent to walk through life without this shield because we are so often mocked by the failure of our hopes and the upsetting of our calculations; but with this shield, however the fates may play, we march always in the ranks of honour.[12]

As a student of history, Churchill disdained political theories and ideologies with glib pseudo-answers to human affairs, like the Marxist dogma that class struggle determines everything. He was a supremely practical man who conceived and asserted arrays of possible means to his ends until he found what worked. Along the way that led to a lot of trials and errors from which his enemies drew ample ammunition with which to attack him. With time he thickened his skin to their barrages, asserting that: 'History judges a man, not by his victories or defeats, but by their results.'[13] More specifically, he found: 'In history lie all the secrets of statecraft.'[14]

He profoundly appreciated complexity, change and paradox:

> The world, nature, human beings do not move like machines. The edges are never clear-cut but always frayed. Nature never draws a line without smudging it. Conditions are so variable, episodes so unexpected, experiences so conflicting, that flexibility of judgment and a willingness to assume a somewhat humbler attitude towards external phenomena may well play their part in the equipment of a modern Prime Minister.[15]

At the very least one should avoid hypocrisy because: 'It is always more easy to discover and proclaim general principles than to apply them.'[16]

An acute awareness of life's evanescence drove Winston Churchill to do all he could with what time he had. During a dinner party, he expressed this universal lament: 'Curse ruthless time. Curse mortality. How cruelly short is the allotted span for all we must cram in.'[17] Mostly he was fatalistic about what was impossible to change: 'Death was certain sooner or later. It only involved a change of state or at the worst a serene oblivion.'[18]

What was the point of it all? For life's deepest mysteries, he found satisfying answers in Zen-like ambiguities rather than dogmatic certainties. He experienced throughout his life a spectrum of devastating failures and exhilarating triumphs. What they shared was that each was a critical turning point that eventually led him to heights of power and fame. For instance, he flunked his first two entrance exams to Sandhurst and would likely have flunked the third had the instructor not had asked for the answer to a question 'which I happened to have learned scarcely a week before'. Had he been asked a question for which he had no answer, 'the whole of my life would have been altered and that I suppose would have altered a great many other lives, which in their turn and so on'.[19] After pondering the roles of will and fate in shaping the course of one's life, he concluded that they 'are identical'. He found a magical analogy for this seeming paradox:

> I have always loved butterflies ... The butterfly is the Fact – gleaming, fluttering, settling for an instant with wings fully spread to the sun,

then vanishing in the shades of the forest. Whether you believe in Free Will or Determination all depends on the slanting glimpses you had of the colour of his wings – which are in fact at least two colours at the same time.[20]

Throughout his life he suffered setbacks that much later proved to be blessings in disguise or, as he put it: 'you never can tell whether bad luck may not after all turn out to be good luck.' For instance, he dislocated his shoulder when disembarking in a turbulent sea at Bombay. That severely crimped his polo playing, kept him from playing tennis and had a tendency to pop out at importune times, like during the exertions of combat. It also inhibited his ability to swing a sabre in battle. And that just might have saved his life at Omdurman when he carried a Mauser pistol instead and shot dead three Arabs who were firing and rushing toward him. This taught him: 'One must never forget when misfortunes come that it is quite possible they are saving one from something much worse; or that when you make some great mistake, it may very easily serve you better than the best advised decision. Life is a whole and luck is a whole and no part of them can be separated from the rest.'[21]

If some dimension of life was determined, what determined it? He was not conventionally religious, rarely attending church other than for high holidays, weddings and funerals. He liked to describe himself as among the Church of England's flying buttresses rather than pillars. He saw the value of organized religion chiefly in helping maintain social order but considered 'too much religion of any kind ... a bad thing' because it demanded blind faith and obedience over detached reason and free choice. He concluded that if a supreme Creator existed 'who gave us our minds as well as our souls, he would be offended if they did not always run smoothly together ... I therefore adopted quite early in life a system of believing whatever I wanted to believe, while at the same time leaving reason to pursue unfettered whatever paths she was capable of treading.'[22] As a young man, he concluded 'that if you tried your best to live an honourable life and did your duty and were faithful to friends and not unkind to the weak and poor, it did not matter much what you believed or disbelieved ... All would come out right. This is what would ... I suppose be called "the Religion of Healthy-Mindedness."' He was certainly open to the possible existence and intervention of higher powers, he just did not have a name for them or an explanation for their origin, reason for being and often puzzling intrusions in human affairs.

He was a classic manic–depressive who seesawed between exhilaration and the abyss, between Eros and Thanatos. He called his down times the 'black dog'. At times he struggled to resist the temptation to end it all. He admitted to his doctor that: 'I've no desire to quit this world, but thoughts, desperate thoughts, come into the head.' Because of that 'I don't like standing near the edge of a platform when an express train is passing through. I like to stand back and if possible to get a pillar between me and the train. I don't like to stand by the side of a ship and look down into the water. A second's action would end everything.'[23] His death drive helped fuel his reckless courage on the battlefield. He once wrote to his wife that a mutual friend had 'interested me a great deal by her talk about her doctor in Germany, who completely cured her depression. I think this man might be useful to me – if my black dog returns.'[24] The depression did indeed return many times but he never ended up on any psychotherapist's couch.

Action was his antidote to depression: 'I like things to happen and if they don't happen I like to make them happen.'[25] He was addicted to adventure, the more perilous the more thrilling. As if with a spirit of each perched on separate shoulders whispering in his ears, he seesawed between prudence and recklessness on military and political battlefields alike. And he justified either type of act with some mix of intellect and intuition. Fortunately for his life and posterity, his reckless courage was immortal, at least for ninety years. He was under fire scores of times at battlefields in Cuba, India, Sudan, South Africa and France but received not a scratch. He explained to his brother that he forced himself to be brave to overcome what he believed was an innate weakness: 'Being in many ways a coward – particularly in school – there is no ambition I cherish so keenly as to gain a reputation of personal courage.'[26] Fatalism bolstered his courage. Once while he was serving in the front-line trenches during the First World War, a shell obliterated his dugout and fellow officer just fifteen minutes after a general called him for a conference. He wrote Clementine about his near-death experience with this lesson: 'Now see from this how vain it is to worry about things. It is all chance and our wayward footsteps are best planted without too much calculation. One must yield oneself simply & naturally to the mood of the game and trust in God, which is another way of saying the same thing.'[27]

His baptism of fire came on his 21st birthday as a liaison officer with the Spanish army fighting Cuban rebels. He described the thrill of being on campaign:

It is still dark, but the sky is paling ... We are on our horses, in uniform; our revolvers are loaded ... long files of armed and laden men are shuffling off toward the enemy. He may be near ... We have nothing to do with their quarrels. Except in personal self-defence we can take no part in their combats. But we feel it is a great moment in our lives … we devoutly hope that something will happen; yet at the same time we do not want to be hurt or killed. What is it then that we do want? It is that allure of youth – adventure for adventure's sake.[28]

He summed up his thrill for battle: 'Nothing in life is so exhilarating as to be shot at without result.'[29] He was a genuine warrior but a reluctant soldier. He hated the tedium of army life and even more being subjected to the orders of others which was why he quit to enter politics.

He glorified and romanticized war no matter how many of its horrors he experienced. He did lament that:

War, which used to be cruel and magnificent, has now become cruel and squalid … It is all the fault of Democracy and Science … Instead of a small number of well-trained professionals championing their country's cause with ancient weapons and a beautiful intricacy of archaic manoeuvre, sustained at every moment by the applause of their nation, we now have entire populations, including even women and children, pitted against one another in brutish mutual extermination and only a set of blear-eyed clerks left to add up the butcher's bill. From the moment Democracy was admitted to or rather forced upon the battlefield, War ceased to be a gentleman's game.[30]

He reflected on the stark differences in the scale and mentality of the Little Wars and the World War that he fought:

It was not like the Great War. Nobody expected to be killed. Here and there in every regiment or battalion, half a dozen, a score, at the worst thirty or forty, would pay the forfeit; but to the great mass of those who took part in the little wars of Britain in the vanished light hearted days, this was only a sporting element in a splendid game. Most of us were fated to see a war where the hazards were reversed, where death was the general expectation and severe wounds were counted as lucky escapes, where whole brigades were shorn away under the steel flail of artillery and machine guns.[31]

He took his first flying lessons in 1911 when he was First Lord of the Admiralty, 37 years old and having just established the Royal Naval Air

Service. He explained the mingled professional and psychological motives that drove him to share the danger of his men: 'Once I had started flying from a motive in which a sense of duty as well as excitement and curiosity played its part, I continued from sheer joy and pleasure.'[32] He survived one crash landing and several of his trainers died when their planes spun out of control. Yet he would have kept flying had his wife Clementine not made him promise to quit.

Being accident-prone compounded the countless risks he took throughout his life. Numerous horses threw him, giving him several concussions. As a boy playing tag he jumped off a bridge to evade his pursuers and the impact rendered him unconscious for three days and bedridden for three months. He looked the wrong way while crossing a New York street and an automobile moving 30 miles an hour struck him; he suffered lacerations but no broken bones. By one count after the Second World War 'he suffered a heart attack, three bouts of pneumonia, two strokes and two operations'.[33] But rather than intimidate him, his accidents spurred him to greater efforts.

The Character

The hundreds of photos of Winston Churchill somehow make him appear larger than he actually was, unless he is depicted standing beside taller others. Actually, at 5ft 6in, his height was below average. He had a large head atop a body that was slender as a youth but fattened steadily from his twenties. As he gained girth, his hair receded until he was almost completely bald. That accentuated his natural baby-face that sometimes beamed angelically and sometimes scowled bulldog-like. He had pale blue eyes. The £25 dead or alive wanted poster that authorities issued after his prison escape during the Boer War added these rather unflattering details: 'walks with a slight stoop, pale appearance, red brown hair, almost invisible small moustache, speaks through the nose, cannot pronounce the letter S ... during long conversations occasionally makes a rattling noise in his throat.'[34]

He was a sensualist who took two languorous daily baths, morning and late afternoon. His skin was sensitive to friction so he wore silk underwear and slept naked. Indeed he was a nudist who indulged himself on secluded beaches and stripped as soon as he arrived home and roamed around unconcerned about what the servants or even his family thought. He chain-smoked seven-inch Cuban cigars, mostly Romeo y Julietas and La Aroma de Cubas. He was pickled for much of his life. He began each morning with a Johnny Walker Red scotch and water, proceeded to champagne and various wines with lunch and dinner, then evening brandies and whiskies until he plodded off to bed. When someone once wondered whether all that drinking was good for him, he replied: 'All I can say is that I have taken more out of alcohol than alcohol has taken out of me.'[35] He was no gourmet but instead gorged on such standard British fare as Irish stew, Yorkshire pudding, fried whitefish, roast beef and chocolate eclairs. He not only loved music but had a soundtrack for his life where certain songs evoked certain periods:

> I have got tunes in my head for every war I have been to and indeed for every critical or exciting phase in my life. Some day ... I am going to have them all collected in gramophone records and then I will sit in a chair and smoke my cigar, while pictures and faces, moods and sensations long vanished return.[36]

He was a night-owl, often keeping guests lively with stories and increasingly incapacitated with alcohol until well after midnight. He was a late riser and often received early visitors in bed. He was anything but punctual, often keeping his colleagues, underlings, guests and even superiors waiting with worsening irritation for his appearance. He had as little common sense of money as he had of time. He gleefully gambled on stock markets and in casinos where he lost prodigious sums. He loved the movies, especially sentimental historic epics like 'That Hamilton Woman' and zany comedies starring Charlie Chaplin or the Marx Brothers. He was a crack shot and erratic driver and flyer. He engaged in massive understatement with this line: 'I have in my life concentrated more on self-expression than self-denial.'[37]

He had an authoritarian personality or, more colloquially, was a control freak. That was hardly surprising. His parents warped his character development in two severe ways – they neglected him emotionally and indulged him with every aristocratic privilege. For each of his ninety years he remained a spoiled child who craved attention and threw tantrums when he could not get it. A friend once remarked: 'Winston is a man of simple tastes. He is always prepared to put up with the best of everything.'[38] And he could be insufferable if he was forced to put up with less. When enraged, he cursed at length with a sailor's gusto and a poet's creativity. It is said that no man is a hero to his butler. Not just Churchill's butler but most of his servants and assistants would be terrified publicly to admit that during his lifetime. Nonetheless, most of them loved him more than they hated him.[39] One Chartwell servant recalled that while Churchill 'could be very ruthless', he was also exciting to be with. 'I had never been in a house like that. It was alive, restless. When he went away it was still as a mouse. When he was there it was vibrating.'[40]

With an ego as bloated as his intellect, Churchill made enemies easily. His self-confidence was nearly always excessive. 'Of course I am an egotist,' he once told Clement Atlee. 'Where do you get if you aren't?'[41] He once explained his view of human nature and himself: 'We are all worms. But I do believe that I am a glowworm.'[42] He was a notorious scene-stealer who craved the limelight. Monarch-like, he dominated talk at dinner tables and drawing rooms which most of his listeners tolerated because his wit and discourses were usually entertaining and insightful. He was not beyond embellishing details. Arthur Balfour once gave him this backhanded compliment: 'I admire the exaggerated way you tell the truth.'[43]

Academically he was a late bloomer. He was regularly at the bottom of his school classes and failed Sandhurst's entrance exams twice before barely squeaking through on his third try. He could only learn what he found interesting or practical so he had mental blocks to subjects like mathematics and Latin that bored him. Yet he was extremely intelligent with a photographic memory for what truly moved him. He could memorize epic poems and prose passages by heart. For two hours each morning he sped-read his way through a stack of newspapers arranged according to his feelings toward the editorial page, starting with the esteemed *Times* and *Daily Telegraph* then descending through the ranks to the despised *Daily Worker*. He was a passionate bibliophile. Indeed for Churchill being with books was akin to lovemaking:

> If you cannot read all your books at any rate handle or, as it were, fondle them – peer into them, let them fall open where they will, read from the first sentence that arrests the eye, set them back on the shelves with your own hands, arrange them on your own plan so that if you do not know what is in them, you will at least know where they are.[44]

Romantic passion apparently skipped a generation in the Churchill line. Unlike his father and son, Churchill was no libertine. He loved only one woman, Clementine, whom he married. They had an affectionate relationship – she fondly called him 'Pig', he called her 'Cat'. After five years of marriage he penned her these revealing words apologizing for causing a spate between them the previous day: 'You know what a prey I am to nerves & prepossessions. I should like to kiss your dear face and stroke your baby cheeks and make you purr softly in my arms. Don't be disloyal to me in your thoughts. I have no one but you to break the loneliness of a bustling and bustled existence.'[45] He could share with her dark secrets that he denied to all others such as:

> You know so much about me, & with your intuition have measured the good & bad in my nature. Alas I have no every good opinion of myself. At times I think I could conquer everything & then again I know I am only a weak vain fool. But your love for me is the greatest glory and recognition that has or will ever befall me … I only wish I were more worthy of you, & more able to meet the inner needs of your soul.[46]

Yet affection rather than passion prevailed between them. Although somehow he managed to sire four children with her, they mostly slept and vacationed separately. His only other relationship with a woman was platonic. In India he began what became a four-year largely epistolary liaison with Pamela Plowden, who finally dumped him after he finally admitted that he was as disinterested in marriage as he was in sex with her.

Biographer William Manchester noted that Churchill delayed marriage until he was 34 years old and was likely a virgin at the altar. He went on to observe that 'he was never really comfortable in the company of women. One explanation may lie in his mother's affairs.'[47] Manchester attributed Churchill's fumbling attempts throughout his life until his mother's death to win her attention and affection explains his ineptness with women: 'He didn't know what to say to them. The only subject which really interested him was himself. He knew none of the delicate moves that could lead to intimacy … In mixed society he was a combination of Wellington and Peel – "I have no small talk," the great duke had said, "and Peel has no manners."'[48] A related reason may have been Churchill's discovery that his father had died of syphilis, a shameful and painful fate that he was determined to avoid. Churchill himself admitted that he sublimated his sexuality with an array of other outlets, especially writing: 'The reason I can write so much is that I don't waste my essence in bed.'[49]

A neglected child often becomes a neglectful parent. Churchill and Clementine were certainly the former and, to varying degrees, the latter. Clementine disliked children in general and barely tolerated her own. She found each pregnancy and its aftermath a torturous ordeal that left her physically and emotionally drained. She delegated as much of her children's upbringing as possible to their nannies and boarding schools. Churchill was not as distant from his children as his own parents were from him. He did occasionally squeeze in time for brief play with them when they were young and conversation with them at the dinner table. He adored his daughters, Diana, Sarah and Mary. He had a tempestuous relationship with his only son, Randolph, with frequent shouting matches between them. Randolph struggled to assert himself in his father's domineering shadow, only to fall far short during his own brief time in Parliament and became notorious as a mean-spirited womanizer and alcoholic.

The Renaissance Man

Winston Churchill was a master writer and speaker of the English language. In his remarks awarding Churchill an honorary American citizenship, President John Kennedy explained: 'He mobilized the English language and sent it into battle.'[50] Churchill himself once quipped: 'In the course of my life I have often had to eat my words and I must confess that I have always found it a wholesome diet.'[51] He admitted that a monetary incentive partly explained his fluency: 'If I found the right words you must remember that I have always earned my living by my pen and by my tongue.'[52] Far more vitally, he experienced sheer delight in literary creation: 'Writing a long and substantial book is like having a friend and companion at your side, to whom you can always turn for comfort and amusement and whose society becomes more attractive as a new and widening field of interest is lighted in your mind.'[53]

During a 1948 Parliamentary debate when assertions arose among the speakers about how history would recall them, Churchill declared: 'For my part, I consider that it will be found much better by all parties to leave the past to history, especially as I propose to write that history myself.'[54] That was no idle boast, or threat, depending on one's point of view. His most prolific biographer, Martin Gilbert, counted 15 million published words and fifty-eight books to his name, including 'seven books of memoirs, sixteen volumes of history (which contained within them his personal memoirs of both world wars), twenty-two volumes of his own speeches, four selections of his newspaper and magazine articles, two volumes of essays, six biographical volumes (four about his illustrious military ancestor John Churchill, first Duke of Marlborough and two about his father Lord Randolph Churchill) and one novel'. In addition, he 'wrote 842 articles in all, 232 of them his eye-witness reports from theatres of war in Cuba, the North-West Frontier, Sudan and South Africa. The first, sent from Cuba, was published in London on 13 December 1895, two weeks after his twenty-first birthday.'[55] He recited rather than wrote nearly all of that extraordinary output. Although he penned his early works, as he acquired fame and money he employed a staff of a dozen researchers, typists and, most importantly, three overworked secretaries who took down the words that he dictated. He could afford that team. During his decades of writing, he was among the world's best-paid authors.

If Churchill is among history's greatest orators, he worked very hard at it, often spending a day or so writing and rehearsing a half-hour speech. A defect in his palate gave him a slight lisp and trouble pronouncing the letter S. He compensated for those deficiencies with his stentorian, grumbling, baritone voice. He made his first public speech at a Conservative Party rally at Bath in November 1898. Even though he had carefully composed his words, he was naturally nervous before he gave it. To his relief, the crowd 'cheered a lot in all the right places when I paused to give them a chance and even at others which I had not foreseen. At the end they clapped loudly and for quite a long time. So I could do it after all.'[56] He gloried in his oratorical powers, admitting that: 'There is nothing that gives greater pleasure to a speaker than seeing his great points go home. It is like the bullet that strikes the body of the victim.'[57]

He was the master of the witty, searing quip. Most erupted spontaneously. Others he forged long beforehand and positioned in his mind's arsenal for the most appropriate moment. He made no secret of the latter. When someone once praised him for some witticism he uttered in a small gathering, he remarked: 'Improvised be damned! I thought of it this morning in my bath and I wish now I hadn't wasted it on this crowd.'[58] Manchester related several hilarious stories that captured the essence of his rapid-fire humour. At the White House, Franklin Roosevelt wheeled himself into the bathroom just as Churchill rose naked from the tub. To Roosevelt's embarrassed apology, Churchill replied: 'The Prime Minister of Great Britain has nothing to hide from the President of the United States.' When he walked into a men's restroom to find Labour Party leader Clement Atlee before one of a line of urinals, he positioned himself at the most distant. Atlee remarked, 'Feeling standoffish today, Winston?' 'That's right,' Churchill retorted. 'Every time you see something big you want to nationalize it.' Perhaps his most celebrated quip was to Lady Nancy Astor's remark that, were he her husband she would poison his soup: 'Nancy, if I were your husband I'd drink it.'[59]

Not only was he a brilliant wordsmith, but he became an accomplished painter of landscapes, seascapes, still-lives and portraits.[60] He was only half-joking when he remarked that:

Happy are the painters for they shall not be lonely. Light and colour, peace and hope will keep them company to the end or almost to the end, of the day ... When I get to Heaven I mean to spend a considerable portion of my first million years in painting and so get to the bottom of the subject. But then I shall require a gayer palette than I get here. There will be a whole range of wonderful new colours which will delight the celestial eye.[61]

Like Leonardo da Vinci, he had a wide-ranging imagination that conceived many inventions that teams of technicians later developed. Roosevelt marvelled that: 'Winston has fifty ideas a day and three or four are good.'[62] At least two revolutionized warfare. During the First World War, he pushed through the tank's development, derided by the military elite as 'Winston's Folly'. The tank was literally and figuratively the decisive breakthrough technology on the Western Front. During the Second World War, he nurtured development of sonar. Sonar won the Battle of the Atlantic and other anti-submarine campaigns. He also conceived such ideas as the Mulberry artificial ports for the Normandy invasion, dropping strips of aluminium foil to blind enemy radar and the undersea oil 'Pluto' pipeline from England to France. He championed the development of radar for military purposes shortly after learning about the concept in 1935. In his 1931 book of essays called *Amid These Storms: Thoughts and Adventures*, he 'predicted the atomic bomb and atomic-powered electrification (and risks to humanity); bioengineering of crops and animals (and perhaps people); and television (which, when it became a reality, he detested)'.[63] His mind did indeed roam among ideas from the sublime to the ridiculous. He backed scientist Geoffrey Pyke's call to create aircraft carriers built from a composite of ice and wood pulp for operations in the North Atlantic beyond the range of land-based aircraft. Usually he played a critical devil's advocate role during meetings with his scientists. For instance, he once posed this puzzle to an expert on the atomic bomb project: 'Uranium is continually halving itself. Why is there any uranium left on earth?'[64] In a speech at Harvard University during the Second World War, he declared that: 'The empires of the future are the empires of the mind.'[65]

The Art of Power

For all his achievements in literature and painting, Winston Churchill will always be best remembered as a statesman. He learned the art of politics and power by studying leading politicians, starting with his father, Randolph Churchill. Twenty-six of the thirty essays in his book *Great Contemporaries* explored the ends and means of such men.[66] He found no underlying principles or characteristics among them. Each had his own unique approach that racked up wins and losses. What worked for oneself in one situation might well work against oneself in the next. As such the ability rapidly to assess and either seize opportunities or blunt threats was crucial. In modern politics, one's ability to inspire a mass public was also critical, although some leaders could be just as successful working behind the scenes. He was well aware of how power can tempt the wielder with corruption and other abuses: 'When one has reached the summit of power and surmounted so many obstacles, there is a danger of becoming convinced that one can do anything one likes.'[67] By cherry-picking the best attributes of his models and avoiding the worst, he sought to excel in all dimensions of politics.

Although Churchill speaks here of war, at every level of politics from global to personal he always sought ways to outfox an adversary if a direct approach failed:

> There are many kinds of manoeuvres in war, some only of which take place upon the battlefield. There are manoeuvres far to the flank or rear. There are manoeuvres in time, in diplomacy, in mechanics, in psychology, all of which are removed from the battlefield, but react often decisively upon it and the object of all is to find easier ways, other than sheer slaughter, of achieving the main purpose. The distinction between politics and strategy diminishes as the point of view is raised. At the summit true politics and strategy are one. The manoeuvre which brings an ally into the field is as serviceable as that which wins a great battle. The manoeuvre which gains an important strategic point may be less valuable than that which placates or overawes a dangerous neutral.[68]

Several key principles guided Churchill's foreign policies. Two related maxims were peace through strength and go to war only after having exhausted all other means to defend or enhance one's national interests. Skilled diplomacy was critical to preserving or enhancing one's national interests. That necessity often rose with the vileness of the regime represented across the table: 'One has to recognize lots of things and people in this world of sin and woe that one does not like. The reason for having diplomatic relations is not to confer a compliment but to secure a convenience.'[69] He believed in being magnanimous in victory because a generous peace tends to last longer than a vindictive peace: 'I have always urged fighting wars and other contentions with might ... till overwhelming victory and then offering the hand of friendship to the vanquished.'[70] One strategy above all should guide British statesmen: 'British policy for four hundred years has been to oppose the strongest power in Europe by weaving together a combination of other countries against the bully ... It is thus through the centuries we have maintained our life and power.'[71]

He saw war as a central and inseparable part of human history: 'The story of the human race is war. Except for brief and precarious interludes there has never been peace in the world; and before history began murderous strife was universal and unending.'[72] He certainly believed that it was better to die on one's feet than live on one's knees: 'You may have to fight when there is no hope of victory, because it is better to perish than live as slaves.'[73] Having experienced war at every level in the field and in government, he was well aware of its bewildering paradoxes: 'The unexpected intervenes in every stage. The will power of the enemy impinges itself upon the prescribed or hoped for course of events. Victory is traditionally elusive. Accidents happen. Mistakes are made. Sometimes right things turn out wrong and quite often wrong things turn out right.'[74] He certainly knew the essence for successfully waging war: 'Almost the first of the great principles is to seize the initiative, to rivet the attention of the enemy on your action and to confront him with a series of novel and unexpected situations which leaves him no time to pursue a policy of his own.'[75] History's greatest military commanders share many outlooks and actions, most importantly the relentless drive to destroy the enemy's will to resist as creatively, rapidly and lightly in lives and treasure as possible. Yet a wide and often unbridgeable gap can separate knowing what to do from actually doing it.

Winston Churchill was a brilliant war leader for inspiration but not for strategy, where his vivid imagination frequently led him astray. His strategic judgment was mostly flawed and often badly executed when it was good. During the rare times when his strategic sense was correct, inept field commanders ruined it, such as in the 1915 Dardanelles and 1940 Narvik campaigns. During the Second World War, Churchill championed ventures that nibbled at the edges of the German, Italian and Japanese empires instead of striking decisively and overwhelmingly as daggers toward their respective hearts.

Churchill was at his very worst in the tug-of-war over strategy with Roosevelt and his administration for the war in Europe. He did everything possible to delay indefinitely the invasion of France by pressuring the

White House to set aside its superior judgment and invade North Africa in November 1942, Sicily in July 1943 and Italy in September 1943. The Italian campaign was a disaster for the Allies, a brutal slog up the mountainous peninsula that drained troops and supplies that should have been deployed on the flat or rolling countryside of France, then the Low Countries and ultimately Germany. Roosevelt finally drew lines in the sand against Churchill's demands for campaigns in the Aegean Sea and Balkans for 1944 that would have further frittered away Allied power in strategic dead-ends. Instead, Roosevelt got him reluctantly to support the invasions of Normandy in June 1944 and the Rivera in August 1944 that eventually led to Germany's decisive defeat on the Western Front. Churchill was nearly as myopic in the Far East. He opposed the effort to keep Chiang Kai-shek and his army supplied even though those Nationalist troops along with the Chinese communists tied down two million Japanese troops. In Burma, he sought to reconquer that entire colony when a parsimonious strategy would have deployed enough troops in the north to retake and defend the Burma Road that helped supply the Nationalist Chinese army, then entice the Japanese to destroy themselves in fruitless attempts to overrun the defenders.

Churchill's most important military advisor was General Alan Brooke, the Chief of Staff. Brooke's journal provides fascinating insights into Churchill, including his strategic myopia: 'Perhaps his most remarkable failing is that he can never see the whole strategical problem at once. His gaze always settles on some definite part of the canvas and the rest of the picture is lost.' During one stretch in early 1944, the prime minister's wild ideas so disturbed Brooke that 'I began to wonder whether I was in Alice in Wonderland ... I ... am honestly getting very doubtful about his balance of mind ... It is a ghastly situation ... I feel like a man chained to the chariot of a lunatic.'[76]

Each war is unique. The strategies and tactics that might work for a nation in one war might work against it in the next. A common failing of many less than great generals is that they keep trying to refight the previous war. They do so from some mix of habit, lack of creativity and desire to purge the ghosts of their previous mistakes that haunt them. Churchill's obsession with the Balkans and Europe's alleged 'soft underbelly' during the Second World War might partly be explained as his attempts to succeed where he failed in the First World War.

Churchill was a better tactician than strategist. During the First World War, he condemned the over the top mass infantry assaults that merely inflicted ever more hundreds of thousands of unnecessary deaths and horrendous wounds to one's fellow countrymen. He explained: 'Battles are won by slaughter and manoeuvre. The greater the general, the more he contributes in manoeuvre, the less he demands in slaughter.'[77] His vision was critical not just in developing tanks but the most effective ways to deploy them on campaign. He envisioned masses of tanks either encircling and destroying masses of infantry or smashing through the enemy's defences and then rolling up the flanks or penetrating deep in the rear to destroy supply depots and communication lines.

Winston Churchill could only become a statesman and strategist after decades of being a politician. He won sixteen of twenty-one elections that he fought between 1899 and 1955. That record may be less impressive than it seems. Both the Conservative and Liberal Parties found him safe seats after he lost contested constituencies. He represented in succession Oldham, Northwest Manchester, Dundee and Epping, although he resided in none of them. Yet, regardless of the outcome, he revelled in each election campaign's intense three weeks, the speeches before often boisterous crowds and the endless handshakes and exhortations. He recognized that: 'No part of the education of a politician is more indispensable than the fighting of elections. Here you come into contact with all sorts of persons and every current of national life ... Dignity may suffer ... much has to be accepted with a shrug, a sigh or a smile; but at any rate one knows a good deal about what happens and why.'[78] Thick skin was essential and the thicker the better because: 'In war you can only be killed once, but in politics many times.'[79]

The House of Commons was Churchill's political temple where he exalted in the speeches and harangues on the floor and the backroom horse-trading and comradery. When that chamber's political course seemed askew, he would remind his colleagues on both sides of floor of certain fundamentals, such as: 'It must be remembered that the function of Parliament is not only to pass good laws, but to stop bad laws', 'Parliament can compel people to obey or submit but it cannot compel them to agree' or 'It is not Parliament that should rule: it is the people who should rule through Parliament'.[80] As for representing the people, he thought Britain's two-party system superior to Europe's multi-party systems:

Much might be said for and against the two-party system. But no one can doubt that it adds to the stability and cohesion of the State. The alternation of Parties in power, like the rotation of crops, has beneficial results. Each of the two Parties has services to render in the development of the national life; and the succession of new and different points of view is a real benefit to the country.[81]

Churchill provoked political controversy wherever he intruded. Those who had to deal directly with him either loved or hated him, with usually far more among the latter. He rubbed a lot of people the wrong way, including countless constituents and powerholders. His enemies condemned him for being an egoist, publicity hound, double-dealer and Machiavellian, accusations that his friends and even he himself could not deny. He once admitted to his mother that: 'I do not care so much for the principles that I advocate as for the impression which my words produce & the reputation which they give me.'[82]

Nonetheless, Churchill was magnanimous in victory or longevity to his political foes. For instance, although he despised Prime Minster Neville Chamberlain's appeasement policies and thought little better of his character, he put them in this perspective: 'It is impossible ... to avoid marking the long series of miscalculations and misjudgements of men and facts, on which he based himself, but the motives which inspired him have never been impugned.'[83] He sought amiability among political rivals because otherwise: 'Hatred plays the same part in government as acids in chemistry.'[84]

A mix of ego, ambition, creed and expediency determined his political alliances. He started out by following his father's footsteps in the Conservative Party, only to break with the Tories after the leaders spurned his reform proposals. He crossed the floor to the Liberal Party and remained with them for a couple of decades until they faced political extinction. He then returned to the Conservative Party. He insisted that he remained loyal to a party as long as it served the nation better than its rival: 'These are the qualifications of a good Party man – you must know how to put your Party before yourself and you must know the occasions when to put nation before Party.'[85]

Churchill ultimately measured his political self-worth by what he did for the British Empire and the peoples living in it rather than for himself. He understood the dynamic between the wealth and power of Britain and the British people: 'To keep our Empire we must have a free people and an educated and a well-fed people. That is why we are in favour of social reform.'[86] Indeed his substance as a reform leader was as great as his style as a war leader. He advocated and achieved an astonishing array of laws and policies that bettered the lives of most Britons, including shorter working hours, higher pay and safer conditions in mines, factories and shops; lowering the retirement age from 70 to 65; providing pensions for the elderly, widows and orphans; alternatives to prison for nonviolent criminals and opportunities for those in prison to improve themselves by learning a trade and expanding their minds; and health insurance and university education for those who could not afford it. He partly paid for these programmes with higher taxes on the rich. Indeed, for better or worse, probably no one was more responsible for the paternity of Britain's welfare state than Winston Churchill. During a broadcast to the nation on March 1943, he insisted that: 'You must rank me and my colleagues as strong partisans of national compulsory insurance for all classes for all purposes from the cradle to the grave.'[87]

Churchill was a great reformer because in belief and behaviour he was at once a progressive and a conservative. As a progressive, he was a pragmatic problem-solver who sought to improve steadily the prosperity, security and glory of Britain and Britons. As a conservative, he prudently sought 'a look before you leap policy and ... a policy of don't leap at all if there is a ladder'.[88] He tried to combine a first do no harm with a speak-your-mind approach to politics: 'In politics when you are in doubt what to do, do nothing ... when you are in doubt what to say, say what you really think.'[89] He definitely believed in gearing one's efforts, political and otherwise, to the stages in one's life: 'Usually youth is for freedom and reform, maturity for judicious compromises and old age for stability and repose.'[90] All along Churchill tried to educate his colleagues and the general public by telling them not what they wanted to hear, but what they needed to hear. And that, of course, continually got him into trouble. Colleagues shunned him and constituents voted against him. But it was as a truth-teller that Churchill transcended the realm of politics into that of statesmanship.

Churchill was truly a great prophet. Indeed, he was a Cassandra most of his life. With his ability to think beyond mental boxes and connect far-flung dots, he clearly foretold events to which virtually everyone else was oblivious. He did so by following this maxim: 'It is only by studying the past that we can foresee, however dimly, the future.'[91] Although he was often blind to the shortcomings of many of his own proposals, he asserted remarkable foresight on the disastrous consequences of the appeasement policies of his fellow British and European leaders. His most critical contributions as a statesman were his continual warnings of the dangers of Communist and Nazi imperialism that could only be thwarted by containment rather than appeasement. A hundred million or so lives would have been spared had the Western Powers throttled those evil regimes in their respective cradles before they grew into the genocidal monsters that he anticipated. In the closing months of the Second World War in Europe, millions of people could have been spared from being swallowed within the subsequent repressive, exploitative communist regimes in Eastern and Central Europe had General

Dwight Eisenhower yielded to Churchill's pleas that the American and British armies race forward to liberate as many people and as much territory as possible. Like other analysts, Churchill struggled to understand the ends and means of Soviet foreign policy. In the dynamic of ideological and national values shaping the Kremlin's behaviour, Churchill assumed that the latter was more important than the former: 'I cannot forecast to you the action of Russia. It is a riddle wrapped in a mystery inside an enigma. But perhaps there is a key. That key is Russian national interest.'[92]

Yet Churchill was certainly not always right and was at times spectacularly wrong. His predictive powers missed as well as hit during the 1930s. For instance, despite Japan's aggression, he saw no threat to British interests, declaring: 'A war with Japan! But why should there be a war with Japan? I do not believe there is the slightest chance of it in our lifetimes.'[93] In another puzzling example, the father of the tank did not foresee the revolutionary effect of his progeny on warfare, but believed that the next world war would be as static as the first: 'One thing is certain about the next war, namely, that the armies will use their spades more than they use their bayonets.'[94] Likewise, although he was among the earliest champions of air power, he suffered a blind spot over its devastating potential, insisting that 'even a single well-armed vessel will hold its own against aircraft'.[95]

Churchill was increasingly pessimistic about humanity's future. As early as 1924, he issued this chilling assessment:

Mankind has never been in this position before. Without having improved appreciably in virtue or enjoying wiser guidance, it has got its hand for the first time on the tools by which it can unfailingly accomplish its own extermination ... Death stands at attention, obedient, expectant, ready to serve, ready to shear away the peoples en masse; ready, if called on, to pulverize, without hope of repair, what is left of civilization. He awaits only the word of command.

And then he envisioned this: 'Might not a bomb no bigger than an orange be found to possess a secret power to destroy a whole block of buildings – nay to concentrate the force of a thousand tons of cordite and blast a township at a stroke?'[96] His pessimism soared after the atomic bomb was developed and dropped to end the war with Japan. No one was safe after the Soviets broke America's nuclear monopoly and massed their own arsenal. He issued this dire warning to the British people: 'You came into big things as an accident of naval power when you were an island. The world had confidence in you.

You populated the island beyond its capacity. Through an accident of air power you will probably cease to exist.'[97]

He saw an antidote to the threat of annihilation. He was nearly as much of an internationalist as he was a nationalist. He became an outspoken promoter for what eventually became the League of Nations, the United Nations, the International Monetary Fund, the World Bank, the General Agreement on Trade and Tariffs, the Council of Europe, the Organization for European Economic Cooperation and the European Union, with all those organizations dedicated to collective security, peace, prosperity and democracy. In a 1938 newspaper article, he at once explained Britain's natural aloofness from Europe and championed a United States of Europe:

We are with Europe, but not of it. We are linked, but not comprised. We are interested and associated, but not absorbed ... The conception of a 'United States of Europe' is right. Every step taken to that end which appeases the obsolete hatreds and vanished oppressions, which makes easier the traffic and reciprocal services of Europe, which encourages its nations to lay aside their threatening arms ... is good for them and good for all. It is, however, imperative that as Europe advances toward higher internal unity there shall be a proportionate growth of solidarity throughout the British Empire and also a deepening self-knowledge and mutual recognition among the English speaking peoples.[98]

The Cold War, the nuclear arms race and seeming imminence of World War III compelled him to propose on 11 October 1950, an even more powerful stage of internationalism: 'The creation of an authoritative, all powerful world order is the ultimate aim towards which we must strive. Unless some effective world super-Government can be set up and brought quickly into action, the prospects for peace and human progress are dark and doubtful. Without a united Europe there is no sure prospect of world government.'[99]

Churchill defined an outstanding leader by these characteristics: 'One mark of a great man is the power of making lasting impressions upon people he meets. Another is so to have handled matters during his life that the course of after events is continually affected by what he did.'[100] However, the greatest of the great are distinguished by championing and realizing grand visions: 'The dominant forces in human history have come from the perception of great truths and the faithful pursuit of great causes.'[101] By these related definitions, Winston Churchill was truly among history's greatest leaders.

Chapter 1

The Child

'I was stubborn. Where my reason, imagination or interest were not engaged, I would not or I could not learn.'

'I began to go to the House of Commons and listen to the great debates.'

Winston Leonard Spencer Churchill was privileged to be born into one of Britain's most distinguished families on 30 November 1874. Of his birth, he later remarked: 'Although present on the occasion I have no clear recollection of the events leading up to it.'[1] His father was Randolph Churchill, who later became a leading member of the Conservative Party, Secretary of State for India and the Chancellor of the Exchequer. Preceding him by nine generations was his most illustrious ancestor, John Churchill, the first Duke of Marlborough, who vies with Arthur Wellesley, the first Duke of Wellington, for laurels as Britain's greatest general. Churchill was born prematurely after only seven months in the womb when his mother slipped and fell on the marble floor of Blenheim Palace, named after Marlborough's most decisive victory. Churchill was half-American. His mother was Jennie Jerome, a New York millionaire's beguiling daughter, who triumphed in her quest to snare a trophy British aristocrat even if he, as the second son, was not the duke. Nonetheless, the Churchills sojourned much of each year at Blenheim Palace where Randolph represented the neighbouring 'rotten borough' of Woodstock with only 1,071 eligible voters. When Parliament was in session, they resided in a mansion in London's upper-crust Mayfair district.

Having produced the requisite heir, his self-indulgent parents had little to do with him or, two years later, with his spare younger brother Jack. They left the care and affection to be bestowed by the nanny, Elizabeth Everest. Randolph and Jennie Churchill were not happily married. Each discreetly cheated on the other. Of Jennie's many lovers, her most prestigious amour was the Prince of Wales, later King Edward VII. Randolph pursued affairs whenever he could find them, including in Europe and prolonged stays in South Africa and India. Churchill helplessly witnessed the coldness between his parents as well as with him.

Many scorned children become rebels; others like Churchill become sycophants who commit countless Sisyphus-like attempts to win their parents' love and esteem then blame themselves for the failures. Churchill adored his parents. He later wrote that: 'My mother always seemed to me a fairy princess: a radiant being possessed of limitless riches and power ... She shone for me like the Evening Star. I loved her dearly – but at a distance.'[2] Among his first books was a fawning biography of his father whose parliamentary career he strove to emulate. And that was despite the harsh reality that his father paid even less attention to him than his mother did. Yet he treasured those fleeting moments. Once at Blenheim Palace he fired his shotgun at a rabbit on the lawn beneath his window. That provoked a 'very angry and disturbed' visit from his father, but 'I then had one of the three or four long intimate conversations with him which are all I can boast ... I listened spellbound to this sudden complete departure from his usual reserve.'[3]

As for academics, Churchill was a late bloomer. At age seven he was packed off to the boarding school of St. George at Ascot from 1882 to 1884. He had mixed feelings about the decision: 'I was no more consulted about leaving home than I had been about coming into the world.' Yet 'I was excited ... by this great change in my life. I thought in spite of the lessons, it would be fun living with so many other boys and that we should make friends together and have great adventures.' He learned the cruel reality shortly after his arrival. He was repeatedly flogged for 'being a troublesome boy'. The sadism permeating the school stunted rather than nurtured Churchill's brilliant mind:

> How I hated this school and what a life of anxiety I lived there for more than two years. I made very little progress at my lessons and none at all at games. I counted the days and the hours to the end of any term, when I should return from this hateful servitude and range my soldiers in line of battle on the nursery floor.

At Ascot he enjoyed only one outlet:

> The greatest pleasure I had in those days was reading ... My teachers saw me at once backward and precocious, reading books beyond my

years and yet at the bottom of the Form. They had large resources of compulsion at their disposal, but I was stubborn. Where my reason, imagination or interest were not engaged, I would not or I could not learn.[4]

He later explained: 'I am always ready to learn, although I do not always like being taught.'[5]

One flogging followed his confusion about Latin nomenclature. He was especially puzzled why the ancient Romans used a term translated as 'O Table,' as if it were some being that deserved special homage. 'But why O table?' the lad asked. The teacher impatiently replied, 'You would use it in speaking to a table.' 'But I never do,' he 'blurted in honest amazement.' The exasperated teacher darkly warned him that: 'If you are impertinent, you will be punished and punished, let me tell you, very severely.' Churchill recalled: 'Such was my introduction to the classics from which, I have been told, many of our cleverest men have derived so much solace and profit.'[6]

After the headmaster inflicted an especially vicious beating that caused him to run home, his mother transferred him to a boarding school run by two elderly spinsters at Brighton where for three years the rod was largely spared and 'I was allowed to learn things that interested me: French, History, lots of poetry by ear and above all riding and swimming.'[7] He passed Harrow's entrance exam and stayed there from 1888 to 1892. Unfortunately Harrow's oral exams inflicted on him a mental flogging that further retarded his learning: 'I should have liked to be asked what I knew. They always tried to ask what I did not know. When I would have willingly displayed my knowledge, they sought to expose my ignorance.'[8] Overall his schooldays were 'an unending spell of worries that did not then seem petty and of toil uncheered by fruition; a time of discomfort, restriction and purposeless monotony'.[9]

It was during his Harrow years that he experienced the first of his countless brushes with death, of which each provoked profound reflection on the nature of life. His parents had sent him, his brother and a tutor on a walking tour of parts of France and Switzerland for several weeks. Churchill and another boy he befriended were rowing far out on Lake Geneva when they 'decided to have a swim, pulled off our clothes, jumped into the water and swam with great delight'. Suddenly they noticed the wind pushing their boat across the water and they swam in pursuit:

Up to this point no idea of danger had crossed my mind. The sun played upon the sparkling blue waters; the wonderful panorama of mountains, the gay hotels and villas still smiled. But now I saw Death as near as I believe I have ever seen Him. He was swimming in the water at our side, whispering from time to time in the rising wind which continued to carry the boat away from us at about the same speed we could swim.

Churchill finally won that race with death and hauled himself into the boat, where he collapsed gasping in the bottom. Once he caught his breath, he rowed back to save his friend.[10]

Throughout his childhood, he suffered bouts of poor health, probably more from stress than from germs, which kept him in bed, the infirmary or at home. He disliked most sports except for swimming and fencing, at which he excelled. He was a voracious reader, with *Treasure Island* his childhood favourite. He had over 1,500 tin soldiers with which he re-enacted history's great battles, including of course those of his brilliant ancestor. His most exciting boyhood experience was attending Buffalo Bill's Wild West show when he was twelve. He daydreamed of travelling the world, having grand adventures and becoming a hero.

Those were not idle dreams. He grew up as the British Empire reached its apotheosis under Queen Victoria's reign.[11] He recalled that: 'I was a child of the Victoria era, when the structure of our country seemed firmly set, when its position in trade and on the seas was unrivalled and when the realization of the greatness of our Empire and of our duty to preserve it was ever growing stronger.'[12] There were still plenty of ways whereby young men could achieve renown. With determination and luck Churchill would exceed virtually everyone in his generation in pursing them.

Of course, all that lay far ahead. For now all he could do was fantasize about someday, somehow following in his father's illustrious political footsteps. In his early teenage years, 'I began to go to the House of Commons and listen to the great debates.' He marvelled as that age's leading politicians jousted with wit and reason across the floor below:

It seemed a very great world in which these men lived; a world where high rules reigned and every trifle in public conduct counted; a duelling ground where although the business might be ruthless … there was ceremonious personal courtesy and mutual respect. But of course I saw this social side only when my father had either intimate friends or persons of high political consequences as his guests.[13]

He revelled in being an integral part of 'English Society' when it still existed in its own form. It was a brilliant and powerful body, with standards of conduct and methods of enforcing them ... In a very large degree every one knew every one else and who they were. The few hundred great families who had governed England for so many generations and had seen her rise to the pinnacle of her glory, were interrelated to an enormous extent by marriage. Everywhere one met friends and kinsfolk. The leading figures of Society were in many cases the leading statesmen in Parliament and also the leading sportsmen on the Turf.[14]

His military career was conceived when his father happened to stop and observe him playing with his toy soldiers and asked him if he would like to become an officer. Churchill recalled that: 'I thought it would be splendid to command an Army, so I said "Yes" at once: and immediately I was taken at my word. For years I thought my father ... had discerned in me the qualities of military genius. But I was told later that he had only come to the conclusion that I was not clever enough to go to the Bar.'[15]

Three times he took the entrance exams for the Royal Military Academy at Sandhurst and barely passed the third time. His low score sent him to the cavalry rather than the infantry. He entered Sandhurst ranked 92nd of a class of 102 cadets. His father sent him these scalding words:

With all the advantages you had, with all the abilities which you foolishly think yourself to possess & been made to make your life easy & agreeable & your work neither oppressive nor distasteful, this is the grand result that you come up among the 2nd rate and 3rd rate class who are only good for commissions in a cavalry regiment ... Make this position indelibly impressed on your mind that if your conduct and action at Sandhurst is similar to what it has been in the other establishments in which it has been sought vainly to impart to you some education, then my responsibility for you is over ... I am certain that if you cannot prevent yourself from leading the idle useless unprofitable life you have had during you schooldays & later months, you will become a mere social wastrel ... and you will degenerate into a shabby unhappy & futile existence.[16]

There was more than a little projection in this cruel polemic; Randolph Churchill wrote them as syphilis rotted his mind and body. His mother wrote him more encouraging words: 'The future now is in your hands to make or to mar it. I have trust that you will make it a success.'[17]

Churchill loved military life, especially riding at which he became an expert. Being an officer in training at Sandhurst had another profound benefit. To his happiness, with his enforced discipline and bearing, as

a gentleman cadet I acquired a new status in my father's eyes. I was entitled when on leave to go about with him, if it was not inconvenient. He was always amused by acrobats, jugglers and performing animals … He took me also to important political parties … where most of the leaders and a selection of the rising men of the Conservative Party were often assembled. He began to take me also to stay with his … friends; and here we had a different company and new topics of conversation which proved equally entertaining. In fact to me he seemed to own the key to everything or almost everything worth having. But if I began to show the slightest idea of comradeship, he was immediately offended.[18]

His father embarked on a round-the-world journey in June 1894. Churchill shared this intriguing recollection: 'I never saw him again, except as a swiftly fading shadow.'[19] Unlike Hamlet, Churchill's glimpse of his father's ghost was unaccompanied by any last message or insight. Syphilis killed Randolph Churchill at the age of 46 on 24 January 1895. Churchill would only learn the cause years later. The loss of his father at once depressed and inspired him: 'All my dreams of comradeship with him, of entering Parliament at his side and in his support were ended. There remained for me only to pursue his aims and vindicate his memory.'[20] His father's death at such a young age atop the deaths of other relatives at similar ages convinced Churchill that he had to live life to the fullest in what time he had.

Around the same time he suffered the loss of someone else he deeply loved, his nanny Elizabeth Everest. Learning that her days were numbered, he hurried to her home in London: 'Death came very easily to her. She had lived such an innocent and loving life of service to others and held such a simple faith, that she had no fears at all and did not seem to mind very much. She had been my dearest and most intimate friend during the whole of the twenty years I had lived.'[21]

Churchill soon had an unshakeable source of support in pursuing his ambitions. To his astonishment and delight, his mother finally took an interest in him after his father died and he became a man. She 'became an ardent ally, furthering all my plans and guarding my interests with all her influence and boundless energy. She was still at forty young, beautiful and fascinating. We worked together on equal terms, more like brother and sister than mother and son ... And so it continued to the end.'[22] What explains his mother's transformation from indifference to enthusiasm over her son's development? Jennie lived through powerful men from whom she extracted wealth, status, adoration and pleasure. She now recognized Winston's potential to achieve worldly triumphs as a worthy investment of her money and time. His brilliant career as a military hero and political leader would brightly reflect back on her own celebrity.

Chapter 2

The Adventurer

'I felt the excitement and very little fear. I rode on my grey pony all along the skirmish line where everyone else was lying down in cover. Foolish perhaps but I play for high stakes and given an audience there is no act too daring or too noble.'

'Whether it was worth it, I cannot tell. At any rate, at the end of a fortnight the valley was a desert and honour was satisfied.'

Churchill was 20 years old when he received Queen Victoria's commission as a second lieutenant on 20 February 1895. He graduated from Sandhurst with honours as number eight in a class of 150. His instructors there had stirred the vast intellectual potential that his schoolteachers had harshly inhibited. In a photo taken shortly thereafter he certainly looked like a storybook young hero dressed in the uniform of the 4th Hussars. He was still lean of body with high cheekbones and a full head of hair. His expression mingles pride and taunt energy. The great adventures and glory that he sought lay ahead far beyond the horizon, but of course for now he could only dream that they would come true.

Instead a scandal engulfed him. A fellow officer, Alan Bruce-Pryce, who was forced to resign the regiment for improprieties, in turn, accused Churchill of 'acts of gross immorality of the Oscar Wilde type', in other words, homosexuality.[1] Churchill employed a lawyer to sue Bruce for £20,000 in damages; he settled for £500 accompanied by a written letter of apology that renounced the accusation. Yet was there any truth to the charge? Although Churchill later admitted that he had once had sex with a man to see what it was like, no evidence exists that he ever repeated the act.[2]

He immersed himself in the comradeship and tedium of regimental life. For the first six months riding school dominated his activities six days a week. He most enjoyed when he and his fellow pupils wheeled from column into line and then charged. He eventually became not just an expert rider but excelled at polo in his spare time with the regiment's team. His most thrilling times 'were the splendid parades when Queen Victoria sat in her carriage at the saluting point and when the whole … garrison, perhaps 25,000 strong, blue and gold, scarlet and steel, passed before her'.[3]

Being an officer certainly had its privileges. An officer was by definition a gentleman and member of the leisured class. During peacetime officers enjoyed plenty of time off from their duties, five months spanning the winter after seven months with the regiment from spring to autumn. Yet, without a war to fight, army life ultimately seemed nothing more than an elaborate facade composed of a series of empty daily rituals broken by an occasional pageant. Churchill and most of his comrades were convinced 'that the British army would never again take part in a European conflict'. They lamented that the 'British army had never fired on white troops since the Crimea and now that the world was growing so sensible and pacific – and so democratic too – the great days were over'. Looking back from his fifties to his twenties, he reflected that: 'Everything I was sure or taught to be sure was impossible, has happened.'[4]

*   *   *

Shortly after receiving his commission, Churchill and a fellow officer, Reginald Barnes, conceived an imaginative way to get a taste of war. A rebellion had erupted in Spain's colony of Cuba. Sir Henry Wolff, a close friend of Churchill's father, was then Britain's ambassador to Spain. Churchill cabled Wolff a request to obtain the Spanish government's permission for them to serve as military observers on the staff of General Juarez Valdez, the army's commander in Cuba. The friends were exultant when they received Madrid's approval.

They sailed first to New York, where Churchill delighted in his introduction to the American half of his heritage. He and Barnes explored the dynamic city, attended high society dinners, visited the United States Military Academy at West Point, toured an American warship and witnessed a court case. In a letter to his aunt, he marvelled: 'What an extraordinary people the Americans are! Their hospitality is a revelation to me and they make you feel at home and at ease in a way that I have never before experienced.'[5] To his brother, he wrote:

This is a great country … Not pretty or romantic, but great and utilitarian, there seems to be no such thing as reverence for tradition. Everything is eminently practical and things are judged from a matter of fact standpoint … A great crude, strong, young people are the Americans … Picture to yourself the American people as a great lusty youth – who treads on all your sensibilities, perpetuates every possible horror of ill manners – whom neither age nor just tradition inspire with reverence – but who moves about his affairs with good hearted freshness which may well be the envy of the older nations of the earth.[6]

Although for centuries countless discerning foreigners have made similar remarks about America, few have risen to the poetry and insights of Churchill's, when he was just 20 years old.

The young officers took the train from New York to Key West, Florida and from there a ship to Havana, where they stepped ashore on 20 November 1895. The British Consul-general introduced them to the Spanish governor who sent them on a 150-mile journey by armoured train to Valdez's headquarters at Sancti Spiritus, where the general cordially welcomed them. For ten days they accompanied Valdez and his troops on an expedition designed to flush and destroy guerrillas in central Cuba. Appropriately he received his baptism of fire on 30 November 1895, his 21st birthday: 'There was a low mist as we moved off in the early morning and all of a sudden the rear of our column was involved in firing … As however, no bullets seemed to come near me, I was easily reassured. I felt like the optimist "who did not mind what happened, so long as it did not happen to him".' After the rearguard chased away the snipers, the column moved forward through the jungle for another hour then halted for breakfast: 'I had been provided with half a skinny chicken. I was engaged in gnawing the drumstick when suddenly, close at hand, almost in our faces it seemed, a ragged volley rang out.' A bullet hit the horse just behind him. As the Spanish troops drove off the rebels 'I could not help reflecting that the bullet which had struck the chestnut had certainly passed within a foot of my head … I began to take a more thoughtful view of our enterprise than I had hitherto done.' He was nearly shot later that day when he joined a group of officers for a swim in a river and rebels fired at them until they scrambled into the forest. The third close call came that night as the rebels fired at their camp:

A bullet ripped through the thatch of our hut, another wounded an orderly just outside. I should have been glad to get out of my hammock and lie on the ground. However, as no one else made a move, I thought it more becoming to stay where I was. I fortified myself by dwelling on the fact that the Spanish officer whose hammock was slung between me and the enemy's fire was a man of substantial physique ... I have never been prejudiced against fat men. At any rate I did not grudge this one his meals. Gradually I dropped asleep.[7]

Such were some of Churchill's grim lessons about how to steel oneself under fire, with a blend of gallows humour, fatalism and stoicism a powerful talisman.

Churchill's baptism of fire was just a harbinger of what lay ahead. The next morning the Spanish column had marched several hours when a large rebel force blocked its path. Valdez deployed his column into line and ordered his troops forward, with the general, his staff and the two British officers trailing about 50 yards behind:

The firing on both sides became heavy. There were sounds about us, sometimes like a sigh, sometimes like a whistle and at others like the buzz of an angry hornet ... and the palm trees smitten by the bullets yielded resounding smacks and thuds ... I was astounded to see how few people were hit amid all this clatter. In our group of about twenty, only three or four horses and men were wounded and not one was killed.[8]

That proved to be the campaign's last skirmish. With provisions dwindling, Valdez led his troops back to their base.

In Cuba, Churchill learned as many valuable lessons about politics as he did about war. He silently sided with the Cubans who had been 'overtaxed in a monstrous manner for a considerable period' with the result that 'industries are paralyzed and development is impossible'. The corruption, exploitation, repression and brutality of Spanish rule appalled him and forced him to conclude that 'a national and justifiable revolt is the only possible result of such a system'.[9] Yet his sympathies spread to embrace both sides after he asked a Spanish colonel why they were trying to destroy the rebels and received this simple reply: 'We are fighting to preserve the integrity of our country.' Churchill 'was struck by this. I had not, no doubt owing to my restricted education, quite realised that these other nations had the same sort of feeling about their possessions as we in England had always been brought up to have about ours. They felt about Cuba ... just as we felt about Ireland.'[10]

* * *

The young British officers parted from their Spanish comrades and began the series of train trips and sea voyages that eventually carried them back to their regiment. There Churchill resumed his light duties and social amusements:

> I now passed a most agreeable six months ... I was able to live at home with my mother and go down to Hounslow Barracks two or three times a week by the Underground Railway. We played polo ... I gave myself over to the amusements of the London Season ... During this vivid summer my mother gathered constantly around her table politicians of both parties and leading figures in literature and art, together with the most lovely beings on whom the eye could beam.[11]

He was thrilled to become a published author when his account of his Cuban experiences appeared in the *Saturday Review*. He resolved to write similar articles about all his military and travel adventures as they unfolded.

He was still in that prolonged, anxious, testosterone-driven, gaff-filled transition from boyhood to manhood. Victorian England imposed demanding standards of propriety for its elite that Churchill struggled to master. At one point, he received the astonishing honour as a mere second lieutenant to be invited to a dinner party hosted by the Prince of Wales, then among his mother's lovers and the future King Edward VII. His regiment's colonel, John Brabazon, was among the guests. Churchill 'realized I must be upon my best behaviour: punctual, subdued, reserved, in short display all the qualities with which I am least endowed'.[12] Alas, he miscalculated the train connections and kept them waiting nearly an hour.

> 'Don't they teach you to be punctual in your regiment, Winston?' said the Prince in his most severe tone and then looked acidly at Colonel Brabazon, who glowered. It was an awkward moment! We went into dinner two by two ... After about a quarter of an hour the prince, who was a naturally ... kind hearted man, put me at my ease again by some gracious chaffing remark.[13]

*   *   *

His regiment received orders to embark for India in September 1896. During the nearly month-long voyage Churchill partly broke the tedium by reaching the semi-finals in the chess contest. His sojourn in India began inauspiciously and painfully when he dislocated his shoulder while trying to disembark at Bombay from a longboat caught in churning waves: 'I had sustained an injury which was to last me my life; which was to cripple me at polo, to prevent me from ever playing tennis and to be a grave embarrassment in moments of peril, violence and effort.'[14]

Churchill reached the subcontinent when the British Empire was nearing its pinnacle with India, known as the Raj, 'the Jewel in the Crown'.[15] Throughout much of the nineteenth century, Britain's imperial leaders acquired the empire's last conquests with a series of 'little wars' against states and tribes mostly in Asia and Africa. The logic of empire prevailed whereby the latest acquisition becomes vulnerable to neighbouring hostile powers which have to be subdued and so on.[16]

The 4th Hussars was posted at Bangalore 600 miles away and 3,000ft up in southern India's jungled hills. There Churchill alleviated the routine with polo, butterfly collecting and his first girlfriend, Pamela Plowden, although the relationship was platonic and mostly epistolary. He wrote newspaper articles and his first and only novel, *Savrola: A Tale of the Revolution in Laurania*.[17] As a diligent, amiable officer he was rewarded with promotion to Brigade Major in February 1897. Most importantly, he tried to fill the daunting gaps in his education by reading good books on history, economics and philosophy for several hours daily.

Wielding her formidable charms, his mother wrangled a three-month leave for him in spring 1897 to cover a pending war between Greece and Turkey. In a series of cables he got the newspaper the *Allahabad Pioneer* to agree to publish his daily 300-word telegram on that war. In Aden, he learned that each side had stepped back from the brink so he sailed to London with hope of pursuing a political career. He asked Fitzroy Stewart, the Conservative Party Secretary and his cousin, if he could run for a seat and was crestfallen to hear that none were vacant. He did make his first political speech at a Conservative rally in a park near Bath.

Churchill then learned of the latest Pathan tribal revolt against British rule on the Northwest Frontier. The British had sooner or later crushed previous rebellions that erupted in 1851–2, 1864, 1879 and 1880. This time the Pathans captured a string of British outposts straddling the Khyber Pass leading from India to Afghanistan. The British had finally vanquished Afghanistan in a war from 1878 to 1880, four decades after the tribes wiped out the first invading British army in 1839–42.[18] Vengeance was only one reason for the second campaign. In what became known as 'the Great Game', the British and Russian empires were expanding toward each other in Central Asia and the leaders of each sought to grab as much territory and people before the other got there.[19]

A family friend, General Sir Bindon Blood, led this 1897 expedition against the rebels. Churchill cabled Blood for permission to join his staff and was elated to receive it. His mother talked the *Daily Telegraph*'s publisher into paying him for the same stories that he was writing for the *Allahabad Pioneer*. Finally, he received his colonel's permission for an extended leave to serve on the campaign. He reached Blood's headquarters in late September. Blood assigned him to the 31st Punjabis to replace an officer who had recently been killed in action.

The campaign pitted a modern nation-state against a mosaic of mutually antagonistic clans and tribes united only by Islam and their fierce desire to drive the infidels from their land. Churchill explained how the Pathan way of war was inseparable from its culture:

> Every man is a warrior, a politician and a theologian. Every large house is a real feudal fortress … Every family cultivates its vendetta; every clan, its feud. The numerous tribes and combinations of tribes all have their accounts to settle with one another. Nothing is ever forgotten and very few debts are left unpaid … Into this … world the nineteenth century brought two new facts; the breech-loading rifle and the British government.[20]

General Blood steadily advanced up the Swat valley. The Pathans sniped at the column, ambushed detachments and evaded pursuers. In turn the British methodically sought to break the enemy's ability to continue the struggle by 'destroying all the crops, breaking the reservoirs of water, blowing up as many castles as possible and shooting anyone who obstructed the process … All night long the bullets flew across the camp; but everyone now had good holes to lie in and the horses and mules were protected to a large extent.'[21] On 30 September, Churchill joined the regiment's assault against the enemy at Agrah. Astonishingly he was not counted among the sixty dead and wounded even though he committed a nearly suicidal act: 'I felt the excitement and very little fear. I rode on my grey pony all along the skirmish line where everyone else was lying down in cover. Foolish perhaps but I play for high stakes and given an audience there is no act too daring or too noble.'[22] The army sidestepped the resistance and continued up the valley. By 12 October, Churchill had been under fire fifteen times.

His fiercest battle came when he and five other officers led eighty-five Sikhs up a hill to drive the enemy from its summit. Then, as hundreds of Pathans manoeuvred to cut them off, they shot their way through back down the hill: 'We carried two wounded officers and six wounded Sikhs with us. That took about twenty men. We left one officer and a dozen men dead and wounded to be cut to pieces.' Churchill stayed at the rear, exchanging shots with the advancing Pathans then: 'I looked all around. I was all alone with the enemy … I ran as fast as I could.' When he found cover he turned and 'fired as carefully as possible thirty or forty shots at tribesmen on the left-hand ridge at distances from eighty to a hundred and twenty yards. The difficulty about these occasions is that one is so out of breath and quivering with exertion, if not with excitement.'[23] He caught up with his comrades who clustered behind cover on a rocky knoll. Eventually the rest of the regiment battled through to rescue them then together they withdrew down the valley. The fighting persisted through the night as Pathans surrounded the army, fired from all directions and crept ever closer until: 'Men grappled with each other; shot each other in error; cannon were fired as you might fire a pistol at an enemy two or three yards away. Four of … ten British officers were wounded. A third of the sappers and gunners were casualties and nearly all the mules were dead or streaming with blood.' The enemy disappeared with the dawn so 'we proceeded to shoot the wounded mules and have breakfast'.[24]

General Blood was determined to inflict a harsh vengeance for his army's bloody repulse. He ordered the troops to devastate the valley:

We proceeded systematically, village by village and we destroyed the houses, filled up the wells, blew down the towers, cut down the great shady trees, burned the crops and broke the reservoirs … So long as the villages were in the valley, this was quite easy. The tribesmen sat on the mountains and sullenly watched the destruction of their homes and means of livelihood. When however we had to attack the villages on the sides of the mountains, they resisted fiercely and we lost for every village two or three British officers and fifteen or twenty native soldiers. Whether it was worth it, I cannot tell. At any rate, at the end of a fortnight the valley was a desert and honour was satisfied.[25]

Churchill pitied the Pathans for far more profound reasons than the devastation their rebellion brought them. He was scathing in the role of Islam in denigrating their lives:

How dreadful are the curses that Mohammedanism lays on his votaries. Beside the fanatical frenzy, which is as dangerous in a man as hydrophobia in a dog, there is this fearful fatalistic apathy. The effects are apparent in many countries. Improvident habits, slovenly systems of agriculture, sluggish methods of commerce and insecurity of property exist wherever the followers of the Prophet rule or live ... No stronger retrograde force exists in the world. Far from being moribund, Mohammedanism is a military and proselytizing faith.[26]

Although Churchill questioned the campaign's strategy, tactics and morality, he wanted to fight on to the end. However, his own regiment's Colonel Brabazon insisted that he had used up his leave and must return immediately. Churchill had no choice but reluctantly to obey. He noted a change in tone among many of his fellow officers after he rejoined them. From jealousy, they were civil but distant. He tried to redeem himself in their eyes by devoting himself to the regiment's polo team when they played their rivals.

Meanwhile he cabled his mother a plea to use her influence to get him back to the Northwest Frontier. This time Jennie's charms failed to produce the desired result. Not only that, but Churchill learned from his brother Jack that their mother's opulent lifestyle threatened their inheritance. He expressed his concern in two letters to her: 'Speaking quite frankly ... there is no doubt we are both ... spendthrifts and extravagant. We both know what is good and we both like to have it.' That, however, had unfortunate consequences: 'In the three years from my father's death you have spent a quarter of our entire fortune in the world. I have also been extravagant: but my extravagances are a very small matter besides yours.'[27]

He spent the winter writing a book about the Northwest Frontier campaign and his own experiences called *The Story of the Malakand Field Force*.[28] To his astonishment and delight, his book was widely praised and sold well: 'I had never been praised before. The comments which had ever been made upon my work at school had been "Indifferent", "Untidy", "Slovenly", "Bad", "Very Bad", etc. Now here was the great world with its leading literary newspapers and vigilant erudite critics, writing whole columns of praise!' The effect was electrifying: 'I felt a new way of making a living and of asserting myself, opening splendidly before me ... I resolved that as soon as the wars ... should be ended ... I would free myself from all discipline and authority and set up in perfect independence in England with nobody to give me orders.'[29]

*   *   *

Churchill learned of a campaign that General Herbert Kitchener was mobilizing in Egypt to ascend the Nile valley to Upper Egypt, today's Sudan, and crush an Islamist state with its capital at Khartoum.[30] That state emerged in 1885, two years after a charismatic Muslim Jihadist named Muhammad Ahmad, who claimed to be the Mahdi or the Prophet Muhammad's successor and thus the Muslim world's leader, led a revolt against Egypt, then a British protectorate. The Mahdi's 30,000-man army besieged Khartoum, whose 7,000-man garrison was commanded by General Charles Gordon, from 13 March 1884 to 26 January 1885. Prime Minister William Gladstone called on Gordon to withdraw with his men, but the general refused, insisting that honour bound him to defend the city from the Jihadists. Gladstone mobilized a relief expedition but low river water and another Jihadist army blocked it far downstream. The Jihadists eventually overwhelmed and butchered Khartoum's defenders. When Ahmad died the following year, the Khalifa Abdullah al-Taashi succeeded him and consolidated his power over Upper Egypt. Word of the massacre of Gordon and his men provoked loud cries in Parliament and across Britain for avenging their deaths and reasserting control over Upper Egypt. But imperial overstretch around the world prevented the British from mounting an expedition for fourteen years.[31]

Kitchener was Britain's most renowned general of the late nineteenth century.[32] Churchill greatly admired him and longed to join his campaign. The feeling was anything but mutual. Churchill's *Story of the Malakand Field Force* outraged Kitchener as it did many officers. They viewed the book's criticisms of the campaign and revelations of its horrors as a betrayal. Kitchener hated Churchill and wanted nothing to do with him. The thought of having him on his staff infuriated him. He politely but firmly rejected Churchill's request, explaining that all his staff positions were filled and there was a long, qualified waiting list for any openings.

Undaunted, Churchill somehow talked his colonel into granting him his latest extended leave. He hurried back to London, arriving on 2 July. The campaign was scheduled to begin sometime in early August. He had to work fast. First, he deployed his most powerful ally, his mother. Jennie did whatever she could to help her son but all was in vain. He had stepped on a lot of very influential toes in his efforts to get to various wars and write about them: 'I now perceived that there were many ill-informed and ill-disposed people who did not take a favourable view of my activities. On the contrary they began to develop an adverse ... even a hostile attitude.'[33] He wangled a meeting on 18 July with Lord Salisbury, then the Prime Minister and

Foreign Secretary.[34] Salisbury had greatly enjoyed Churchill's book for the same reasons that Kitchener detested it – it was a lively, critical analysis of what went right, what went wrong and why. Salisbury told Churchill that 'I was able to form a truer picture of the kind of fighting that has been going on in these frontier valleys from your writings than from any other documents which it has been my duty to read'.[35] He then cabled Kitchener to request that he accept Churchill on his staff or elsewhere in his army. Kitchener once against explained that his staff was full. However, a few days later the War Office informed Churchill that a lieutenant's position was open with the 21st Lancers commanded by Colonel Robert Martin.

Churchill signed a contract with the *Morning Post* to pay him £15 for each article he sent them then made haste to catch up with his latest regiment. He reached the 21st Lancers' headquarters at Cairo on 2 August. Half the troops had already headed up the Nile. He embarked with the remainder early the following morning. Taking a series of trains and steamboats, they finally joined the army 1,200 miles up the Nile.

Kitchener's 25,800-man army comprised 8,200 British and 17,600 Egyptians and Sudanese. Awaiting them at Khartoum were 52,000 Jihadists. Upon learning of Kitchener's approach on September 1, Taashi led his army a dozen miles north of the city beyond a village called Omdurman and aligned his men along a string of hills with the Nile anchoring their right and cavalry their left. Half a dozen miles north, Kitchener's army was similarly deployed but with half as many troops stretched far thinner. The 21st Lancers were deployed a few miles before the army as a screen and Churchill's company was posted a mile beyond that.

When the Mahdist army came into view, Churchill's captain ordered him to ride back and inform Colonel Martin, who in turn, had him carry the news to Kitchener. The latter mission filled Churchill with trepidation:

> So I was to meet Kitchener after all! Would he be surprised to see me? Would he be angry? Would he say, 'What the devil are you doing here?'' He dutifully rode back to the main army and, after spotting the general and his staff, 'approached at an angle, made a half circle, drew my horse alongside and slightly in rear of him and saluted. It was the first time I had ever looked upon that remarkable countenance … He turned his grave face upon me. The heavy moustaches, the queer rolling look of the eyes, the sunburnt and almost purple cheeks and jowl made a vivid manifestation upon the senses.

To Churchill's relief, Kitchener 'listened in absolute silence to every word, our horses crunching the sand'. Kitchener dismissed him to return to his regiment. There was no fighting that day. The 400 troopers of the 21st Lancers were withdrawn as a screen half a mile before the army.[36]

The battle began shortly after dawn the following day, 2 September. The Khalifa ordered his army forward. Typically Churchill volunteered to lead a detachment to a ridgeline on the right to observe the approaching enemy. He witnessed an extraordinary sight:

> There was our army ranked and massed by the river. There were the gunboats lying expectant in the stream. There were all the batteries ready to open. And meanwhile, on the other side, this large oblong gay-coloured crowd in fairly good order climbed swiftly up to the crest ... Ancient and modern confronted one another. The weapons, the methods and the fanaticism of the Middle Ages were brought by an extraordinary anachronism into dire collision with the organization and inventions of the nineteenth century.

Suddenly a group of Madhist riders detached from the army and galloped toward them, 'dark, cowled figures, like monks on horseback – ugly sinister brutes with long spears. I fired a few shots at them from the saddle and they sheared off.' He then received an order to withdraw with his men to the regiment as the army was about to open fire.[37]

The fusillade of massed British rifles, machine guns and artillery along the line and gunboats on the river decimated the Jihadists. Kitchener then ordered the 21st Lancers to pursue and slaughter the fleeing enemy. The 21st cut a swath with lance and pistol through them. Churchill

> saw the gleam of his curved sword as he drew it back for a hamstringing cut ... I fired two shots into him at about three yards. As I straightened myself in the saddle, I saw before me another figure with uplifted sword. I raised my pistol and fired. On my left was an Arab horseman in a bright-coloured tunic and steel helmet, with chain-mail hangings. I fired at him. He turned aside

Churchill found himself alone and observing the scene until Jihadists began to converge on him: 'Then for the first time that morning I experienced a sudden sensation of fear ... What a fool I was to loiter like this in the midst of the enemy.' A wounded Jihadist 'staggered towards me raising his spear. I shot him at less than a yard. He fell on the sand and lay there dead. How easy to kill a man! But I did not worry about it.'[38]

Kitchener ordered the infantry forward to complete the rout. The troops advanced all the way to Khartoum, slaughtering thousands of wounded or straggling Jihadists before them. In Khartoum Kitchener ordered the Mahdi's tomb destroyed. That appalled Churchill who wrote:

If the people of the Sudan cared no more for the Mahdi, then it was an act of vandalism and folly to destroy the only fine building which might attract the traveller and interest the historian. It is a gloomy augury for the future of the Sudan that the first action of its civilized conquerors and present ruler should have been to level the one pinnacle that rose above the mud houses. If on the other hand, the people of the Sudan still venerate the memory of the Mahdi – and more than 50,000 had fought hard only a week before to assert their respect and belief – then I shall not hesitate to declare that to destroy what was sacred and holy to them was a wicked act.[39]

The British victory at Omdurman was among the most lopsided in history. In all the British killed about 12,000 jihadists, wounded 13,000 and captured 5,000, while losing 48 dead and 428 wounded. The 21st Lancers suffered 22 per cent casualties; of the 310 men who rode into battle, 21 were killed and 49 were wounded. The Khalifa himself escaped with thousands of followers and would not be destroyed until 1899. Although once again Churchill escaped combat without a scratch, he suffered excruciating pain when he donated a skin graft to a severely wounded officer.

Kitchener tried to humiliate Churchill by charging him with herding the camels on the 1,400-mile trudge back to Cairo. An enraged Churchill ripped up his orders and remained with the Lancers all the way to London, where he rode with them in the victory parade. He later avenged himself against Kitchener in his book, *The River War*, which revealed the mistakes the general made and the atrocities he ordered.[40] Then Churchill hurried back to India before his leave expired. This time he stayed long enough to participate in the polo tournament in February 1899. The following month he resigned his commission and left India for London.

* * *

He sought to exploit his swelling fame by following his father's footstep as a rising star in the Conservative Party. The Tory leaders picked Churchill as the sacrificial lamb for a by-election in the working-class constituency of Oldham in Lancashire. Two seats were open and contested by two men each from the Conservative and Liberal Parties. He recalled that: 'The fight was long and hard. I defended the virtues of the Government, the existing system of society, the Established Church and the unity of the Empire ... Our opponents deplored the misery of the working masses, the squalor of the slums, the glaring contrast between riches and poverty.'[41] When the votes were counted on 6 July 1899, the Liberal candidates won both seats with 12,976 and 12,770 votes, while Churchill came in third with 11,477.[42] He recalled returning to London 'with those feelings of deflation which a bottle of champagne or even soda water represents when it is half emptied and left uncorked for a night'.[43] His sunken spirits lifted when the senior Conservative Arthur Balfour assured him that: 'This small reverse will have no permanent ill effect upon your political fortunes.'[44]

*   *   *

With his political ambitions temporarily stymied, Churchill embarked on his latest adventure. His imagination riveted on South Africa where war raged between that British colony and the Boer Orange Free State and Transvaal.[45] The British had annexed Transvaal in 1877, but the Boers won back their independence in 1881. The discovery of gold there in 1886 inspired a rush of prospectors who eventually outnumbered the Boers. Transvaal President Paul Kruger denied the newcomers any political rights and formed an alliance with the Orange Free State. In 1899, the mostly British foreigners in Transvaal petitioned Queen Victoria to secure their political rights. Negotiations between the British and Boer governments broke down and fighting erupted. The Boers invaded the British colony of Natal and besieged General George White's army in Ladysmith. Other Boer forces launched raids deep into Natal and South Africa. The British government declared war and resolved to conquer the Boer states once and for all.

Churchill talked the *Morning Post* into sending him there as a reporter with a £250 monthly salary and all expenses paid. He boarded a ship at Southampton on 11 October 1899 and stepped ashore at Cape Town on the 31st. He made his way to the front by a series of train and boat trips until the front reached him. On the morning of 15 November, he boarded an armoured train of two cars pulled by an engine with Captain Aylmer Haldane and 150 troops at Escourt. At Chievely, Haldane received a telegraphed order to return to Frere where Boer commandoes were reported present. The engineer ran the train backwards. Just beyond Frere, Boers fired at the train. The engineer opened the throttle to evade the fusillade and ploughed into a huge boulder the enemy had placed on the tracks. The last two wagons derailed but the engine remained on the track. The Boers fired rifles and cannons as the uninjured men struggled to extract themselves and the wounded from the wreck. Outnumbered and surrounded, Haldane surrendered. Churchill was determined to escape so he

> turned and ran between the rails of the track ... Two bullets passed ... I flung myself against the banks of the cutting ... Another glance at the figures; one was kneeling to aim. Again I darted forward ... Again two soft kisses sucked in the air, but nothing struck me ... .I scrambled up the bank ... struggling to get my wind. On the other side of the railway a horseman galloped up, shouting to me and waving his hand ... I reached for my Mauser pistol ... I had left the weapon in the cab of the engine in order to be free to work at the wreckage ... Death stood before me, grim sullen Death without his light-hearted companion, chance. So I held up my hand and ... was herded with the other prisoners.[46]

A Boer detachment conveyed the captives all the way to Pretoria, where, on 18 November, they were incarcerated in a school converted into a prison. Churchill appealed for his release as a journalist to authorities up the chain of command all the way to Boer Secretary of War Louis de Souza, to no avail. He wrote to his mother and the Prince of Wales to intercede on his behalf, but they were powerless. For a man of action to suffer imprisonment is a painful fate. Churchill felt 'a sense of constant humiliation in being confined to a narrow space, fenced in by railings and wire, watched by armed men and webbed about with a tangle of regulations and restrictions. I certainly hated every minute of my captivity more than I have ever hated any other period of my whole life.'[47]

He and two officers conceived a way to escape. It was a short drop from a bathroom window to a garden with several sheds to hide behind. Two sentries patrolled the garden but at times faced the opposite direction or stopped to chat with each other. It might be possible to slip past them some dark night. On 11 December, Churchill was the first to go over the wall and lay in the shadows waiting for the others to follow. He waited an hour and heard a loud whisper that the guards were watching his comrades who they suspected were plotting something. Churchill was on his own. When the two sentries met for a smoke, he walked as quietly and swiftly as possible across the garden and down the road from them. People were still strolling in the streets and paid no attention to him as he zigzagged through Pretoria's streets to the periphery until he reached the railway tracks stretching eastward. He hopped aboard a slow-moving freight train, rode it until near dawn then jumped off as it approached a town. He walked around the town and followed the tracks until the sun rose then hid in the brush throughout the day. He caught another train that night and got off toward dawn at a town. Famished and filthy, he decided to try his luck by asking for help.

He knocked on the door of the first house he encountered. When a man opened it, he claimed that he had fallen off the train and asked for help. Once again his extraordinary luck saved him. When the man expressed scepticism, Churchill told him the truth. To that the man identified himself as John Howard, the manager of a local coal mine and exclaimed: 'Thank God you have come here! It is the only house for twenty miles where you would not have been handed over. But we are all British here and we will get you through.'[48] Astonishingly one of them was actually from Oldham and promised to vote for him the next time he ran there. They hid Churchill in the mine for three days and supplied him with a mattress, candles, a leg of mutton, roast chicken, cigars and whisky. His solitude was broken by black miners during the day, who gave him a wide berth, fearing he was a ghost and the rats that scurried over him whenever he blew out the candle. Meanwhile, his escape was discovered the morning after at roll and a manhunt was launched with a £25 reward for his capture. One day a police officer came to the house to ask Howard if he knew anything about the fugitive; Howard distracted him by challenging him to a shooting contest which cost him a £2 bet to deliberately lose.

On the fourth night Howard extracted Churchill and hid him on a train wagon filled with bales of wool bound for Portugal's colony of Mozambique. One of the Britons journeyed in a passenger carriage and managed to bribe officials who sought to search the wool wagon. The end of the line was the port of Lourenco Marques. Churchill hurried to the British consulate which supplied him with funds and telegraphed his escape to London. He took a steamer to Durban where he found himself 'a popular hero. I was received as if I had won a great victory. The harbour was decorated with flags. Bands and crowds thronged the quays. The Admiral, the General and the Mayor pressed on board to grasp my hand.'[49]

The British were preparing two offensives into the Boer heartland. With Field Marshal Lord Roberts the commander and Kitchener as chief of staff, the main army would march from Cape Town to break the Boer siege of Kimberly then push on to capture Bloemfontein. General Sir Redvers Buller commanded the army that would march north from Durban to relieve Ladysmith. Churchill was aware that Roberts shared the animosity of Kitchener and many other officers against him so he stayed clear of them for now. Instead, he made his way to Buller's headquarters and asked to join his campaign. At first Buller was reluctant, citing the War Office's recent rule that officers could not double as journalists, provoked by Churchill's previous bouts. Finally, he agreed to assign Churchill as a lieutenant to Colonel Julian Byng's South African 10th Hussar regiment, with permission to roam freely between combats.

During this campaign, Churchill was exhilarated as he engaged in nearly daily firefights and the battles of Spion Kop and Doornkloof. He recalled:

> The two months fighting for the relief of Ladysmith make one of the most happy memories of my life … We had one skirmish after another with casualties running from half a dozen to a score … Day after day we rode out in the early morning on one flank or another and played about with the Boers, galloped around or clambered up the rocky hills, caught glimpses of darting, fleeting horsemen in the distance, heard a few bullets whistle, had a few careful shots and came … home to a good dinner and cheery, keenly intelligent companions … Meanwhile I dispatched a continual stream of letters and cables to *The Morning Post* and learned from them that all I wrote commanded a wide and influential public. I knew all the generals and other swells, had access to everyone and was everywhere well received.[50]

The Boer War became a Churchill family affair when not just his brother Jack but his indomitable mother joined him on campaign. Jennie had gathered £41,597 in contributions from wealthy Americans, commissioned a hospital ship and sailed to Durban, South Africa. Among her first patients was Jack, who was shot in the calf while serving beside Churchill at the battle of Hussar Hill.

Buller's army finally drove the Boers from Ladysmith and relieved that garrison on 28 February, 1900. That ended the fighting on that front. Churchill sought permission to join Roberts's army. Unfortunately his request coincided with an article in which he called for reconciling rather than punishing the Boers and criticized a spiteful sermon by the army's head chaplain. Many officers found these words especially offensive:

> Beware of driving men to desperation. Even a cornered rat is dangerous. We desire a speedy peace and the last thing we want is that this war should enter upon a guerrilla phase. Those who demand 'an eye for an eye and a tooth for a tooth' should ask themselves whether such barren spoils are worth five years of bloody partisan warfare and the consequent impoverishment of South Africa.[51]

The Boer War lasted another two years.

Roberts and Kitchener did what they could to prevent Churchill from joining their army, but Lord Salisbury overrode them. Churchill attached himself to General John French's cavalry division although he 'disapproved of me' and 'completely ignored my existence and showed me no sign of courtesy or good will'. Churchill understood that:

> I was that hybrid ... of subaltern officer and widely followed war correspondent which was not unnaturally obnoxious to the military mind. A young lieutenant, discussing the greatest matters of policy and war with complete assurance ... distributing blame among veteran commanders, apparently immune from regulation of routine and gathering war experience and medals all the time.[52]

He experienced his latest near-death experience on 22 April, when he rode with Captain Angus McNeil's Scouts with the mission of overrunning a Boer commando company on a distant hill. The Boers opened fire as the Scouts approached the hill. Assuming they would assault the enemy on foot, Churchill dismounted just as McNeil ordered a withdrawal. As Churchill struggled to remount, his terrified horse broke free and galloped off. Luckily he was able to scramble up behind another trooper and they rode to safety.

As the Boers abandoned Johannesburg and the British army prepared to enter it, Churchill embarked on his latest perilous adventure. He and a Frenchman, who knew Johannesburg, donned civilian clothes and bicycled into the city. Had the Boers captured Churchill they would have summarily shot him because 'I was an officer holding a commission in the South African Light Horse, disguised in plain clothes and secretly in the enemy lines'. But he was determined to be the first in Johannesburg for a thrilling story in which he was the hero. The British army bloodlessly occupied Johannesburg on 1 June, then, four days later, entered Pretoria, with Churchill again leading the way. His first stop was his former prison where he led the prisoners in disarming the guards and liberating themselves.

Having literally come full circle, he decided that was an appropriate way to end his campaign. He resigned his commission and spent a month in Ladysmith writing his latest book, *London to Ladysmith via Pretoria*; it would be a bestseller, with 11,000 copies bought in the first six weeks alone. He then headed by train to Cape Town.[53] Guerrillas attacked the train near Kopjes Station. Churchill took command and got the engineer to reverse course. As it neared the town he spotted 'under the burning bridge a cluster of dark figures. These were the last Boers I was to see as enemies. I fitted the wood stock to the Mauser pistol and fired six or seven times at them. They scattered without firing back.'[54] He was only able to resume his journey after British forces chased away the Boers and repaired the tracks.

Colonel Ian Hamilton recommended Churchill for a Victoria Cross for 'conspicuous gallantry' in various battles, but Kitchener and Roberts blackballed the application. Churchill sailed from Cape Town on 7 July and disembarked at Southampton on 20 July 1900, eager to exchange soldiering for politics.

Chapter 3

The Reformer

'If we carry on in the old happy-go-lucky way, the richer classes ever growing in wealth and in number, the very poor remaining plunged or plunging ever deeper into helpless, hopeless misery, then I think there is nothing before us but the savage strife between class and class and an increasing disorganization, with the increasing waste of human strength and human virtue.'

After returning home, Churchill's first important engagement was social rather than political. On 27 July 1900, he attended a wedding that was the talk of high society. His mother, then 45 years old, had fallen in love with George Cornwallis-West, a dashing army captain who was the same age as her eldest son. Churchill wrote to his brother Jack that the wedding 'went off very well. The whole of the Churchill family ... was drawn in a solid phalanx and their approval ratified the business.'[1]

With that behind him, Churchill devoted himself to politics. His fame as a Boer War hero made him a highly desirable candidate. The Conservative Party in eleven constituencies solicited him to be their candidate in the next election. Churchill, however, was determined to win Oldham, the scene of his first, failed attempt to take a parliamentary seat. Prime Minister Lord Salisbury dissolved Parliament on 17 September. Two days later, Churchill announced his candidacy and began two weeks of hard campaigning with several speeches daily before diverse audiences. The votes were counted on 1 October . This time he won one of the district's two seats, with his 12,931 votes only 16 less than the candidate with the most, a Liberal candidate and 221 votes ahead of the other Liberal candidate.[2]

Yet he did not attend the brief parliamentary session in December. Instead, hard-up for cash, he embarked on a promotional tour for his just-published fifth book, *Ian Hamilton's March*, that took him to cities in Britain, the United States and Canada. When his book appeared on 12 October, he quipped that he had written 'as many books as Moses'.[3] In America the loftiest celebrities that he met were President William McKinley, New York

Governor Theodore Roosevelt and Mark Twain. His publicist talked Twain into introducing him at his first lecture, held at New York's Waldorf Astoria Hotel. The introduction was not what Churchill expected. Twain praised Churchill but denounced the imperialist wars of Britain against the Boers and America against the Filipinos. Although Churchill bristled at the rebuke, he got Twain to add his signature beside his own in the thirty books for sale. In one, Twain wrote: 'To be good is noble; to teach others how to be good is nobler & no trouble.'[4] Twain's wit was among Churchill's models. After nearly six weeks in North America he sailed home on 21 February 1901.

While Churchill was away, symbolically if not substantively, Queen Victoria brought the era named after her to an end when she died on 22 January 1901 after a 64-year reign. Looking back thirty years later, he recalled a British world 'very different in the days of Queen Victoria. Then the world seemed set in a frame and the paths of progress were clearly marked before us. Free trade, the Gold Standard, our Indian Empire, a supreme Navy, universal education, the sweeping away of class privilege and the gradual but constant extension of the franchise.'[5] The Victorian era's true demise, however, would come thirteen years later on 4 August 1914, when the First World War erupted in Europe. Her son, the Prince of Wales, took the throne as King Edward VII. Jennie Churchill counted Edward among her sexual conquests and had repeatedly got him to wield his influence to advance her son's ambitions. Now Edward would have even more power to lend to that task.

Winston Churchill first sat in Parliament on 14 February 1901, an appropriate date given that politics was the great love of his life. He gave his maiden speech on the 24th. All went well until, in a plea for tolerance and conciliation to end the war against the Boers, he uttered this line: 'If I were a Boer fighting in the field … and if I were a Boer, I hope I should be fighting in the field.' That provoked an eruption of protests that briefly flummoxed him. But he rallied and finished to general applause and cheers. That controversial assertion was the first of countless others over the next six decades. The Conservative Party's leaders soon recognized that their 26-year-old star was a maverick who did not hesitate to break ranks when his principles or ego led him elsewhere.[6] He explained his outlook of that era: 'I became anxious to make the Conservative party follow Liberal courses. I was in revolt against "jingoism". I had a sentimental view of the Boers. I found myself differing from both parties in various ways … I did not understand the importance of party discipline and unity.'[7]

His next assertion was to condemn the army budget's near doubling from £17 million in 1894 to £30 million in 1901, with Secretary of War St John Brodrick proposing to expand the army to three corps which would cost millions more to underwrite. Churchill condemned Brodrick's proposal because

> any danger that comes to Britain would not be on land, it would come on the sea. With regard to our military system we must be prepared to deal with all the little wars which occur continually on the frontiers of the Empire ... We cannot expect to meet great wars ... for I think our game essentially is to be a naval and commercial power. I cannot look upon the army as anything but an adjunct to the navy ... I hope that in considering the lessons of the South African war we shall not be drawn from our true policy, which is to preserve the command of markets and the seas.[8]

In this he won his first victory in Parliament when Brodrick resigned. But his blunt criticisms and maverick positions split the Conservative Party between those for and those against him. He formed a dinner club called The Hooligans that convened each Thursday night with different invited guest speakers from across the political spectrum.

Tariffs were the third issue over which Churchill defied his party. To the outrage of most of his colleagues, he embraced classic liberal economic theory by denouncing protectionism and advocating free trade. In a speech he demanded that his listeners answer this barrage of rhetorical questions: 'Will the shutting out of foreign goods increase the total amount of wealth in this country? Can foreign nations grow rich at our expense by selling us goods under cost price? Can a people tax themselves into prosperity? Can a man stand in a bucket and lift himself up by the handle?'[9] Although 'no' is the only answer to the last question, 'it depends on how it is done and what other countries are doing' is the best reply to the other questions. However, he moved from shaky to firm historic ground when he made this comparison:

> Socialism seeks to pull down wealth, Liberalism seeks to raise up poverty. Socialism would destroy private interests; Liberalism would preserve private interests ... by reconciling them with public right. Socialism would kill enterprise. Liberalism would rescue enterprise from the trammels of privilege and preference. Socialism assails the pre-eminence of the individual; Liberalism seeks ... to build up a

minimum standard for the mass. Socialism exalts the rule; Liberalism exalts the man. Social attacks capital; Liberalism attacks monopoly.[10]

Regardless, in championing free trade, Churchill not only opposed his party but most of his working-class constituents. Mercantilism shielded British industries and their workers from competitive foreign products. Stripping away that protection would force British industrialists to cut costs to survive, which usually meant some mix of raising efficiency, firing surplus workers and slashing wages. In the short term, workers bore the worst burden even if the industry eventually survived and even thrived. Theoretically that burden would be alleviated as new enterprises hired the jobless and everyone enjoyed cheaper prices in the competitive marketplace. Churchill also pointed to a strategic rationale for free trade. He argued that America would supply Britain with cheap food and raw materials. Ideally, Britain's national security would increase as economic interdependence thickened between those countries. If another great power or powers warred against Britain, America logically would back Britain to protect the profits from its exports to the realm.[11]

Intellectually and ethically Churchill achieved a breakthrough after reading Sebum Rowntree's *Poverty: A Study of Town Life*.[12] Having been born into the cocoon of upper-class privilege, he was imbued with the conservative conceit that bad character impoverished lives. Now he understood the vicious cycle of abysmal economic, social, educational and political conditions that trapped people in poverty and he became a champion for breaking those chains. He summed up the dilemmas and misplaced policy priorities with this line: 'I see little glory in an Empire which can rule the waves and is unable to flush its sewers.'[13] He tried to rally the Conservative Party to join him during a conference at Blackpool in January 1902, but initially attracted a mere dozen followers.

After Salisbury resigned on 11 July 1902, Arthur Balfour took his place as prime minister, with his right-hand man Colonial Secretary Joseph Chamberlain. They debated whether to condemn or somehow co-opt Churchill by offering him a minor ministry. But Churchill was determined to transform the party or, if that failed, join the Opposition. His open revolt came on 13 July 1903, when he announced the establishment of the Free Food League with sixty Conservative members compared to only thirty members in the Tariff Reform League led by Balfour and Chamberlain. Churchill took his campaign to the people with a speaking tour around Britain. When Balfour refused to denounce Churchill or endorse the high tariff policy,

Chamberlain resigned on 12 September. Balfour then pressured the three free trade advocates in the Cabinet also to resign. On 2 October, Balfour announced that the Conservative Party would pass a protectionist bill. The Conservative Party pressured the Oldham branch to denounce Churchill, which it did on 8 January 1904. Churchill offered to resign, knowing that he would likely win a subsequent by-election as a Liberal Party candidate. That forced Oldham's Tories to back down.

A turning point came on 28 March 1904, when Prime Minister Balfour and Postmaster General Austen Chamberlain walked out while Churchill was delivering a speech critical of Conservative Party policies. After Churchill angrily castigated the leaders for disrespecting him, the rest of the Cabinet and most other Tories joined their leaders outside, while only about thirty Conservative allies remained. Churchill's campaign to transform the party had failed disastrously.

Churchill negotiated the terms of his defection with Liberal Party leaders, especially Herbert Asquith. The Liberal Association of the Northwest Manchester district asked him to be a candidate. Churchill accepted on 18 April. The stress of being a turncoat was driving him toward an emotional breakdown. When he rose to speak on 22 April, his mind went completely blank. He sat back down and buried his head in his hands as his enemies howled in derision. On 31 May 1904, he strode across the floor of the Commons chamber to sit on the Liberal Party's side. That defection led to him being booted out of the Conservative Carlton Club and Hurlingham Club. And he had inadvertently jumped from the proverbial frying pan into the fire. What neither he nor anyone else at the time could anticipate was that the Liberal Party was peaking as a political force and would become nearly extinct within a generation. Indeed as a junior member of the opposition party, Churchill could do little more than hone his rhetorical skills over the next twenty months.[14]

Exhausted by the political struggles within and beyond his party, Prime Minister Balfour resigned on 4 December 1905. King Edward VII asked Liberal Party leader Henry Campbell-Bannerman to take his place and form a Cabinet. Campbell-Bannerman promptly dissolved Parliament and scheduled a general election from 12 January to 8 February 1906. With the votes counted, the Liberal Party took 397 seats; Churchill was among eight Liberals who won seats in Manchester. The Conservative Party plummeted from 402 seats to 156; Balfour was among those who lost his seat. The Irish Nationalist Party and Labour Party won 82 and 29 seats, respectively.[15]

Meanwhile, Churchill was appointed the Undersecretary of State at the Colonial Office, headed by Victor Bruce, Lord Elgin, in the government that Campbell-Bannerman formed in December 1905. His first major project was to draft a constitution for the newly-conquered Transvaal. He presented what was his first state paper on 2 January 1906. His theme was Boer home rule as a dominion beneath British sovereignty. Nothing else could conciliate that conquered people and entice diehard guerrillas from the field. He presented a similar constitution for the Orange Free State in December 1906. Boers dominated the Transvaal parliament and elected Louis Botha the prime minister in March 1907. In another human rights issue, Churchill pressed for the immediate liberation and repatriation of Chinese coolie labour from South Africa; mine owners kept the Chinese in abysmal, near slave conditions. The government approved and implemented that proposal as well.

Churchill embarked for a five-month journey that took him through France to Egypt and up the Nile valley all the way to Kenya where the highlight was a hunting safari. Typically he mixed business with his pleasure trip that was supposed to be an official inspection. He earned £1,150 for a series of articles that he wrote for *Strand Magazine*, then later made more money when he bundled the articles into a book called *My African Journey*. He turned from adventure to reform in an article entitled 'The Untrodden Field in Politics' for *The Nation* in March 1908. His core argument was that political freedom was inseparable from social and economic development which the state was obliged to nurture by providing universal schooling, technical training, a minimum living wage, health care and pensions.[16]

That same month Churchill was seated beside a young woman at a dinner party who he had first met at a ball four years earlier. He had made a terrible first impression. The beauty, grace and aloofness of then 19-year-old Clementine Hozier had stunned him. He could not think of anything to say to her, not even to ask her to dance; he just rudely stared at her in wonder. His second performance was slightly less awful. He dominated the conversation which was pretty much all about himself then ended by asking her if he had read his biography of his father. When she replied that she had not, he promised to send her a copy but broke his promise. Later that spring he initiated an epistolary relationship with her. His brother Jack's wedding that summer inspired him to follow suit. Churchill got his cousin the Duke of Marlborough to invite Clementine to Blenheim Palace for the weekend and on Sunday mustered the courage to ask her to marry him. She had already been engaged twice but terminated both. Now she accepted her third offer and, for better or worse, was determined to keep this one. They publicly announced their engagement on 15 August and married at St. Margaret's Church, Westminster on 12 September 1908. He leased a home for them in the upscale neighbourhood of Pimlico. Churchill's whirlwind matrimony campaign all took place as he received a post that empowered him to pursue his ambitious reform agenda.

When ill health forced Campbell-Bannerman to resign on 3 April 1908, Herbert Asquith succeeded him as prime minister. Asquith tapped Churchill to be the President of the Board of Trade, but there was a catch. The rules then required anyone with a new Cabinet portfolio to undergo a by-election in his district. Churchill lost by 429 votes, with 4,988 to his opponent's 5,417, but the Liberal Party found him a safe seat in Dundee on 9 May, which he won.

Now politically secure, Churchill embarked on his reform campaign in partnership with David Lloyd George, the Chancellor of the Exchequer.[17] He lyrically explained the virtuous cycle of prosperity, political freedom and security he sought to bring to Britain:

> Every forward step was followed by swiftly reaped advantages: the wider the franchise, the more solid the State; the fewer the taxes, the more abundant the revenue; the freer the entry of goods into the island, the more numerous and richer were the markets gained abroad ... to enforce frugality upon Governments, to liberate the native genius of the country, to let wealth fructify in the pockets of the people, to open a career broadly and freely to the talents of every class, these were the paths ... to tread.[18]

Churchill's first reform was to ameliorate the dismal pay and working conditions in the coal mining industry. In July 1908, he introduced the Coal Mines Regulation Act that reduced the working day to eight hours. He justified his proposal with this argument: 'The general march of industrial democracy is not toward inadequate hours of work, but towards sufficient hours of leisure.'[19] He sought for workers balanced lives between earning and enjoying. He called for Labour Exchanges where unemployed workers could go to find jobs. The act passed, the first of five reform bills that he helped spearhead through Parliament, which also included the Children's Act, the Companies Consolidation Act, the Old Age Pension Act and the Statute Law Revision Act.[20]

To pay for his reform programmes, Churchill sought two sources. Higher taxes would supply the lion's share. However, he pledged to tax 'not wages, but wealth'. He would not 'lay any taxes on the wealthy classes which could not be justified in equity or … be borne without trenching on their comforts or even elegances. We, in short, propose to tax luxuries, monopolies and superfluities, but we scrupulously avoid taxing the necessities of life.'[21] For additional revenue, he joined Lloyd George to urge diverting the cost of two of six dreadnoughts or state-of-the-art battleships to be built in 1909 as advocated by Reginald McKenna, First Lord of the Admiralty. Prime Minister Asquith appeased both sides by agreeing to the diversion while allocating enough money to build four dreadnoughts in 1909 and four more in 1910. Churchill explained that 'a curious and characteristic solution was reached: The Admiralty had demanded six ships: the economists offered four and we finally compromised on eight.' As for initially wanted to cut back the number of dreadnoughts he admitted that while he and Lloyd George 'were right in the narrow sense, we were absolutely wrong in relation to the deep tides of destiny'.[22]

What Churchill referred to was Germany's ambitions to supplant Britain as the world's greatest naval power. The tensions provoked by that fierce arms race contributed to the outbreak of the First World War in August 1914.[23] He was privileged to get a glimpse of what might lie ahead as Kaiser Wilhelm II's guest at the German Army manoeuvres of 1906 and 1908. The Kaiser 'was then at the height of his glory. As he sat on his horse surrounded by Kings and Princes while his legions defiled before him in what seems to be an endless procession, he represented all that his world has to give in material things.' Churchill was far more impressed with the German army than its leader: 'Wilhelm II had none of the qualities of the modern dictators, except their airs. He was a picturesque figurehead in the centre of the world stage.'[24]

In September 1908, Churchill resolved the first labour dispute brought before him. The Electrical Workers Union protested the threat by electrical power plant managers to fire anyone who did not accept wage cutbacks. By a vote of 4,606 to 3,739, the union approved his compromise that it take a smaller cut in return for the owners' promise not to cut wages again for half a year.[25] He tried to persuade those reluctant to support these reforms with arguments like these:

If we carry on in the old happy-go-lucky way, the richer classes ever growing in wealth and in number, the very poor remaining plunged or plunging ever deeper into helpless, hopeless misery, then I think there is nothing before us but the savage strife between class and class and an increasing disorganization, with the increasing waste of human strength and human virtue ... The greatest danger to the British Empire and to the British people is not to be found among the enormous fleets and armies of the European Continent, nor ... any danger in the wide circuit of colonial and foreign affairs. No, it is here in our midst, close at hand in the vast growing cities of England and Scotland ... It is there that you will find the seeds of Imperial ruin and national decay.[26]

Churchill and Lloyd George succeeded in getting Parliament to pass more reforms in 1909, including the complimentary Trade Boards Bill and the Labour Exchange Board Bill that regulated wages, working hours and conditions and provided job opportunities, with the government to arbitrate any deadlocked disputes. They also introduced the National Health Insurance Act although Parliament did not pass it until 1911. To help pay for the expanding array of reforms, they got a People's Budget passed that raised taxes on petrol, whisky, pub licences, inheritance, unused land and capital gains, along with higher taxes on Britons who enjoyed annual incomes higher than £3,500, then around 11,500 or so people. Conservative criticisms that Churchill was 'a traitor to his class' rose to a crescendo.

Churchill's progeny in 1909 was not confined to progressive laws. Clementine gave birth to their first child, a daughter they named Diana. The pregnancy and birth exhausted Clementine and she needed months to recuperate. She endured the whole process of conception, delivery and childrearing out of duty rather than desire. She was not fond of children and left as much of that tedious intrusion as possible to nannies. However, like most traditional women, she was devoted to her husband and his career which gave her wealth and status. She actually saved his life at Bristol's railway station on 15 November 1909. A suffragette named Theresa Garnet attacked Churchill with a whip and then shoved him toward the edge of the platform as a train rumbled down the tracks. Clementine grabbed his coat and pulled him back just in time. As police arrested Garnet, the would-be murderer snarled, 'You brute, why don't you treat British women properly?'[27]

Churchill favoured women's rights, to a point. He loathed the radical feminists led by Emmeline Pankhurst who not only committed acts of civil disobedience but also terrorism by smashing windows and planting bombs.[28] He declared: 'Nothing would induce me to vote for giving women the franchise. I am not going to be henpecked on a question of such great importance.'[29] Nonetheless, when two suffragettes were arrested for disrupting one of his speeches in Manchester, he had the good political sense masked as gallantry to offer to pay their fine. They refused to be co-opted and stayed in jail for a week. During another protest at one of his speeches, he pointed out that Sylvia Pankhurst, Emmeline's daughter, was holding her 'Votes for Women' sign upside down, then invited her on stage to express her views. When the crowd roared against her, he tried to hush them, exclaiming: 'Will everyone please be quiet.' Voices shouted that they had come to hear him. He tried to placate the crowd by declaring: 'We should be fair and chivalrous to ladies. They come here asking us to treat them like men. That is what I particularly want to avoid. We must observe courtesy and chivalry to the weaker sex dependent on us.'[30] At that, an enraged Pankhurst strode away.

In a Cabinet shakeup, Asquith rewarded Churchill for his decisive role in pushing through reforms by naming him Home Secretary on 14 February 1910. At 35, he was the youngest Home Secretary since Robert Peel. Given his own brief stint in captivity, he was determined to add Britain's prison system to his reform agenda with this underlying value: 'The first real principle which should guide anyone trying to establish a good system of prisons should be to prevent as many people as possible getting there at all.'[31] He sought to alleviate their bleak tedium with libraries and lectures and reduce the then 184,000 inmates with early releases for the one in three there for relatively minor offenses like drunkenness or failure to pay fines for various infractions. Thanks to Churchill the number of debtors in prison dropped from 95,686 to 5,264 and drunks from 62,822 to 1,670. As for suffragettes, he let them wear their own clothes, speak with each other, bathe and receive packages. He established a Central Agency that helped released prisoners readjust to life outside. While he exalted in being able to make these reforms, he found one duty of the Home Secretary terribly distressing, deciding whether a judge's decision for capital punishment was warranted.[32]

Asquith asked Churchill to spearhead a bill to curb the power of the House of Lords to veto spending bills. On 31 March 1910, Churchill rose in the House of Commons to deliver these incendiary lines:

> We have reached a fateful period in British history. The time for words is past, the time for action has arrived. Since the House of Lords … have used their Veto to affront the Prerogative of the Crown and to invade the rights of the Commons, it has now become necessary that the Crown and the Commons, acting together, should restore the

balance of the Constitution and restrict forever the Veto of the House of Lords.[33]

That did the trick, at least with the pending budget, which the Lords passed on 28 April. Asquith then prepared to ask Edward VII to appoint 500 Liberal lords to dilute that conservative body. He waited too late. On 6 May, Britain got a new king when Edward VII died and his more conservative son took the throne as George V. Asquith and Churchill decided to delay that request for six months as the new king settled into his duties.

Like his predecessor, George V was concerned about the growing tensions between London and Berlin as the German navy expanded to catch up with Briton's. Churchill had twice accepted invitations to attend Germany's annual September army manoeuvres, once as Colonial Undersecretary in 1906 and then as the President of the Board of Trade in 1909. In May 1910, aware of his experiences, George V wrote to Churchill for his assessment of the German threat. In his reply, Churchill downplayed any danger from Germany and advised a conciliatory attitude toward Berlin.

Churchill resolved his latest labour conflict in November 1910 when 25,000 coal miners went on strike and riots broke out at Rhondda, Wales. He deployed 400 troops to back 1,500 police mobilized from across the country to reimpose order. He then cut a deal whereby the miners returned to work in exchange for his promise to promote bills that alleviated working conditions for them and other labourers. He would be good to his word. He had no sooner ended that strike when violence shattered London's East End. An anarchist group on a crime spree murdered three policemen then holed up in a tenement. A standoff ensued as police blocked off the streets but dared not assault the heavily armed men. Churchill arrived at the scene and took charge. Suddenly smoke and flames seeped from the tenement. A dispute arose between firemen who wanted to put out the blaze and policemen who wanted the fire to drive out the anarchists. Churchill sided with the police but the anarchists died in the flames, apparently intentionally. He weathered harsh criticism from his handling of both the coal and anarchist crises, for using troops to suppress the miners and rejecting the firemen's pleas to extinguish the fire.

The Conservative Party made a comeback in the election held from 3 to 10 December 1910, winning 271 seats, just one behind the 272 Liberal Party seats, while the Irish Parliamentary Party and the Labour Party won 72 and 42 seats, respectively. The Liberal Party made the most of its razor-thin victory by promoting several key reforms in 1911. Churchill got Parliament to pass his Coal Miners Bill that imposed safety and working hour standards. However, business groups pressured enough parliamentarians to kill his Shops Bill that would have cut the work week from eighty hours to sixty, imposed sanitation standards and given bonuses for overtime, meal breaks and a weekly early closing day. Finally, Churchill was instrumental in helping draft the Unemployment Insurance Bill that Parliament passed.

These progressive steps merely whetted labour's appetite for more. Communist and anarchist agitators provoked huge strikes and demonstrations in 1912, first by 80,000 workers in the docklands and then by 200,000 workers and their supporters in the railways. Once again Churchill wielded the stick and carrot by deploying massive numbers of police backed by troops to restore order while trying to talk the strike leaders into standing down in return for more reforms.

Churchill's most remarkable act during this stage of his political career was to predict how the opening six weeks of a war between Germany and France would unfold.[34] As Home Secretary he served on the Committee of Imperial Defence. On 13 August 1911, he submitted a memorandum that analysed the most likely war scenario between France and Germany. He anticipated a German attack through Belgium that outflanked the French army on the Meuse River by the twentieth day. The Germans would then rout the French and march on Paris unless the British deployed an army in Flanders to threaten their right flank. He foresaw that by the fortieth day the Germans would be exhausted and overextended, thus providing the allied French and British armies the chance for a counter-attack that drove them back. That is pretty much what happened in August and September 1914 that culminated with the Battle of the Marne. He would play critical roles in Britain's land and sea strategy during those fateful weeks.

Chapter 4

The Scapegoat

'We must at all costs win. Victory is a better boon than life and life without it will be unendurable. It rests with us to make sure that these sacrifices are not made in vain.'

'This is living History. Everything we are doing is thrilling – it will be read by a thousand generations, think of that! Why I would not be out of this glorious delicious war for anything the world could give me.'

P rime Minister Herbert Asquith appointed Winston Churchill First Lord of the Admiralty on 24 October 1911. Churchill immediately embarked on a set of initiatives to expand and modernize the navy. He accelerated the transformation begun by the former First Sea Lord, Admiral Sir John Fisher, who had developed and deployed the dreadnought class of battleships, then the world's largest, with 13.5in guns that fired 1,400lb shells, a huge advance over the previous largest guns with 12in bores that fired 850lb shells. He then developed a new super-dreadnought class with eight 15in guns, 13in armour plate and more powerful engines that propelled those behemoths at a nominal 25 knots. They were also oil rather than coal-fired, which extended a ship's range 40 per cent before refuelling. He scrapped obsolete ships. He promoted officers committed to a technologically cutting-edge navy and purged those who were opposed. Finally, he massed the fleet in British waters to counter Germany's rising naval power.[1]

As for strategy, he upheld the nation's venerable tradition: 'Hitherto all British naval arrangements had proceeded on the basis of the two-Power standard, namely, an adequate superiority over the next two strongest Powers.'[2] As for tactics, to win approval for the more powerful class of dreadnoughts, he typically made his case before Parliament with vivid imagery:

If you want to make a true picture in your mind of a battle between two great modern iron-clad ships, you must not think of it as if it were two men in armour striking at each other with heavy swords. It is more like a battle between two egg-shells striking each other with hammers … The importance of hitting first and hitting hardest and keeping on hitting … really needs no clearer proof.[3]

The conversion to petroleum required a new foreign policy. With no oil fields in the home islands or across the empire, Britain had to acquire rights to develop that resource elsewhere. Geologists estimated that Persia had large, relatively easily extractable oil fields. Churchill got Parliament to allocate £5 million to acquire a controlling interest in the existing the Anglo-Persian Oil Company, which was established in 1901. Under the agreement, Persia received 16 per cent of all profits, which meant the British government and private investors split 84 per cent according to their respective shares. The Anglo-Persian Company soon signed deals with the Ottoman Empire to establish subsidiaries that developed oil fields in today's Iraq, Georgia and Azerbaijan. Other government funds were invested in building huge oil storage and processing facilities.

The development of submarines posed a clear threat to all surface ships, including battleships. The Royal Navy needed a sanctuary far enough from Germany's growing submarine fleet yet close enough to sail forth to protect Britain from a potential invasion. Churchill chose Scapa Flow in the Orkney Islands north of Scotland. Anti-submarine nets were stretched across its mouth to shield the fleet which could sail south into the North Sea or south-west into the Atlantic if need be.

Churchill established the Royal Naval Air Service not just for reconnaissance but eventually equipped with planes large enough to attack targets at sea. Characteristically, as a hands-on leader he insisted on learning how to fly. Clementine tried to put a stop to that after two of his trainers were killed in a crash the day after one of his lessons. He promised to stop for now with these words: 'I will not fly any more until … the risks may have been greatly reduced.' Yet doing so would be a sacrifice:

I have been up nearly 140 times, with many pilots & all kinds of machines, so I know the difficulties, the dangers & the joys of the air … it was an important part of my life during the last seven months & I am sure my nerve, my spirit & my virtue were all improved by it. But at your expense my poor pussy cat! I am sorry.[4]

Of all the perks of being First Lord, Churchill most enjoyed the Admiralty yacht, *Enchantress*, which became my office, almost my home; and my work my sole occupation and my amusement. In all I spent eight months afloat in the three years before the war. I visited every dockyard, shipyard and naval establishment in the British Isles and in the Mediterranean and every important ship. I examined for myself every point of strategic consequences ... I could put my hand on anything that was wanted and knew thoroughly the current state of our naval affairs.[5]

Germany's naval build-up was Churchill's biggest worry. He hoped that behind-the-scenes diplomacy might end the naval arms race between Germany and Britain. For a special envoy he selected Sir Ernest Cassel, who was born in Prussia but became a British citizen, converted from Judaism to Catholicism and made a fortune in an array of mining, manufacturing and financial ventures. In early 1912, he sent Cassel to Berlin to inform Wilhelm II that until he 'dropped the naval challenge' the British would view Germany 'with deepening suspicion and apprehension'. Cassel returned with a disturbing message from the Kaiser: Germany's naval build-up would not just continue but accelerate with fifteen rather than twelve new dreadnoughts along with four more large cruisers, twelve smaller cruisers and fifty submarines that were scheduled to join the fleet within six years, while the Kiel Canal that linked the North and Baltic Seas would be deepened to let the largest warships transit.[6]

Churchill then wielded public diplomacy in an attempt to freeze the arms race. In a speech before Parliament on 9 March 1912, he called for all the great powers to take a one-year 'naval holiday' or suspension of warship construction. During that year, he hoped to negotiate a naval arms limitation treaty. He felt that his public diplomacy would succeed no matter what happened: 'If the Germans refuse I shall have made my case for action. If they accept, it will be a big event in the world's affairs.'[7] After Berlin ignored his appeal, he got Parliament to approve a naval budget of £50,694,800 for 1914.[8] He hoped to make the case for a naval limitation treaty directly to the Kaiser after being invited to attend the German navy's review at Kiel in June 1912. However, Prime Minister Asquith and Foreign Secretary Edward Grey convinced him that attending might be perceived as approving Germany's naval build-up, while rejecting the invitation would send the opposite message. All along Churchill remained confident that the awareness among the great powers of the horrors of modern warfare would deter them from actually fighting one another. That hope proved to be severely misplaced.

Although it was not in Churchill's official bailiwick, Asquith asked him to resolve the conflict between Ireland's Nationalists and Unionists. Catholics were the majority except the six northern counties of Ulster, where two-thirds of the people were Protestants. Nearly all Catholics wanted independence while most Protestants insisted on remaining in the United Kingdom. Each side was heavily armed and prepared to fight for its cause with the Catholic Irish Republican Army versus the Protestant Ulster Volunteer Force or Orangemen. Churchill sought to bridge that chasm with the Home Rule Bill that would grant Ireland dominion status within the British Empire. Although after he submitted the bill on 11 April 1912, the House of Commons twice passed it, a majority in the House of Lords blocked it each time. To bypass that roadblock, Churchill advocated a referendum for each Irish county to decide whether to remain in the United Kingdom or become a dominion. Those measures became unnecessary in March 1914, when the Home Rule bill became law after passing the House of Commons for the third time; the House of Lords can only veto a bill twice. But Whitehall suspended the process of transforming Ireland into a dominion after the First World War erupted in August 1914.

*   *   *

The causes of the First World War were complex and diverse, with each of Europe's great powers responsible more or less.[9] A general peace had prevailed in Europe from 1815, with Napoleon's final defeat at the Battle of Waterloo and the 'Concert' of great powers that thereafter worked to ensure that crises over local conflicts did not ignite a continental conflagration. The First World War would have been unlikely without the brilliant statesmanship of Prussian Otto von Bismarck, who unified Germany under Berlin's leadership in three wars, against Denmark in 1864, Austria in 1866 and France from 1870 to 1871. Yet just because Germany surpassed France and Russia in economic and military might on the continent did not make a world war inevitable. Indeed, Bismarck was determined to prevent that by encouraging the great powers to sublimate any tensions by cooperating on divvying up much of Africa, Asia and the Pacific Islands among their respective empires. However, to that end, he wielded potential military power to pressure the British and French to accept a German overseas empire. He formed an alliance between Germany and Austria in 1879, then expanded it to a Triple Alliance with Italy in 1882.

But in 1890, Kaiser Wilhelm II dismissed Bismarck and adopted a more aggressive policy on the continent and beyond. The Kaiser's most critical departure from Bismarck's policies was for Germany to try to supplant Britain as the greatest naval power. The subsequent naval arms race between Britain and Germany raised tensions among all the great powers. The more powerful its fleet, the more Berlin flexed its naval muscle. Wilhelm II's belligerent rhetoric and behaviour worried Germany's neighbours the French and Russians more than the British, secure in their island realm. In 1894, France and Russia formed a defensive alliance. Although the French wanted an alliance, in 1904 the British agreed only agreed to sign an entente cordiale whereby they accepted each other's existing empires and spheres of influence.

Britain feared Russia far more than Germany since their empires were expanding toward each other in Central Asia.[10] The defensive alliance that Britain and Japan formed in 1902 was an attempt by both to contain the mutual Russian threat. Tragically that emboldened Tokyo to be more assertive in north-east Asia where Japan and Russia had overlapping spheres of influence and ambitions. The Russo-Japanese War from 1904 to 1905 was a devastating military, economic and political defeat for Russia. In 1907, Britain tried to reset the skewed power balance by signing a convention with Russia that France joined later that year. Although Britain had only ententes with France and Russia, it had an obligation to uphold the neutrality of Belgium that dated to 1839. Thus were the great powers tied into two huge mutually suspicious blocks of countries that split Europe and other regions around the world. These alliances and ententes both contributed to and helped resolve crises among the great powers over Morocco in 1906 and 1911.

Meanwhile the Ottoman Empire steadily crumbled. Bulgaria declared independence on 22 September 1908, Austria annexed Bosnia-Herzegovina on 5 October the same year, and Italy began its conquest of Libya by occupying Tripoli on 3 October 1911. The Turks were powerless to prevent any of these events. Then in 1912, the Balkans erupted in war as Albania, Macedonia and Thrace revolted against Ottoman rule. Eventually Greece, Romania and Bulgaria joined the fighting that persisted well into 1913.

Despite the rising tensions, virtually no one in Britain imagined that war, let alone a horrendous four-year world war, lay just beyond the political horizon. Churchill recalled: 'All around flowed the busy life of peaceful, unsuspecting, easy-going Britain. The streets were thronged with men and women utterly devoid of any sense of danger from abroad. For a hundred years the safety of the homeland had never been threatened.'[11] And he shared the belief that peace would prevail, that Europe's statesmen would continue to manage with reason and compromises any crisis from spiralling into war. Yet, just to be on the safe side, he 'began to make inquiries about vulnerable points ... about sabotage and espionage and counter-espionage'.[12]

The triggering event that made the First World War likely happened by chance. On 28 June 1914, the Serbian terrorist Gavrilo Princip shot to death Austrian Archduke Franz Ferdinand and his wife Sophie when their chauffeured automobile took a wrong turn and stopped in front of him in Sarajevo, Bosnia-Herzegovina's capital. Over the next four weeks, Austria's Emperor Franz Josef and his ministers debated how to respond as Austrian spies gathered more intelligence. On 23 July, Vienna issued an ultimatum to Belgrade that condemned Serbian officials and officers for sponsoring the terrorist group the Black Hand that committed the murders and demanded that Serbia arrest and prosecute all those involved in the conspiracy, halt anti-Austrian propaganda and let the Austrians oversee that process.

Upon hearing of Vienna's ultimatum, Asquith convened the Cabinet to discuss the implications. Churchill recalled his reaction: 'it was an ultimatum such as had never been penned in modern times ... it seemed ... impossible that any State in the world would accept it or that any acceptance ... would satisfy the aggressor.'[13] Anticipating the chain reaction as the members of each alliance mobilized, he strode back to the Admiralty and drew up a list of seventeen separate standing orders that would mobilize the navy for war when the time came.

Wilhelm II sent an unofficial envoy, the industrialist Albert Ballin, to meet Churchill and determine how Britain might react if a war that began between Austria and Serbia expanded to include Berlin backing Vienna and St. Petersburg and Paris backing Belgrade. Churchill chose his words carefully but pointedly: 'it would be a great mistake to assume that England would necessarily do nothing and I added that she would judge events as they arose.' Ballin then asked if Britain would remain on the sidelines if Germany guaranteed that it would only take territory from France's overseas colonies, not any more of its land in Europe. To that Churchill was noncommittal.[14] He reported the exchange to the Cabinet. To his alarm, he found that his colleagues were 'overwhelmingly pacific' with 'at least three-quarters ... determined not to be drawn into a European quarrel unless Great Britain were herself attacked'.[15] He argued that war could best be deterred by asserting strength and determination shoulder to shoulder with France and Russia as long as Serbia offered reasonable compensation. The counterargument prevailed that by not supporting those countries they would be less likely to declare war against Austria and Germany.

Serbia's reply to the ultimatum came on 25 July. Belgrade agreed to all the conditions except allowing an Austrian representative to participate in any legal proceedings against the terrorist suspects. Instead, Serbia proposed submitting the process to the International Court at The Hague. The following day Vienna rejected Belgrade's conciliatory position.

That same day King George V expressed the bewilderment and uncertainty of himself and most of his ministers to visiting Germany's Crown Prince Heinrich: 'I don't know what to do, we have no quarrel with anyone and I hope we shall remain neutral. But if Germany declared war on Russia and France joins Russia, then I am afraid we shall be dragged into it. But you can be sure that I and my government will do all we can to prevent a European war.'[16] Astonishingly, Asquith did not convene a Cabinet meeting to discuss the latest escalation of the crisis until 27 July. Once again the consensus was to remain neutral. Churchill sidestepped that consensus the next day by ordering the Channel Fleet at the Isle of Wight to sail into the North Sea as a show of force against the Germans.

Austria declared war against Serbia on 28 July. The result was a chain reaction as the allies of each side mobilized their armies while insisting that they were merely reacting defensively against the aggression of others. When word reached Berlin on 30 July that Tsar Nicholas II had mobilized his reserves, Wilhelm II declared that: 'England, Russia and France have agreed among themselves ... to take the Austro-Serbian conflict for an excuse for waging a war of extermination against us ... The famous encirclement of Germany has finally become a complete fact ... We squirm isolated in the net.'[17] He demanded that Russia rescind its mobilization. When Russia refused, Germany began mobilizing on 31 July. That same day, Berlin asked Whitehall to stay on the sidelines in return for its promise not to invade the Netherlands or take any French territory in the subsequent war. Foreign Secretary Edward Grey rejected the request. That night Churchill wrote Clementine that:

Everything tends towards catastrophe & collapse. I am interested, geared up & happy. Is it not horrible to be built like that? The preparations have a hideous fascination for me. Yet I would do my best for peace, & nothing would induce me wrongfully to strike the first blow ... I feel sure however that if war comes we shall give them a good drubbing.[18]

Asquith had convened the Cabinet on 30 July. Twelve of eighteen ministers rejected Churchill's call for mobilizing the navy and declaring support for France. That evening Churchill talked Asquith into issuing an order to mobilize the fleet despite the opposition of most ministers. He then hurried back to the Admiralty and issued his seventeen standing orders that most importantly included sending the First and Second Fleets to Scapa Flow, cancelling all leave, calling up the reserves, building fuel and ammunition stocks to capacity and dispatching destroyers, submarines and minesweepers into the North Sea. The next morning, faced with Asquith's act, the opponents angrily agreed to support it which King George reinforced it with a royal proclamation. Churchill then dealt with a delicate command issue. The Home Fleet's commander, Admiral Sir George Callaghan, suffered from ailments that left him little mental or physical energy. Churchill pressured him to retire and replaced him with Admiral Sir John Jellicoe.

Britain's first clear if limited warning to Germany did not come until 2 August, when Grey informed Berlin that Britain would not tolerate any German naval movements in the North Sea or English Channel as part of an attack on France. That same day the German army invaded Luxembourg. Germany formally declared war against France and Russia as German troops marched into Belgium on 3 August. Until then the Cabinet was split over whether or not to go to war. It was an appeal by Belgian King Albert to King George for Britain to uphold its 1839 treaty commitment that finally united the Cabinet. The Germans had not just violated international law by invading Belgium, more vitally they violated British national security by threatening to dominate the Low Countries and decisively tip the continent's balance of power in their favour. Grey issued an ultimatum to Berlin to withdraw its army before midnight on 4 August.

*   *   *

When the deadline passed on 4 August, the British government declared war against Germany. While that fatal decision plunged the rest of the Cabinet into deep gloom, the First Sea Lord was exultant. An insider recalled that 'in burst Churchill, radiant, smiling, a cigar in his mouth and satisfaction upon his face. "Well," he exclaimed, "the deed is done!"'[19] Being a critical part of the war effort exhilarated him. A few weeks later during a dinner party at Walmer Castle, he happily exclaimed to Lady Asquith: 'This is living History. Everything we are doing is thrilling – it will be read by a thousand generations, think of that! Why I would not be out of this glorious delicious war for anything the world could give me.'[20]

Looking back from April 1918, Foreign Secretary Grey believed that war was inevitable. In 'questioning whether by foresight or wisdom I could have prevented the war … I have come to think no human individual could have prevented it.'[21] That certainly is true but collective farsighted diplomacy among the great powers could have kept them from going to war between 23 July and 2 August, although the odds of doing so obviously dwindled during those nine days. At some point in those last days, railway timetables supplanted diplomacy in each country. Years before each nation's General Staff had meticulously prepared a contingency plan grounded on the belief that getting to the front first with the most military might would determine who won or lost the war.[22]

The Cabinet met early on 5 August and agreed to send six divisions or 120,000 troops led by Field Marshal Sir John French across the Dover Strait to northern France. It would take two weeks to mobilize and funnel all those men to the English Channel and then ferry them to the far side. Thanks to Churchill's earlier orders to the Channel Fleet, warships now formed a cordon across the approach from the North Sea and those troops could cross in safety.

Meanwhile the first combat by British forces was at sea.[23] On 6 August, a British light cruiser sank a German minesweeper then was sunk herself by a mine laid by that vessel. Churchill was eager to strike back but what he suggested might have won a limited victory at the cost of a strategic defeat. He urged the Cabinet to authorize an expedition to seize the Dutch island of Ameland to be fortified as a base to hem in and launch attacks against Germany's North Sea fleet. Asquith and the other ministers adamantly rejected any attack against the neutral Dutch that would drive them to ally with Germany. When Churchill learned that two German warships had anchored in the Dardanelles Strait, he called for a blockade. Once again the Cabinet rejected his idea as likely to push Turkey into Germany's arms. On 12 August, the Cabinet did approve Churchill's plan to blockade Germany's North Sea and Baltic ports with warships and submarines and send a flotilla to liaison with Russia's Baltic Fleet. He envisioned supplying the Russians with enough transport ships to convey an army to invade northern Germany.

Churchill's roaming mind did not distract him from overseeing the navy's critical task of ferrying 80,000 troops, 30,000 horses and 315 guns across the Channel to France between 12 and 22 August. That was just the first wave. By the end of the year, he could boast that the Royal Navy had ferried

'809,000 men, 203,000 horses, 250,000 tons of stores, 20,000 vehicles, 65,000 wounded, 5,000 refugees and 4,884 German prisoners of war … without the loss of a single man'.[24]

* * *

Germany's war strategy was designed as early as 1897 by Chief of the General Staff Alfred von Schlieffen and thereafter was annually updated. The strategy assumed a two front war with France and Russia whereby initially Germany and Austria would defend against a Russian attack while most German forces attacked France in a huge arc through Luxembourg and Belgium that destroyed the French army, captured Paris and imposed the latest humiliating peace treaty at Versailles. That done, Germany could then mass its forces for a similar campaign against Russia. That strategy nearly succeeded.[25]

The German army marched rapidly through eastern and central Belgium to capture Liège on 16 August, Brussels on 17 August and Namur on 25 August. Those were devastating Allied defeats. Having passed through the forested hills of the Ardennes to seize the Moselle River valley and central Belgium, the Germans could now march swiftly across the rolling open terrain of western Belgium into northern France. The first good military news came from the Balkans where the Serbs drove back the Austrian invaders on 20 August after a fierce four-day battle. From the other side of the world came word that on 23 August, Japan declared war against Germany with the excuse the 1902 Anglo–Japanese defensive alliance. Tokyo's real motivation was to seize the easy pickings of Germany's empire in the Far East, namely in Shantung in China and the island groups of the Marianas, Carolines and Marshalls.[26] On the Eastern Front, 150,000 German troops routed 230,000 Russian troops during the Battle of Tannenberg from 26 to 30 August, inflicting 160,000 casualties at the cost of 15,000. That was the first of a series of German and Austrian attacks that pushed back Russian forces.[27]

Germany's western juggernaut collided with Britain's 80,000 troops at Mons in Belgium on 23 August and drove them south, with each side suffering about 1,500 casualties. That was a relative skirmish compared to the Battle of the Marne that raged between 1,071,000 French and 1,485,000 German troops in an arc 20 miles north and east of Paris from 5 to 12 September. The French hit the Germans' right flank and eventually forced them to retreat, with the former sustaining 263,000 casualties and the latter 256,000.[28]

Thereafter the war of manoeuvre transformed into a war of attrition as each side fortified itself within mazes of trenches protected by machine guns, rolls of barbed wire and massed artillery behind the lines that stretched 460 miles from the North Sea to Switzerland. For more than four years tens of millions of men fought and millions died or were maimed on the Western Front, whose contours changed very little. The Eastern Front was less rigid but nearly as blood-soaked. Then there was the Italian-Austrian front in which a million or so men died after Italy joined the Allies on 23 May 1915. Other fronts included those between Serbia and Austria and between Britain and Turkey in the Middle East and the Dardanelles Straits and battles for Germany's colonies in Africa and the Far East.[29]

* * *

Churchill meanwhile received the Cabinet's approval for a series of proposals in late August. He established a naval division and ordered one of its brigades to land at Ostend to secure that critical port and divert some German attention from their drive against the British and French armies. He ordered the building of landing craft for future beach assaults. At Dunkirk, he set up a naval air base whose first mission was to attack Zeppelin sheds near Cologne, Dusseldorf and Friedrichshafen that destroyed six dirigibles. His expertise in air power prompted Secretary of State for War Lord Kitchener to assign him Britain's air defence on 3 September. Churchill established the headquarters at Hendon and began relocating aircraft there.

Starting on 10 September, Churchill repeatedly crossed from Dover to Dunkirk then back again as he mobilized naval, land and air forces for a thrust against German supply lines across central Belgium. Then came the disturbing word on 23 September that Belgium's government was going to abandon Antwerp. Once the Germans secured Antwerp and protected their northern flank, they could mass forces for an offensive against Dunkirk and Calais to sever the British army from its supply bases across the English Channel. Churchill flew to Antwerp to urge King Albert to keep fighting with a promise that British troops would soon bolster the city's defence. He was good to his word as 2,000 marines reached Antwerp on 4 October. The following day he telegraphed Asquith his offer to resign as First Lord in exchange for a lieutenant general's commission and command over the forces defending Antwerp. Asquith insisted that he return promptly to London and leave that city's defence in the hands of General Henry Rawlinson who would soon arrive. Churchill delayed his return as long as possible. On 6 October, two understrength naval brigades arrived and he deployed them in the trenches surrounding Antwerp. Those reinforcements raised the number of British troops to 8,000.

Despite that heartening contribution, King Albert, his government and his army's remnants were demoralized by two months of devastating defeats and wanted to give up. Churchill exerted all his persuasive powers to keep them in the fight. On 7 October, Rawlinson reached Antwerp. After briefing the general and together inspecting the defences, Churchill flew back to England. That same day, Clementine gave birth to their third child, Sarah. Bad news trailed him home. Rawlinson reported that the German forces converging around Antwerp were so overwhelming that not only should the 40,000 additional troops being readied to reinforce the city be withheld but the 8,000 British troops there should be withdrawn as soon as possible. After a heated debate, the Cabinet accepted Rawlinson's appeal.

In all, Churchill's 'Antwerp campaign' had distracted the German offensive and won the British army a six-day reprieve in France at the cost of only 57 British lives, 158 wounded and 2,500 captured along with 20,000 Belgian captives. Yet his critics blasted him for presiding over a defeat since the Germans captured Antwerp. A bitter Churchill lamented that his foes had transformed a successful rearguard action into 'the Antwerp Blunder'. He did admit that 'Antwerp was a blow and some aspects of it have given a handle to my enemies and perhaps for a time reduced my power to be useful'.[30] That was only a harbinger of the storm of criticism for an even more ambitious Churchill plan that lay ahead.

Meanwhile, Churchill stirred controversy within the government when he requested that the retired Admiral Fisher be recalled as First Sea Lord.[31] King George V protested the notion of recalling a man whose acerbic temper had offended him when he had held the office from 1904 to 1910. Churchill convinced Asquith that Fisher's experience and wisdom were indispensable and the prime minster in turn won the king's reluctant approval on 30 October. Churchill would come to deeply regret that decision. He soon learned that Fisher was 'harsh, capricious, vindictive, gnawed by hatreds arising often from spite, working secretly or violently … by methods which the typical English gentlemen or public school boy are taught to dislike and avoid'. Fisher liked to say that 'If any subordinate opposes me, I will make his wife a widow, his children fatherless and his home a dunghill.' Worst of all, he rejected the Royal Navy's tradition of seeking decisive battles with the enemy: 'He could not bear the idea of risking ships in battle. He settled … upon a doctrine widely inculcated among our senior naval officers that the navy's task was to keep open our own communications, blockade those of the enemy and to wait for the Armies to do their proper job.'[32]

Clearly some new mix of strategy and tactics had to be devised to reverse what appeared to be a losing war at sea.[33] So far German warships, submarines or mines had sunk a battleship and four cruisers along with dozens of smaller naval and merchant vessels, while German warships had bombarded the towns of Whitby, Scarborough and Hartlepool. Churchill longed for a decisive naval battle that would never come. With Britain's fleet at Scapa Flow superior to Germany's fleet at Wilhelmshaven, Berlin wisely did not risk it. The war's only major fleet action, off Jutland from 30 May to 1 June 1916, was indecisive and came after Churchill had left the Admiralty.[34]

Amid a daily stream of grim war news Churchill suffered a personal loss with word that his cousin had been killed at the front. He sent these words to his aunt:

> We must at all costs win. Victory is a better boon than life and life without it will be unendurable. The British Army has in a few weeks of war revived before the whole world the glories of Agincourt and Blenheim and Waterloo and in this Norman has played his part. It rests with us to make sure that these sacrifices are not made in vain.[35]

Comparing Mons to Waterloo was hyperbole at its most blatant, but one hopes his aunt believed it and found some solace for the loss of her son.

Churchill despaired at the quagmire that weekly killed an average of a thousand British soldiers and maimed thousands more: 'A policy of pure attrition between armies so evenly balanced cannot lead to a decision ... Unless this problem can be solved ... we shall simply be wearing each other out on a gigantic scale and with fearful sacrifices without ever reaping the reward.'[36] That did not stop each side from launching devastating self-defeating attacks on the other:

> There existed at this period no means of taking the offensive successfully in France; the centre could not be pierced and there were no flanks to turn. Confronted with this deadlock, military art remained dumb; the Commanders and their General Staffs had no plan except ... frontal attacks ... no policy except ... exhaustion ... It was not even a case of exchanging a life for a life. Two and even three British or French lives were repeatedly paid for the killing of one enemy and grim calculations

were made to prove that in the end the Allies would still have a balance of a few millions to spare.[37]

Churchill conceived a possible solution to that horrific dilemma and, on 5 January 1915, shared it with Asquith:

It would be quite easy in a short time to fit up a number of steam tractors with small armoured shelters, in which men and machine guns could be placed, which would be bullet-proof. Used at night, they would not be affected by artillery fire to any extent. The caterpillar system would enable trenches to be crossed quite easily and the weight of the machine would destroy ... wire entanglements. Forty or fifty of these ... prepared secretly and brought into position at nightfall, could advance quite certainly into the enemy's trenches, smashing away all away the obstructions and sweeping the trenches with their machine gun fire and with grenades thrown out of the top. They would then make so many point d'apuis for the British supporting infantry to rush forward and rally on them. They can then move forward to attack the second line of trenches.

He asked for permission to develop the new war machine, arguing that the 'cost would be small' and if the experiment failed, 'what harm would be done?'[38]

Asquith forwarded Churchill's appeal to Kitchener who established a committee to discuss the notion. Fearing that the War Office would fail to realize his vision, Churchill formed his own committee on 20 February 1915, not to discuss but actually to develop a prototype of what would be called the tank. The name came much later from the deliberately misleading label on the plywood case containing each vehicle when it was sent to the front. After his committee submitted him a design, he allocated £70,000 from the navy budget to build a prototype.

The more that Churchill tried to work with Kitchener and his underlings the more he recognized that he was a gross liability to Britain's war effort:

Kitchener had not made a scientific professional study of war on the largest scale, nor did he understand the staff or the organization connected with it as they were understood in the great armies of Europe ... It was disastrous in these circumstances that he should not have at his disposal a really competent military staff ... Of the officers who took their places in the War Office, the majority were overawed by the old Field Marshal's formidable prestige and were discouraged from attempts at argument or persuasion when their views and suggestions were consistently ignored.[39]

Asquith had found the Cabinet too ponderous for decision making. To streamline that task, on 1 December 1914, he formed a War Council composed of himself, Foreign Secretary Grey, Chancellor David Lloyd George, Kitchener and Churchill. In consultation with Fisher, Churchill promoted two plans before the War Council. One was for an expedition to capture the German North Sea island of Borkum and use it as a staging area for landing a British army in north-west Germany. The War Council rejected that idea for lack of troops. His other plan involved a British offensive at the other end of Europe.

It was the British and French declarations of war against Turkey on 5 November 1914 that inspired Churchill with an idea that he envisioned might decisively shift the conflict in favour of the Allies. The German and Austrian armies had devastated and routed the Russian army. Genuine fears arose that Russia might cut its losses and sign a separate peace with the Central Powers. That would let Berlin and Vienna shift their armies from the Eastern Front to join their armies on the Western Front where the sheer mass of their guns and troops would likely crush the British and French armies before them. Yet the alliance of Turkey with Germany and Austria provided an opportunity along with a new threat. Turkey might well surrender if a British armada punched through the Dardanelles Strait and anchored with its massed guns pointed toward Constantinople. Then the armada could sail on to join the Russian front whose left flank was anchored on the Black Sea. The weight of that British army might be enough to drive back the Austrians which might then encourage the rest of the Russian army to counter-attack the enemy before them. That in turn might entice Romania, Bulgaria, Italy and Greece to join the Allies. This array of possibilities certainly made the Dardanelles campaign worth trying.[40]

The War Council approved the Dardanelles campaign with Admiral Sir Sackville Carden in command on 28 January 1915. At first Carden insisted that the navy alone could battle its way to Constantinople, followed later by an army to fight alongside the Russians. But the War Council eventually decided that troops should accompany the navy to take and hold the fortified Gallipoli Peninsula at the entrance to the straits. The question was where to find those troops. On 16 February, the War Council diverted three divisions of 30,000 Australians and New Zealanders then in Egypt and bound for the Western Front to the Dardanelles along with 18,000 men of the 29th Division, 8,500 men of the Royal Naval Division and 18,000 French troops.

Three days later, Carden's fleet shelled the forts guarding the Dardanelles' entrance. Although the bombardment destroyed those forts, the fleet did not immediately steam toward Constantinople. The excuse was that the Turks were mining the straits and there were no minesweepers to remove them or troops to occupy the high ground. Carden had committed a grave mistake that would have devastating consequences. He had ordered a premature bombardment that warned the Turks that a full-fledged attack was pending and thus enabled the enemy to deploy masses of troops on the heights and masses of mines in the sea to block that future assault.

It was not until 12 March that the War Council got around to appointing a commander for the army earmarked for the Dardanelles. General Sir Ian Hamilton would need a week to journey from London to the front. Meanwhile, Carden ordered then cancelled minesweeping operations when the vessels came under enemy fire even though no one was killed or wounded. That prompted an incredulous Churchill to telegraph Carden these carefully-chosen words:

> Your original instructions laid stress on caution … and we approved highly the skill and patience with which you have advanced … without loss. The results to be gained are, however, great enough to justify loss of ships and men … We do not wish to hurry you or urge you beyond your judgment, but we recognize clearly that at a certain period in your operations you will have to press hard for a decision and we desire to know whether you consider that point has now been reached … I do not understand why minesweeping should be interfered with by fire which causes no casualties. Two or three hundred casualties would be a moderate price to pay for sweeping as far as the narrows.[41]

That criticism in turn spurred Carden to send his fleet of one dreadnought, one battlecruiser, sixteen British and French pre-dreadnought battleships, and a score of smaller warships into the straits on 18 March, while the waters were still strewn with mines. The result was a disaster. After mines sank four battleships and damaged three others, Carden called off the attack. Churchill expected that a chastised Carden would either resume trying to sweep mines from the straits or order the fleet forward regardless of losses, but the admiral refused to commit either act until the army secured the Gallipoli Peninsula on the Strait's north shore.

The first wave of 30,000 troops hit two Gallipoli beaches on 25 April. Turkish fire killed or wounded more than a thousand of those men and subsequent reinforcements that packed the beaches. The troops remained pinned down along the shore because no one ordered them to advance atop the ridge and hold it. The Turks massed ever more men, munitions and supplies along the ridge and dug more elaborate trenches. The carnage spread to the navy on 10 May, when a Turkish torpedo boat sank a battleship and 570 sailors drowned. Rather than cut their losses and withdraw, the Allies committed hundreds of thousands of more troops. The Dardanelles stalemate lasted another eight months, cost the Allies 120,000 casualties of 470,000 troops deployed there and encouraged Bulgaria to join the Central Powers on 11 October 1915. The War Council finally agreed to cut their losses and evacuate the army on 19 December 1915.

In analysing the Gallipoli disaster, Churchill identified a critical element in any invasion of an enemy shore:

> Time was the dominating factor. The extraordinary mobility and unexpectedness of amphibious power can ... only be exerted in strict relation to limited periods of time. The surprise, the rapidity and the intensity of the attack are all dependent on the state of the enemy's preparations at a given moment. Every movement undertaken on one side can be matched by a counter-movement on the other ... A week lost was the same as a division. Three divisions in February could have occupied the Gallipoli Peninsula with little fighting. Five could have captured it after March 18. Eleven might have taken it at the end of April. Fourteen were to prove insufficient on August 7. Moreover, one delay breeds another.[42]

Rage at the blood-soaked Dardanelles and Gallipoli deadlock by politicians, the press and the public rose with the casualty lists. Pressure soared for those responsible to resign. During the War Council meeting on 14 May 1915, Churchill pointed out that the war effort had a foot on two stools with each sliding in the opposite direction: 'Kitchener and the British Government had to make their choice between the Western and Eastern policies. They were drawn into a compromise between them.'[43] He called on his colleagues not to despair but to double down in the Straits: 'Stop these vain offensives on the Western Front ... Concentrate the available reinforcements upon the

Dardanelles and give them as much ammunition as was necessary to reach a decision there at the earliest possible moment.'[44]

His colleagues rejected his plea. The War Council needed a scapegoat to atone for the debacle. On 15 May, Fisher was the first to go even though Kitchener was responsible for all army operations. With Fisher gone the political spotlight shifted to his boss, Churchill. Asquith spearheaded the campaign to sacrifice him to placate the political scalp-hunters and form a national government that included members from all the parties. With extreme bitterness and humiliation, Churchill vacated his position as First Lord of the Admiralty for former Tory Prime Minister Arthur Balfour on 23 May 1915. Churchill admitted that he may have been partly to blame: 'If I have erred it has been in seeking to attempt an initiative without being sure that all the means & powers to make it successful were at my disposal.'[45] Yet he was incensed that Asquith

> threw me over without the slightest effort even to state the true facts on my behalf & still more that thereafter in all the plenitude of his power he never found for me a useful sphere of acting which would have given scope to my energies & knowledge … he has treated me with injustice, & has wasted qualities which might have been used in many ways to the public advantage in this time of war.[46]

Clementine later recalled that: 'The Dardanelles campaign haunted him for the rest of his life. He always believed in it … I thought he would die of grief.'[47]

Asquith appointed a Dardanelles Commission of Enquiry to investigate just what went wrong and who was responsible. Churchill would remain in political limbo until the Commission issued its report, assuming that it vindicated him. For half a year Churchill holed up at a rented Tudor country house near Godalming and took up painting to sublimate his tortured feelings. Asquith rejected his requests for minor posts in the new coalition government or as a brigadier general on the Western Front. He concluded that the only honourable path for him was to join a regiment at the front. On 18 November 1915, he left England for France as Major Winston Churchill.

*   *   *

Field Marshal Sir John French, the British army commander, welcomed him to his headquarters at Saint Omer for a fine dinner and soft bed. They had established a cordial working relationship when Churchill was First Lord of the Admiralty. Churchill contrasted French with his successor Douglas Haig as the British army commander: 'French was a natural solider. Although he had not the intellectual capacity of Haig, nor perhaps his underlying endurance, he had a deeper military insight. He was not equal to Haig in precision of details; but he had more imagination and he would never have run the British Army in the same long drawn-out slaughters.'[48]

Early the next morning, Churchill was driven to the front 35 miles away to train with the Grenadier Guards near the destroyed village of La Gorgue. He would remain in the trenches there and another section of the line for most of the next six months, sharing the constant fear, filth, cold and tedium of trench warfare. The Germans shelled that stretch of the lines every few days. One day a barrage opened up fifteen minutes after he had been recalled to confer with a general. After the shelling stopped, he returned to the front to find his dugout destroyed and his fellow officer obliterated. He vividly described another near miss:

> The shell arrived with a screech and a roar & tremendous bang & showers of bricks & clouds of smoke, & all the soldiers jumped & scurried & peeped up out of their holes & corners. It did not make me jump a bit – not a pulse thickened … I felt 20 yards more to the left & no more tangles to unravel, no more anxieties to face, no more hatreds & injustices to encounter … a good ending to a chequered life, final gift – unvalued – to an ungrateful country.[49]

More than ever he envisioned tanks as the way to decisively break the stalemate and he fired off letters to urge those responsible to hasten their development and deployment for a mass attack.

Haig replaced French on 19 December 1915. On New Year's Day 1916, Haig promoted Churchill to lieutenant colonel and assigned him to command a battalion of the 6th Royal Scots Fusiliers near Ploegsteert 10 miles northeast. His rank permitted him comforts that he had not enjoyed as a major in his old unit, including hot baths and ample supplies of champagne and fine wines. But that did not stop him from leading patrols into no man's land, something few lieutenant colonels did. At one point he asked a lieutenant to join him in a stroll atop the entire thousand-yard stretch of front that his battalion defended. His troops marvelled at his acts of reckless courage. In the trenches he learned a critical reason behind the bloodbaths launched by the Allied commanders – ignorance of the horrendous consequences of their orders: 'This was one of the cruellest features of the war. Many of the generals in the higher commands did not know the conditions with which their troops were ordered to contend, nor were they in a position to devise the remedies which might have helped them.'[50] He lost his command when his understrength battalion was merged with another Scottish battalion and a senior officer took over. Without a unit, he had no choice but to send his resignation to Kitchener. He hosted a farewell lunch for his officers on 6 May, then departed for England.

*   *   *

Back in London Churchill once again found himself in political limbo with no foreseeable chance of re-entering the government. The Dardanelles debacle had politically tainted him so darkly that for now not even a dangerous stint on the Western Front could purge the stigma. All along, the War Council presided over one devastating defeat after another that inflicted hundreds of thousands of British dead and wounded yet remained politically unshakeable. The Conservative Party's power and attitude explains the discrepancy. The Tories still despised him for defecting to the Liberals nearly a decade before and blackballed any notion of rehabilitating him. And since they were now critical partners in the national coalition government their will was unquestionable.

The most Churchill could do was wangle a meeting with Asquith over the tank. The War Council had decided to deploy the fifteen existing tanks to support the infantry during the ongoing Battle of the Somme. He argued against doing so then in that way. Tanks should spearhead an offensive, not support it and should only be unveiled in 1917 when they numbered the several hundred needed for a decisive breakthrough. The current plan would prompt the Germans rapidly to develop their own version and Britain's advantage would be forever lost. His words were wasted. Asquith informed him that nothing would alter the ongoing plan. A deeply dejected Churchill later wrote that 'the immense advantage of novelty and surprise was thus squandered while the number of the tanks was small, while their condition was experimental and their crews almost untrained. This priceless conception, containing if used in its integrity and on a sufficient scale, the certainty of a great and brilliant victory, was revealed to the Germans for the mere petty purpose of taking a few ruined villages.' Then, during the Battle of Passchendaele from 31 July to 10 November 1917, General Haig tossed away Britain's advantage in tanks even after massing large numbers of them:

'Instead of employing them all at once in dry weather on ground not torn by bombardment in some new sector where they could operate very easily and by surprise, they were plunged in fours and fives as a mere minor adjunct of the infantry into the quagmires and crater fields.'[51]

Churchill's only other defence was of himself and here too Asquith hobbled him. The Dardanelles Commission of Enquiry was still massing evidence for an eventual report. Churchill was as prepared as he was permitted to be when he was called to testify on 28 September. He had spent five months refining arguments to counter each charge against him, but the prime minister forbad him from using War Council documents that could definitively clear his name. Here Asquith blatantly abused his power to protect himself and his coterie. The War Council minutes would vindicate Churchill while implicating Asquith and other key ministers along with Admiral Carden, General Hamilton and many of their underlings. Churchill's only hope lay in the eventual publication of the Commission's final report to placate those in Parliament, the press and the public most appalled by the Dardanelles disaster.

Meanwhile, a far worse disaster was unfolding. The Battle of the Somme lasted from 1 July to 19 November 1916, when the Allied high command finally called it off. After four and a half months of slaughter, the Allies had captured several square miles of devastated earth at the cost of 794,238 British and French dead and wounded to German casualties of 537,918. Never have so many men died for so little gain.[52]

Prime Minister Asquith was forced to resign on 6 December 1916, when Secretary of State for War David Lloyd George and several other ministers threatened to withdraw from the government rather than serve under him. The king asked Lloyd George to form a government. Against vociferous opposition, Prime Minister Lloyd George offered Churchill a minor post, but Churchill refused to accept anything that would not return him to the War Council.[53]

At least Churchill still held his seat in Parliament from which he made eloquent and often critical speeches about Britain's war effort. Among his more notable addresses came on 5 March 1917, when he called for more vigorously developing and deploying cutting edge technologies to give British arms decisive strategic and tactical advantages that would reduce the carnage and shorten the war with an Allied victory: 'Machines save life. Machine-power is a substitute for man-power. Brains will save blood. Manoeuvre is a great diluting agent to slaughter.' He then pleaded with the government not to launch another Somme-type offensive for 1917 that would inevitably result in hundreds of thousands of British dead or maimed for no discernible gain.[54]

The Dardanelles Commission's report finally appeared in March 1917. The report did not single out Churchill or anyone else for blame yet did not absolve him of the serious charges that had swirled in Parliament and the press against him. So Churchill, along with Fisher, who had also resigned, remained scapegoats in countless British minds then and ever since. The following month, an event happened that would have a decisive effect on the war.

* * *

In attempts to sever France and Britain from American supplies, Germany conducted unrestricted submarine warfare three times, from March to August 1915, from February to March 1916 and from 9 January 1917 until the end of the war. The first two times, Berlin did so hoping to bring Paris and London to their knees before Washington intervened, but backed off when that policy appeared to backfire. When a submarine sank the British liner *Lusitania* on 7 May 1915, 128 Americans were among the 1,198 people who drowned. President Woodrow Wilson called on Kaiser Wilhelm to end his unrestricted submarine warfare. Viewing Wilson as weak-willed, the German government continued the policy until a submarine sank the British passenger ship *Arabic* on 19 August, killing forty-four people including three Americans. Once again Wilson protested. This time the Kaiser and his ministers promised on 28 August that henceforth submarines would only sink passenger ships after warning them and letting their crew and passengers escape. That seeming concession satisfied Wilson.

The German announcement on 9 January 1917, that it was resuming unrestricted submarine warfare prompted Wilson's latest protest. Then on 19 January, British intelligence intercepted and decoded a message from German Foreign Minister Arthur Zimmerman to the ambassador in Mexico, authorizing him to encourage Mexico to go to war against the United States in return for German military aid and support for winning back territory that America won from Mexico in 1848. The British passed that intelligence to Wilson on 24 February and he released it to the press four days later. The resulting uproar decisively shifted American public opinion against Germany. Then in March, German submarines sank five American merchant ships. On 2 April, Wilson sent a war declaration message to Congress. On 6 April, the Senate voted 86 to 6 and the House of Representatives 373 to 50 in favour. The weight of American military, industrial and financial power would break the stalemate on the Western Front.[55]

*　　*　　*

Lloyd George was willing to take the political heat if he could tap Churchill's knowledge, energy and ideas in the Cabinet.[56] On 16 July 1917, he asked Churchill to join the government with his pick of any post. Churchill eagerly chose the Ministry of Munitions where he hoped to realize his visions for new war machines and the strategies and tactics to decisively wield them. He devoted considerable time to supervising improved versions of the tank then mass manufacturing them. He also proved to be an able manager. He reorganized the ministry from fifty departments into ten with each head serving on a council which he chaired. Seventy-five committees linked relevant personnel and sections among the departments. The council's secretariat assisted the departments and committees in implementing the council's decisions. The only thing he failed to do was get the prime minister to add the Minister of Munitions to the War Council.

As a hands-on manager, Churchill seized every excuse to fly to the front and observe his machines in action. Just getting there and back by air was hazardous enough. Biographer William Manchester noted Churchill's latest batch of extraordinarily close brushes with death and his coldblooded indifference to them:

> Once his plane caught fire over the Channel. Another of his planes somersaulted after take-off the pilot made a forced landing. Later, when he was piloting himself in a dual control aircraft over Croydon airfield, the guiding stick failed. Their speed was about sixty miles per hour and they were seventy or eighty feet above the ground. The plane nose-dived and crashed. Winston's co-pilot was badly injured; he himself was bleeding and badly bruised. Nevertheless, he insisted on driving off and delivering a speech. Those who urged him to see a doctor were curtly dismissed.[57]

Then there was the front line where he courted death. An aide recalled a typical incident:

> Winston was attracted by the sight of shells bursting in the distance – irresistible! Out we got, put on our steel helmets, hung our gas-masks

round our necks and walked for half an hour towards the firing. There was a great deal of noise, shells whistling over our heads and some fine bursts in the distance ... and the firing died down, so we went back.[58]

Tragically, despite the tank's advent, the Allied generals failed to appreciate just how it could revolutionize warfare. Instead, they persisted in launching the same over-the-top mass infantry attacks with the same horrific results. On 31 July 1917, Haig launched an assault of fifty British and six French divisions against the German lines around Passchendaele. When he finally called off the assault three and a half months later on 10 November, the Allies had suffered 448,000 casualties, inflicted 410,000 and advanced half a dozen miles.[59]

Ten days after that battle ended, Churchill showed what massed tanks were capable of achieving. He exulted as 381 British tanks overran six miles of the enemy's front near Cambrai on 20 November 1917. By the time the high command ended the offensive on 7 December, the British had captured 42 square miles and inflicted 45,000 casualties while suffering equal numbers of dead and wounded along with 179 knocked-out tanks.[60] In all, the tank-led offensive at Cambrai had seized more ground in one-tenth the time and with one-tenth the casualties than the British infantry alone had squandered at Passchendaele.

He watched 456 Allied tanks rumble into battle near Amiens on 8 August 1918. Over the next four days, with infantry crouching behind each tank, the attackers smashed through the German lines, killing and wounding 25,000, capturing 50,000 and advancing a dozen miles at the cost of 22,000 casualties each for the British and French.[61] An exuberant Churchill wrote to Prime Minister Lloyd George that 'this is the greatest British victory that has been won in the whole war and the worst defeat that the Germans army has yet sustained'. It could have been much more. Actually the victory was limited when it could have been decisive, as the prime minister pointed out: 'Had Haig flung his army into the gap created and pursued the broken and demoralized Germans without respite, an even greater victory was within his grasp. When the enemy was scattered and their reserves were not yet up, Haig did not press forward with relentless drive and the Germans were given time to recover and reform their lines.'[62]

But it was American troops rather than tanks that would break the stalemate. The American army in France took a long time to form. President Wilson appointed General John Pershing to command the American army in France and dispatched the first division of 14,000 troops there in June 1917.

It was another nine months before the American troops reached 287,000 and occupied a stretch of the front and would number 1,944,000 when the war ended. Churchill was so moved by witnessing an American offensive that this most loquacious and eloquent of men was rendered nearly speechless: 'When I have seen in the last few weeks the splendour of American manhood striding forward on all the roads of France and Flanders, I have experienced emotions which words cannot describe.'[63]

During a series of Allied offensives in the summer and autumn of 1918, the weight, spirit and skill of those American troops was decisive in punching through and routing the Germans before them. Allied troops on other fronts were just as successful. Bulgaria signed an armistice on 30 September, Turkey on 30 October and Austria on 3 November. On 7 November, a German delegation crossed the lines under a white flag and requested an armistice. The Allied high command issued the Germans a list of terms and gave them 72 hours to accept them. The armistice was signed at five o'clock on the morning of 11 November and would go into effect at eleven o'clock later that morning.

Churchill described what it was like in Central London when the word arrived:

It was a few minutes before the eleventh hour of the eleventh day of the eleventh month. I stood at the window of my room looking … toward Trafalgar Square, waiting for Big Ben to tell that the war was over. My mind strayed back across the scarring years to the scene and emotions of the night at the Admiralty when I listened for these same chimes in order to give the signal of war against Germany … And now was all over! … I was conscious of reaction rather than elation … The whole vast business of supply … all of a stroke vanished like a nightmare dream, leaving a void behind … And then suddenly the first stroke of the chime … Then from all sides men and women came scurrying into the street. Streams of people poured out of all the buildings. The bells of London began to clash … Almost before the last stroke of the clock had died away, the strict, war-straightened … streets of London had become a triumphant pandemonium.[64]

Chapter 5

The Cassandra

'Two things I confess have staggered me after a long parliamentary experience in these debates. The first has been the dangers that have so swiftly come upon us in a few years, and have been transforming our position and the whole outlook of the world. Secondly, I have been staggered by the failure of the House of Commons to react effectively against those dangers ... I say that unless the House resolves to find out the truth for itself it will have committed an act of abdication of duty without parallel in its long history.'

'Was there ever a more awful spectacle ... than ... the agony of Russia? This vast country ... .not only produced enough food for itself, but, before the war, it was one of the great granaries of the world ... It is now reduced to famine ... because the theories of Lenin and Trotsky have ... driven man from the civilization of the twentieth century into a condition of barbarism ... racked by pestilence and deprived of hope.'

The First World War was disastrous for every country that participated regardless of whether it was among the victors or losers when it ended. Twice as many Britons died in the First World War as would die in the Second. In all, Britain and its empire lost 908,371 dead, 2,090,212 wounded and 191,652 missing and presumed dead from August 1914 to November 1918. Of that the British army suffered 702,410 and the navy 32,287 dead or 11.8 per cent of those mobilized and 1.6 per cent of the total population.[1] And those were just the physical deaths, maimings and lesser wounds. Hundreds of thousands of Britons returned from the front crippled in mind and spirit. They and those they left behind in mass graves would haunt British politics for a generation before the government reluctantly led the nation into the next global conflagration.

To varying degrees the losses were also horrendous for the other great powers, including Germany with 2,037,000 dead and 4,207,028 wounded; Russia with 1,811,000 dead and 1,450,000 wounded; France with 1,398,000 dead and 2,000,000 wounded; Austria with 1,100,000 dead and 3,630,000 wounded; Turkey with 804,000 dead and 400,000 wounded; Italy with 578,000 and 947,000 wounded; and America with 114,000 dead and 205,690 wounded. As a portion of the population, Turkey suffered the worst with its dead accounting for 3.7 per cent, followed by France's 3.4 per cent, Germany's 3.0 per cent, Austria's 1.9 per cent, Italy's 1.6 per cent, Russia's 1.1 per cent and America's 0.1 per cent. For all the belligerents, around 9,450,000 soldiers and 7,000,000 civilians died, perhaps as many from disease and starvation as from combat. As unprecedented as the dead and wounded were the numbers of men mobilized for war, with Russia leading with 15,800,000, followed by Germany with 13,000,000, Britain with 8,400,000, France with 7,900,000 and America with 4,300,000, although only about half of those forces served on the front lines.[2] Overall no country suffered worse than Russia with not just ten million or so casualties during the war but a revolution, civil war, famine and genocide in the following years and decades inflicted by the communist dictatorship that clung to power until 1991.

Then there were the direct financial costs, with the Allies expending $147 billion and the Central Powers $61.5 billion. Britain was the biggest spender with $45.307 billion, followed by America with $35.731 billion, Germany with $32.388 billion, France with $30.009 billion, Italy with $12.892 billion and Russia with $11.778 billion. From 1914 to 1919 the national debt soared to $30.432 billion in Britain, $25.423 billion in France, $24.144 billion in America, $15.133 billion in Germany and $7.364 billion in Italy. Washington kept the Allies in the war as much with money as with men by distributing $9.6 billion in loans of which Britain borrowed $4.3 billion. Wartime inflation devoured wealth in each country, with Austrians suffering the worst with 1,162 per cent followed by Russia with 473 per cent, Germany with 304 per cent, France with 213 per cent, Britain with 210 per cent and America with 164 per cent.[3]

Only America and Japan emerged from the war economically stronger than when they entered it. Indeed, the United States took over the United Kingdom's role as the global banker and widened its already considerable lead as the world's largest and most dynamic economy. Washington assumed the global banker role reluctantly but responsibly for a decade. Self-interest rather than altruism in an economically interdependent world demanded nothing less. Yet America also spurned membership of the League of Nations with its principle of collective security. Then came New York's stock market collapse in October 1929, after which Washington abandoned economic internationalism for nationalism. Protectionist policies globalized the Great

Depression and Americans clung fiercely to isolationism for a dozen years until Pearl Harbor.

The negotiations to resolve the First World War began in Paris on 18 January 1919 and ended with the signature of a treaty at the Palace of Versailles on 28 June 1919. The controversy over the process and results began then and has persisted ever since.[4] At first a Council of Ten among the Allies met to cut a deal among themselves and then present it to the Germans, who initially were not invited. Eventually thirty-two belligerent or neutral countries attended the conference although they formally convened for only eight sessions. Those arrangements proved to be unwieldy as each delegation asserted its own wish list. By March, the conference was overshadowed by separate haggling among the Big Four, who called themselves the Supreme Council, which included Britain's Prime Minister Lloyd George, France's Prime Minister Georges Clemenceau, Italy's Prime Minister Vittorio Orlando and America's President Woodrow Wilson. With the common enemy that had united them defeated, each leader asserted his own version of a just peace that mingled how he interpreted his nation's interests through the psychological matrix of his own experiences, values, emotions and ambitions. However much Lloyd George, Clemenceau and Orlando differed in character from one another, they were worldly realists well versed in the complexities of European great power politics. Geographically and ideologically, Wilson was the group's outlier. Yet it was Wilson's internationalist vision that most shaped the subsequent peace.

Woodrow Wilson was the son of a southern Presbyterian minister whose weekly Bible thumping sermons imbued in him a good-versus-evil, black-and-white world view.[5] Education failed to challenge that idealistic vision and may have bolstered it as he made his way up the ranks to graduate from John Hopkins University with a doctorate in political science, teach at Princeton University, eventually serve as its president and along the way write nine books on American politics. Looking for an honest, bright, progressive leader, New Jersey's Democratic Party bosses convinced him to run as their candidate for governor. He won on a reform agenda whose gist he subsequently got the state assembly to approve in Trenton. He then ran for the presidency in 1912 with a reform agenda for America. Once elected, he worked with Congress to enact much of it. In 1916, he campaigned for re-election with the slogan 'He kept us out of the war'. Germany's resumption of unrestricted submarine warfare in January 1917, during which five American ships were sunk, forced him to betray that promise. On 2 April, he submitted a declaration of war to Congress which approved it four days later. He elaborated his justifications for American participation in the war with his Fourteen Points speech before Congress on 8 January 1918. Eight points offered proposals to resolve specific European conflicts and the other six asserted principles for international relations that included disarmament, open diplomacy, freedom of the seas, free trade, national self-determination and a League of Nations to keep the peace and address other problems.

None of his ideals provoked more controversy than national self-determination. Indeed his demand that all peoples be free helped loosen a political Pandora's Box that will likely persist to the end of time. His own Secretary of State, Robert Lansing, deplored that potentially explosive principle: 'It will, I fear, cost thousands of lives. In the end it is bound to be discredited, to be called the dream of an idealist who failed to realize the danger until it was too late to check those who attempt to put the principle into force.'[6] In a rare candid moment, Wilson later ruefully admitted before the Senate Foreign Relations Committee that: 'When I gave utterance to those words I said them without the knowledge that nationalities existed which are coming to us day after day.'[7]

Wilson was one of those idealistic, preachy, straight-laced types of people that Churchill loathed. Although the two never met, Churchill devoured what reports he could of him. He did not like much of what he learned. He condemned Wilson for delaying for three years America's entry into the war, describing him as:

> the inscrutable and undecided judge upon whom the lives of millions hung ... He did not truly divine the instinct of the American people. He underestimated the volume and undervalued the quality of the American feeling in favour of the Allies. Not until he was actually delivering his famous war message to Congress ... did he move forward with confidence and conviction.[8]

Here Churchill misunderstands Wilson and American sentiment. Wilson genuinely wanted to avoid war and only asked Congress for a declaration after German submarines sank five American vessels. The public was divided in their own sentiments. Certainly millions of Americans of German, Irish and Polish heritage leaned toward the Central Powers. Wall Street, however, firmly backed the Western Allies whose governments and businesses owed American financiers billions of dollars. That money would disappear forever if the Central Powers won and imposed crippling reparations on the losers.

Of all Wilson's ideals none disgusted and terrified Churchill more than his demand for self-determination for all peoples. He foresaw mass death and destruction as subsumed peoples fought to free themselves. Yet he did find himself in agreement with the president on two issues. Like Wilson, Churchill called for a lenient peace as the best means of avoiding the bitterness that could lead to a future war of vengeance. He also supported a League of Nations devoted to collective security whereby the members worked together to keep the peace. He later wrote:

> The whole history of the world is summed up by the fact that when nations are strong they are not always just and when they wish to be just they are often no longer strong. I desire to see the collective forces of the world invested with overwhelming power ... Let us have this blessed union of power and justice.[9]

The Supreme Council did not invite Germany to send a delegation to Paris until 14 April and then kept its 180 members cooling their heels until the finished treaty was presented to them on 7 May. The Germans were stunned by what they read. They spent several weeks composing a tenet by tenet alternate version to what they decried as a draconian peace that blamed them for the war and forced them to cede enormous amounts of land, people and money to the victors. Although to varying degrees each of the Big Four harboured doubts about the treaty's justice, collectively they refused to budge and insisted that the Germans accept the existing treaty by 24 June. Lloyd George later explained that 'I could not accept the German point of view without giving away our whole case for entering the war'.[10]

The official signing took place at the Hall of Mirrors in the Palace of Versailles on 28 June 1919, the fifth anniversary of the assassinations at Sarajevo. In the treaty, President Wilson had won his insistence that for symbolic reasons the opening tenets would authorize the establishment of a League of Nations. A cluster of tenets provided for the eventual creation, recreation, aggrandizement, diminishment or recognition of fifteen countries from the ruins of the German, Austrian, Russian and Ottoman empires in Europe: France, Italy, Poland, Czechoslovakia, Hungary, Austria, Bulgaria, Romania, Yugoslavia, Albania, Greece, Finland, Estonia, Latvia and Lithuania. Germany would lose 13 per cent of its territory and 10 per cent of its population to its neighbours. Germany and Austria could not merge into one country. A section restricted Germany's army to 100,000 troops, its navy to 15,000 sailors and forbade military aircraft, submarines and tanks. A tenet required Germany to surrender almost all existing warships to the British Royal Navy. Tenets transferred Germany's overseas colonies to the victors as 'mandates' to be groomed for eventual independence. The treaty's most controversial clause made Germany the war's scapegoat that owed reparations to the victims. The final bill came to $31,530,500,000, with $5 billion due immediately. To enforce that Allied troops were authorized to occupy Germany's Ruhr and Saar industrial regions.

At Versailles and thereafter Britain and France made two grievous mistakes. First, they insisted on imposing onerous restrictions and penalties upon Germany. They then compounded that by failing to enforce them. The first mistake filled most Germans with a desire for vengeance, the second opened the way for them to realize that desire. Churchill was among those protested this 'Carthaginian peace', warning that it would enflame the Germans to restore their lost honour, territory and power.

That might not have mattered had the United States ratified the treaty and joined the League of Nations. If America had stood shoulder to shoulder with Britain and France to rally the League against Japanese aggression in Manchuria in 1931, it might well have not only prevented that but deterred the subsequent decade of aggression by Japan, Italy and Germany that culminated in the Second World War. Instead, the Senate rejected the Treaty of Versailles and two amended versions. Wilson's argument for ratifying the treaty was as much emotional as rational. At one point he declared: 'Dare we reject it and break the heart of the world?'[11] Here Wilson universalized his own deeply-wrought feelings for his beloved creation. Washington later signed separate peace treaties with Berlin, Vienna and Budapest.

One critical festering problem preceded the treaty. The Germans had accepted an armistice before their country was invaded and overrun. The Germans had marched up the Champs Elysée to the Arc de Triomph in 1871. The Allies would not march down the Unter den Linden and through the Brandenburg Gate in 1918. Although subsequently Allied troops would occupy parts of the Ruhr and Saar valleys, for most Germans their military defeat was an abstraction rather than a horrific reality. The myth persisted that the German army was invincible against its foreign enemies, but instead was defeated on the home front. The political slogan for that belief echoed ever louder over the next two decades. It was coined during a meeting between General Erich Ludendorff, who commanded the German army and Major Neil Malcolm, who headed Britain's military mission in Berlin. When Malcom asked Ludendorff why he believed that Germany had lost, the general replied that the people had let down the army, referring to the revolution that overthrew the Kaiser. 'Do you mean that you were stabbed in the back,' Malcolm asked. 'Yes, that's exactly it. We were stabbed in the back.'[12] That phrase would become one of the most virulent weapons in Adolf Hitler's political arsenal.

*   *   *

However fascinated Winston Churchill was with the ongoing events in Paris, he was too busy with new duties to give them more than an occasional glance. With the war finally over, Prime Minister David Lloyd George dissolved the House of Commons and scheduled an election for 14 December 1918. The Conservatives won a resounding victory by taking 379 seats to 127 for Lloyd George's Coalition Liberals, 73 for Sinn Fein, 57 for the Labour Party and 36 for Herbert Asquith's Liberal Party. Despite this, Lloyd George remained the prime minister and simply reshuffled the seats in his national coalition Cabinet. He asked Churchill, whose constituents overwhelmingly re-elected him, to become the Minister for War and Air with two immediate challenges, demobilizing the British army and determining British policy towards Russia's worsening civil war.[13]

Churchill managed demobilization swiftly and efficiently with just one significant glitch. By late January 1919, he had withdrawn nearly a million troops to Britain and shipped half a million Imperial troops to their respective countries. A crisis erupted when a regiment mutinied after being sent to England and then in a mix-up returned to France. Haig surrounded the regiment with loyal troops and declared his intention to execute the ringleaders. Churchill tried to convince him not to do so, arguing that: 'Unless there was serious violence attended by bloodshed and actual loss of life, I do not consider the infliction of the death penalty would be justifiable.'[14] Haig eventually followed Churchill's advice; the ringleaders received prison terms while the rest of the regiment was returned to England.

What to do about the Russian Civil War was a far tougher policy to determine. A communist revolution in Russia and subsequent civil war was not inevitable, but increasingly likely in the years following Tsar Nicholas II's declaration of war against the Central Powers on 2 August 1914.[15] The German, Austrian, Ottoman and Bulgarian armies decimated the Russian army in one campaign after another along a thousand-mile front. The Tsarist regime extracted ever more money, manpower and other resources from the population to fight a war that increasingly seemed unwinnable and senseless. Millions of Russians were killed, crippled or captured during the first two and a half years of fighting. In Russia's Duma or national assembly, a coalition of liberal and socialist political parties pressured Tsar Nicholas to abdicate in favour of Grand Duke Michael on 15 March 1917. Alexander Kerensky's Provisional Government promised civil rights for all, amnesty for all political prisoners and eventually free elections and a liberal constitution. But the new government failed to provide what most Russians wanted, peace and food, and proved to be just as inept as its predecessor in waging war.

The ranks of the outlawed Bolshevik or Communist Party swelled as its leaders promised the people peace, food and prosperity after taking power. Communist Party Chairman Vladimir Lenin and his cabal staged a carefully planned coup that violently took power in St. Petersburg and Moscow on 8 November 1917. They consolidated power by rapidly distributing food from warehouses following by signing an armistice with the Central Powers on 15 December and opening peace negotiations on 22 December. The Russian empire began breaking up. Finland was the first to declare independence on 6 December 1917, followed by Ukraine on 28 January 1918, Lithuania on 16 February, Estonia on 23 February, Belarus on 25 March, Georgia on 26 May, Armenia on 28 May, Latvia on 18 November and Azerbaijan on 5 December. Apart from Finland, the communists would sooner or later crush each of those countries and reincorporate them in the Russian empire, renamed the Soviet Union. But for now the Communist Party accelerated the Russian Empire's dissolution by signing the Treaty of Brest Litovsk on 3 March 1918, whereby Russia exited the war while paying six billion German gold marks to Berlin, ceding the Baltic states to Germany and Kars Oblast to the Ottoman Empire and recognizing Ukraine's independence.

Generals Nicholai Yudenich, Anton Denikin and Lavr Kornilov and Admiral Alexander Kolchak turned their forces, soon known as the White Army, against the forces loyal to the Lenin's regime called the Red Army. Japan was the first foreign power to intervene when Japanese landed and secured Vladivostok on 30 December 1917. Tokyo hoped to carve away the Russian Empire's Far East provinces and join them with Japan's empire. Eventually British, American and French forces deployed on the fringes of the Russian Empire to guard the huge supply depots that they feared the communists would seize and give to the Central Powers.[16] Whitehall first sent British troops to Murmansk then, with a French contingent, to Archangel. The Americans also sent troops to Archangel. British troops dispatched from Salonika in Greece and Tehran in Persia secured the Baku-Batum railway. By spring 1918, there were 13,000 British troops in Archangel and Murmansk, 2,000 along the railway and 1,000 in Vladivostok, all deployed to guard the enormous stocks of munitions and provisions that the Allies had sent Russia in their fruitless attempt to keep it in the fight. Having secured those supplies, the question became whether the Allies should simply extract those supplies back to their respective countries or support the White Russian armies fighting the communist Red Army.

Within the Cabinet, in the House of Commons and through the mass media, Churchill advocated massively aiding the anti-communist forces. To a *Times* reporter, he declared: 'Of all the tyrannies in human history, the Bolshevik tyranny is the worst, the most destructive and the most degrading.'[17] In a letter to the *Weekly Review*, he wrote:

> Bolshevism means in every country a civil war of the most merciless kind between the discontented, criminal and mutinous classes on one hand and the contented or law-abiding on the other ... Bolshevism, wherever it manifests itself openly ... means war of the ruthless character, the slaughter of men, women and children, the burning of homes and the inviting in of tyranny, pestilence and famine.[18]

Communism was a totalitarian system whereby the party suppressed and exploited the masses and mass murdered any opponents:

> Was there ever a more awful spectacle ... than ... the agony of Russia? This vast country ... not only produced enough food for itself, but, before the war, it was one of the great granaries of the world ... It is now reduced to famine ... because the theories of Lenin and Trotsky have ... driven man from the civilization of the twentieth century into a condition of barbarism ... racked by pestilence and deprived of hope.[19]

He explained the insidious nature of the communist threat:

> The Bolshevist aim of world revolution can be pursued equally in peace or war. In fact, a Bolshevist peace is only another form of war. They do not for the moment overwhelm with armies, they can undermine with propaganda. Not a shot may be fired along the whole front ... yet invasion may be proceeding swiftly and relentlessly. The peasants are roused against the landlords, the workmen against their employers, the railways and public services are induced to strike, the soldiers are incited to mutiny and kill their officers, the mob are raised against the middle classes to murder them, to plunder their houses, to debauch

their wives and carry off their children, an elaborate network of secret societies entangles honest political action; the Press is bought whenever possible.[20]

Yet Churchill recognized the difficulties of fighting in Russia given its merciless winters and vast landscapes. He did not want British and other Allied troops directly to combat the communists, but to support the anti-communist forces and only then if they were capable of winning: 'It is highly important to know what the Russians can & will do for themselves. If they put up a real fight, we ought in my view to back them in every way possible. But without them it is not good our trying.'[21]

Churchill's warnings were in vain. Most members of the Cabinet and the public opposed military involvement in Russia's civil war. During a Cabinet meeting on 12 February 1919 Prime Minister Lloyd George estimated that the scale of fighting for both the numbers of troops and expanse of territory in the Russian civil war was so great that the British would need to field at least half a million men to tip the balance. Politically and economically that was a non-starter without massive contributions of French troops and American dollars. He would ask Presidents Clemenceau and Wilson what their governments could do after he arrived at the Paris Peace Conference. The Big Three leaders quickly concluded that their respective populations would reject a war against Russia's communists. Each would withdraw his respective troops from Russia and encourage the Japanese to do likewise. However, they did favour supplying the anti-communist forces with surplus military weapons, munitions and equipment.

That decision deeply depressed Churchill. He later wrote that: 'If I had been properly supported in 1919, I think we might have strangled Bolshevism in its cradle, but everybody turned up their hand and said, "How shocking!"'[22] The destruction of communism 'would have been an untold blessing to the human race'.[23] To that end he then advocated that the British and their allies wield all means to help defeat the communists short of directly fighting them. As the Red Army inflicted ever more defeats on the Whites, he urged the anti-communist leaders to cut a political deal with the communists whereby they would share power. He offered to mediate peace between them. But Lenin and his cabal wanted total victory over their enemies and total control of Russia as the first stage in promoting communist revolutions around the world.

Lenin's regime had two critical advantages over the White forces. First, the communists had superior leadership and organization and a more appealing ideology and so could mobilize far more manpower, money and other resources. Second, the Red Army fought on interior lines and so could transfer forces from front to front to mass forces that routed each White Army before it. By October 1922, the Red Army had destroyed all the counterrevolutionary forces and reconquered all the countries apart from Finland that had liberated themselves from the Russian Empire, now the Soviet Union.

* * *

By late 1920, War Office politics, especially the endless battles over funding, had burned Churchill out on that post. He asked Lloyd George if he could take another, more politically powerful ministry like the Foreign Office or the Treasury, stepping stones to 10 Downing Street. Indeed the Chancellor of the Exchequer's residence is right next door at No. 11. On 14 February 1921, the prime minister gave Churchill an especially appropriate Valentine's Day present, the Colonial Office. There Churchill could apply his interests and experiences in the empire by administering it. But there was a catch. British imperial policies would be increasingly complicated by the new League of Nations.

During the opening days of the Paris Peace Conference on 25 January 1919, the delegations agreed to establish a commission to design a League of Nations dedicated to promoting international peace and prosperity. The Covenant or constitution setup an international organization with four bodies, a Secretariat or administration; an Assembly in which each member state would have one vote; an executive Council of ten states; and a Permanent International Court of Justice. Whitehall enjoyed an advantage in the Assembly as its dominions of Canada, Australia, New Zealand and South Africa could be expected to vote with Britain on the issues, especially critical ones involving war and peace.[24]

The League of Nations was no sooner established than the great powers began to manipulate that international body to promote their own respective national interests. The division of war spoils among Britain, France, Italy and Japan took a giant stride forward during the London Conference of 12–24 February, 1920, elaborated that understanding at Sam Remo, Italy Conference of 18–26 April 1920 and codified it with the Treaty of Sèvres on 10 August 1920. The German, Austrian and Ottoman Empires were dissolved and the colonies distributed to the winners as mandates, theoretically to be nurtured for eventual independence. There were three types of mandates. Class A mandates were Ottoman Empire provinces that had reached a development level that could lead to independence in a generation or so. France got the provinces of Syria and Lebanon. Britain got Palestine and the three Mesopotamian provinces of Basra, Baghdad and Mosul that it combined into a new country called Iraq. Class B mandates included Germany's African colonies which had a low development level and thus would be controlled for the foreseeable future. Belgium received Rwanda, Britain Tanganyika; France and Britain split Cameroun and Togoland between them. Class C mandates included the former German colonies of Southwest Africa for South Africa; the Pacific island groups of the Marianas, Carolines and Marshalls for Japan; Papua New Guinea for Australia; and Samoa for New Zealand. Each Class C trustee country could administer its mandates indefinitely as part of its own territory. Mandates turned out to be financial burdens for most governments that received them as their administrative costs far exceeded any revenues.

Sentiment as much as reason determined Prime Minister Lloyd George's choices of Middle East mandates for Britain, akin to a boy in a sweetshop with only so much pocket change. Historian Arnold Toynbee was then the prime minister's aide and later recalled:

Lloyd George, to my delight, had forgotten my presence and had begun to think aloud. 'Mesopotamia ... yes ... oil ... irrigation ... we must have Mesopotamia. Palestine ... yes ... the Holy Land ... Zionism ... we must have Palestine. Syria ... h'm ... what is there in Syria? Let the French have that.[25]

President Clemenceau captured the moral arguments behind the Ottoman Empire's dismantling:

There is no case to be found either in Europe or Asia or Africa in which the establishment of Turkish rule in any country has not been followed by a diminution of material prosperity and a fall in the level of culture; nor is there any case to be found in which the withdrawal of Turkish rule has not been followed by a growth in material prosperity and a rise in the level of culture.[26]

Turkey was reduced to a rump state confined to south-west Asia, with the Dardanelles and Bosporus Straits and intervening Sea of Marmara internationalized and demilitarized, at least in theory.[27] For now British,

French and Italian troops occupied Constantinople and key forts along the European side of the straits and Chanak on the south side of the Dardanelles. Greece received Thrace and Smyrna (Izmir). Britain and France split Turkey's Middle East provinces between them.

Tragically, the Greeks were not satisfied with that vast expansion of their territory but wanted much more. The Greek army, assisted by British, French and Italian naval forces, had already occupied Smyrna in May 1919. In October 1920, the Greeks advanced along the coast and inland to secure regions with predominantly Greek populations and expel the Turks. The Turks blunted the Greek offensive at the Battle of Inonu on 30 March 1921. The Greeks resumed their offensive in June 1921, seeking to overrun Anatolia and capture Ankara. The Turks defeated them at the Battle of Sakarya River that raged from 23 August to 13 September 1921. The British, French and Italian governments rejected Greek appeals for military help but did offer to mediate a peace treaty. General Mustafa Kemal Ataturk, Turkey's de facto ruler, rejected any talks as long as the Greek army remained in Anatolia. Meanwhile, he massed Turkish forces and on 26 August 1922, launched an offensive that routed the Greek army. On 9 September, the Turks captured Smyrna then advanced to the Straits and massed forces around Chanak, held by British forces.

Prime Minister Lloyd George, Foreign Secretary George Curzon and Colonial Secretary Churchill debated whether to resist or accept Turkey's conquest of lands allocated to Greece. British forces were stretched thin and the budget to uphold them thinner around the world. The public would not support joining Greece in a war against Turkey. Yet acquiescing might encourage Turkey and other ambitious countries to further aggression. They hoped that standing firm at Chanak would deter the Turks from attacking north of the Dardanelles. They decided to dispatch 5,000 troops to reinforce the 3,500-man garrison. The trouble was that those reinforcements would not reach Chanak until 9 October at the earliest. By late September, Ataturk had massed 23,000 troops around Chanak and demanded that its garrison withdraw. So far not a shot had been fired. The garrison's provisions were dwindling. Ceding to the Turkish demand would be a tremendous blow to British prestige.

Lloyd George, Curzon and Churchill decided to hang tough. On 29 September, the prime minister instructed General Charles Harrington, who commanded British forces in Turkey with his headquarters at Constantinople, to warn the Turks to withdraw from Chanak's perimeter or the British troops would open fire. Ataturk offered a swap. The Turks would back off from Chanak if the British garrison withdrew to the north shore. Harrington opened talks with him. A deal was cut for the Turks to withdraw 10 miles from Chanak and another British post at Ismid. When that withdrawal was complete, the British troops were ferried across the strait back to Europe. A face-saving compromise had averted war. With the Treaty of Lausanne, signed on 24 July 1923, Turkey got eastern Thrace and Constantinople, which Ataturk renamed Istanbul. A million and a half Greeks and half a million Turks were forced to abandon their homes and move to Greece and Turkey, respectively.

Elsewhere a similar mingling of mutually-hostile peoples proved impossible to resolve; indeed British policy contributed to what would be a blood-soaked deadlock. During the First World War, the British made conflicting promises to the Arabs and Jews to entice their support.[28] The High Commissioner to Egypt, Henry McMahon, exchanged letters with Hussein bin Ali, the Sharif of Mecca, from 14 July 1915 to 30 January 1916, in which he pledged support for Arab independence from the Ottoman Empire if those tribes joined British forces against the Turks. On 9 May 1916, British diplomat Mark Sykes and French diplomat François Picot secretly signed what became known as the Sykes-Picot Agreement, which committed their countries to splitting the Middle East between them as spheres of influence after the war. The Arab tribes revolted on 5 June 1916. On 2 November 1917, Foreign Secretary Balfour wrote to Walter Rothschild, Britain's most prominent Jewish leader, this message: 'His Majesty's Government views with favour the establishment of a national home for the Jewish people and will use their best endeavours to facilitate the achievement of this object' as long as it did not 'prejudice the civil and religious rights of existing non-Jewish communities in Palestine'. The letter was published on 9 November. That promise was embedded in the August 1920 Sèvres Treaty that dissolved the Ottoman Empire in the Middle East and awarded the provinces as mandates either to Britain or France.

The British faced worsening challenges to their mandate for Palestine.[29] The Arabs grew increasingly enraged as ever more Jews emigrated to their territory, enticed by the Zionist insistence that Palestine was 'a land without people for a people without a land'. In reality, by 1922, Palestine's 752,048 people included 668,258 Arabs and 83,790 Jews or 88.9 per cent and 11.1 per cent, respectively, according to the British mandate census. The Zionists established their own shadow government including police and paramilitary forces to protect and expand their land holdings and businesses. Violence worsened between Arabs and Jews.

Churchill decided to see the situation first-hand. Colonel Thomas Edward (T.E.) Lawrence 'of Arabia' was among his three-man staff. Lawrence was fluent in Arabic and had helped lead the Arab revolt against the Ottoman Empire during the First World War. On the eve of Churchill's departure, Chaim Weizmann, the president of the World Zionist Organization, sent him a letter demanding that the Jewish homeland include not just all of Palestine but Transjordan as well, even though Arabs comprised nearly all its inhabitants. Churchill's first stop was Cairo for a conference from 12 to 22 March 1921, held to determine who would rule which countries. Acting on Lawrence's advice, Churchill picked Emir Feisal and Emir Abdullah to head Iraq and Transjordan, respectively. He charged Herbert Samuel, Palestine's high commissioner, to work with the Zionists to develop a Jewish homeland. On 23 March, Churchill, Abdullah and their entourages took the train to Gaza. The next morning Palestinians massed in the streets to protest the Jewish homeland and demand independence for themselves. As Churchill reached Jerusalem on 27 March, Arabs rioted against Jews in Haifa.

The following day, an Arab delegation asked Churchill to end Jewish immigration and to support the Palestinian people's right to their own state. He promised them that British authorities would help them protect their property and eventually govern themselves. Yet he insisted that: 'It is manifestly right that the Jews, who are scattered all over the world, should have a national centre and a National Home where some of them might be reunited. And where else could that be but in this land of Palestine, with which for more than 3,000 years they have been intimately and profoundly associated.'[30]

During Churchill's visit to the Hebrew University's future site on 29 March, he publicly endorsed a Jewish national home:

> The hope of your race will be gradually realized here, not only for your own good but for the good of the world ... Every step you take should therefore be also for the moral and material benefit of all Palestinians ... If you do this, Palestine will be happy and prosperous and peace and concord will always reign.[31]

He then announced that 'I am now going to plant a tree and I hope that in its shadow peace and prosperity may return once more to Palestine.' A ceremony that was intended to symbolize hope instead became a metaphor for broken promises and lives. The tree snapped in two as someone handed it to him. There was no other tree in reserve. Someone found a small potted palm but it died after it was transferred to the unsuitable soil.[32]

Back in London, Churchill drafted a constitution for Palestine that, among other things, protected the right of Jews to immigrate and invest there. He suffered a political embarrassment when the House of Lords repudiated his endorsement of a Jewish homeland by a vote of 60 to 20. However, in the House of Commons he was able to rally 292 votes in favour to 35 against. He authorized a Zionist monopoly over irrigation and electricity development, hoping that Jewish ingenuity in those pursuits would serve as a model for the Arabs. Instead, it just gave the Arabs another excuse to hate the Jews and the British mandate. On 22 July, the League of Nations approved these steps that Britain had taken for Palestine. Churchill may have failed to alleviate the worsening hatreds between Arabs and Jews in Palestine, but he was able to pare British administrative costs from £8 million in 1920 to £4 million in 1921 and to £2 million in 1922.[33]

Elsewhere in the Middle East, Churchill was prominent among those responsible for Iraq's paternity. Iraq was constructed from the Ottoman provinces of Basra, Baghdad and Mosul up the Tigris and Euphrates River valleys, a region known from ancient times as Mesopotamia. The new country harboured severe religious and ethnic cleavages that only the sternest authority could prevent from warring against each other. The population was roughly 80 per cent Arab and 20 per cent Kurd and roughly 60 per cent Shiite Muslim, 35 per cent Sunni Muslim and 5 per cent Christian, Jewish, Zoroastrian and Yazidi. In 1920, Churchill wrote this about British involvement in Iraq that has echoed loudly in more recent decades:

> There is something very sinister to my mind in this Mesopotamian entanglement … [We seem] compelled to go on pouring armies and treasures into these thankless deserts … Week after week and month after month we shall have a continuance of this miserable, wasteful, sporadic warfare, marked from time to time certainly by minor disasters and cuttings off of troops and agents and very possibly attended by some very grave occurrence.[34]

Churchill faced an explosive situation far closer to London. Whitehall's worries over Ireland's loyalty worsened during the First World War.[35] On 18 September 1914, a month after Britain declared war, Prime Minister Asquith first got Parliament to pass the Irish Home Rule Bill then suspend it for the duration of the war with a Conscription Bill for Ireland, thus promising future autonomy in exchange for the immediate drafts of Irishmen to fight in the trenches. After Irish Republicans revolted during Easter in April 1916, British authorities crushed them with martial law, arrests of hundreds of suspects and execution of fifteen ringleaders. During the December 1918 general election, the Irish Republican party Sinn Fein ('Ourselves Alone') won 73 of Ireland's 105 seats in Parliament. On 21 January 1919, Arthur Griffith, Sinn Fein's head, led its members to form a government in Ireland that declared independence. Fighting broke out between the Irish Republican Army (IRA) and the combined forces of the British Army, Royal Irish Constabulary (RIC), Ulster Special Constabulary, Ulster Volunteer Force, Dublin Metropolitan Police and Protestant Black and Tan militia. Irish Republican sympathizers conducted strikes, especially transport workers who refused to carry any military equipment or personnel.

Prime Minister Lloyd George pushed the Government of Ireland Act through the House of Commons on 23 December 1920. During Ireland's elections on 11 May 1921, Sinn Fein won 124 of 128 seats and in turn elected Eamon de Valera the president. George V called for negotiations between de Valera and Lloyd George. De Valera would talk only if in protocol he was treated superior as a president to Lloyd George, who was merely a prime minister. Lloyd George rejected the notion. A series of terrorist attacks by both sides resumed. A face-saving way was found to resolve the protocol issue. De Valera sent Michael Collins and Arthur Griffith to negotiate with Lloyd George and they signed a truce on 11 July 1921. On 10 October, Lloyd George greeted the Sinn Fein and Protestant Unionist delegations at 10 Downing Street, then had Churchill lead negotiations with them.[36]

Churchill presided over the three-way negotiations that ground on for six tense weeks from 11 October until a preliminary treaty was signed on 6 December 1922. He swiftly bonded with Collins as a fellow warrior and nationalist. When Collins angrily complained about the £5,000 dead-or-alive reward that Churchill had issued for him, Churchill replied, 'You are not the only one', then showed him the framed £25 dead or alive reward that the Boers had issued for him after his escape. 'At any rate it was a good price – £5,000. Look at me – £25 dead or alive. How would you like that?' Collins laughed heartily and they were soon trading war stories over cigars and whisky.[37] Churchill was just as sly in getting Collins and the Unionist leader James Craig to negotiate: 'They both glowered magnificently, but after a short commonplace talk I slipped away on some excuse and left them together. What these two Irishmen, separated by such gulfs of religion, sentiment and conduct, said to each other, I cannot say. But it took a long time.' After several hours 'I ventured to look in. They announced to me complete agreement reduced to writing. They wanted to help each other in every way.'[38]

It was Churchill's proposal that broke the stalemate and led to an agreement. On 12 November, he recommended splitting the island between the twenty-six mostly Catholic central and southern counties which would become the Irish Free State as a Dominion within the British Empire and the six mostly Protestant northern counties of Ulster that would stay in the United Kingdom. Churchill then bent heads with Griffith to design a constitution for the Irish Free State. They established a two-house parliament with budgets originating in the lower chamber. The British monarch would serve as Ireland's head of state and appoint a governor general to preside over the government in Dublin. The Free State would pay taxes to Britain. The Irish army would be small and the navy confined to a few gunboats. When Collins signed the treaty on December 6, he quipped: 'I may have signed my actual death warrant.'[39]

Ireland's parliament approved the treaty by 64 to 57 votes on 9 January 1922. Now De Valera resigned in protest at the treaty that split Ireland. Collins took his place on 15 January. That same day the British turned over Dublin Castle to the Irish Free State. Collins struggled to end IRA attacks on Unionists. Churchill tried to soften Irish nationalist bitterness for their failure to take over the entire island by passing word that the government would not execute several IRA terrorists who had received death sentences. He promised that Ulster's police would be half Catholic and half Protestant. He earmarked £500,000 to alleviate poverty in Ulster. When he introduced the Irish Free State Bill in the House of Commons on February 16, 1922, he struggled to win a majority with rhetoric like this:

If you wish to see Ireland degenerate into a meaningless welter of lawless chaos and confusion, delay this Bill. If you wish to see increasingly serious bloodshed all along the borders of Ulster, delay this Bill. If you want this House to have on its hands, as it has now, the responsibility for peace and order in Southern Ireland, without the means of enforcing it, delay this Bill.[40]

On 31 March 1923, the House of Commons vote was 302 for and 60 against.

The Irish Free State held its first elections on 22 June 1923. The Griffith-Collins and de Valera factions respectively won 58 seats and 36 seats, with another 34 seats distributed among other parties and independents. By putting together a coalition, the pro-treaty party had 93 against 35 seats. The coalition elected Griffith president and Collins prime minister. De Valera and his men were sore losers. Having failed at the polls, the radicals resorted to violence, this time against their fellow Irish Catholics. The IRA took over the Four Courts in Dublin, where all the legal records were stored. Collins ordered an attack by his own militia on 28 July, but failed to dislodge the radicals. He turned down Churchill's offer to send British troops from Ulster. The following day, Collins resumed the battle but the radicals repulsed the attack. On 30 July, after setting fire to the Four Courts, the radicals surrendered. The Irish government experienced convulsive changes. A heart attack killed Griffith on 12 August, then the IRA ambushed and murdered Collins on 22 August. The Irish Free State, however, endured with William Cosgrave as prime minister and then president. In all more than 1,400 people died in the sporadic fighting between the Easter Rising and Cosgrave government. For months Churchill himself feared being assassinated and slept with a pistol within reach.

*   *   *

Although the Senate had rejected the Versailles Treaty that would have committed the United States to the League of Nations, the White House promoted international peace and prosperity on its own. President Warren Harding invited the foreign ministers of Britain, France, Italy and Japan to meet with Secretary of State Charles Hughes to negotiate limits on the size and power of their respective navies. The conference began on 21 November 1921 and concluded on 6 February 1922 with the Treaty of Washington. The treaty limited battleships and cruisers to a ratio in tonnage of 5 for the United States and Britain, 3 for Japan and 1.75 for France and Italy, with guns no larger than 16in. Aircraft carriers were limited to 33,000 tons each. All other warships could not exceed 10,000 tons each. Six years later, those five naval powers signed the Treaty of London on 22 April 1930, that committed them to an array of restrictions on cruisers, destroyers and submarines.

While those cutbacks and limitations would prove to be huge cost-savers in the long run, it was an immediate psychological blow to Britain. To realize its quota the British had to scrap 657 ships. For the first time in their history, the British would accept another country with a navy the same size as its own. Until then British policy was to keep a navy as large as the next two largest navies combined. Churchill accepted this restriction only because the United States was that other power. War with America was unimaginable while their combined fleets would rule the waves and defeat any enemy alliance.

During the Washington Conference the great powers attempted further to solidify peace with two other treaties. The Four Power Pact committed the United States, Japan, Britain and France to non-aggression against each other, to uphold the Pacific Basin's status quo and not seek further territory and to consult whenever a serious problem arose; that pact replaced the 1902 Anglo-Japanese Alliance. The Nine Power Pact between the United States, Japan, China, Britain, France, Italy, Portugal, Belgium and the Netherlands committed them to uphold China's sovereignty and free market, 'the open door'. That web of treaties appeared to entangle the Pacific Basin in peace, trade and growing prosperity. Tragically, the Great Depression and the rise of Japanese fascism destroyed that system.[41]

* * *

Paralleling the series of critical international events in which Churchill was either directly or indirectly involved, were a series of critical events in his private life. He suffered two devastating losses during the summer of 1921. At age 67, his mother fell down the stairs and suffered a compound leg fracture. Gangrene festered. A haemorrhage killed her on 29 June. In a letter to a friend, Churchill was heartbroken yet philosophical about her passing:

> She suffers no more pain; nor will she ever know old age, decrepitude, loneliness ... I wish you could have seen her as she lay at rest – after all the sunshine & storm of life was over. Very beautiful and very splendid she looked ... She recalled to me the countenance I had admired as a child when she was in her heyday and the old brilliant world of the eighties & nineties seemed to come back.[42]

Biographer William Manchester paints this revealing scene of the funeral: 'After the others had left, Winston stood alone by the open grave. He wept and threw in a spray of crimson roses. But he was mourning his own lost youth and the imperial glory of those years, as much as his mother.'[43] His sorrow deepened when meningitis killed his 2½-year-old daughter, Marigold, on 24 August.

During 1922, Churchill experienced two wonderful events followed by two wretched ones. He bought Chartwell Manor set among eighty bucolic

acres in Kent about 30 miles south-east of London and Clementine gave
birth to Mary, their fourth child who would live into adulthood. Then, on
16 October, he suffered excruciating pains in his stomach and was rushed
to the hospital where his appendix was removed. As he recovered another
crisis erupted.

*   *   *

The Conservative Party split bitterly over whether to remain junior partners
in the Coalition Cabinet. Austen Chamberlain's faction wanted to stay.
Stanley Baldwin led those who wanted to withdraw and thus precipitate an
election that the party might well win.[44] The decision came during a party
conference at the Carlton Club on 10 October 1922. By a vote of 185 to 88,
the Tories agreed to abandon the coalition on 19 October. That forced Lloyd
George to resign as prime minister. On 23 October, King George V asked
Conservative leader Andrew Bonar Law to form a caretaker government.
Law promptly called for a general election to be held three weeks later on
15 November. The Conservatives won a sweeping victory with 344 seats.
The Labour Party came in second with 142 seats. The Liberals suffered a
catastrophe, with David Lloyd George's National Liberals retaining only 62
seats and Herbert Asquith's faction falling to 53. Baldwin became the Tory
Cabinet's prime minister.[45]

Churchill was among those who lost his seat. After twenty-two years in
Parliament and a succession of posts in a succession of governments, he was
now an unemployed 48-year-old. To lick his wounds and figure out what to
do next, he holed up in a villa near Cannes on the French Rivera for half
a year, writing his memoirs and painting. He left meticulous instructions
for Chartwell's renovation while he was gone but returned twice for several
weeks to oversee the work. In London he stayed at the Ritz where he wrote
and entertained influential people who might help him make a political
comeback. His core effort was trying to reunite the Liberal Party by healing
the rift between Asquith and Lloyd George.

The opportunity came on 6 December 1923, with the latest general
election. Baldwin made a severe miscalculation. By calling an election, rather
than reinforce his party's hold on power, he diminished it. Conservative
seats dropped to 258, while Labour and Liberal seats rose to 191 and 158,
respectively. Churchill urged Asquith to form a coalition with the Tories,
but he chose to join a government led by Labour Party leader Ramsay
MacDonald who became prime minister on 22 January 1924 and would

remain so until 21 November that year, when Baldwin returned to Downing Street.[46]

This proved to be a catastrophic turning point in Britain's political history. Thereafter the centrist Liberal Party became an impotent third party while British politics polarized between the Conservative and Labour Parties. In that tug-of-war, the Socialists steadily pulled the Tories ideologically closer to themselves.[47] Churchill condemned the cancerous effects of Socialism, spearheaded by the Labour Party,

> as a disaster to the British people ... with a decline in the progress of democracy, with a marked discrediting of universal suffrage and with the decay of the parliamentary institutions by which the liberties of England were won. A crudeness and a dullness has been brought into the discussion of every question ... The promulgation ... of a programme of nationalising all the means of production, distribution and exchange ... has produced in Europe violent reactions towards the extremes of nationalism and the tyrannies of dictatorship.[48]

Churchill sidestepped this election. There were no safe seats and he feared that a loss would permanently end his political career. A by-election emerged in the conservative district of Westminster. Hat in hand, Churchill went to Baldwin and asked to be allowed to rejoin the Conservative Party and run for that seat. Baldwin acquiesced but a Conservative candidate opposed him. Churchill lost that election on 19 March 1924 by the razor-thin margin of seventy-three votes. This time he dealt with his defeat by remaining in London and trying to forge ties between the Conservative and Liberal Parties against the Labour Party. He rallied around fifty Liberal MPs who were appalled by Asquith's Faustian bargain with the Socialists.

For Churchill's conciliatory efforts, Baldwin rewarded him with a safe seat for Epping, a district in London's north-east suburbs. During the general election on 29 October 1924, Churchill won, one of 412 Tory seats in a resounding victory. Labour fell to 151 seats and the Liberals plummeted to a mere 40 seats. To those who condemned him for once again turning coat, Churchill replied: 'Anyone can rat but it takes a certain amount of ingenuity to re-rat.'[49] Yet he remained firmly his own man. He saw little political difference between Baldwin and MacDonald: 'Nominally the representatives of opposing parties, of contrary doctrines, of antagonistic interests, they proved in fact to be more nearly akin in outlook, temperament and method than any other two men who had been prime minister since that office was known to the Constitution.'[50] For Churchill himself, the critical difference was that he would serve under one but not the other.

* * *

Baldwin rewarded Churchill's defection by appointing him Chancellor of the Exchequer. There Churchill once again proudly trod one of his father's political footsteps. Randolph Churchill's last government post was Chancellor. He had resigned out of principle over a trifling dispute with Prime Minister Lord Salisbury and was never recalled to power. Churchill was determined to redeem his father with his own contributions. The trouble was that he knew next to nothing about economics but thought that he did. He was armed with free trade and Gold Standard nostrums but they backfired against him and the country when he tried to ground policy on them. Of his four-and-a-half-year stint at the Treasury, he later admitted: 'Everyone said I was the worst Chancellor of the Exchequer that ever was and now I am inclined to agree with them.'[51]

He had the right instincts about old and new wealth. On 14 December 1924, he shared his thoughts with key Treasury officials:

> The creation of new wealth is beneficial to the whole community. The process of squatting on old wealth though valuable is a far less lively agent. The great bulk of the wealth of the world is created and consumed every year. We shall never shake ourselves clear from the debts of the past and break into a definitely larger period, except by the energetic creation of new wealth. A premium on effort is the aim and a penalty on inertia may well be its companion.[52]

Yet Churchill was clueless over just how to encourage the creation and distribution of wealth.

With America and Japan the exceptions, the First World War devastated the victors nearly as much as the losers. The war left Britain and most other former belligerents trapped in a vicious economic cycle of worsening growth, productivity, debt, inflation, joblessness, homelessness, strikes, bankruptcies and despair. Free trade and a fixed gold-backed currency only worsened matters as cheaper-priced goods flooded markets and destroyed British industries. Economist John Maynard Keynes argued that the vicious cycle could be broken only if the government nurtured key industries with protective tariffs, subsidies and investments in infrastructure. That practical approach, however, was anathema to free trade and Gold Standard purists.[53]

Churchill returned Britain to the Gold Standard on 28 April 1925. When Keynes heard what Churchill had done, he remarked: 'Why did he do such a silly thing.'[54] The Gold Standard walloped Britain's economy exactly as Keynes and other naysayers had warned. The high-priced pound benefited British consumers with low-priced imports. British producers, however, suffered a double whammy of diminishing sales at home and abroad as cheaper imports meant more costly exports that priced British goods out of all markets. The pound's fixed rate to gold straitjacketed the Treasury's ability to expand the money supply to stimulate the economy; with the gold supply fixed so too was the currency supply. Much later after he left the Treasury, Churchill repented his faith in the false gold god: 'To hell with it! It has been used as a vile trap to destroy us. I would pay the rest of the American debt in gold as long as the gold lasted and then say – "Henceforward, we will only pay in goods. Pray specify what goods you desire".'[55]

During the 1920s Britain's economic woes climaxed with the General Strike of May 1926. Churchill sympathized with the worker demands for a minimal wage. The challenge was to convince most Cabinet ministers and business chiefs that granting that demand was actually good for Britain. He invited Labour Party leader Ramsay MacDonald to Chartwell for secret talks on 1 September, with a follow-up in London two days later. MacDonald arranged a secret meeting between Churchill and the miners' leaders. Churchill got them to accept a minimum wage that would not do the economy more harm than good. He then invited the mine owners to Chartwell for secret talks but was frustrated when they adamantly rejected any minimum wage. He then delivered a speech before the House of Commons in which he called the strikers back to work while he established an independent National Tribunal with legally binding decisions in arbitrating disputes between workers and owners. The workers refused to return to their jobs and the corporate chiefs rejected any notion of neutral arbitration. Churchill was back at square one while the deadlock strangled the economy. Eventually the workers returned to their jobs but the conflicts and animosities festered.

Some of Churchill's economic measures did bring some relief to millions of desperate people. He tried to alleviate poverty by reducing the retirement age from 70 to 65, abolishing means tests for welfare recipients, paying stipends to war widows and orphans, providing universal health care, cutting taxes by 40 per cent for the poor, and raising taxes on the rich and on luxury goods like cars, trucks and petrol. His proudest achievement was getting stipends for '344,000 children, 236,800 widows, 450,000 Britons over sixty-five years old and 227,000 over seventy'.[56] Yet his welfare policies may have worsened rather than lessened the economic vicious cycle. Tax hikes on the rich underwrote only a portion of the higher spending. The rest came from borrowed money that increased the national debt and dampened economic growth.

Although America replaced Britain as the financial, commercial, manufacturing and technological engine of global economic growth in the late nineteenth century, Washington did not begin to assume a political role commensurate with its economic power until after the First World War.[57] Self-interest forced the White House and Wall Street jointly to assume that critical role. Virtually every country owed money to American creditors. By the war's end Britain alone had racked up £4,933,701,642 in debt whose annual interest payments came to £35 million. Britain had trouble making those payments not just because its own economy was weak but because the economies of other countries that owed Britain money were as bad or worse. Britain, France, Belgium and Italy relied on German reparations payments to help underwrite what they owed America, but hyperinflation engulfed Germany and rendered its deutschmarks worthless. In 1924 and 1929, Berlin announced that it would suspend payments in gold. Doing so threatened to destroy the global economy by ending the circulation of money through the system. Each time Washington overcame the crisis by bringing together representatives of the major economies and convincing them to follow America's lead in reducing interest rates, extending the years for payment and writing off some of the debt. When it came to the reparations bill imposed by the Allies, Germany got off quite lightly, paying only about $4.5 billion of the $31.5 billion it owed from 1918 to 1932 or less than what Paris paid Berlin after the Franco–Prussian War.[58]

Churchill successfully lightened Britain's debt to the United States. In January 1925, he attended an international debt conference in Paris where he cut several interrelated deals. The Americans agreed to reschedule Britain's payments to American creditors equal to what Britain received from the array of countries that collectively owed £2 billion to British creditors. Typically he distilled his lessons in money management to a maxim: 'In finance, everything that is agreeable is unsound and everything that is sound is disagreeable.'[59]

Churchill spent most weekdays in London struggling to manage the economy, occasionally making rousing speeches when Parliament was in session and living at 11 Downing Street. He passed most weekends at his beloved Chartwell. The £5,000 he had paid for it seemed a good deal at the time but the mansion proved to be a fixer-upper. He ended up investing another £18,000 in repairs and additions including electricity, plumbing and a detached studio for painting. Clementine never took to the place and avoided it when she could. But it was Churchill's dream home and he loved inviting distinguished quests for long weekends of talking, drinking and eating. Perhaps his most famous sojourners were Lawrence of Arabia and Charlie Chaplin. One consistent guest was Oxford University Professor Frederick Lindemann, a quiet genius on the cutting edge of science and mathematics whose brain Churchill relished picking for ideas and inventions.

Churchill typically managed to squeeze in some long trips abroad during his tenure at the Treasury. His most notable encounter was with Benito Mussolini in January 1927. During a press conference, he lauded the dictator as a great leader for Italy and for 'your triumphant struggle against the bestial appetites and passions of Leninism'. He promised Mussolini that eventually 'we shall succeed in grappling with Communism and choking the life out of it'.[60] Although he retained his fierce hatred of communism until his last breath, his view of Mussolini would greatly change from the mid-1930s. During that same trip he met Pope Pius XI. In the negotiations preceding the audience he rejected the protocol of kneeling before the pontiff but did agree to make three short bows as he might before any monarch.

* * *

In the election on 29 May 1929, Labour surged ahead of the Conservatives, winning 287 to 260 seats, while the Liberals finished with 59. Ramsay MacDonald formed a coalition government with the Liberal Party. Although Churchill retained his seat, he lost his job at the Treasury on 4 June. He was flabbergasted that so many Britons had voted for MacDonald and his fellow socialists.

Churchill soon had a falling out with Baldwin over strategy.[61] He insisted 'that the Conservative Opposition should strongly confront the Labour Government on all great imperial and national issues ... Mr. Baldwin felt that ... the hope for the Conservative Party in accommodation with Liberal and Labour forces and in adroit, well timed manoeuvres to detach powerful moods of public opinion and large blocks of voters from them.' Looking back, Churchill admitted that Baldwin's strategy was successful: 'He was the greatest party manager the Conservatives ever had. He fought, as their leader, five general elections, of which he won three.'[62] They broke over

India. Baldwin and most Conservatives favoured India's transition to self-rule. Adamantly opposed, Churchill resigned in protest from the Shadow Cabinet on 27 January 1931. In doing so he relegated himself to the back benches after having enjoyed a front-row seat on either side of the House almost continuously since 1905.

As usual after a setback, Churchill hit the road, this time to North America, typically journeying in a style that far exceeded his income. His friend Bernard Baruch, a powerful New York lawyer, got corporate giant Charles Schwab to lend him his private railway car for a vast circuit that took him north to Montreal, across the continent to Vancouver, down the west coast to San Francisco and Los Angeles and finally east to Washington and New York. He was mostly unimpressed with the childlike William Randolph Hearst whom he met at his hilltop palace near San Simeon, California, although he did marvel that the multi-millionaire somehow kept his wife and mistress in amiable company on either side of him. He readily agreed to Hearst's request that he write periodic essays for his newspaper empire.

Churchill was staying at New York's Savoy-Plaza Hotel when the stock market crashed on 24 October 1929. That night he joined a coterie of New York's financial elite for dinner at Baruch's Fifth Avenue mansion and provoked more grimaces than grins by raising his glass and toasting my 'friends and former millionaires'.[63] The value of half of Churchill's investments was among the $30 billion wiped out when that speculative bubble burst. That left Churchill devastated but not bitter. He visited the Stock Exchange the next day to laud 'the march of a valiant and serviceable people who by fierce experiment are hewing new paths for man and showing to all nations much that they should attempt and much that they should avoid'.[64]

Britain's economy sank steadily lower as America's Great Depression globalized and strikes crippled the economy.[65] The impotence of the Labour-Liberal coalition to prevent that collapse caused the government to fail and both parties to shatter. The Labour Party split between MacDonald's National Labour and Arthur Henderson's Labour factions. The Liberal Party broke into three parts led by John Simon's Liberal National, Herbert Simon's Liberal and David Lloyd George's Independent Liberal factions. The Conservative Party remained united.

King George V refused MacDonald's offer to resign and instead asked him to remain prime minister of a 'National Government' composed of Labour, Liberal and Conservative members, followed by an election. The Conservatives made an extraordinary comeback on 27 October 1931, winning 471 seats, while Labour took 52, National Labour 13, Liberal National 35,

Liberal 33 and Independent Liberal 4.[66] Churchill held his seat resoundingly with two-thirds of the votes cast.

Despite the overwhelming Tory victory, Baldwin declined the king's offer to be prime minister. He insisted instead that MacDonald remain prime minister in a coalition government that included eleven Conservatives, five National Liberals and four National Labour members. Two primary motives drove that decision. He wanted to preserve the façade of national unity amidst the Great Depression and to use MacDonald as a fall guy if the coalition failed to revive the economy. MacDonald appointed Baldwin Lord President of the Council and, thus, de facto deputy prime minister and Neville Chamberlain Chancellor of the Exchequer. Churchill would not have accepted a seat had he been offered one in a Cabinet headed by the socialist MacDonald even if he were a figurehead.

Churchill left behind his political woes in the wake of a ship bound for New York. He journeyed to America to make lots of money. He had signed two contracts, one for £10,000 to deliver forty lectures around the country and another for £8,000 to write a series of essays on America for the *Daily Mail*. As usual, he was living in style, this time at the Waldorf-Astoria Hotel, while hanging out with Bernard Baruch and his coterie. On 12 December 1931, he hailed a taxi to dine at Baruch's Fifth Avenue mansion overlooking Central Park but could not recall the address. Believing that he could find it better on foot he asked the driver to let him out. He looked the wrong way down Fifth Avenue then stepped from the curb. A car moving 30 miles an hour hit him and dragged him several yards before it screeched to a halt. Astonishingly he was not killed, but suffered two cracked ribs, lacerations and bruises. He admitted his own responsibility to the driver. A taxi took him to Lennox Hill Hospital's emergency room where he identified himself as 'Winston Churchill, a British statesman'.[67] The accident wounded his psyche worse than his body. He had faced death numerous times before but this brush deeply depressed him. He was 57 years old; his political career was stalled with his ambition to become prime minister more elusive than ever; he was deeply in debt; and now he was too battered physically and emotionally to deliver the lectures and essays that would earn him a small fortune. He needed three weeks of agonizing bedridden recovery before he felt strong enough to write and speak for a public audience. Eventually he was able to fulfil both contracts.

Nonetheless, overall Churchill's years in the political wilderness were as pleasant as they were productive. In between parliamentary sessions, he wrote books and newspaper articles, hosted dinner parties with fascinating people, supervised labourers at Chartwell building cottages and a heated swimming pool and composed speeches that warned the House of Commons of worsening dangers facing Britain. In all, 'I never had a dull or idle moment from morning to midnight and with my family around me dwelt at peace within my habitation'.[68]

* * *

During the 1930s, a new threat to liberal democratic countries joined that of communism. Fascism is an ideology with four key related components, authoritarianism, nationalism, mercantilism and imperialism.[69] Nationalism is what makes fascism possible in the modern world and so distinguishes it from premodern monarchies where one's nation was a hazy notion to nearly everyone outside the ruling elite. By this definition, Napoleon was the grandfather of fascism since he was the first to mobilize and command all the components. The father, however, was Benito Mussolini who coined the term.[70]

Mussolini began his political career as a socialist who shed that ideology's internationalist pretentions during the First World War and instead espoused nationalism. Despite all his flag-waving, he was no war hero. He talked officials into discharging him from the army after a grenade exploded during training and lightly wounded him. He was a brilliant politician if not soldier. He knew how to compose polemical essays and speeches that rallied ever more people behind him. He was a master of political theatre who dominated a series of increasingly larger stages where he strutted the role of the dictator who would transform Italy into a modern version of the Roman Empire. He was a skilled grassroots organizer who founded the Fascist Party in Milan on 11 December 1914. As the Fascist Party's chief, he commanded his followers to surge to the polls or into the streets in ways that aggrandized his movement's power. Spearheading his movement were his Blackshirts, a paramilitary organization that bullied rival parties with threats of violence, actual beatings and even murders.

An act of terrorism brought Mussolini to power. On 28 October 1922, he threatened to march at the head of his followers to Rome if he was not made prime minister. That was a stunning act of chutzpah if not madness on two counts. First, his Fascist Party held only 37 seats of 535 in the Chamber of Deputies. Second, Italy's army far outgunned his Blackshirts. Nonetheless, the following day King Victor Emmanuel III authorized him to form a coalition government. Once installed in power, Mussolini wielded all of the state's patronage, appointment and communication power to swell his movement with millions of new adherents. On 28 November 1923, he got parliament to pass the Acerbo Law which empowered the party that won the largest share of the votes, if it was more than 25 per cent of the total, to receive two-thirds of the seats in the Chamber of Deputies. In the election of 6 April 1924, the Fascist Party and allied parties in a National List won 65 per cent of the vote and received 374 seats. With that power, Mussolini was not only the prime minister but also headed the ministries of foreign affairs, war, navy, aviation, corporations, colonies, interior and public works. With all those titles he preferred simply being called *il Duce* or the leader. Although theoretically Italy remained a multi-party democracy with a constitutional monarch, Mussolini and his Fascist Party amassed and asserted dictatorial powers. He explained this reality on his third anniversary of taking power. Henceforth 'all would be for the state, nothing outside the state and no one against the state'.[71] Parallel assemblies, the state's Chamber of Deputies and the party's Grand Council, rubber-stamped Mussolini's laws and decrees. He established a secret police and tribunals to persecute political opponents. Nonetheless, his dictatorship was not genocidal. Of the 13,547 people who were brought to trial, only 43 were sentenced to death and only 22 actually were executed from 1927 to 1943.[72]

Adolf Hitler idolized Mussolini and used him as a model for his own Nazi version of Fascism and how he took and wielded power, with some wrenching twists.[73] Failure and bitterness filled his early life as he dropped out of high school, got bad reviews as an aspiring painter and lived as a pauper in Vienna. In May 1913, he moved to Munich, Germany where he hoped to find a market for his paintings but only met more rejections. He joined the German army after the First World War erupted. It was through combat that he found meaning for his life; the army rewarded his heroism with the Iron Cross First and Second Class. After the war, he returned to Munich where, on 12 September 1919, he joined the far right German Workers Party, founded by Anton Drexler, which espoused a nationalistic version of socialism. On 24 February 1920, the leaders renamed their party the National Socialist German Worker's Party, better known as the Nazi Party. Hitler's zealous devotion and electrifying demagoguery won him promotions up through the party's ranks until he was elected chairman with absolute powers on 28 July 1921. Hitler formed a paramilitary wing called the *Sturmabteilung* (SA) or Brownshirts for the colour of their uniforms, on 5 October 1921. Four years later he founded the *Schutzstaffel* (SS) or Blackshirts, an elite paramilitary organization within the SA. As the Nazi

Party's symbol, Hitler adopted the swastika, a design found in many ancient cultures around the world, to express how the Nazis embodied the German people's primordial roots and historic glories.

Hitler's first bid to taking over Germany was a quixotic fiasco. On 9 November 1923, he, his coterie and his Brownshirts tried to instigate a rebellion in Munich, the so-called 'Beer Hall Putsch'. The police and army swiftly crushed the revolt and arrested the leaders. Hitler received a five-year prison term but was released after nine months for good behaviour. In prison he wrote his autobiography *Mein Kampf* or 'My Struggle,' in which he revealed his vision for Germany, with a Nazi dictatorship, the nation's territory expanded to include all German speakers, and all Jews and other 'undesirables' eliminated to purify the German race. His book became a best seller and made him increasingly wealthy.

Germany was governed by a republic that had been formed after revolutionaries forced Kaiser Wilhelm II to flee to exile in the Netherlands on 9 November 1918 and the German army to agree to an armistice on 11 November. The provisional government that originated in Weimar moved to Berlin but continued to be called the 'Weimar Republic' until Hitler took power. The new constitution established a bicameral legislature with an upper Bundestag of representatives sent by the state governments and a lower house whose varying numbers of seats were elected by proportional representation that encouraged a score or more parties to participate. The result was that in each of the seven elections held from February 1919 to March 1933 no party ever won a majority of seats and so had to form a coalition government. Executive powers were split. Every seven years starting in 1919 the people elected a president who served as the head of state and appointed the chancellor who headed the coalition government.

Hitler took power legally under this system.[74] His Nazi Party did poorly during the three elections of the mid-1920s, with the best showing in May 1924 with 6 per cent of the vote and thirty-two seats. But voters increasingly embraced extremist parties with the Nazis on the right and the Democratic Socialists and Communists on the left as centrist-liberal and conservative parties failed to prevent Germany from falling into the abyss of the Great Depression. The Nazi Party's portion of votes and number of seats rose to 18 per cent and 107 seats in September 1930, 37 per cent and 230 seats in July 1932 and 33 per cent and 198 seats in November 1932. Although the Nazis had the most seats following the 1932 elections, other party leaders managed to form rickety governing coalitions that excluded them. When the latest coalition collapsed on 30 January 1933, President Paul von Hindenburg felt compelled to appoint Hitler the chancellor.

Hitler accepted the Nationalist Party as his Nazi Party's junior partner. After a communist set fire to the Reichstag on 27 February, he got Hindenburg to grant him emergency powers. In an election on 5 March, the Nazis won 43 per cent of the vote and 288 seats. He bolstered his coalition with more parties, then, on 23 March, won a Reichstag vote of 444 to 84 for the Enabling Act that granted him dictatorial powers. He ordered the first of what would be millions of arrests of his real or imagined political opponents. He set up the first concentration camp for political prisoners at Dachau outside Munich, with a network of fifty more erected by the end of the year. On 1 April, he decreed a boycott of Jewish businesses. On 26 April, he formed the Gestapo or secret police to work with the Security Service (*Sicherheitsdienst*, SD) founded the previous year. On 10 May, the Nazis expressed their hatred of any views contrary to their own by igniting piles of books by forbidden authors. During the election on 12 November 1933, the Nazis won 92 per cent of the vote and all 661 seats. Hitler had achieved his dream of becoming Germany's dictator and had only begun to reveal what he intended to do with it.

Japan developed its own version of fascism.[75] By the 1920s, Japan, like Italy and Germany, had a working democracy with universal male suffrage and a multiparty electoral system and parliament. Unfortunately, as in Italy and Germany, Japanese democracy was illiberal rather than liberal since its democratic institutions were embedded in a thoroughly authoritarian culture. Unlike Italy and Germany, Japan's transition from democracy to fascism was prolonged rather than abrupt, led by a coterie rather than one charismatic leader and committed aggression before authoritarianism extinguished liberalism. Japan's Emperor Hirohito was a figurehead manipulated by an association of fascist military and civilian leaders. Like Germany and unlike Italy, Japan committed horrific atrocities that murdered tens of millions of people.

The first major act of fascist aggression that led to the Second World War occurred on 18 September 1931, when Japanese troops began taking over China's north-east region known as Manchuria.[76] The excuse for doing so was that Chinese rebels threatened Japan's economic interests there. Actually anarchy and civil war had engulfed most of China. The two largest contenders for power were the Nationalist Party led by General Chiang Kai-shek and the Communist Party led by Mao Zedong; consumed in a life and death struggle against each other, neither could spare forces to fight the Japanese in Manchuria. All that Chiang's rump government could do was issue a protest at the League of Nations on 19 September. The League of Nations condemned Japan's aggression on 24 October and called on all Japanese troops to leave Manchuria by 16 November. Secretary of State Henry Stimson declared on 7 January 1932 that the United States would not recognize Japan's takeover of Manchuria. On 14 January, a League of Nations delegation led by Victor Bulwer-Lytton disembarked at Shanghai to investigate Japan's imperialism. On 18 February, the Japanese completed their conquest of Manchuria and announced that the region was now an independent country called Manchukuo under Japan's protection. On 2 October, the Lytton commission issued its report that detailed and condemned Japan's brutal conquest of Manchuria. And that ended the League of Nations response. There was no follow up with diplomatic, economic or military sanctions against Japan. Mussolini and Hitler carefully watched the Japanese get away with blatant aggression and they began planning to do the same.

*   *   *

During the 1920s and 1930s, most Britons were as indifferent or fatalistic about the rising Fascist threat as they were to the horrors of Communism. The British government's policy of appeasement bridged the opposing sides of the House of Commons and was championed in turn by three prime ministers, Ramsay MacDonald of the Labour Party from 5 June 1929 to 7 June 1935, followed by Conservative Party leaders Stanley Baldwin to 28 May 1937 and Neville Chamberlain to 10 May 1940. That policy at once shaped and reflected public opinion.[77]

Perhaps as many Britons revered their government's appeasement policy then as fervently as most people have reviled it ever since. The sources of that stance are complex but understandable. Most vitally, the First World War ravaged the lives and psyches of millions of Britons and French, the two nations with the greatest power and thus duty for upholding collective security through the League of Nations. Compounding that was the belief common among humanitarians and democrats that everyone is as goodhearted as they are; that any differences can be overcome with reason, kindness and compromise; that aggression is learned not innate; and that wars result from escalating fear and miscalculations, not intent. Communist agents infiltrated Britain's trade unions and universities to promote their central creed and recruit agents. Much of the intelligentsia adopted communism as much out of fashion as conviction. That affiliation led some of them to treason like the notorious 'Cambridge Five,' Harold 'Kim' Philby, Donald Maclean, Guy Burgess, Anthony Blunt and John Cairncross who spied for the Soviet Union.

Pacifism was nowhere more deeply embedded than among the students of Britain's most prestigious universities. In March 1927, Cambridge University's student union resolved that 'lasting peace can only be secured by the people of England adopting an uncompromising attitude of pacifism' by 213 to 138 votes. Not to be outdone, in February 1933, Oxford University's student union debated the resolution 'that this House will in no circumstances fight for its King and Country', then approved it by 275 to 153 votes.[78] Sentiments like that from Britain's future elite appalled Churchill. He contrasted the attitudes of British college students to what he had seen during his post-war trips to Germany: 'I think of Germany with its splendid clear-eyed youth marching forward on all the roads of the Reich singing their ancient songs; demanding to be conscripted into an army, eagerly seeking the most terrible weapons of war; burning to suffer and die for their fatherland.'[79]

Explaining appeasement's catastrophic consequences was the theme of Winston Churchill's Second World War memoirs: '

It is my purpose, as one who lived and acted in these days, to show how easily the tragedy ... could have been prevented; how the malice of the wicked was reinforced by the weakness of the virtuous; how the structure and habits of democratic states, unless they are welded into larger organisms, lack those elements of persistence and conviction which can alone give security to humble masses; and how, even in matters of self-preservation, no policy is pursued for even ten or fifteen years at a time.[80]

Pacifism was hardly confined to Britain. Most people in every country that had experienced the horrors of the First World War sought to avoid future conflagrations. At its Geneva headquarters, the League of Nations convened a World Disarmament Conference on 1 February 1932.[81] For more than two and a half years, the delegates discussed such possibilities as imposing 200,000-man ceilings for the armies of France, Italy, Germany and Poland, eight-month stints for conscripts, 500-plane ceilings for each air force with the reductions completed by 1939; and banning of air bombardments, submarines, aircraft carriers and chemical and biological weapons.

Verification was a sticky issue. Britain's envoy actually joined with Germany's to reject a French plea for mandatory inspections to ensure that each signatory lived up to their obligations. This was despite the fact that spies at Britain's embassy in Berlin had determined that Germany was violating the Treaty of Versailles by building a secret air force. Britain's ambassadors to Germany from 1928 to 1940, Horace Rumbold, Eric Phipps and Neville Henderson, sent a stream of reports to Whitehall detailing German rearmament and Hitler's ambitions, but MacDonald, Baldwin and Chamberlain ignored those warnings.

A major obstacle to progress appeared on 30 January 1933, when Adolf Hitler became Germany's chancellor and insisted that his nation was no longer bound by the Treaty of Versailles' restrictions on its military. The other delegates could only hope that Hitler was simply asserting a hard line before making concessions. A truly serious blow followed on 27 March, when Japan's delegation announced their withdrawal from both the League of Nations and the World Disarmament Conference in protest against the Lytton Commission's conclusion that Tokyo committed aggression in Manchuria.

The Conference received a desperately-needed boost on 16 May 1933, when President Franklin Roosevelt sent word to all fifty-four League members that an American delegation would join the talks to promote this goal: 'If all nations will agree wholly to eliminate from possession and use the weapons which make possible a successful attack, defences automatically will become impregnable and the frontiers and independence of every nation will become secure.'[82] But Hitler inflicted the death blow on 14 October 1933, when he withdrew Germany from the League of Nations and the World Disarmament Conference. Although the remaining delegations lingered debating well into 1934, there was no chance of a treaty with the absence of two of the greatest military and economic powers, Japan and Germany.

And for Churchill that was just as well: 'I am very glad that the Disarmament Conference is passing out of life into history … It is the greatest mistake to mix up disarmament with peace. When you have peace you will have disarmament.'[83] The effort was doomed because its premises were convoluted: 'If you wish for disarmament, it will be necessary to go to the political and economic causes which lie behind the maintenance of armies and navies. There are very serious economic and political dangers at the present time and antagonisms which are by no means assuaged.'[84] He explained the prevailing psychology: 'The removal of the just grievances of

Second Lieutenant Winston Churchill in the dress uniform of the 4th Queen's Own Hussars at Aldershot in 1895. (*Library of Congress*)

Churchill, on the right, pictured whilst being held as a prisoner of war in the Second Anglo–Boer War. He was captured whilst working as a war correspondent for the *Morning Post* when the armoured train he was travelling in was shelled and derailed. (*via Historic Military Press*)

Winston Churchill watching German Army exercises near Breslau, Germany in 1906. (*US Library of Congress*)

Winston Churchill (second from left), the then Home Secretary, pictured at the Siege of Sidney Street in London's East End in January 1911. (*via Historic Military Press*)

A portrait of Winston Churchill in the uniform of the First Lord of the Admiralty that is dated 16 September 1914. (*via Historic Military Press*)

Major Winston Churchill, wearing his French helmet, stands with General Émile Fayolle and other officers at the headquarters of XXXIII Corps, French Army, at Camblain L'Abbé in the Pas-de-Calais while visiting the French front line on 15 December 1915. Churchill's visit came during the training he was undertaking with the Grenadier Guards. (*Historic Military Press*)

Lieutenant Colonel Winston Churchill pictured in uniform during the winter of 1915/16. (*Courtesy of Jon Wilkinson*)

A portrait of Prime Minister Winston Churchill at his seat in the Cabinet Room at No.10 Downing Street, London, during the Second World War. (*National Museum of Denmark*)

Prime Minister Winston Churchill tours a section of the South Coast to see anti-invasion defences and preparations in the summer of 1940. It is believed that this image was taken in the Dover area circa 28 August 1940. (*Polish National Archives*)

Inspecting the damage caused by the first day of the Blitz, Winston Churchill is pictured here on the corner of Winchester Street and Factory Road by the smouldering ruins of the Silvertown Rubber Company, on 8 September 1940. (*Historic Military Press*)

Taken using only the light of fires burning as the result of an air raid on London in early 1944 – the original caption is dated 9 March 1944 – this image was captured when Churchill decided to venture out to see the work of the emergency services first-hand. He was accompanied by his daughter, Mary Spencer-Churchill, who can be seen to his right in her ATS uniform. (*Historic Military Press*)

Winston Churchill chats with Field Marshal Sir Alan Brooke, Chief of the Imperial General Staff (to the left of the Prime Minister in this view), on the bridge of the 'K' class destroyer HMS *Kelvin* during his voyage across the English Channel en route to General Bernard Montgomery's headquarters in Normandy on 12 June 1944. (*NARA*)

The 'Big Three', Churchill, Roosevelt and Stalin, pictured in the courtyard of the Livadia Palace during the Yalta Conference in February 1945. (*USNHHC*)

The King and Queen, Princess Elizabeth, Princess Margaret and Winston Churchill waving at the crowds that have gathered in front of Buckingham Palace on 8 May 1945, VE Day. (*Historic Military Press*)

Winston Churchill enjoys a moment away from the military and political world by undertaking some repairs to a wall at his home, Chartwell. (*National Museum of Denmark*)

During a visit to Denmark, Winston Churchill is seen being driven over the Knippelsbro Bridge in Copenhagen, 9 October 1950. (*National Museum of Denmark*)

the vanquished ought to precede the disarmament of the victors ... Nobody keeps armaments going for fun. They keep them going for fear.'[85]

Yet Churchill was deeply disturbed when the withdrawals of Japan and Germany from the League of Nations struck devastating blows to that international organization's legitimacy and power. More than ever he championed the League's collective security principle but worried that Britain and France lacked the political will to rally other members into containing international lawbreakers like Japan. To overcome that he sought this balance: 'Some people say: "Put your trust in the League of Nations." Others say: "Put your trust in British rearmament." I say we want both.'[86] Tragically during the 1930s a succession of prime ministers and most Members of Parliament wanted neither. Looking back from 1943, Churchill concluded:

> It is said that the League of Nations failed. If so, that is largely because it was abandoned and later on betrayed because those who were its best friends were ... infected with a futile pacifism: because the United States, the originating impulse, fell out of the line: because, while France had been bled white and England was supine and bewildered, a monstrous growth of aggression sprang up in Germany, in Italy and Japan.[87]

* * *

Meanwhile Hitler continued to expand his dictatorial powers.[88] On 30 January 1934, a year after he took power, he signed a law that outlawed all political parties except the Nazi Party. On 30 June, he turned against potential enemies within the Nazi ranks by ordering 150 Brownshirt leaders arrested and executed. When Hindenburg died on 2 August, Hitler announced that he had merged the office of president with that of chancellor with himself as Germany's '*Führer*' or Leader. Although in doing so, he violated the constitution, no one dared challenge him. During a plebiscite on 18 August, 38 million of 42 million Germans who voted, or 90 per cent, approved his assumption of dictatorial powers. Hitler subsequently required all military officers to swear an oath of loyalty to him personally, not the nation. A succession of laws steadily Nazified German public affairs, requiring bureaucrats, teachers and business and labour leaders to be party members. Despite these increasingly onerous measures, Hitler remained popular because his economic policies that constructed infrastructure and subsidized industries revived growth and incomes while lowering inflation and unemployment. Nearly all Germans were grateful to Hitler for materially and emotionally bettering their lives.

Hitler sent agents to form Nazi parties among other German-speaking peoples who then agitated for their incorporation into the Third Reich. In the spring of 1934, he sought to bully Austria into joining Germany with a terrorist campaign of bombings and murders that peaked when a Nazi hit squad murdered Austrian Chancellor Engelbert Dollfuss at the chancellery building in Vienna on 25 July. His successor, Kurt von Schuschnigg, ordered a crackdown that captured thirteen terrorists who were tried and executed. Hitler then suspended his terrorist campaign and concentrated on expanding Austria's Nazi Party to take power through elections as he had in Germany.

In 1934 Churchill rose repeatedly in the House of Commons to warn that Germany was violating the Versailles restrictions on its military and to call for greater British military spending, especially for the air force. And he was just as repeatedly ignored by virtually all his colleagues. In a speech before Parliament on 28 November 1934, Prime Minister Baldwin pledged that: 'His Majesty's Government is determined in no condition to accept any position of inferiority with regards to what air force may be raised in Germany in the future.'[89] But that is exactly what happened in both Britain and France as economic austerity trumped the worsening security threat. Looking back, Churchill wrote: 'If Great Britain and France had each maintained quantitative parity with Germany they would together have been double as strong and Hitler's career of violence might have been nipped in the bud.'[90]

Hitler's first blatant violation of the Treaty of Versailles and test of the League's resolve came on 16 March 1935, when he decreed the army's expansion from 100,000 to 300,000 soldiers and the navy's from 15,000 to 45,000 sailors; he had already secretly ordered the construction of battleships, cruisers, submarines and military aircraft. On 11 April, the foreign ministers of Britain, France and Italy met at Stresa in Italy to condemn the violations and pledge to uphold Austrian independence. The League of Nations echoed those protests and formed a committee to investigate Germany's treaty violations. Those concerns soared on 25 April, after Hitler revealed his naval build-up. Hitler then finessed the swelling international opposition on 21 May with a Reichstag speech in which he promised to keep Germany's navy only 35 per cent and 15 per cent the size of the respective British and French navies and declared that 'Germany neither intends nor wishes to interfere in the internal affairs of Austria, to annex Austria or to conclude an Anschluss'.[91] For clarity, he might have added 'at that moment', but of course his intent was to bamboozle the appeasers as much as possible. He warned that Germany would rejoin the League of Nations only if it repudiated the Versailles treaty. The international community took him at his word. Indeed, Whitehall committed its first act of appeasement when Foreign Secretary John Simon called for codifying Hitler's fleet proposals in a treaty. Hitler dispatched Joachim von Ribbentrop to London. Under the treaty signed by British and German diplomats on 18 June, Germany's navy would be 35 per cent of Britain's in all categories of warships including submarines.

*   *   *

For now, British politicians, including Churchill, were distracted by the jockeying for power at home and the worsening agitation in parts of the empire, especially India. Baldwin and MacDonald traded places on 7 June 1935. Baldwin now was prime minister and MacDonald, whose declining health prompted his resignation, became Lord President of the Council. Baldwin despised Churchill and rejected any suggestion to invite him into his Cabinet. Churchill was philosophical, at least many years later, at all the machinations the prime minister wielded to keep him out of the government: 'Mr. Baldwin certainly had good reason to use the last flickers of his power against one who had exposed his mistakes so severely and so often. Moreover, as a profoundly astute party manager, thinking in majorities and aiming at a quiet life between elections, he did not wish to have my disturbing aid.'[92] Indeed, looking back, Churchill reflected that 'Baldwin knew no more than I how great was the service he was doing me in preventing me from becoming involved in all the Cabinet compromises and shortcomings of the next three years'.[93]

The fate of India rather than the swelling threat from Hitler's Germany consumed increasing time in the Cabinet and Parliament. That pressure had been building for a generation. Britain had granted dominion status to Canada in 1867, Australia in 1901, New Zealand in 1907 and South Africa in 1910. After the First World War India's Congress Party led by Jawaharlal Nehru and a mass movement led by Mahatma Gandhi demanded the same for the subcontinent. That was only fair, they argued, given India's contribution of a million men and £500 million to the war effort.

A horrific massacre in the Punjab city of Amritsar boosted the independence movement's numbers. After learning that a British woman had been sexually molested, General Reginald Dyer forced all Indians living or working on the street where she was assaulted to crawl its length on their hands and knees. He also authorized policemen to whip anyone who approached them. Several thousand Punjabis gathered to protest in a square near the Sikh Golden Temple on 13 April 1919. Dyer ordered his troops to surround the square and open fire on the crowd. The fusillade killed 379 people and wounded 1,500 more. Whitehall actually rewarded Dyer for his massacre by promoting him to major general.[94]

Parliament, however, responded with the Government of India Act that became law on 23 December 1919. The act transformed the Legislative Council into a bicameral parliament. The Legislative Assembly had 144 members with 104 elected and 40 nominated by the princely states for three year terms. The Council of States had sixty members with thirty-four elected and twenty-six nominated by the princely states for five-year terms. Each state had autonomy over education, agriculture and health. The British government retained sovereignty and India remained a crown colony. The king continued to appoint a viceroy or governor general with powers over finance, defence, foreign affairs and international trade. The system was called a dyarchy. Nehru, Gandhi and their followers protested the act and vowed to continue resisting until they achieved independence.

Churchill adamantly opposed dominion status let alone independence for India. For him, 'India is an abstraction ... India is no more a political personality than Europe. India is a geographic term. It is no more a united nation than the Equator.'[95] In numerous speeches he reiterated the same arguments, that India was a cultural and religious mosaic; that Britain brought peace, unity, efficiency and modernity to the subcontinent; and that if Britain abandoned its burden the result would mire 400 million people in a vicious cycle of anarchy, poverty, corruption, incompetence, exploitation and violence. He scorned the Indian independence movement, especially its charismatic leader, who he skewered in a 1931 speech:

> It is alarming and nauseating to see Mr. Gandhi, a seditious Middle Temple lawyer, now posing as a fakir ... striding half-naked up the steps of the Viceregal palace while he is still organizing and conducting a defiant campaign of civil disobedience, to parley on equal terms with the representative of the King Emperor. Such a spectacle can only increase the unrest in India and the danger to which white people there are exposed. It can only encourage all the forces which are hostile to British authority.[96]

A new Government of India Act was proposed in 1935. This version would transform the diarchy into a Federation of India. Parliament would consist of an upper Council of State with 260 members, 156 elected and 104 appointed and a lower Assembly with 375 members, 250 elected and 125 appointed. Yet the British government continued to deny India dominion status by retaining emergency powers, appointing provincial governors, refusing to include a bill of rights and giving the princes considerable political clout. Churchill opposed even these limited concessions and motioned to halt any further consideration of the India Act. He and his supporters lost by 283 votes to 89 on 26 February. Parliament passed the India Act by 382 votes to 122 on 2 August 1935. That ended Churchill's somewhat quixotic crusade to prevent Indians from having any significant rights and powers. He had dropped out of the government in protest against its embrace of reforms. Now he felt free to re-enter the government. The trouble was that Baldwin and virtually all other prominent leaders had no desire to invite him back.

In the election held on 14 November 1935, the Tories retained their majority with 386 seats, although they lost 83 seats. The Labour Party vote split among three factions, with Clement Atlee's 154 Labour seats, Ramsay MacDonald's eight National Labour seats and James Maxton's four Independent Labour seats. The Liberal Party vote divided between John Simon's thirty-three National Liberal seats and Herbert Samuel's twenty-one Liberal seats.

* * *

Meanwhile, Mussolini increasingly worried Churchill. Having observed the League of Nations appease Japan's takeover of Manchuria and Hitler's repudiation of the Treaty of Versailles, Mussolini reasoned that it would be just as impotent as he asserted his own imperial ambitions. Abyssinia (Ethiopia) was one of two countries on the African continent that had escaped European imperialism, the other being Liberia. Mussolini was determined to change that. On 3 October 1935, he ordered his army in Italy's neighbouring colony of Somalia to invade Abyssinia. Although inferior in numbers, manpower and training, Abyssinia's army valiantly resisted. The Italian army battled its way upward into Abyssinia's highlands.

Churchill favoured standing firm against Italian aggression. With somewhat of an unintended mix of irony and hypocrisy that tireless champion of the British Empire condemned 'Mussolini's designs upon Abyssinia' as 'unsuited to the ethics of the twentieth century. They belonged to those dark ages when white men felt themselves entitled to conquer yellow, brown, black or red men and subjugate them by their superior strength and weapons.'[97] He called for League sanctions backed by increased defence spending. The Labour leader Clement Atlee half agreed with him: 'We want effective sanctions, effectively applied. We support economic sanctions. We support the League system.' So far so good, Churchill reasoned until he heard Atlee utter this zinger: 'We are not persuaded that the way to safety is by piling up armaments. We do not believe that in this time there is such a thing as national defence.'[98]

The League of Nations did indeed condemn Italy's aggression and impose economic sanctions. But both those acts were symbolic rather than substantive. The British, French and other governments did not want to assert measures too harsh against Italy that might prompt an alliance between Mussolini and Hitler. So oil was not included in the sanctions. Actually, Whitehall could have stopped Italy's invasion in its tracks simply by forbidding Italian vessels packed with supplies and troops from sailing through the Suez Canal, which Britain controlled.[99]

Hitler welcomed Mussolini's Abyssinia adventure to distract the world from the Third Reich's next aggrandizement. At dawn on 7 March 1936, he ordered 20,000 troops to enter the Rhineland and occupy the major cities in direct violation of the Versailles and Locarno treaties. The British government responded with its latest act of appeasement. Baldwin and most of the Cabinet rejected the idea of condemning the Rhineland invasion and calling for League of Nations sanctions. Baldwin dispatched Foreign Secretary Anthony Eden to Paris to inform Prime Minister Albert Sarraut and Foreign Minister Pierre Flandin that Britain would ignore the transgression. That deflated the French leaders who hoped for a united stand against the aggression. Sarraut authorized Flandin to outflank the appeasers by issuing before a press conference this appeal: 'Today the whole world and especially the small nations, turn their eyes toward England. If England will act now, she can lead Europe ... all the world will follow you and you will prevent war. It is your last chance. If you do not stop Germany now, all is over.'[100] But Baldwin and his ministers clung to their appeasement policy. That in turn frightened Belgium's King Leopold III into withdrawing his country from its alliance with Britain and France into neutrality, thus ignoring his realm's experience just a generation earlier. Neutrality then had not deterred Germany's opening offensive of the First World War directly through Belgium.

Churchill would look back on Hitler's military occupation of the Rhineland as a turning point:

> Up till the middle of 1936, Hitler's aggressive policy and treaty breaking had rested, not upon Germany's strength, but upon the disunion and timidity of France and Britain and the isolation of the United States. Each of his preliminary steps had been gambles in which he knew he could not afford to be seriously challenged. The seizure of the Rhineland and its subsequent fortification was the greatest gamble of all. It had succeeded brilliantly. His opponents were too irresolute to call his bluff.[101]

Hitler had indeed launched his most reckless pre-war gamble. He later admitted that: 'The forty-eight hours after the march into the Rhineland were the most nerve-racking in my life. If the French had then marched into the Rhineland, we would have had to withdraw with shame and disgrace for the military resources at our disposal would have been wholly inadequate for even a moderate resistance.'[102]

The Rhineland invasion was also Churchill's turning point. He reprised his Cassandra role, this time issuing repeated warnings that Britain must rally the world against the Nazi menace. He painted the threat in apocalyptic Manichean terms: 'We are in the midst of dangers so great and increasing, we are the guardians of causes so precious to the world, that we must, as the Bible says, "Lay aside every impediment" and prepare ourselves night and day to be worthy of the Faith that is in us.'[103] He urged the Cabinet to establish a Munitions or Supply Ministry to coordinate the development and production of weapons and military equipment with army, navy and air force needs. On 28 July, he made this plea behind closed doors to Baldwin and the Committee of Imperial Defence:

> First, we are facing the greatest danger and emergency of our history. Second, we have no hope of solving our problem except in conjunction with the French Republic. The union of the British Fleet and the French Army, together with their combined Air Forces operating from close behind the French and Belgian frontiers, together with all that Britain and France stand for, constitutes a deterrent in which salvation may reside.[104]

After Hitler's takeover of the Rhineland, Churchill rethought his views on Italy's war against Abyssinia. He now warned that Hitler's looming threat in Europe far surpassed in importance any possible results of Mussolini's faraway ambitions in East Africa. On 6 April, during a House of Commons debate on whether to retain the economic sanctions against Italy, he denounced them, arguing that they had failed to deter Mussolini's aggression while pushing him into Hitler's arms. On 5 May, the Italians captured Addis Ababa, the capital. On 12 May, Abyssinian Emperor Haile Selassie appeared before the League of Nations Assembly and pleaded for the members to uphold the Covenant's duty for all members to join against any aggressor. On 2 July, the League of Nations rewarded Mussolini for his conquest by lifting the sanctions. On 21 October, Germany and Italy signed a secret alliance which Mussolini publicly described as an Axis ten days later. On 25 November, diplomats from Germany, Italy and Japan signed the Anti-Comintern Pact, ostensibly directed against the Soviet Union and communist movements around the world. The three Fascist powers were now formally allied.

These latest disturbing developments prompted a debate in the House of Commons during which Churchill declared:

> Two things I confess have staggered me after a long parliamentary experience ... The first has been the dangers that have so swiftly come upon us in a few years and have been transforming our position and the whole outlook of the world. Secondly, I have been staggered by the failure of the House of Commons to react effectively against those dangers ... I say that unless the House resolves to find out the truth for itself it will have committed an act of abdication of duty without parallel in its long history.[105]

* * *

Amidst the worsening threat of Japanese, Italian and German aggression, a political distraction arose that at the time appeared to be a full-fledged constitutional crisis. On 20 January 1936, King George V died and his son took the throne as Edward VIII. On 10 November 1936, the king informed Prime Minister Baldwin that he intended to marry Wallis Simpson, a twice-divorced Baltimore femme fatale. Wallis was that rare kind of woman who compensated for a lack of natural beauty with charms in and out of bed that drove many men crazy with desire. Baldwin, backed by the Cabinet, warned Edward that he could either keep the throne or marry the divorcee, but he could not have both. As king, Edward was head of the Church of England which did not then permit remarriage after divorce. Atop that most Britons would not want a divorced American woman as their queen. Edward proposed a morganatic marriage whereby he remained king but Simpson would not be the queen. Baldwin rejected that notion. Churchill was virtually alone in backing Edward. Edward finally buckled under the pressure and abdicated on 16 December 1936. The coronation of his brother the Duke of York as George VI took place on 20 May 1937.

Eight days later, Stanley Baldwin asked the new monarch to allow him to resign. George VI accepted and asked Neville Chamberlain to form a government. Churchill later compared these two prime ministers:

> Stanley Baldwin was a wiser, more comprehending personality, but without detailed executive capacity. He was largely detached from foreign and military affairs. He knew little of Europe and disliked what he knew. He had a deep knowledge of British party politics ... Neville Chamberlain ... was alert, businesslike, opinionated and self-confident ... Unlike Baldwin, he conceived himself able to comprehend the whole of Europe and indeed the world ... He kept the tightest and most rigid control over military expenditures ... He had formed decided judgments about all the political figures of his day, both at home and abroad and felt himself capable of dealing with them. His all-pervading hope was to go down to history as the great peacemaker and for this he was prepared to strive continually in the face of facts and face great risks ... I should have found it easier to work with Baldwin ... than with Chamberlain, but neither of them had any wish to work with me except in the last resort.[106]

Of course, Chamberlain is notorious for being the great appeaser who unwittingly led Europe to war rather than peace. Although Baldwin is little known today, his policies also empowered rather than throttled Hitler.[107] Churchill did not hesitate to expose Baldwin's dark side: 'Occasionally he stumbled over the truth, but hastily picked himself up and hurried on as if nothing had happened.' Churchill could not avoid this indictment: 'I wish Stanley Baldwin no ill, but it would have been much better if he had never lived.'[108] The same might be said for Chamberlain.

Although Churchill remained in the political wilderness, Hitler and his henchmen targeted him as their most dangerous British critic. Joachim von Ribbentrop, Germany's ambassador to Britain, buttonholed Churchill to determine whether an understanding could be reached. What Germany required was a free hand in Eastern Europe to obtain 'living space' for the German people. Would Whitehall go along? After asserting that no British government would accept that, Churchill vividly recalled Ribbentrop's chilling retort: 'In that case, war is inevitable ... The Führer is resolved. Nothing will stop him and nothing will stop us.' Churchill then issued this warning: 'When you talk of war, which no doubt will be a general war, you must not underrate England ... Do not judge by the attitude of the present government ... If you plunge us into another Great War she will bring the whole world against you, like last time.'[109]

In a speech before Parliament on 14 April 1937, Churchill explained the horrible dilemma that the civilized world might soon face, standing with either Nazism or Communism against the other:

I will not pretend that, if I had to choose between Communism and Nazism, I would choose Communism. I hope not to be called upon to survive in the world under a Government of either ... I feel unbounded sorrow and sympathy for the victims. We seem to be moving, drifting, steadily, against our will, against the will of every race and every people and every class, towards some hideous catastrophe. Everyone wishes to stop it, but they do not know how. We have talks of Eastern and Western Pacts, but they make no greater security. Armaments and counter-armaments proceed apace and we must find something new.[110]

* * *

The relentless succession of crises in Europe from 1935 to 1939 obscured tragic news from the Far East. The worst event was the outbreak of war between Japan and China in July 1937. After conquering China's north-eastern region of Manchuria in September 1931, Tokyo spent the next six years consolidating and exploiting its control. Meanwhile, Japanese agents infiltrated neighbouring regions to play off rival warlords against each other and make them dependent on Tokyo for money and guns. Although Tokyo did not plan the eruption of fighting between Japanese and Chinese troops at the Marco Polo Bridge near Beijing on 7 July, it used it as an excuse to declare war against China. Three massive armies overran different regions of China and eventually converged, one from Manchuria that captured Beijing and drove south, another that captured Shanghai and drove west up the Yangtze River valley and a third that captured Canton and drove north. On 13 December 1937, Japanese troops overran Nanjing and for the next month committed robbery, rape and mass murder that slaughtered as many as 200,000 people. That was just the beginning of Japan's genocidal policy against 'inferior Asians' that resulted in the massacres of at least 10 million Chinese and millions more people from other Asian countries. In that the Japanese were just as murderous as the Nazis. But no matter how many people the Japanese murdered and how deep into China they penetrated, they could not conquer China. The result was that China was to Japan's imperial ambitions what Russia was for Germany's, a quagmire that devoured rather than enhanced its power.[111]

Japan's war against China from 1937 to 1945 complicated an ongoing civil war in China between Chiang Kai-shek's Nationalist Party and Mao Zedong's Communist Party that lasted from 1927 until the communist victory in October 1949. After the Japanese invasion, Chiang transferred his capital to Chungking far west up the Yangtze valley. Mao's capital was at Yenan near Mongolia. Although Nationalist and Communist troops continued to clash on the frontier between their respective realms, they turned most of their guns against the Japanese.[112]

* * *

Hitler summoned Austrian Chancellor Kurt von Schuschnigg to meet him at his Alpine home at Berchtesgaden on 11 February 1938. After the Austria leader arrived, Hitler subjected him to eleven hours of threats and demands. At one point Hitler declared that 'I have a historic mission and this mission I will fulfil because Providence has destined me to do so'.[113] Finally, Schuschnigg broke and signed a promise to legalize the Nazi Party, free all Nazi prisoners and accept three Nazis in his Cabinet, most notoriously Arthur Seyss-Inquart as his interior minister and Edmund von Glaise-Horstenau as his war minister.

This set off alarm bells at the White House if not at 10 Downing Street.[114] President Roosevelt sent Prime Minister Chamberlain a proposal to convene a summit between the German, Austrian, British, French and Italian leaders in Washington where he would try to help them resolve their differences. Chamberlain may have grovelled before Hitler and Germany but he despised Roosevelt and America. This would-be 'great peacemaker' abhorred sharing a stage with anyone, especially some upstart from a former colony. The very notion offended his overweening faith in his own superior knowledge, intellect and pedigree. Churchill explained: 'Thus it was that President Roosevelt's proposal to use American influence for the purpose of bringing together the leading European Powers to discuss the chances of a general settlement, this of course involving, however tentatively the mighty power of the United States was repulsed by Mr. Chamberlain.' Churchill blistered Chamberlain's rejection of 'the proffered hand stretched out across the Atlantic' for the 'lack of all sense of proportion, even of self-preservation'.[115]

Schuschnigg announced on 9 March that a national referendum would be held on 13 March over whether Germany should annex Austria. Hitler demanded that Schuschnigg cancel the vote and instructed Austria's Nazi Party to protest violently in the streets. When Schuschnigg refused to back down, Hitler ordered his army to invade Austria the day the referendum was scheduled. The 38,000-man Austrian army did not resist. After the Germans arrested Schuschnigg, Arthur Seyss-Inquart took his place as chancellor and also assumed the power of president. Hitler triumphantly entered Vienna on 14 March. A rigged plebiscite on 10 April resulted in 99.9 per cent of Austrians voting to join their nation to Germany. Concentration camps were established to imprison thousands of political opponents and other undesirables.

Chamberlain and his ministers discussed what to do and decided to do nothing. In Parliament, Churchill called for a military alliance between Britain and France that would defend all countries threatened by Nazi Germany. He then flew to Paris to lobby members of France's government and national assembly. On 14 March, Chamberlain tried to justify his appeasement policy and undercut Churchill's unauthorized diplomacy with this assertion in the House of Commons: 'The hard fact is that nothing could have arrested what actually have happened unless this country and other countries had been prepared to use force first.'[116] And that was exactly what should have happened, Churchill insisted. But in a speech on 24 March, Chamberlain rejected that idea because he feared that it would 'aggravate the establishment of exclusive groups of nations which must ... be inimical to the prospects of European peace'.[117]

*   *   *

After Germany digested Austria, Hitler turned toward Czechoslovakia in September 1938 and demanded that Prague cede the western, mostly

German-speaking Sudetenland region.[118] President Edvard Beneš rejected that demand. Hitler warned Beneš to cede the Sudetenland before 1 October or else the German army would invade Czechoslovakia. Determined to be renowned in history as a great peacemaker, Chamberlain journeyed to Berchtesgaden and met with Hitler on 15 September. Hitler harangued Chamberlain for hours, trying to bully him into acquiescing in the takeover. An exhausted Chamberlain finally agreed to the 'self-determination' of the Sudetenland Germans if it kept the peace. He then invited French Prime Minister Edouard Daladier and Foreign Minister Georges Bonnet for talks in London on 18 September, when he talked them into accepting what they were not willing militarily to prevent. The following day Chamberlain and Daladier had their ambassadors in Prague meet Beneš and warn him that if he did not surrender the Sudetenland, his country would face the German army alone. Beneš stood firm.

Once again Churchill tried to reverse the appeasement tide through public warnings and private diplomacy. He issued the press this statement:

> The mere neutralization of Czechoslovakia means the liberation of twenty-five German divisions which will threaten the West front; in addition to which it will open up for the triumphant Nazis the road to the Black Sea. It is not Czechoslovakia alone which is menaced, but also the freedom and the democracy of all nations. The belief that security can be obtained by throwing a small State to the wolves is a fatal delusion. The war potential of Germany will increase in a short time more rapidly than it will be possible for France and Great Britain to complete the measures necessary for their defence.[119]

He met Colonel Ewald von Kleist, from German's *Abwehr* (military intelligence) and handed him this written statement: 'I am sure that the crossing of the frontier of Czechoslovakia by German armies ... will bring about renewal of renewal of the World War. I am as certain as I was at the end of July 1914, that England will march with France ... Do not, I pray you, be misled upon this point.'[120] Of course, that was a completely unauthorized, desperate attempt to undercut Chamberlain's appeasement policy.

Chamberlain flew to Bad Godesburg for his latest meeting with Hitler on 22 September. Hitler angrily rejected Chamberlain's suggestion of a plebiscite for Sudetenland and demanded its cession to Germany along with all its fortifications, weapons, munitions, other military equipment and factories no later than 26 September. Beneš reacted to that ultimatum by ordering the Czech army to mobilize.

Churchill managed to wangle a meeting with Chamberlain and Halifax on 26 September, during which he urged them to get Britain, France and the Soviet Union to issue a statement declaring that they would not tolerate Germany's invasion of Czechoslovakia. The prime minister and foreign secretary rejected his plea. Instead, Chamberlain redoubled his efforts to bully Beneš into yielding to Hitler's demands. Chamberlain explained the rationale for his appeasement policy to the British people in a radio broadcast on 27 September . He unwittingly admitted his utter ignorance and naivety over the crisis with this line:

> How horrible, fantastic, incredible it is that we should be digging trenches and trying on gas masks here because of a quarrel in a faraway country between people of whom we known nothing … However much we may sympathize with a small nation confronted by a big and powerful neighbour, we cannot … undertake to involve the whole British Empire in a war simply on her account. If we have to fight, it must be on larger issues than that. I am a man of peace to the depths of my soul.[121]

In desperation Chamberlain got Hitler to agree to a summit in Munich which would also include Daladier and Mussolini on 29–30 September. The four leaders agreed to sign a document that transferred the Sudetenland to Germany in return for Germany's guarantee to respect Czechoslovakia's remaining territorial integrity and sovereignty; the German army would occupy the Sudetenland on 1 October. They then had a courier convey that document to Beneš in Prague. Beneš had no choice but to submit.

With enormous relief, Chamberlain flew back to London. When he stepped from his chauffeured car before 10 Downing Street, he turned toward a small expectant crowd that had gathered, smiled triumphantly, raised his copy of the agreement and proclaimed: 'My good friends this is the second time in our history that there has come back from Germany to Downing Street peace with honour. I believe it is peace for our time.'[122]

Churchill was with Violet Bonham Carter when he learned of the Munich deal. She recalled that 'I saw the tears in his eyes … His last attempt to salvage what was left of honour and good faith had failed … Then Churchill spoke: "What are they made of? The day is not far off when it won't be signatures we'll have to give but lives – the lives of millions".'[123] Yet he was still literally crying in the political wilderness. On 4 October, during the Parliamentary debate over Munich, a deafening chorus of jeers erupted when he asserted:

> We have sustained a total and unmitigated defeat and France has suffered even more than we have ... All is over. Silent, mournful, abandoned, broken, Czechoslovakia recedes into the darkness ... It must now be accepted that all the countries of central and eastern Europe will make the best terms they can with the triumphant Nazi Power.

He went on to argue that

> there can never be friendship between the British democracy and the Nazi power ... which vaunts the spirit of aggression and conquest, which derives strength and perverted pleasure from persecution ... What I find unendurable is the sense of our country falling into the power, into the orbit ... of Nazi Germany ... I have tried my best to urge the maintenance of every bulwark of defence – first the timely creation of an Air Force superior to anything within striking distance of our shores; secondly the gathering together of the collective strength of many nations; and thirdly, the making of alliances and military conventions, all within the [League of Nations] Covenant, in order to gather together forces at any rate to restrain the onward movement of this Power. It has all been in vain.[124]

Hitler recognized Churchill as his British nemesis but dismissed his influence: 'After all, Churchill may have ... 30,000 votes behind him ... but I have 40 million behind me.'[125] So did lawmakers in both Britain and France, who overwhelmingly backed the Sudetenland deal, the House of Commons by 369 to 150 and the Chamber of Deputies by 535 to 75. Only one man in Chamberlain's Cabinet resigned in protest at the sell-out, Duff Cooper, the First Lord of the Admiralty. Everyone else sat tight. Galeazzo Ciano, Italy's foreign minister and Mussolini's son-in-law, offered this insight into the appeasement mentality that afflicted most of Briton's ruling elite: 'These men are not made of the same stuff as the Francis Drakes and the other magnificent adventurers who created the empire. These, after all are the tired sons of a long line of rich men and they will lose their Empire.'[126]

The latest phase of Hitler's terrorism against the Jews took place two days after a Jewish teenager, whose father had been arrested by the Nazis, murdered an official at Germany's embassy in Paris. On 9 November 1938,

Propaganda Minister Joseph Goebbels broadcasted a call on Germans to punish Jews by whatever means they thought appropriate. The result was 'Crystal Night' or a twenty-hour attack of vandalism, robbery, rape and murder of Jews by German thugs; over 7,500 businesses were pillaged. To prevent insurance companies from going bankrupt, Berlin then imposed a billion-mark fine on the Jews to pay for the damage to their own property.

Hitler's latest vicious anti-Jewish pogrom prompted Churchill to compare the two totalitarianisms that threatened humanity: 'Like the Communists, the Nazis tolerate no opinion but their own. Like the Communists, they feed on hatred. Like the Communists, they must seek, from time to time and always at shorter intervals, a new target, a new prize, a new victim.'[127] Stalin was indeed as tyrannical and genocidal as Hitler, but subtle rather than flamboyant.[128]

*   *   *

Once again, Hitler asserted his latest stage of imperialism after half a year of consolidating his previous gain. During that time he had asserted pressure on Czechoslovakia's national and regional leaders to acquiesce in Germany's takeover of the rest of the country. In the face of overwhelming military force, the Czech government finally surrendered. In an open car, Hitler led a military parade through Prague on 15 March 1939. He demanded £6 million worth of gold that the Czech government had transferred to the Bank of England for safe-keeping. Chamberlain rejected Churchill's plea that Britain retain that gold. The prime minister insisted that the Czechs had legally liquidated their country and all its assets to Germany, including the gold entrusted to Britain. To consolidate their power, the Nazis broke up the country into regions and eventually murdered over 250,000 people, acts ideologically justified because as Slavs, the Czechs, Slovaks and Ruthenians were members of 'a degenerate race'.

Germany's conquest and breakup of the rest of Czechoslovakia prompted Churchill, Cooper and around thirty other Tories to call on 28 March for a 'national government' with members from all the parties. Chamberlain rejected that appeal but did issue an astonishing declaration on 31 March:

I now have to inform the House that ... in the event of any action which clearly threatens Polish independence and in which the Polish Government accordingly considers it vital to resist with their national forces, His Majesty's Government will feel themselves bound at once to lend the Polish Government all support in their power. They have given the Polish Government an assurance to this effect. I may say that the French Government have authorized me to make it plain that they stand on the same ground as do His Majesty's Government.[129]

Of Chamberlain's abrupt discovery of his backbone, Churchill noted the irony:

History, which, we are told, is mainly the record of the crimes, follies and miseries of mankind, may be scoured and ransacked to find a parallel to this sudden and complete reversal of five or six years' policy of easygoing placatory appeasement and its transformation almost overnight into a readiness to accept an obviously imminent war on far worse conditions and on the greatest scale.[130]

That extraordinary step demanded another.

During a speech in June 1939, Churchill reminded Chamberlain and his fellow ministers of their ultimate duty: 'There are two supreme obligations which rest upon a British government. They are of equal importance. One is to strive to prevent a war and the other is to be ready if war should come.'[131] He feared that war was not just imminent but that the Nazi war machine might well triumph if it combined with Italy against Britain and France while the United States remained mired in isolationism. He told the American journalist Walter Lippmann: 'I for one would willingly lay down my life in combat rather than, in fear of defeat, surrender to the menaces of these most sinister men. It will then be for you, for the Americans, to preserve and to maintain the great heritage of the English-speaking peoples.'[132]

Churchill's gift of prophecy extended to the hazy far side of the world. Pondering East Asia, he concluded: 'I do not believe that Japan, deeply entangled in China ... her strength ebbing away in a wrongful and impossible task and with the whole weight of Russia upon her in the north of China, will wish to make war upon the British Empire until she sees how matters go in Europe.'[133] Once again he was prescient. Just as they had done during the First World War, vulture-like, the Japanese watched carefully and waited patiently to seize any weakly defended opportunities in the Far East that resulted from a war in Europe. Those opportunities would soon arise.

Poland was next on Hitler's conquest list. With a million troops and a large territory, Poland would not be easy to overrun, especially if Britain, France and the Soviet Union came to that country's rescue. Germany would likely have lost a two-front war at this time. In April 1939, London and Paris made separate and different appeals to Moscow to join them in guaranteeing the sovereignty of Poland and Romania; the British wanted a simple statement, the French an alliance. Foreign Minister Maksim Litvinov replied that the Soviet Union would join a triple alliance that could deter Hitler but not a bilateral alliance with France that might fail to deter him. Chamberlain rejected any notion of formally allying with the Soviet Union. On 19 May, Churchill blistered Chamberlain for his latest blunder:

> When you … examine … the interest … of the Russian Government in this matter, you must not be guided by sentiment. You must be guided by a study of the vital interests involved. The vital major interests of Russia are deeply engaged in cooperation with Great Britain and France to prevent further acts of aggression … If you are ready to be an ally of Russia in time of war, why should your shrink from becoming an ally of Russia now, when you may by that very fact prevent the breaking out of war?[134]

Spurned by London, Moscow would accept Berlin's courtship four months later. Meanwhile, the best France could do was sign with Poland a treaty forming a bilateral defensive alliance on 19 May 1939. Chamberlain refused to back up his 31 March pledge with a concrete military commitment to France and Poland.

Not to be outdone by Hitler, Mussolini had his army invade Albania on 7 April 1939. This latest stage of Fascist imperialism provoked a reaction not at 10 Downing Street, but at the White House. President Roosevelt wrote to both Hitler and Mussolini, asking them to promise not to commit any more aggression for 'twenty-five years, if we are to look that far ahead'. On 28 April, Hitler replied with a long speech before the Reichstag in which he justified his takeovers and insisted that he was devoted to peace.[135]

Three international agreements became the foundation for Hitler's next act of imperialism. On 22 May 1939, Hitler and Mussolini signed their 'Pact of Steel' military alliance; thereafter, each would unconditionally back the other's conquests. On 24 July, Hungarian Prime Minister Paul Teleki wrote letters to Hitler and Mussolini pledging his country's allegiance with Germany and Italy. Poland's fate was sealed on 23 August 1939 with a public nonaggression pact between Berlin and Moscow and a secret deal that split that country between them.

The German army's first 'blitzkrieg' or 'lightning war' was unleashed in the invasion of Poland on 1 September 1939.[136] Armoured divisions followed by mechanized infantry punched through vulnerable stretches of the Polish defences and encircled and wiped out the troops. Tactical aircraft like Stuka dive-bombers devastated front-line Polish troops while heavy bombers destroyed strategic positions like airfields, supply depots, railway stations, bridges and headquarters. Within two weeks, the German army overran and gutted the Polish army west of the Vistula River and captured Warsaw along with other cities. By the time Stalin ordered the Red Army to attack on 17 September, the Polish army had largely ceased to exist. The Soviets mopped up and imprisoned the remnants in eastern Poland, of which the communists murdered 22,000 Polish officials and officers, each by a pistol shot in the back of his head and buried them in mass graves in the Katyn Forest.[137]

Hitler had ordered the invasion confident that the British and French would not attack Germany while most of the German army was overrunning its share of Poland. Once again his confidence was justified. Despite the Franco-Polish alliance, the million-man French army did not invade Germany to relieve pressure on the Poles. Instead, the French troops remained safe in the Maginot Line and other positions far from any fighting that might endanger them. Indeed they would enjoy eight and a half months of what became known as the 'Phoney War' before a German blitzkrieg devastated them.

Typically, London and Paris failed to coordinate their responses to news of the German invasion. Ironically, Chamberlain's government, which was not allied with Warsaw, was the first to issue an ultimatum to Berlin, demanding that a withdrawal from Poland by noon on 3 September. Daladier's government, which was Allied with Warsaw, did not issue such an ultimatum until the morning of 3 September with the deadline five o'clock that afternoon. Britain and France formally went to war after their respective deadlines passed.

The subsequent debate in the House of Commons over the war's ends and means invoked a near transcendental experience in Churchill:

> As I sat in my place listening to the speeches, a very strong sense of calm came over me, after the intense passions and excitement of the last few days. I felt a serenity of mind and was conscious of a kind of uplifted detachment from human and personal affairs. The glory of Old England, peace-loving and ill prepared as she was, but instant and fearless at the call of honour, thrilled my being and seemed to lift our fate to those spheres far removed from earthly facts and physical sensation.[138]

Chapter 6

The Commander

'This cannot be an accident. I was kept for this job.'

'Might it not be thought rather cynical if it seemed we had disposed of these issues, so fateful to millions of people, in such an offhand manner?'

Prime Minister Neville Chamberlain probably mentally held his nose when he summoned his nemesis, Winston Churchill, on 3 September 1939 and offered him his old post as First Lord of the Admiralty with a seat in the War Cabinet. News of the appointment provoked a spectrum of reactions. Those who feared and loathed Churchill in Britain and beyond were sickened. For instance, the commander of the Luftwaffe, Hermann Göring, grimly noted: 'That means war is really on. Now we shall have war with England.'[1] Meanwhile, Churchill's admirers rejoiced.

Churchill was thrilled to receive a congratulatory letter and offer of cooperation from President Franklin Roosevelt. 'My Dear Churchill,' the letter began, 'It is because you and I occupied similar positions in the World War that I want you to know how glad I am that you are back again in the Admiralty … I shall at all times welcome it, if you will keep me in touch personally with anything you want me to know about.'[2] This was the first step in a deepening four-year relationship as Allied leaders and friends that was critical for how the war was fought and eventually won.[3] They had met long before, on 29 July 1918, as guests at a War Cabinet dinner. Roosevelt vividly recalled the encounter; Churchill was hazy, as perennial centres of attention usually are. Nonetheless Churchill greatly admired Roosevelt for the array of socioeconomic reforms he enacted first as New York's governor, then as president.

During the two weeks following Germany's invasion of Poland, the critical question in London and Paris was whether the Soviet Union would resist or acquiesce. It was then that Churchill issued his celebrated prognosis:

I cannot forecast to you the action of Russia. It is a riddle wrapped in a mystery inside an enigma: but perhaps there is a key. That key is Russian national interest. It cannot be in accordance with the interest of the safety of Russia that Germany should plant itself upon the shores of the Black Sea or that it should overrun the Balkan States ... That would be contrary to the historic life-interests of Russia.[4]

That may have been true in an objective sense, but Stalin judged otherwise. He clung to his nonaggression pact with Hitler like a security blanket until 22 June 1941, when he learned that the German army had invaded the Soviet Union. Meanwhile the Soviets were just as aggressive and murderous as the Germans. In September and October 1939, the Red Army not only conquered eastern Poland but the Baltic states of Estonia, Latvia and Lithuania as well. Moscow issued an ultimatum to Helsinki to yield territory within artillery range of Leningrad. Helsinki refused. Stalin ordered his army to invade Finland on 30 November. The Finns fought valiantly against overwhelming odds but finally sued for peace on 6 March 1940.

An extraordinary event occurred on 10 January 1940, that revealed the 'Phoney War' would soon become real. A German staff officer's plane flew off course, ran low on fuel and landed in Belgium, where officials arrested him and confiscated his papers. What they found was an intelligence gold mine, the German plan for outflanking the Maginot Line by invading the Low Countries. Brussels shared the intelligence with London and Paris, but, incredibly, none of the three governments subsequently adjusted their existing plans.

Churchill remained a Cassandra, but this time within the British government which at least tried to coordinate a defence strategy with its counterparts. He personally warned France's leading generals about a panzer-led German invasion through the Ardennes: 'Remember that we are faced with new weapons, armour in great strength, on which the Germans are no doubt concentrating and that forests will be particularly tempting to such forces since they will offer concealment from the air.'[5] Whitehall warned Brussels that the German army would soon spearhead its offensive through their territory in 1940 just as it had in 1914, 'but the Belgian King and his Army staff merely waited, hoping that all would turn out well'.[6] And, even more tragically, the French government did not adapt its strategy either.

Meanwhile Chamberlain was determined to ensure that Churchill's presence in the War Cabinet was more symbolic than substantive. He shot down many of Churchill's ideas, most notably his proposal to lay thousands of mines in the Rhine or along Norway's coast to impede the flow of German war materials. To his later regret, the prime minister did go along with one of his First Lord's plans. As with the Gallipoli campaign, the Norway campaign made strategic sense but was ineptly executed and Churchill would become the failure's scapegoat.

Eleven million of the fifteen million tons of iron ore annually consumed by Germany's industries came from Sweden's Gallivare region near the Arctic Circle. During the summer, that ore was conveyed by train south to Baltic ports where it was loaded on ships bound for Germany. During the winter, that ore went by train westward to Narvik in Norway, where it was safely shipped within the neutral waters of first Norway and then Denmark nearly all the way to Germany.

Almost simultaneously in December 1939, Churchill and Hitler realized how vulnerable the Narvik route was and they determined to capture it despite Norway's neutrality.[7] A British raid caused both sides to accelerate their plans. Churchill received intelligence that a German supply ship with 299 captured British sailors aboard was steaming south within Norway's waters toward Germany. He authorized British warships to intercept the ship and liberate the prisoners on 14 February 1940. The operation succeeded, although local Norwegian officials protested the violation of their nation's sovereignty. When Hitler learned of the seizure, he ordered his staff to prepare to invade Norway on 9 April 1940. Meanwhile the War Cabinet rejected Churchill's proposal to mine Norwegian waters but did approve seizing the ports of Stavanger, Bergen, Narvik and Trondheim. The Germans beat the British to Norway as flotillas disgorged troops that captured those ports along with Oslo and Kristiansand. Over the next two months the British took Narvik and several smaller ports but the Germans boxed them in. Britain's worst defeat during the campaign came when the German battlecruisers *Gneisenau* and *Scharnhorst* sank the aircraft carrier HMS *Glorious* and two destroyers, killing 1,500 men. Atop those losses, throughout the campaign the British suffered 5,000 causalities and a cruiser and five destroyers sunk. By 8 June, the remaining British troops along with Norway's government had escaped. As for Norway's fate, while the Germans controlled most of the coastline and installed a puppet regime under Vidkun Quisling in Oslo, they fought guerrillas throughout the war.

Although the Norway campaign losses were a fraction of those of Gallipoli, Churchill was well aware that his latest military disaster made him liable to resignation and he acknowledged that 'it was a marvel that I survived'. He was partly shielded by Chamberlain's sinking approval ratings along with the public's understanding that 'for six or seven years I had predicted with truth the course of events and had given ceaseless warnings, then unheeded but now remembered'.[8] He also benefited from publicly admitting and apologizing for his role in the debacle. In the House of Commons debate on the controversy, Lloyd George argued that 'I don't think the First Lord was responsible for all the things that happened in Norway'. Churchill rose and declared: 'I take full responsibility for everything that has been done by the Admiralty and I take full share of the burden.'[9] Beyond that Churchill was poised to shoulder the heaviest burden of all, one that he had dreamed of for decades.

The Labour Party and many of his fellow Tories erupted in rage against Chamberlain in the Commons on 8 May, blistering him for all the disasters that he had unwittingly instigated from Munich to Narvik. Technically Chamberlain survived the no confidence vote by 281 to 200, although 39 Tories voted against him and 60 others abstained. The scorching criticism topped by his greatly reduced majority demoralized him. He confided to Churchill that he felt he should he resign but Churchill talked him out of it. On 9 May, Chamberlain called for a meeting between Churchill, Foreign Secretary Lord Halifax and Labour Party leaders Clement Atlee and Arthur Greenwood, during which he asked for an all-party Cabinet. Atlee and Greenwood replied that they would have to consult their party which was then convening at Bournemouth. It took hours for the Labour Party to reach a consensus. Atlee relayed the blunt message that Labour would join a coalition only if Chamberlain did not head it. Chamberlain had no choice but to hurry to King George VI and resign.

Churchill mingled irony with disingenuousness when the king summoned him on 10 May:

His Majesty received me most graciously and bade me sit down. He looked at me searchingly and quizzically for some moments and then said, 'I suppose you don't know why I have sent for you?' Adopting his mood, I replied, 'Sir, I simply could not imagine why.' He laughed and said, 'I want to ask you to form a government.' I said I would certainly do so.[10]

Inwardly he was bursting with triumph. He confided to his secretary that: 'This cannot be an accident. I was kept for this job.'[11] He later recalled:

Thus at the onset of this mighty battle, I acquired the chief power of the State ... I was conscious of a profound sense of relief. At last I had the authority to give directions over the whole scene. I felt as if I were walking with destiny and that all my past life had been a preparation for this hour and for this trial. Eleven years in the political wilderness had freed me from ordinary party antagonisms. My warnings over the last six years had been so numerous, so detailed and were now so terribly vindicated, that no one could gainsay ... Therefore, although impatient for the morning, I slept soundly and had no need for cheering dreams. Facts are better than dreams.[12]

That same day Hitler unleashed a blitzkrieg against France and the Low Countries.[13] In hard power, the Germans had the edge over the French and British, with 2.5 million troops, 2,574 tanks and 2,750 aircraft versus 2 million troops, 3,609 tanks and 1,700 aircraft. But that alone was not enough to prevail.[14] Germany triumphed with vital elements of soft power – superior strategy and tactics and better led and motivated troops. Berlin's strategy was a revised and expanded version of its 1870 and 1914 offensives. Once again the decisive thrust was via the Ardennes forest of northern Luxembourg and southern Belgium to outflank the bulk of French forces massed along the Rhine River; General Gerd von Rundstedt's army of seven armoured divisions and thirty-eight infantry divisions dashed westward through the forest to capture the critical Meuse River fortress cities of Liège, Sedan and Namur on 10, 15 and 23 May, respectively. However, this time an additional army overran the Netherlands and captured the key port of Rotterdam. And, most critically, rather than turn south toward Paris, most German armoured divisions turned north toward the English Channel. As for tactics, the Germans perfected the integration of tanks, paratroopers, infantry, artillery, fighter planes, fighter-bombers and heavy bombers relentlessly pounding, encircling and destroying the enemy.

Meanwhile, the House of Commons endorsed Churchill's coalition government by a vote of 381 to zero on 13 May. In his acceptance speech, Churchill declared these immortal words:

I have nothing to offer but blood, toil, tears and sweat. You ask, what is our policy? I will say: It is to wage war, by sea, land and air, with all our might ... That is our strategy. You ask, what is our aim? I can answer in one word: It is victory, victory at all costs, victory in spite of all terror, victory however long and hard the road may be; for without victory, there is no survival.[15]

Churchill obtained from Parliament 'extraordinary powers … for requiring persons to place themselves, their services and property at the disposal of His Majesty as appear to him to be necessary or expedient for securing the public safety, the defence of the realms, the maintenance of public order or the efficient prosecution of any war in which His Majesty may be engaged'.[16] He was both the prime minister and defence minister and for a while the Chancellor. He chaired the five-member War Cabinet and the 25-strong full Cabinet. Some faces changed during the war but the key people sooner or later included Clement Atlee as Deputy Prime Minister; Halifax and then Antony Eden as Foreign Secretary; Albert Alexander as First Lord of the Admiralty; Herbert Morrison as Home Secretary; Kingsley Wood then John Anderson as Chancellor of the Exchequer; William Aitken, Lord Beaverbrook as Aircraft Production Minister then Supply Minister then War Production Minister; Duff Cooper then Brendan, Viscount Bracken as Information Minister; Hugh Dalton as Economic Warfare Minister; Ernest Bevin as Labour Minister; and Stafford Cripps as Lord Privy Seal then ambassador to the Soviet Union. Churchill presented Chamberlain the consolation post of Lord President of the Council, but cancer, undoubtedly aggravated by stress, killed him six months later. Churchill's Imperial General Staff included as Chiefs Edmund Ironside, Dudley Pound, then Alan Brooke; First Sea Lords Dudley Pound then Andrew Browne; Army Chief John Dill; Air Chiefs Cyril Newall then Charles Portal; and Combined Operations Chiefs Roger Keyes then Louis Mountbatten. Churchill established a Joint Planning Committee that included military and intelligence officers. The War Cabinet initially met at 10 Downing Street but Germany's bombing campaign forced them into the New Government Office's basement a hundred yards away across from St. James Park.

Although Churchill brilliantly fulfilled his role as the nation's 'inspirer in chief', he irritated many ministers for how he presided over them. He worked at least sixteen hours a day.[17] He began his morning between six and seven o'clock, laboured steadily until early afternoon when he took a short nap within a two-hour break, then often continued until well past midnight. He explained that his 'siesta' was critical to his ability to squeeze a day and a half's worth of work into a day.[18] Few of his ministers or underlings could keep pace with that gruelling schedule, further harshened by Churchill's frequent rages against those around him. Clementine cautioned him of the 'danger of you being generally disliked by your colleagues and subordinates because of your rough sarcastic & overbearing manner ... You are not so kind as you used to be.'[19] Atlee wrote him an official letter of complaint in January 1945, that his failure to read his briefing papers before meetings made him

> inimical to the successful performance of the tasks imposed upon us as a Government and injurious to the war effort ... Often half an hour or more is wasted in explaining what could have been grasped by two or three minutes reading of the document. Not infrequently a phrase catches your eye which gives rise to a disquisition on an interesting point only slightly connected with the subject matter. The result is long delays and unnecessarily long Cabinets.[20]

Among those who worked most closely with Churchill was General Alan Brooke who became chairman of the Chiefs of Staff Committee on 5 March 1942. Brooke found Churchill's 'ideas often unrealistic, his habits of mind irrational and infuriating, his methods of work frustrating and exhausting and his temper sometimes vile', yet still greatly admired the prime minister.[21]

*   *   *

French Prime Minister Paul Reynaud telephoned Churchill on 15 May 1940 and blurted out that France was defeated. That prompted the first of Churchill's four journeys to France over a month to bolster the confidence of Reynaud and his ministers while trying to coordinate strategy between the French army and the 250,000-man British Expeditionary Force. On 20 May, a German panzer division rumbled into Abbeville at the mouth of the River Somme, cutting off the British army and what was left of France's First Army from the other French armies. Two days later British troops in Boulogne withdrew up the coast to Calais and then Dunkirk, where the British army and the First French Army's remnants massed in a horseshoe defence. An extraordinary event happened as the German panzer divisions were poised to overrun the Allied defences at Dunkirk. On 24 May, Hitler called off that attack and instead ordered Göring to destroy with air power that army and any vessels that tried to rescue it.

Churchill flew to Paris to try to convince the French to attack the German flank with their reserves. He was stunned to learn that the French had no reserves; all French troops were either deployed on the front lines, were isolated in pockets surrounded by German forces or had been killed, wounded or captured. Reynaud expressed doubt that the French army could resist much longer. In later analysing French strategy in spring 1940, Churchill concluded that the blunder was not in building and defending the Maginot Line but in failing to mass mobile strategic reserves that could rush to overwhelm any enemy breakthrough. After noting that 'the policy of the Maginot Line has often been condemned' for engendering 'a defensive mentality', he offered this balanced view:

> Yet it is always a wise precaution in defending a frontier of hundreds of miles to bar as much as possible by fortifications and thus economise in the use of troops in sedentary roles and 'canalise' potential invasion. Properly used in the French scheme of war, the Maginot Line would have … been viewed as presenting a long succession of invaluable sally ports and above all as blocking off large sections of the front as a means of accumulating the general reserves or 'mass of manoeuvre'.[22]

The French did the former but neglected the latter and thus lost the campaign after the Germans outflanked the Maginot Line. The French had more and better tanks than the Germans but dispersed them among infantry divisions rather than concentrated them in armoured divisions.

Churchill returned to London to convey the grim news to the War Cabinet on 27 May. Although Chamberlain was no longer prime minister, his spirit of appeasement lingered in his mind and those of several colleagues. Foreign Secretary Lord Halifax actually proposed trying to engage Mussolini as a go-between for peace with Hitler. Churchill warned that Mussolini would demand colonies like Malta or Gibraltar as the price of peace. Halifax suggested that Hitler could be also appeased with the return of Germany's African colonies that were taken by the 1919 Treaty of Versailles. Not surprisingly, Chamberlain piped up in favour of Halifax's proposal. A disgusted Churchill spiked that notion by insisting that Britain would fight on alone if need be and expressed his confidence that everyone in the Cabinet would be willing to die along with his family rather than submit to the Nazis. The firm support of Atlee and Greenwood for Churchill silenced Halifax and Chamberlain. With the War Cabinet's approval, Churchill ordered the navy to evacuate the troops from Dunkirk.[23]

Churchill and Atlee flew to Paris on 30 May. Reynaud had appointed the First World War hero Marshal Phillipe Pétain to head the army. Both Frenchmen appeared resigned to their country's imminent defeat. Churchill tried to rouse them to rally their nation for a fight to the death with these words:

> The British Government was prepared to wage war from the New World, if through some disaster England herself were laid waste. If Germany defeated either ally or both, she would give no mercy; we should be reduced to the status of vassals and slaves forever. It would be far better that the civilization of Western Europe with all its achievements should come to a tragic but splendid end than that the two great democracies should linger on, stripped of all that made life worth living.

Churchill's defiant spirit briefly animated Reynaud but 'Pétain's attitude, detached and sombre, gave me the feeling that he would face a separate peace. The influence of his personality, his reputation, his serene acceptance of the march of adverse events, apart from the words he used, was almost overpowering to those under his spell.'[24]

Britain's navy and air force coordinated their efforts to successfully evacuate Dunkirk. Eventually 335,480 Allied troops, 224,318 British and 111,172 French, were rescued. The Germans sank 30 of the 222 Royal Navy vessels involved in the operation. The British got the edge in the air battles over the evacuation, shooting down 394 German planes while suffering 114 losses, a ratio of three-and-a-half to one.[25] On 4 June, Churchill announced the operation's successful completion then declared:

> Even though large tracts of Europe ... have fallen or may fall into the grip of the Gestapo and all the odious apparatus of Nazi rule, we ... shall go on to the end, we shall fight in France, we shall fight on the seas and oceans, we shall fight with growing confidence and growing strength in the air ... we shall never surrender ... And even if, which I do not for a moment believe, this island ... were subjugated and starving, then our empire beyond the seas, armed and guarded by the British Fleet, would carry on the struggle until ... the New World, with all its power and might, steps forward to the rescue and the liberation of the old.[26]

Italy declared war on France and Britain on 10 June. Churchill wrote to Mussolini asking whether it was 'too late to stop a river of blood from flowing between the British and Italian peoples?' He warned the dictator that no matter what happened on the continent, 'England will go on to the end, even quite alone, as we have done before and I believe with some assurance that we shall be aided in increasing measure by the United States and indeed by all the Americas'.[27]

That same day Churchill flew to France for his fourth summit. The government had evacuated Paris and had stopped briefly at Tours before hurrying all the way to Bordeaux. Churchill had hoped to convince Reynaud and Pétain to defend Paris street by street and house by house. They disabused him of that hope. Paris was an open city and would be spared death and destruction. He then pressed them to conduct a guerrilla campaign in the countryside. They dismissed that notion as well for bloodying the entire nation. He urged them to hold out at least several more weeks. They grimly told him that the end was near. The Germans entered Paris without resistance on 14 June.

Although the French army still numbered 250,000 troops, its leaders were more interested in finding scapegoats than fighting the enemy. Astonishingly, Reynaud tried to blame America for the criminal incompetence with which he and France's other politicians and generals had appeased Germany over the previous half-dozen years, culminating with the looming catastrophic and humiliating defeat. On June 14, he sent this message to Roosevelt, warning that if he failed to give 'France in the coming days a positive assurance that the United States will come into the struggle in a short space of time ... you will see France go under like a drowning man after having thrown a last look toward the land of liberty from which he was expecting salvation'.[28]

With France's surrender imminent, Churchill's priority was to evacuate the 150,000 British and Canadian troops deployed in north-western France. That operation took several days, with most troops funnelled to Cherbourg and from there ferried across to Britain. Meanwhile Churchill faced his own domestic enemies who sought to scapegoat him. On 8 June, he staved off a motion in the House of Commons to investigate the disaster in France by arguing that nearly everyone was responsible in varying degrees and ways over half a dozen years:

> They seek to indict those who are responsible for our affairs. This also would be a foolish and pernicious process. There are too many in it. Let each man search his conscience and search his speeches. I frequently search mine. Of this I am certain, that if we open a quarrel between the past and the present, we shall find that we have lost the future.

He went on to explain: 'The battle of France is over. The battle of Britain is about to begin.'[29] On 18 June, he broadcasted a version of that speech:

> I speak to you ... as Prime Minster, in a solemn hour for the life of our country, of our Empire, of our Allies and above all of the cause of freedom ... We have differed and quarrelled in the past; but now one bond unites us all – to wage war until victory is won ... Upon this battle depends the survival of Christian civilization. Upon it depends our own British life ... If we fail, then the whole world ... will sink into the abyss of a new Dark Age ... Let us therefore brace ourselves to our duties and so bear ourselves that if the British Empire and its Commonwealth last for a thousand years, Men will still say, 'This was their finest hour'.[30]

Pétain surrendered France to Hitler on 22 June. Under the agreement, Hitler reduced France to a rump state with its capital at Vichy, in the centre of the country.[31] The German army would occupy France's coastlines and northern half. Hitler could now reinforce Germany with much of France's vast military and economic assets.

Churchill ordered all French vessels in British ports and Alexandria in Egypt to be seized on 3 July. The authorities captured over 200 ships in the United Kingdom and interned a battleship and four cruisers at Alexandria. But for now, with one exception, the French battleships, cruisers and other warships in the ports of France or its colonies were beyond the Royal Navy's power to capture or sink. The exception was the French base of Mers-el-Kébir, near Oran, where two battleships and two battlecruisers were anchored with Admiral Marcel Gensoul in command. Admiral James Sommerville commanded the British squadron composed of an aircraft carrier, two battleships, a battlecruiser, three cruisers and smaller warships that approached Mers-el-Kébir on 3 July. Sommerville gave Gensoul four choices. He could join forces with him against the Axis, head to a British or American port or sink his warships. Gensoul played for time while awaiting instructions from Admiral Jean Darlan. British intelligence intercepted and passed to Sommerville Darlan's order to Gensoul to stall as long as possible as other French warships steamed to join forces and fight the British. Sommerville ordered his warships to open fire on the French fleet. The British salvos destroyed every warship except for a French battlecruiser that escaped; 1,297 French sailors died in the fighting. Pétain reacted by condemning the attack and severing diplomatic relations with Britain.[32]

Churchill had other attacks in mind, not just against Vichy France but against German and Italian forces wherever they could be hit. On 22 July, he established the Special Operations Executive (SOE) or, as he unofficially dubbed it, 'the Ministry of Ungentlemanly Warfare', to conduct espionage, sabotage and assassinations behind enemy lines. He tapped Hugh Dalton, then the Economic Warfare Minister, to be the SOE's chief. He ended his extensive briefing for Dalton on what he had in mind with these words: 'And now, go set Europe ablaze.'[33]

Churchill received an extraordinary visitor on 8 June one who would cause him much frustration and anger throughout the war. Reynaud had appointed General Charles de Gaulle his deputy for national defence and sent him to London to convince Churchill to commit Britain's entire air force to France. De Gaulle accepted Churchill's explanation that he had to retain the air force in Britain to prevent a German invasion. Churchill's initial impression of de Gaulle was positive, that he was patriotic and committed to fighting on no matter what. Those feelings would worsen with each subsequent meeting. Nonetheless, Churchill recognized de Gaulle as the Free French leader on 28 June. Then came the debacle at Dakar, Senegal, when Vichy troops repelled repeated attacks by combined British and Free French forces from 23 to 25 September 1940.

* * *

The next obvious step for Germany was to invade Britain. But that was impossible without command of the air and the sea and for that Germany had to win simultaneous battles over Britain and across the Atlantic.[34] The two countries had asymmetrical air and naval power. Germany's bomber and fighter planes vastly outnumbered Britain's, but the Royal Navy vastly outnumbered Germany's navy. To prevail the Germans had to conduct three different but critically related operations. The Luftwaffe had to destroy Britain's air force then bomb to rubble Britain's industries and infrastructure. The Luftwaffe and U-boats had to sink as many warships guarding and merchant ships sailing to and from the United Kingdom as was possible. Enough ships and landing craft had to be collected to convey overwhelming numbers of troops across the intervening seas.

The Royal Air Force had several advantages despite being outnumbered three to one in planes and pilots. Air Chief Marshal Sir Hugh Dowding was the RAF Fighter Command's farsighted commander. As early as 1937, he foresaw how radar could give Britain a decisive edge and ordered the development and deployment of that critical technology. By June 1940, fifty carefully-positioned radar stations along the coast tracked aircraft up to 30,000ft above Britain and over the surrounding seas 120 miles away. Britain's two fighter planes, Hurricanes and Spitfires, had different, complementary strengths; Hurricanes were more strongly built so they could take more punishment and dive faster while the more lightly armoured Spitfires were more manoeuvrable and had longer ranges. By scrambling whenever German aircraft approached, British pilots had plenty of fuel to manoeuvre and follow the enemy aircraft which were running short of fuel and had an hour or so flight back to their bases. Most British pilots whose planes were shot down were able to bail out in time and parachute safely to their homeland; German pilots who did so ended up in prisoner of war camps or the sea.

Nonetheless Germany's air force steadily ground down Britain's in a war of attrition from 10 July to 30 August. Göring's strategy was to attack British air bases and factories with overwhelming numbers of bombers protected by fighter planes. Although the Royal Air Force usually shot down more enemy planes than it lost, eventually the Germans would prevail through sheer numbers. In a speech in the House of Commons on 20 August 20, Churchill immortalized Britain's fighter pilots with these words: 'Never in the field of human conflict was so much owed by so many to so few.'[35]

Then Hitler made a decision that saved Britain's air force from destruction and seesawed the battle. On 24 August, an off-course German bomber dropped its load on London. The next day Churchill ordered eighty RAF bombers to attack Berlin. That provoked Hitler to order Göring to shift the bombing campaign from air fields to cities and from day to night. The first major raid came on 30 August against London's docks and continued for a week. The attacks on the city iteself began on 7 September and persisted for months while steadily spreading to other cities. The British shot down few bombers with anti-aircraft guns and none with fighters which then did not have effective night-fighting capabilities. The result was that German bombs killed or wounded tens of thousands of people and destroyed swaths of cities but missed most air bases and war production factories.

The British called the bombing of their cities the Blitz. In a 11 September broadcast, Churchill assured Britons that they would eventually avenge the devastation that they were suffering by destroying Hitler's regime:

This wicked man, the repository and embodiment of many forms of soul-destroying hatred ... has now resolved to try to break our famous

island race by a process of indiscriminate slaughter and destruction ...
He has lighted a fire which will burn with a steady and consuming flame
until the last vestiges of Nazi tyranny have been burnt out of Europe
and until the Old World and the New World can join hands to rebuild
the temples of man's freedom and man's honour upon foundations
which will not soon or easily be overthrown.[36]

And to that end, Churchill believed that nothing was more vital than air
power:

The Navy can lose us the war, but only the Air Force can win it.
Therefore our supreme effort must be to gain overwhelming mastery in
the air. The Fighters are our salvation, but the Bombers alone provide
the means to victory. We must, therefore, develop the power to carry
an ever increasing volume of explosives to Germany so as to pulverize
the entire industry and scientific structure on which the war effort and
economic life of the enemy depend, while holding him at arm's length
from our Island.[37]

Vengeance was a powerful motivation for the bombing strategy. Churchill
admitted that 'I hail it as an example of sublime and poetic justice that those
who have loosened these horrors upon mankind will now in their homes and
persons feel the shattering strokes of just retribution'.[38]

*   *   *

The Battle of the Atlantic overlapped with and continued long after British
airmen won the battle of Britain and ended only with Germany's surrender,
a total of five years, eight months and five days. Of all the war's decisive
battles, none was more vital. Churchill later admitted: 'The only thing that
ever really frightened me during the war was the U-boat peril ... The Battle
of the Atlantic was the dominating factor all the war. Never for one moment
could we forget that everything ... elsewhere, on land, at sea or in the air
depended ultimately on its outcome.'[39]

That battle began hours after Britain declared war against Germany on
3 September 1940. Berlin ordered its submarine captains to torpedo any
enemy war or merchant ships. By the end of September, German submarines
had sunk twenty-six merchant and three war ships, including the passenger
ship *Athenia* in which 28 Americans were among the 112 dead.[40] That was

just the grim beginning. Month after month Germany's U-boat campaign sank a steadily rising number of merchant ships sailing to or from the British Isles along with British warships guarding the home waters or patrolling the high seas. After the Allies adopted the convoy system of massed cargo ships protected by warships, the Germans deployed 'wolf-pack' tactics of massed U-boats that trailed and picked off vessels from the convoys. U-boats diverted enormous amounts of enemy resources even when they were not torpedoing ships. Naval base commanders struggled to protect their anchored vessels with underwater steel nets, sunken obsolete ships, patrol boats, coastal batteries, searchlights, minefields, radar and, eventually, sonar. Even then a few intrepid submariners somehow zigzagged that maze of defences. One sank the battleship *Royal Oak* in Scapa Flow, entombing 833 sailors beneath those waters on 14 October 1940. Aircraft played supporting roles. German long-range aircraft searched for convoys and attacked shipping, while Allied bombers sought German warships and surfaced U-boats at sea and port.

Compared to Germany's U-boats and even aircraft, its surface fleet was more distracting than genuinely threatening. Germany's navy was outnumbered by one to ten in battleships and cruisers and had no aircraft carriers. At best, German captains could steam into shipping lanes and sink merchant vessels and hopefully any warships that they encountered. Throughout the war, of all the German 'kills' of enemy vessels, surface ships accounted for less than 1 per cent, aircraft around 4 per cent and U-boats around 95 per cent. The German surface navy's power was mostly psychological. Britain's strategy was to hunt and destroy German warships that ventured onto the high seas with flotillas of warships and aircraft or destroy them in their lairs with submarines and bombers. The campaigns to find and sink the *Graf Spee* in the South Atlantic and the *Bismarck* in the North Atlantic were white-knuckled for the sailors who endured them, but were footnotes in the context of the world war.

The Battle of the Atlantic was a war of attrition that the Allies eventually won for many reasons, most critically the soaring productivity of American shipyards. Eventually the Americans built 2,710 cargo or 'Liberty' ships with 38.5 million tons, a capacity two and a half times greater than the 14 million tons that the Germans sank. And that was just American production. Shipyards in Britain, Canada and dozens of other countries produced hundreds of their own vessels. Ultimately, the Allies paid an exorbitant price in lives, vessels and treasure to keep the Atlantic and its adjacent North, Mediterranean and Caribbean seas open. The Germans sank 5,151 Allied ships, including 175 warships, in which 30,132 seamen lost their lives and shot down at least 741 planes and killed hundreds of pilots. German losses were also heavy, 783 submarines and a score of warships, with at least 30,000 sailors killed.[41]

* * *

Churchill's fervent hope that the New World would rescue the Old came true, but only after years passed and millions died. It took two years and three months after war erupted in Europe for the United States to enter the war and another thirty-two months to defeat Italy, forty months to defeat Germany and forty-three months to defeat Japan. Until the Japanese attack on Pearl Harbor on 7 December 1941, isolationism pervaded Congress and public opinion. That forced President Roosevelt to take a series of small steps to aid Britain and China against their enemies, while avoiding the assertion of military force. Roosevelt explained the chasm between what many people believed and how America's government could act in a radio speech after Germany's invasion of Poland in September 1940: 'The nation will remain a neutral nation, but I cannot ask that every American remain neutral in thought as well. Even a neutral cannot be asked to close his mind and conscience.'[42]

Roosevelt did more than simply root silently for the Allies and then Britain after France was overrun.[43] He aided Britain in two vital ways long before the United States formally went to war against Germany. Diplomats signed a deal critical to Britain's defence on 24 July 1940. Washington committed itself to producing 14,375 aircraft of various kinds for Britain over the next 21 months. Similar deals were struck for the Americans to supply tanks, trucks, weapons, munitions and other equipment. Britain desperately needed more destroyers which, with their speed, manoeuvrability and relatively small size, could best hunt submarines. On 2 September 1940, envoys signed a deal whereby Washington swapped fifty obsolete destroyers to London in return for base rights in Newfoundland, Bermuda, Antigua, the Bahamas, British Guiana, Jamaica, St Lucia and Trinidad. That freed British forces in those bases to redeploy to bases elsewhere far closer to the fighting.

The trouble with the production deal was that Britain was running out of gold and cash to pay for all of it. Churchill sent pleas to Roosevelt for America to loan Britain money with which to buy American weapons and equipment. Roosevelt had Harry Hopkins, his political advisor and alter-ego, fly to London and speak confidentially to Churchill.[44] Hopkins explained that the president sympathized but his political hands remained tied by

Congressional isolationists and misers. Roosevelt certainly could do nothing before that year's presidential and congressional elections.

Franklin Roosevelt overwhelming won re-election against Republican Party candidate Wendell Willkie by 54.7 per cent to 44.8 per cent of the vote and 449 to 83 in the Electoral College on 5 November 1940. Meanwhile, the Democratic Party widened its domination of Congress with 267 to 169 in the House of Representatives and 69 to 23 in the Senate. The results left Churchill relieved and ecstatic. In his congratulatory letter to Roosevelt, he confided: 'I did not think it right for me, as a foreigner, to express my opinion upon American politics while the Election was on, but now I feel you will not mind my saying that I prayed for your success and that I am truly thankful for it.'[45]

With that electoral mandate, Roosevelt now confidently asserted the next critical stage of assistance for Britain, China and other countries threatened by fascist imperialism. Although their styles differed, Roosevelt was just as brilliant an orator as Churchill. The president had a gift for putting complex issues in words that most Americans could easily understand. For instance, during a press conference on 17 December 1940, he justified his proposed Lend-Lease programme with this analogy: 'Suppose my neighbor's house is on fire and I have a length of garden hose four or five hundred feet away. If he can take my garden hose and connect it up to his hydrant, I may help him to put out the fire.'[46] During one of his 'fireside chats' on December 29, 1940, he told his radio listeners that: 'We must be the great arsenal of democracy. For us this is an emergency as serious as war itself.'[47]

Having carefully prepared the political ground, Roosevelt presented his Lend-Lease Bill during his State of the Union Address before Congress on 6 January 1941. He sugar-coated the programme with American ideals that he called the Four Freedoms, of speech and religion and from want and fear. He pledged America's support for all countries that sought to keep or gain those freedoms. The Lend-Lease Bill passed the House of Representatives by 260 to 165 votes and the Senate by 66 to 31 votes, revealing that the power balance had tipped from isolationists to realists, although the former still had plenty of support. Roosevelt signed the bill into law on 11 March 1941. Eventually the United States would send $50.1 billion worth of weapons, munitions, provisions, tanks, trucks, petroleum, aircraft and an array of other supplies to its Allies, an amount that accounted for 17 per cent of America's war costs. Of the total, Britain received the lion's share with $31.4 billion followed by the Soviet Union with $11.3 billion, France with $3.2 billion, China with $1.6 billion and the other $2.6 billion spread among a score of lesser allies. Contrary to the bill's name and political marketing, virtually all of that military aid was a gift rather than sale or loan. America supplied around 10 per cent of Soviet military equipment and weapons and equipment, the critical difference between the Soviets being conquered by the Germans or driving them back all the way to Berlin.[48] Although hard American national security interests underwrote all that aid, Churchill also rightfully described Lend-Lease as 'the most unsordid act'.[49]

Roosevelt followed up his Lend-Lease victory by flying Averell Harriman, one of his leading advisers, to London for weeks of discussions with Churchill and his government over how America could best aid Britain short of war. Roosevelt then made two big defence commitments in June 1941. He extended the American navy's patrols out to the mid-Atlantic which let the Royal Navy withdraw its ships from that region eastward to waters closer to home. He stationed American troops in Iceland which freed British troops there to be deployed elsewhere.

* * *

As in other dimensions of warfare, each side developed cutting-edge technologies to locate its enemies, struggled to break ever more complex enemy codes and fired more sophisticated versions of weapons to destroy its enemies. As usual Churchill took a keen interest in novel gadgets that could revolutionize warfare. As prime minister he finally had the power to push projects to fruition through the bureaucratic and political maze where they were easily lost. Sonar was the key technology whose development Churchill spurred during the Second World War that compared to his paternity for tanks during the First World War. He also conceived two ideas critical for sustaining the invasion of France, the 'Mulberry' artificial ports and the 'Pluto' undersea cross-Channel oil pipeline. As for 'Mulberry', Churchill issued these instructions for his engineers to work out: 'They must float up and down with the tide. The anchor problem must be mastered. The ships must have a side flap cut in them and a drawbridge long enough to overreach the moorings of the piers. Let me have the best solution worked out. Don't argue the matter. The difficulties will argue for themselves.'[50] General Percy Hobart developed a series of special types of tanks, including Crocodiles mounting flamethrowers and Flails with a roll of revolving chains extended before the tank that exploded mines.

The most critical technology involved code-breaking. For that the government established a top secret team of hundreds of Britain's most brilliant and often eccentric mathematicians and other thinkers at Bletchley Park 50 miles north-west of London.[51] Indeed, after spending several hours at the site speaking with many participants, Churchill quipped to the director: 'I told you to leave no stone unturned to get staff but I had no idea you had taken me so literally.'[52] The programme began on 15 August 1939 and peaked with a sprawling complex with 9,000 personnel in January 1941. Germany's main encryption machine was called the 'Enigma' and the intelligence reports produced from the intercepts were codenamed 'Ultra'. Eventually they succeeded through brilliant calculations and lucky captures of several of the machines. They also struggled to break the codes of Italy, Japan and the Soviet Union. Meanwhile, the Americans had cracked Japan's diplomatic 'Purple' code in August 1940 and would crack the naval 'Magic' code in January 1941.[53] These Allied code-breaking efforts saved countless lives and shortened the war by years.

Finally there was atomic power. During the Second World War, five countries tried to develop atomic bombs, the United States, Britain, Germany, Japan and the Soviet Union. Britain's atomic bomb effort was originally code-named 'Maud' for Military Application of Uranium Detonation, led by Henry Tizard. On 19 August 1943, Churchill and Roosevelt agreed to combine their atomic bomb programmes. That effort eventually led to the first successful test of an atomic bomb in the New Mexico desert on 16 July 1945 and the bombings of Hiroshima and Nagasaki on 6 and 8 August, respectively. On 14 August, Tokyo announced that it would surrender and formally did so on 2 September. Thus did the atomic bombs save millions of Japanese lives and hundreds of thousands of American and other Allied lives that would have been lost in an invasion.

*   *   *

Germany, Italy and Japan signed the Tripartite Pact on 27 September 1940. Both allies proved to be as much liabilities as assets for Germany. Ideally, in June 1941, the Japanese would have attacked the Soviet Union from the east as the Germans invaded from the west; the combined weight of those offensives would have crushed the communist regime and broken up the Soviet Union. Instead, the Japanese kept strictly neutral in the war between Hitler and Stalin. Japan's war against America eventually led to the destruction of all three fascist regimes. Italy was nearly as much of a burden.

Mussolini kept invading countries and getting defeated, then called for help from Berlin which diverted considerable military forces from fighting the Soviet Union, enough to rob Germany of victory there.[54]

Mussolini ordered the 80,000-man Italian army in Libya, led by General Rodolfo Graziani, to attack the British army defending Egypt on 13 September 1940. Spearheaded by 300 tanks, the Italian offensive initially caught the British by surprise and drove them back in confusion. General Archibald Wavell managed to rally his troops and reinforce them west of the port of Mersa Matruh, 181 miles from Alexandria. Graziani halted his army and entrenched it at Sidi Barrani, 260 miles west of Alexandria.

The first British counter-attack was against Italy's navy rather than army. British carrier-borne torpedo bombers attacked the Italian fleet at Taranto, in southern Italy on 12 November 1940. The raid sank three of the six battleships and damaged other warships there. Two of the battleships were out of action for four to six months, and repairs to the third were not completed before the Italian surrender in 1943. This would be followed by an even more decisive British attack.

General Richard O'Connor launched his 30,000-man Eighth Army in Egypt in a carefully prepared flank and rear attack that routed Italy's 60,000 troops at Sidi Barrani on 8 December. This battle was Britain's first large-scale victory of the war. Within a week, the 39,000 Italian prisoners outnumbered the British army. O'Connor finally halted his offensive just across the Libyan frontier. General Annibale Bergonzoli took over the Italian army's remnants and rallied them at Bardia. Reinforcements boosted his army to 45,000 men. With merely 16,000 troops, O'Connor launched a flank attack that crushed the Italian army between 3 and 5 January 1941. In one of the more lopsided victories in military history, the British captured 36,000 men, killed 1,703 and wounded 3,740, while losing only 130 killed and 328 wounded. Reinforced to 100,000 men, O'Connor's Eighth Army hurried west along the coast, mopping up Italian detachments and seizing supplies all the way to Derna, a hundred miles beyond Tobruk. By February 1941, the Eighth Army had inflicted 25,000 dead and wounded, captured 130,000 and destroyed 400 tanks. Although the Italians still had 125,000 troops in Libya, they were low on morale, food, munitions and tanks. Most were at Benghazi but the rest were strung out in detachments back to Tripoli. O'Connor was readying his forces for a final offensive to overrun the rest of Libya when he received an order that stopped the Eighth Army dead in its tracks. He was to detach 62,000 troops and send them to Greece. When he protested, Britain's best general of the Second World War was replaced by one of numerous mediocrities, Philip Neame. Those absurd orders originated with the prime minister himself.[55]

Thus did Churchill snatch defeat from the jaws of victory in North Africa and instigate a devastating British debacle in the Balkans. It represented Churchill the strategist at his very worst when fantasy trumped common sense. He diverted 62,000 British and Imperial troops from North Africa to fight alongside Greeks and Yugoslavs against Germans, Italians and Bulgarians, who routed them. The Royal Navy did inflict heavy losses an Italian flotilla that steamed from Taranto to attack a convoy bound for Greece, sinking three cruisers and two destroyers and damaging a battleship. Meanwhile, the Allied army's remnants along with the Greek King George II and his government fled to Salonika and then sailed to Crete. On 20 May, a German airborne division landed on Crete and eleven days later forced the Allied forces to surrender. Of the troops that Churchill committed to the Greek campaign, 16,000 were casualties along with 100 tanks lost on the mainland and another 22,000 were casualties on Crete along with two cruisers and six destroyers sunk and an aircraft carrier, four cruisers and eight destroyers damaged in various related naval operations.[56]

Meanwhile, Hitler sent General Erwin Rommel, arguably the best of his numerous excellent panzer generals, along with 80 tanks and 20,000 troops to take command in Libya. Rommel launched his Afrika Korps against the Eighth Army's flank at El Agheila on 24 March 1941, routed the British, captured Benghazi and Derna and besieged Tobruk with 22,000 defenders. For Churchill, the lost prestige was worse than the lost territory: 'Far more important than the loss of ground is the idea that we cannot face the Germans and that their appearance is enough to drive us back many scores of miles. This may react evilly throughout the Balkans.'[57] Churchill here was blind to his own ultimate culpability in Britain's latest defeat. Had he retained rather than transferred O'Connell and 62,000 battle-hardened troops elsewhere, the Eighth Army could have overrun Libya and defeated Rommel. Although Churchill did send O'Connor back to retake command from the hapless Neame, German troops captured both generals and their staff. Britain's best general of the war spent the rest of it in a prisoner of war camp.

Adding to Churchill's woes was word that in Baghdad in Iraq on 1 April 1941, a pro-Nazi faction led by Rashid Ali El Gailani had overthrown the pro-British government led by Regent Abd al-Ilah and Prime Minister Nuri as-Said. Britain had granted Iraq independence in 1932, with side agreements that kept Iraqi oil flowing to Britain and a British air force base at Habbaniya, 50 miles west of Baghdad. Rebel forces besieged Habbaniya, defended by 2,200 British troops. Hitler sent German officers and aircraft to assist the rebels. Churchill dispatched an Indian brigade commanded by General William Slim from Alexandria by ship to Basra. After stepping ashore on 18 April, Slim and his men packed into trucks and drove north. Over the next three weeks, those troops first routed the rebels around Habbaniya, then pursued and drove them from Fallujah and finally hounded the remnants from Baghdad, where they reinstalled the pro-British government. Although the campaign involved relatively small numbers of men, the stakes were potentially huge. Had the pro-Nazi regime defeated the British attempt to depose it, later that year oil would have been trucked from Iraq across neutral Turkey to its Black Sea ports and then shipped across to German-held ports in the Soviet Union.[58]

The British enjoyed a priceless asset on the North Africa front. Naval and air forces on Britain's colony of Malta commanded the direct sea and air links between Italy and Libya. The Germans and Italians lost scores of ships, thousands of men and hundreds of thousands of tons of war supplies in that gauntlet. In return, the German and Italian air forces bombed Malta off and on for nearly two years. That bombing never succeeded in destroying Britain's forces on the islands. Hitler resisted repeated temptations to invade Malta and end that source of depredations against Axis shipping which by 1943 was losing two of three vessels that sailed within a couple of hundred miles of the island.[59]

* * *

During the German blitz against Britain, Churchill predicted that the *Führer* would eventually turn against the Soviet Union. He confided to an aide that: 'Hitler must invade or fail. If he fails, he is bound to go east to Russia and fail he will.'[60] He wrote a letter to Stalin and entrusted Stafford Cripps, a socialist and the new ambassador to Moscow, to deliver it to him. The letter warned Stalin that Hitler would attack him and called for better relations between Britain and the Soviet Union. Stalin dismissed the warning and offer, then passed on word to Hitler of what had transpired.[61]

The German army's invasion of the Soviet Union came on 22 June 1941.[62] Hitler had mobilized 2.8 million troops, 3,350 tanks, 7,200 guns and 2,770 aircraft along the Soviet frontier. To defend that front, Stalin initially deployed only 2.9 million of the Red Army's 5.7 million troops along with 11,000 tanks, 10,000 guns and 9,000 aircraft. Over the next six months, the German blitzkrieg encircled and destroyed one Soviet army after another, killing, wounding or capturing over four million Soviet troops at a cost of 800,000 German and allied troops. In early December the German offensive stalled on the outskirts of Leningrad and Moscow and a stretch of the Don River in eastern Ukraine. Winter and supply shortages were the key reasons why the German blitzkrieg ultimately failed. Hitler's hatreds were nearly as important. Had his war been to liberate rather than liquidate Slavs, millions would have joined his army to fight against a communism that was guilty of mass repression, exploitation and murder. Otto Brautigam, a key Ministry for Occupied Eastern Territories' official, explained in October 1942: 'In the Soviet Union we found on our arrival a population weary of Bolshevism' that 'greeted us with joy as liberators and placed themselves at our disposal.'[63]

In a speech broadcasted the evening of the German invasion, Churchill put the war between the totalitarian, genocidal ideologies of Nazism and Communism, in perspective:

> The Nazi regime is indistinguishable from the worst features of Communism … It excels all forms of human wickedness in the efficiency of its cruelty and ferocious aggression. No one has been a more consistent opponent of Communism than I have … But all this fades away … We are resolved to destroy Hitler and every vestige of the Nazi regime … Any man or state who marches with Hitler is our foe … It follows … that we shall give whatever aid we can to Russia and the Russian people.[64]

Churchill swiftly forged an alliance between London and Moscow. On 10 July, the British and Soviet navies signed a cooperation agreement to protect supply convoys going to and coming from Murmansk and Archangel. On 12 July, Stafford Cripps, the British ambassador, and Foreign Minister Molotov signed a treaty that pledged mutual assistance and no separate peace with Germany. On 19 July, Stalin first asked Churchill to open a second front against the Germans in Norway or France. Churchill explained that any landing was unthinkable for the foreseeable future because not enough troops could be massed, conveyed and sustained to defeat the Germans and thus could not avoid suffering a disastrous defeat. That rational explanation would not discourage Stalin from making repeated and increasingly insistent demands for a second front over the next three years. Yet for now Churchill was able to supply Stalin with something far more valuable. The Bletchley Park team achieved a breakthrough on 27 June 1941, when it cracked the Enigma code used by the German army that invaded the Soviet Union.

Churchill arranged for critical information to be shared with Stalin in a way that masked the true source and attributed it to other possible sources.

* * *

For most Europeans and Americans, a decade of brutal Japanese imperialism in the Far East from September 1931 to December 1941 was at most abstract but was a living hell to its tens of millions of victims. President Roosevelt, however, was increasingly concerned that the Japanese would conquer China and thus decisively shift the Pacific's power balance in their favour. Tragically, Congress passed three neutrality laws in 1936, 1937 and 1938 that prevented him from assisting the Chinese or any other victim of imperialism with money, arms and other vital supplies. It was not until 1940 that Roosevelt got Congress to begin undoing those neutrality laws. He was also able to double the army's size army from 135,000 troops when he took office in 1933 to 268,000 troops in 1940. Then the 1940 German blitzkrieg that conquered France, Belgium, the Netherlands and Luxembourg and besieged Britain changed a lot of American hearts and minds. Congress quadrupled defence spending to $10.5 billion and passed a one-year renewable conscription act that expanded the army to 1.5 million troops by the end of that year. Nonetheless, the fact that the bill passed by just one vote in the House of Representatives revealed how embedded isolationism remained among Americans.

Nine years after Japan invaded Manchuria, Roosevelt imposed the first economic sanctions on 2 July 1940. He did so after Tokyo bullied France's Vichy regime to let Japanese troops occupy northern French Indochina. Under the Export Control Act, the United States halted exports of aviation fuel, scrap metal and copper to Japan and barred Japanese vessels from the Panama Canal. Under the Lend–Lease Act, Washington provided credit to China to purchase American military equipment. The United States had two critical strategic assets in the Pacific Ocean, the Philippines as a colony and the Hawaiian Islands as a territory, along with smaller strategic islands like Guam, Wake and Midway. Pearl Harbor and Manila were 2,500 and 7,300 flying miles, respectively, across the ocean from Los Angeles.

The Japanese had an economic and thus military Achilles heel. They imported 80 per cent of their oil, 75 per cent of their scrap iron and 90 per cent of their copper from the United States. If that supply ended, Japan's war and economic machine would eventually grind to a halt. To offset that possibility, Tokyo had huge oil storage tanks filled with a year and a half's supply. In addition, the Japanese hoped to conquer the oil fields of the Dutch East Indies. The flaw was that the productivity of those oil wells was a fraction of what the Americans sold to Japan. Tokyo's self-imposed dilemma was to seek economic, military and political autarky for its expanding empire that practically was impossible to achieve. Like German and Italian imperialism, Japan's imperialism was ultimately self-defeating.

On 21 July 1941, Tokyo forced Vichy France to let Japanese forces occupy bases in Indochina's southern half. The Roosevelt administration reacted on 26 July by freezing Japan's financial assets in the United States. That prevented Tokyo from paying for critical American products, with oil the most vital. Japan's leadership faced a tough choice. They could yield to American demands that Japan withdraw from all its conquests that started with Manchuria in September 1931, in return for which Washington would lift the sanctions or they could attack the United States along with Britain and the Netherlands in the Pacific basin. Tokyo chose the latter. While the Japanese prepared for that offensive, their diplomats in Washington redoubled their efforts to get Secretary of State Cordell Hull to recognize Japan's conquests in Asia and the Pacific basin.[65]

*   *   *

Meanwhile, on 24 July 1941 Churchill received an invitation from Roosevelt for them to meet as soon as possible. Their first of eleven summits during the war took place from 9 to 14 August at the tiny port of Argentia in Newfoundland. Both men arrived aboard warships protected by flotillas of smaller vessels that anchored together in Placentia Bay. They immediately hit it off in what became one of history's greatest partnerships and friendships among statesmen.[66] Churchill later wrote that 'to encounter Roosevelt with all his buoyant sparkle, his iridescent personality and his sublime confidence was like opening your first bottle of champagne'.[67]

Roosevelt promised to do what he could to aid Britain's defence short of directly fighting the Germans and Italians or violate laws passed by Congress that limited his powers. That required some adept political and military manoeuvring. The first step involved signing a declaration of principles by America and Britain against tyranny and aggression. The president then handed the prime minister a document. What would be called the Atlantic Charter committed their governments to a just peace that renounced any territorial gains for themselves; adjusted territory according to the desires of most people involved; upheld the right of all nations to self-determination and democratic government; promoted international free trade and economic development; protected freedom of the seas; disarmed aggressor states; and reduced the militaries of the victors. Churchill was hesitant to sign, fearing that to do so would acquiesce in the breakup of the British Empire along with all other empires. But Roosevelt was insistent and Churchill eventually went along. On 14 August, the two leaders publicly released the Atlantic Charter for all the world's peoples to ponder.[68] Churchill later explained the Atlantic Charter's purpose: 'We had the idea ... that without attempting to draw up final and formal peace aims, it was necessary to give all peoples and especially the oppressed and conquered peoples, a simple, rough and ready wartime statement of the goal towards which the British Commonwealth and the United States meant to make their way.'[69]

Back in Washington, Roosevelt was good as his word. He convinced majorities in both houses of Congress to rescind the law that prevented merchant ships from arming themselves. He also deployed more destroyers to escort convoys to the mid-Atlantic where British warships took over. But he worried that public opinion and congressional majorities still favoured peace even after two attacks by German submarines that damaged one American destroyer and sank another, with 11 killed on the former and 115 killed of the 159-man crew on the latter. The president believed that only a direct attack on the United States would provoke Congress to declare war.

* * *

That attack came early on the morning of 7 December 1941, but from Japan rather than Germany.[70] Two weeks earlier, on 25 November, Tokyo issued orders for a series of meticulously planned offensives across the Pacific Basin to be spearheaded by the attack on Pearl Harbor. Those orders followed a message from the Washington embassy that Secretary of State Hull had rejected Japan's demand that the United States recognize all Japanese conquests and lift its economic embargo. Instead Hull repeated his demand that the Japanese withdraw from all their conquests since 1931, starting with Manchuria.

A Japanese fleet of four carriers protected by scores of other warships and supply ships launched two waves of bombers that devastated America's naval and air power in Hawaii. In all, the Japanese sank six battleships, damaged two battleships and six other warships, destroyed 180 warplanes, damaged 128 warplanes and killed over 3,600 military and civilian personnel. That victory, however, was far from decisive. The Pacific Fleet's three aircraft carriers were elsewhere when the Japanese attacked. Their worrisome absence, in turn, persuaded Admiral Chuichi Nagumo to withdraw his fleet to safety rather than dispatch a third wave of bombers targeted against oil storage tanks and ship repair facilities. The biggest lost opportunity, however, came in the pre-campaign planning when Tokyo decided not to conquer the Hawaiian Islands. Had the Japanese overrun Hawaii they would have driven America's defence back to the West Coast and delayed most of America's subsequent war efforts across the Pacific while at best propping up Britain across the Atlantic. That in turn might well have decisively tipped the Soviet and North African campaigns in favour of the Germans and Italians. Better still for the Axis powers would have been for Japan scrupulously to avoid attacking the United States and instead concentrate on conquering the British and Dutch empires in Asia and the Pacific. That would have deprived Roosevelt of any reason to ask Congress for a declaration of war and thus sidelined America from the war indefinitely.

Although Japan's attack preceded Tokyo's issuance of an official declaration of war against the United States, Washington was aware that war was imminent. The Americans had cracked Japan's latest diplomatic code in August 1940, although not its military code until early 1942. Analysis of Japan's diplomatic traffic indicated that Tokyo would likely launch an attack somewhere in the Pacific basin in late November or early December 1941, although there was no evidence that it would be against American territory. On 24 November, Washington ordered the commanders in the Philippines and Hawaii to ready their forces for a possible attack. Hawaii's navy and army chiefs, Admiral Husband Kimmel and General Walter Short, assumed that the only threat they faced was from saboteurs from the local Japanese population, so they ordered ships anchored closer together in Pearl Harbor and planes parked closer together on the tarmac. In the Philippines, General Douglas MacArthur dismissed the warning and made no preparations.

After learning of the attack, Churchill telephoned Roosevelt and asked, 'Mr. President, what's this about Japan?' Roosevelt sombrely replied, 'It's quite true. They have attacked us at Pearl Harbor. We are all in the same boat now.' 'That certainly simplifies things,' Churchill stated. 'God be with you.' Although he commiserated with Roosevelt and America, he was exultant: 'We had won the war ... Britain would live; the Commonwealth of Nations and the Empire would live. How long the war would last or in what fashion it would end no man could tell, nor did I at this moment care.' His next step was to call on the Cabinet to meet the next day. Once the ministers had convened, the 'War Cabinet authorized the immediate declaration of war upon Japan for which all formal arrangements had been made ... Under the British constitution the Crown declares war on the advice of Ministers and Parliament is confronted with the fact.'[71] Thus did Britain declare war against Japan before Roosevelt got Congress to do the same on 8 December. That done, Churchill prepared to journey to Washington for his first wartime summit with Roosevelt.

Hitler and Mussolini helped seal their eventual fates by declaring war against the United States on 11 December, to which Congress promptly reciprocated. Now the war was effectively global. In the timeless logic of the maxim 'the enemy of my enemy is my friend', the German and Italian declarations of war against the United States made Washington and Moscow de facto allies. Roosevelt and Churchill would make a series of Faustian pacts with one evil communist empire in order to destroy three more immediately threatening evil fascist empires.

Churchill reached the White House on 22 December, for what would be a three-week sojourn, broken by a five-day vacation at Miami, Florida.[72] The talks began inauspiciously when he suffered a mild heart attack the day he arrived. On 26 December, he addressed Congress, where loud applause greeted these lines referring to the Japanese: 'What kind of people do they think we are? Is it possible they do not realize that we will never cease to persevere against them until they have been taught a lesson which they and the world will never forget?' He ended with this: 'Lastly, if you will forgive me for saying it, to me the best tidings of all is that the United States, united as never before, have drawn the sword for freedom and cast away the scabbard.'[73]

Roosevelt and his advisors had already made vital advances in organization and personnel that would mobilize and direct American power to victory in the Second World War.[74] The most important strategic decision the president and prime minister made was first to defeat Germany and then Japan. As for the opening campaign, the British rejected the American proposal, presented by General George Marshall, the army Chief of Staff, to invade France in late 1942. That was much too soon, Churchill and his generals argued. The Americans needed experience against secondary enemies before they squared off with the Wehrmacht. They finally talked Roosevelt and his advisors into an Allied invasion of French North Africa. The American and British chiefs of staff formed a Combined Chiefs of Staff Committee to facilitate planning.[75] The Americans initially included Marshall for the army, Admiral Harold Stark for the navy in the Atlantic, Admiral Ernest King for the navy in the Pacific and General Henry 'Hap' Arnold for the air force.

The British included General Alan Brooke for the army, Dudley Pound for the navy and Charles Portal for the air force.

Churchill made his own concessions, although they were more symbolic than substantive. On New Year's Day 1942, he agreed to a joint statement of war principles and goals by the then twenty-six Allied and occupied countries or 'the United Nations', as Roosevelt called them. He grudgingly accepted Roosevelt's effort to add India to the United Nations which then included America, Britain and its dominions of Australia, New Zealand, Canada and South Africa, the Soviet Union, China, the occupied European countries Poland, Yugoslavia, Belgium, Norway, Greece, the Netherlands and Luxembourg, and the Latin American countries of Panama, Cuba, Costa Rica, El Salvador, the Dominican Republic, Honduras, Guatemala, Nicaragua and Haiti. He disagreed with the president's attempt to include China with America, Britain and Russia as great powers.

Churchill nearly failed to make it home. The pilot of his flying boat went off course and nearly flew to Brest, France, where German anti-aircraft gunners might have opened fire or fighter planes scrambled in pursuit. The pilot's abrupt correction after he realized his mistake nearly provoked the same potentially fatal results when they approached Plymouth from Brittany. Back in London, Churchill broadcasted to the British people the exhilarating results of his Washington summit:

> I crossed the Atlantic again to see President Roosevelt. This time we met not only as friends but as comrades, standing side by side ... the power of the United States and its vast resources ... with us ... till ... victory ... That is what I dreamed of ... and worked for and now it has come to pass.[76]

George Marshall and Harry Hopkins, Roosevelt's closest advisor, visited London for several days of debate over strategy in mid-April. The Americans pressed for a limited cross-Channel campaign that took and held Cherbourg at the tip of France's Normandy peninsula before the end of the year. Seizing that vital port would be the first step in a full-scale invasion of north-western France early the following year. Churchill rejected the plan as premature and likely to lead to a disaster as overwhelming numbers of German troops converged to wipe out the invaders. He insisted that the Americans uphold their pledge to invade French North Africa later that year. The American army was green and needed to cut its teeth on second rate enemy troops in a secondary theatre before they fought Germans.

The Allied strategy remained in abeyance. In late May, Soviet Foreign Minister Molotov arrived in Washington for several days of talks with Roosevelt, Hull and other key officials. Molotov conveyed Stalin's urgent demands for billions of dollars' worth of Lend-Lease aid and for the Americans and British to open a second front in France later that year. Roosevelt promised to increase military aid but could only agree to a second front if Churchill was in accord. Molotov journeyed to London where Churchill explained that although an invasion of France was impossible that year the mere threat was tying down dozens of German divisions that otherwise might be fighting on the Russian front. Churchill then sent Louis Mountbatten, a charismatic, highly decorated naval commander, to Washington to nail down Roosevelt's support for the North African campaign. That diplomatic campaign succeeded.

* * *

Japan's attack on Pearl Harbor was the opening act in what became a six-month offensive that stretched across vast expanses of the South-west Pacific and South-east Asia. The next blow was against the Philippines on 8 December. Although General MacArthur had nearly twenty-four hours to prepare after learning about Pearl Harbor, he did nothing. Japanese bombers flying from Taiwan destroyed America's air force on the ground and much of the fleet in Manila Bay. The Japanese army invaded the main Philippine island of Luzon on 22 December, routed the American and Filipino troops, pursued them to the Bataan Peninsula and besieged them for the next three and a half months. Leaving General Jonathan Wainwright in command, MacArthur and his staff escaped by boat to safety in Australia on 11 March 1942. Wainwright surrendered 75,000 American and Filipino troops on 9 April; the Japanese murdered nearly half of them in a 'death march' to prison camps in central Luzon. Corregidor, a small fortress island in Manila Bay, surrendered on 6 May.[77]

The British suffered their own series of devastating defeats in South-east Asia. Japanese torpedo bombers sank the battleship HMS *Prince of Wales* and the battlecruiser HMS *Repulse* off Malaya on 10 December 10. Churchill was ultimately responsible because he had ordered those warships into those waters without air support. An aide recalled that after learning of the sinkings, Churchill 'moped about, wept and sat staring off to nowhere for days.' All along he kept repeating: 'I don't understand what happened. I don't understand it.'[78] Actually the answer was quite simple. It was a classic case of cognitive dissonance whereby Churchill clung to his belief that naval power was impervious to air power despite countless examples over the preceding year and a half that it was untrue.

Far worse disasters followed. The Japanese deployed 50,000 troops around Hong Kong and forced its 14,000 British defenders to surrender on 25 December. From Indochina, General Tomoyuki Yamashita's army invaded northern Malaya and repeatedly routed the British army down the peninsula even though the British had twice as many troops, 140,000 to 70,000; the Japanese, however, had ten times more tanks, 200 to 23; twice as many aircraft, 568 to 252; and, most vitally, far superior generalship. British General Arthur Percival holed up with his remaining 85,000 men in Singapore. Yamashita's army neared Singapore on 1 February. Singapore had two weaknesses that rendered it indefensible from the land – all its heavy guns pointed seaward and all its water was piped from reservoirs in Malaya. The Japanese turned off the tap as they massed cannons along shore. After a two-week bombardment, Percival surrendered on 15 February. In the entire Malaya campaign, the British and Imperial forces suffered devastating losses of 8,708 casualties and 130,000 prisoners to 5,710 Japanese dead and wounded. The Japanese won one of military history's most lopsided victories along with two great prizes, Malaya with its tin mines and rubber plantations and Singapore with its deep-water port commanding the Malacca Straits between the Pacific and Indian Oceans.[79]

For this latest series of disasters, Churchill could offer only candour, resolve and hope:

> Singapore has fallen. All the Malay Peninsula has been overrun. Other dangers gather about us out there ... This ... is one of those moments when the British race and nation can show their quality and their genius ... Here is the moment to display that calm and poise combined with grim determination which not so long ago brought us out of the very jaws of death. Here is another occasion to show as so often in our long story that we can meet reverses with dignity and ... renewed ... strength. We must remember that we are no longer alone ... Three-quarters of the human race are now moving with us. The whole future of mankind may depend upon our action and upon our conduct ... We shall not fail now.[80]

The Japanese did not rest on their laurels. Their conquest of the Dutch East Indies, today's Indonesia, overcame a spirited but doomed air defence and limited ground fighting that netted 90,000 prisoners, with Java the first to be overrun in just a week and a half from 28 February to 9 March. Further east, Japanese troops occupied strategic points in the Solomon Islands and New Guinea's north coast from January through April. Meanwhile, another offensive targeted Burma. Japan's bombing campaign and raids began in mid-January followed by an invasion on 22 January that captured Rangoon on 8 March, then drove steadily north to sever the Burma supply road between India and China. Japanese troops took over the Andaman Islands in the eastern Indian Ocean. Admiral Chuichi Nagumo's carrier strike force steamed to Australia's north coast to bomb Darwin in late March then turned west to bomb Colombo, Ceylon and sink a British aircraft carrier, two cruisers and a destroyer in early April. Fortunately, a lack of fuel and need for repairs forced Nagumo to return to Singapore. That was a tremendous relief to Churchill and his War Cabinet who feared that Nagumo's task force would steam all the way to the Persian Gulf and invade Iraq for its rich oil fields.[81]

With Britain's army and fleet in the Pacific wiped out, only America potentially had the military means to blunt further Japanese advances and eventually lead an offensive that culminated with Japan's defeat.[82] Roosevelt made a political decision that extracted both scapegoats and a hero from the ruins of Pearl Harbor and the Philippines. Hawaii's commanders, Kimmel and Short, were court-martialled while MacArthur was given a Medal of Honor and command of American forces in the south-west Pacific. The first gift to MacArthur, whose troops dubbed him 'Dugout Doug' for holing up at his headquarters, was completely unmerited. The second gift proved to be a strategic calamity.

Initially Roosevelt intended for MacArthur simply to hold the south-west Pacific against a further Japanese advance while Admiral Chester Nimitz's armada of aircraft carriers, other warships and transports packed with marines took a series of key islands across the central Pacific directly toward Japan, which eventually would be invaded. Tragically, Roosevelt succumbed to MacArthur's insistence that his own offensive proceed parallel to Nimitz's offensive. Thus were countless human and material resources destroyed or squandered for political rather than strategic reasons for the next three and a half years. That had a disastrous multiplier effect as other fronts around the world desperately needed assets that were diverted to MacArthur's offensive, especially landing craft and fuel.[83]

As for hard power, the Americans had considerable existing assets. The most important was that the army already numbered 1.5 million troops, although virtually all were novices, along with a powerful navy despite the losses at Pearl Harbor. Actually the sinking of five battleships and damaging of four others was a blessing in disguise. That devastation decisively shifted the navy's mentality by revealing that battleships were obsolete and that aircraft carriers were now the key elements of naval warfare. America's most important elements of hard power was its vast financial, commercial, manufacturing, transportation, communication, mineral, petroleum, technological and scientific assets in an economy with 130 million people. Washington would mobilize that economic power into extraordinary military power.

America had some existing technologies and weapons that provided some tactical advantages. The deployment of the Norden Bomb Sight in 1935 let bombardiers flying three miles above a target drop bombs that hit within 200ft of it. The B-17, B-24 and B-25 were first-rate heavy and medium bombers. The air weakness was in fighter planes; the P-40 was then America's best but inferior to Japan's Zeros and Germany's Me 109s. It would take a couple of years before the Americans developed cutting edge fighters like the F-6 Hellcat and P-51 Mustang, fighter-bombers like the P-38 Lightning and P-47 Thunderbolt, and the B-29 super-bomber that far exceeded the B-17 in range and payload.

America's most important immediate tactical naval assets were the three aircraft carriers, although they were outnumbered four to one by Japanese carriers. America's first offensive assertion of carrier warfare was a high-risk gamble with a soft power payoff. On 18 April 1942, the USS *Hornet* steamed within 650 miles of Japan and launched sixteen B-25s that bombed Tokyo. Although the physical damage was miniscule, the psychological blow was significant. The Japanese recognized their vulnerability while the Americans cheered at their first act of vengeance. A month later Japanese suffered and Americans exulted at a strategic as well as emotional American triumph. The battle of Coral Sea from 4 to 8 May was a tactical draw since each side lost a carrier then steamed away in opposite directions. Strategically it was a decisive American victory since it blunted the Japanese advance in the south-west Pacific. Never again would a Japanese carrier task force try to sever the sea-lanes between America and Australia. It was also the first carrier war in history where the warships were far beyond the horizon from each other. The Pacific War's turning point came with the Battle of Midway from 3 to 7 June 1942. Planes launched from America's three carriers sank all four Japanese carriers while Japanese bombers sank only one American carrier. Thereafter the United States was almost continuously on the offensive and steadily pushed back Japan's empire across the Pacific. America's first ground offensive in the Pacific came with the invasion of Guadalcanal Island on 7 August. The result was a land, sea and air battle that raged for half a year until the island was finally secured on 9 February 1943. During that time, the Japanese and Americans suffered 19,200 to 17,100 casualties, 38 to 29 warships sunk and 880 to 615 planes destroyed.[84]

*   *   *

Churchill could only observe rather than contribute to these critical events in the Pacific.[85] With Britain's South-east Asian colonies lost, he had to ensure that India did not suffer that same fate. He dispatched General William Slim with reinforcements to the Burma front to stave off any further Japanese advance westward. The result was a seesaw battle in that region that ground on for three and a half years.[86] Meanwhile, he became increasingly concerned about the threat that swelling Indian nationalism posed to British rule. He sent Stafford Cripps to India to try to talk Gandhi into pledging his 'Quit India' independence movement's loyalty to Britain for the duration of the war in return for dominion status after it. Gandhi argued that the British presence in India attracted Japanese aggression and insisted on independence as soon as possible. The result for now was a political stalemate. During a speech in November 1942, Churchill expressed his determination not to make any further concessions: 'I have not become the King's First Minister in order to preside over the liquidation of the British Empire.'[87]

India's independence movement had a distant but very important sympathizer if not outright ally. To Churchill's irritation, Roosevelt favoured eventual freedom not just for India but for the rest of the British Empire.[88] The president informed the prime minister in Washington that 'the feeling is almost universally held ... that the deadlock has been caused by the unwillingness of the British government to concede to the Indians the right of self-government'.[89] In his memoirs, Churchill criticized Roosevelt for putting idealism before practical problems: 'The President's mind was back in the American War for Independence ... I, on the other hand, was responsible for preserving the peace and safety of the Indian continent, sheltering nearly a fifth of the population of the globe. Our resources were slender and strained to the full.'[90]

In his exchanges with Roosevelt and other Americans officials over the fate of the British Empire and India, Churchill was usually diplomatic in not pointing out America's own foibles, especially its race relations, but during a dinner party at the White House he could not restrain himself. Seated beside him was Helen Ogden Reid, the *New York Herald Tribune*'s formidable owner. Indian independence was among the pet causes she championed on her editorial page. She archly asked him: 'What are you going to do about those wretched Indians?' Churchill promptly replied: 'Before we proceed further let us get one thing clear. Are we talking about the brown Indians in India, who have multiplied alarmingly under benevolent British rule? Or are we talking about the Red Indians in America, who, I understand are almost extinct?' The quip rendered Reid speechless and convulsed Roosevelt with laughter.[91]

*   *   *

Rommel's Afrika Korps outflanked General Neil Ritchie's Eighth Army at Bir Hacheim and routed it on 26 May 1942. Fortunately, the reserve corps of General John Gott held up Rommel's advance for eight critical days while the rest of the army escaped complete destruction. Ritchie left behind 33,000 troops under General Henrik Klopper in Tobruk, hoping they would stall the enemy advance while he regrouped further east. Rommel besieged Tobruk and forced Klopper to surrender on 21 June. Rommel then led his troops eastward before finally halting his advance on 1 July, at El Alamein, the best defensive position along North Africa's coast with the Qattara Depression 20 miles south and Alexandria just 70 miles east. In a brilliant whirlwind campaign, the Afrika Korps had inflicted on the British over 50,000 casualties and 1,188 destroyed or captured tanks, at the cost of 3,300 casualties and 400 tanks.[92]

Churchill was in Washington meeting with Roosevelt when he received word of the disastrous loss of 33,000 troops at Tobruk. When Roosevelt asked how he could help, Churchill requested as many tanks as the Americans could possibly spare. Roosevelt diverted 300 Sherman tanks and 100 self-propelled guns that were earmarked for American troops to Alexandria, Egypt. When a U-boat sank one of the six ships conveying those tanks and guns, the president promptly ordered that lost load to be replaced and forwarded. Some of Churchill's colleagues were less forgiving. In the House of Commons, Aneurin Bevan called for a censure vote against Churchill with this argument: 'The prime minister wins debate after debate and loses battle after battle. The country is beginning to say that he fights debates like a war and the war like a debate.'[93] The motion was defeated by 475 votes to 25.

Churchill travelled to Cairo to assess first-hand the situation, arriving on 31 July. En route he pulled rank to have a specially modified oxygen mask that let him chain-smoke cigars in the unpressurized Liberator bomber. Following the Gazala and Tobruk debacles, the depleted and demoralized Eighth Army desperately needed a vigorous, decisive new commander. Churchill replaced the disgraced Ritchie with General Claude Auchinleck then, at reports that he had failed to revitalize the army, transferred him to the Middle East command. Churchill gave the Eighth Army to General Gott, who had blunted Rommel's advance for eight days. Tragically a German fighter plane shot down Gott's plane as he was returning to Cairo. Churchill then turned to General Bernard Montgomery, arguably Britain's most controversial general of the Second World War.[94]

That done, Churchill then flew on to Moscow via Tehran, arriving on 12 August. All along his mind churned with his undertakings' ironies and moral dilemmas: 'I pondered on my mission to this sullen, sinister Bolshevik State I had once tried so hard to strangle at its birth and which, until Hitler appeared, I had regarded as the mortal foe of civilized freedom. What was it my duty to say to them now?' What followed were three days of terse talks with Stalin over strategy, supply and, most persistently on the tyrant's part, a second front on the Continent that year. Churchill insisted that his Mediterranean strategy that he had talked Roosevelt into would 'attack the soft belly of the crocodile'. To his relief, 'Stalin seemed suddenly to grasp the strategic advantages'. Nonetheless, by the time he departed 'I had been offended by many things which had been said at our conferences. I made every allowance for the strain under which the Soviet leaders lay, with their vast front flaming and bleeding along nearly two thousand miles and the Germans but fifty miles from Moscow and advancing toward the Caspian Sea.'[95] After returning to Cairo on 17 August, he gave this assessment of his impact on Stalin: 'I believe that I made him feel that we were good and faithful comrades in this war but that, after all, is a matter which deeds, not words, will prove.'[96] Stalin's bottom line was for the British and Americans to invade Europe as soon as possible and his anger and resentment swelled steadily against his Allies as that failed to happen.

The day that Churchill returned to Cairo, a Canadian division launched a raid on the small French port of Dieppe. The result was a debacle, the latest for which Churchill was ultimately responsible even though his close friend Louis Mountbatten was in actual command. The Canadian troops and British warships suffered over 5,000 casualties before the survivors were evacuated. In his memoirs, he put the best possible spin on the Dieppe raid, justifying it for all the alleged lessons learned. But he also wielded the failure of Dieppe as part of his campaign to avoid a cross-Channel invasion.[97]

Montgomery launched the Eighth Army against the Afrika Korps on 23 October 1942. The battle was classic Montgomery, a meticulously planned bulldozer offensive after months of build-up that gave him overwhelming odds of six to one in tanks and troops and two to one in artillery. He enjoyed two other critical advantages. 'Enigma' intercepts led to the sinking of three ships filled with fuel bound for the Afrika Korps. Atop that Rommel was on medical leave back in Germany, leaving in command General Georg Stumme, who was killed on the first day. Despite such overwhelmingly favourable odds, the Eighth Army still needed ten days to pulverize the Afrika Korps with near-constant artillery barrages and carpet bombings before Rommel, who had hastily flown back, ordered a retreat with his remaining 10,000 German and 25,000 Italian troops and mere 60 tanks, after suffering 59,000 casualties of whom 34,000 were German. The Eighth Army recaptured Tobruk on 13 November.[98]

President Roosevelt tapped General Dwight Eisenhower to command America's North African campaign.[99] Eisenhower accepted the mission with mixed feelings. He was happy to head an army but wanted to lead it in Europe rather than Africa. 'This is the blackest day in history' was his bitter reaction to the target.[100] Churchill succinctly expressed to Roosevelt the logic behind attacking North Africa rather than France: 'The first victory we have to win is to avoid a battle.'[101]

Ideally, the Allied invasion would be bloodless because the French would not resist. That depended on convincing Admiral Jean Darlan, Vichy's military commander, to join rather than resist the Allies when they came ashore. Before the invasion on 9 November, Eisenhower flew his deputy General Mark Clark and Free French General Henri Giraud to Algiers to meet Darlan and talk him into defecting with the French fleet, army and air force to the Allies. Darlan explained that he and all other officers had sworn an oath of allegiance to Vichy President Pétain, not to France. It would be dishonourable to break his oath or so Darlan's logic went.

A fatal flaw lay in the core of planning for Operation Torch. American General George Patton was assigned to land his corps at four ports in Morocco, with the nearest German troops a thousand miles away, while the corps of American General Lloyd Fredendall and British General Kenneth Anderson would bring their corps ashore at Oran and Algiers, respectively, with the German front line 350 miles from Anderson's corps. Countless lives and precious time would have been spared in the North African campaign had Patton and Anderson traded places. Although Patton's greatest military glories lay ahead, he had already earned a reputation for being America's most aggressive and ingenious commander.[102] He was trained as a cavalryman who switched to tanks in the First World War and saw them as armoured horses ideal for spearheading rapid offensives that encircled and destroyed the enemy. In contrast, Anderson was an infantryman who had fought in the trenches on the Western Front and retained that over-the-top mind-set of massed troop attacks supported by tanks.

The defending and invading forces were nearly equal, with 110,000 French facing 107,000 Allied soldiers, which included Patton's 33,000, Fredendall's 39,000 and Anderson's 35,000 troops. Conveying and protecting the invaders were 500 transports and 350 warships. On 8 November, when Allied troops hit the beaches, French resistance was sporadic but deadly, especially at Casablanca. The Allies suffered around 500 dead and 720 wounded and the French 1,300 dead and 1,900 wounded before Darlan agreed to a ceasefire on 10 November. Yet that was a relatively light cost to pay for a couple of thousand miles of North African coast along both the Mediterranean Sea and Atlantic Ocean and studded with half a dozen ports. Upon learning of the successful invasion, Churchill at once lauded that achievement and put it into perspective: 'Now this is not the end. It is not even the beginning of the end. But it is, perhaps, the end of the beginning.'[103]

In North Africa, the worst fighting lay ahead for Eisenhower's army. Hitler reacted to word of the Allied invasion by ordering the German army to overrun and secure Vichy France on 10 November. Although the Vichy regime's army acquiesced in the takeover, the navy committed a massive act of passive resistance that provided the Allies with enormous relief. Darlan kept his promise never to surrender the French fleet. As a German column raced toward Toulon on 27 November, the French captains scuttled their warships in the harbour.

Hitler ordered General Hans-Jurgen von Arnim, who commanded the Fifth Panzer Army in Tunisia, to retake French North Africa and sent 250,000 reinforcements to Tunisia to ensure victory. In the subsequent campaign, the Germans enjoyed three critical advantages over the Allies. Most of their troops were combat veterans; their Panzer IV tanks, with 75mm guns, were superior to the American Grants; and Arnim was as nimble at devising and asserting strategy as Anderson was plodding. Even the weather favoured the Germans. The winter rains turned the dirt roads into quagmires that slowed the Allied advance to a slog. The German advantage in generalship was the most critical. Arnim repelled two offensives by Anderson into Tunisia before both sides settled into defensive lines.

*   *   *

Meanwhile, the latest summit between Churchill and Roosevelt took place in Casablanca, Morocco from 14 to 24 January 1943.[104] The most critical issue was where next to attack. The Allies split in a vigorous and at times heated debate over this question. Churchill led the British charge for first invading Sicily and then crossing over to Italy's toe and fighting up the mountainous peninsula. After securing northern Italy, the Allies would veer north-east and battle their way over the Alps toward Vienna. Roosevelt and his staff called for seizing Sardinia and Corsica as forward bases for invading the French Riviera and advancing up the broad rolling Rhone valley, fine tank country. As German forces converged to attack those invaders, another Allied army would land in northern France, capture Paris and catch the Germans in a giant pincer movement. Once the Allied armies joined forces they would then surge into Germany with Berlin the ultimate objective.

The relative merits of these two plans should have been as obvious then as they are now. The Allies capitalized on their vast advantage in numbers of troops and tanks whenever they fought on flat or rolling terrain and they sacrificed that advantage whenever they tried to bludgeon their way through a mountainous region. And that was just the American plan's overwhelming military advantage. The political advantage of advancing toward Berlin, the Nazi empire's capital, rather than Vienna, also should have been just as evident then as it has been ever since. But the British minds were firmly shut to those military and political advantages and Churchill ultimately was responsible for that wilful ignorance. Worst of all, Churchill and his cohorts pressured the Americans to yield. The result was that the war in Europe lasted until 8 May 1945, when it might have ended sometime in 1944, thus sparing millions of dead and wounded and tens of billions of dollars' worth of destruction. As importantly, the American and British armies would have advanced at least as far as the Oder River and possibly as far as the Vistula, thus sparing tens of millions of people from the subsequent communist tyranny that would repress and exploit them.

The debate then shifted from the sublime to the ridiculous. An issue that was as irritating as it was potentially vital was just who should lead the Free French military and political movement. The two contenders, Generals Charles de Gaulle and Henri Giraud, despised each other. Both were war heroes, egoists and hypersensitive to any affront, although de Gaulle far surpassed Giraud in the latter two wretched characteristics. Giraud, at least, was as pleasant and cooperative as de Gaulle was petulant and petty. Indeed, de Gaulle's reaction to the Allied 'liberation' of fascist North Africa was, 'I hope the Vichy people throw them into the sea! You don't go into France like a pack of burglars!'[105] That alone might have been enough for the Allied leaders to cast him into political obscurity if not prison. Roosevelt certainly would have insisted upon that had Churchill not talked him into giving de Gaulle his latest reprieve. It took the combined statesmanship of Churchill and Roosevelt just to get de Gaulle to submit to meeting Giraud, shaking hands and then the four of them sitting down together for a news photo to display 'Allied unity' to the world.

The squabble to head the Free French movement would have been worse had not a third contender recently been eliminated. Admiral Jean Darlan was assassinated in Algiers on 24 December 1942. Security guards captured the assassin, one Ferdinand Bonnier de la Chappelle. The interrogation revealed that Chappelle was not an agent of the other rivals nor the Germans, but was a French royalist trained by Britain's SOE. The agency disclaimed any responsibility for the act. However, in yet another awkward twist, MI6 Chief Stewart Menzies just happened to be dining down the street during the murder.

During the news conference on the last day, Roosevelt asserted what became a key Allied political goal, nothing less than the 'unconditional surrender' of the Axis powers. That revelation annoyed Churchill. The prime minister and president had discussed but not decided what surrender terms to present Germany, Japan and Italy. Now Roosevelt had publicly committed them. Churchill soon got Roosevelt to limit unconditional surrender solely to Germany and Japan in hope that by omitting Italy it would provoke divisions there.[106] In a later speech before the House of Commons, he explained that 'unconditional surrender does not mean that the German people will be enslaved or destroyed … It does not mean that they are entitled to behave in a barbarous manner … If we are bound, we are bound by our own consciences to civilization.'[107]

* * *

Of course, the Allies had to win the war before they could impose terms. In North Africa Arnim blocked Anderson in western Tunisia while Montgomery had advanced only as far as Tripoli against Rommel who withdrew to the

Mareth Line's fortifications on the Libyan-Tunisian border. With nothing to fear from Montgomery, Rommel left a skeleton force in the Mareth Line and massed most of his army to join Arnim for an attack westward. The offensive began on 19 February 1942, with the goal of shattering Fredendall's army, capturing the key supply depot at Tebessa, then swinging north to Thala behind Anderson's lines. It was a brilliant plan that nearly succeeded. The panzer divisions of Rommel and Arnim smashed through the American lines at Gafsa and at Sidi Bouzid, respectively and converged at Kasserine Pass. By the time that Axis offensive finally ground to a halt with its fuel and munitions exhausted on 26 February, it had inflicted 10,000 casualties and knocked out 183 tanks at a cost of 2,000 casualties and 34 tanks. Churchill and Eisenhower reacted by agreeing to replace the inept Anderson and Fredendall with Generals Harold Alexander and George Patton, respectively. Patton never got a chance to square off against Rommel. Devastated by a cocktail of diseases including malaria, Rommel flew back to Germany to recuperate on 9 March, leaving Arnim in command of all Axis forces.

Montgomery gingerly advanced his Eighth Army to the Mareth Line in early March. After building up his forces, on 19 March he ordered a massive frontal assault that the Axis troops repelled with heavy losses. In late March, Eisenhower coordinated an offensive for the two Allied armies whereby Patton advanced toward the rear of the Mareth Line while Montgomery outflanked it westward. To escape destruction, the Germans and Italians withdrew into a hedgehog defence around Tunis where overwhelming Allied air and naval power prevented any escape. The 275,000 Axis troops, including 100,000 Germans, surrendered on 13 May 1943.

*   *   *

Bad news from the Atlantic darkened the good news from North Africa. German U-boats and bombers sank 721,700 tons of Allied shipping in November 1942, the worst losses to date and, it turned out, of the war. Especially disastrous that November was the sinking of Britain's aircraft carrier *Ark Royal* near Gibraltar and the battleship *Barham* near Tripoli. The losses were nearly as severe in December, capped when Italian frogmen attached limpet mines to the hulls of the battleships *Queen Elizabeth* and *Valiant*; the mines detonated and sank both warships in Alexandria's harbour. Two reasons caused the worsening losses. The Germans were building and deploying more submarines than the Allies could destroy. Atop that the

Germans had cracked Britain's merchant marine code and so knew when and where the convoys sailed.

Nonetheless, the Allies received a lucky break that eventually saved thousands of lives and hundreds of ships. On 9 May 1942, a British destroyer shot up a surfaced German submarine then a boarding party retrieved the Enigma machine and code book. It still took the Bletchley Park team until December 1942 to figure out how the machine and code worked together. Thereafter Allied naval and air forces systematically scoured the seas of German U-boats as Allied shipping losses steadily diminished, with an occasional month experiencing an upward spike. The tide had finally turned in the Battle of the Atlantic that had raged since September 1940.

* * *

The latest summit between Roosevelt and Churchill took place from 12 to 27 May 1943, partly at the White House and partly at what the president called Shangri-La, now Camp David, atop the Catoctin Mountains 60 miles north-west of Washington. The Americans scored a decisive victory by pressuring the British to accept 1 May 1944, as the date for the cross-Channel invasion, codenamed 'Overlord'. Churchill in return wanted a Briton to head Overlord. Here too Roosevelt and his staff prevailed, arguing by then American forces and supplies would surpass the British contribution so an American commander would be appropriate. Yet another critical issue was Britain's still rudimentary effort to develop an atomic bomb. The British had hoped to obtain the necessary uranium and heavy water from Canada only to discover that Ottawa had signed a contract to sell its annual supplies solely to Washington. That effectively ended Britain's programme. When Churchill raised that issue with Roosevelt on 25 May, the president immediately proposed that America and Britain combine their nuclear development efforts. Churchill agreed. They assigned a team to work out the details in an agreement to be signed at their next summit.[108]

Typically, Churchill flew not home but back to North Africa, first to Algiers and then Tunis to inform the commanders of the latest summit's decisions. In Algiers, he lauded Generals de Gaulle and Giraud for papering over their mutual loathing and agreeing to become co-presidents of the Committee of National Liberation for France. He returned to London via Lisbon and Plymouth on 5 June. He was nearly killed not once but twice during his latest overseas trip. His flying boat was struck by lightning over the Atlantic. On the same day that he flew the leg from Lisbon to Plymouth, a German aircraft shot down another flying boat on that route; among the passengers was the actor Leslie Howard. Churchill later recalled: 'It was a painful shock to me to learn what had happened to others in the inscrutable workings of Fate.'[109]

*   *   *

Eisenhower designated Generals Patton and Montgomery to command the American and British armies to invade Sicily. The campaign opened on 3 July 1943, with the week-long air bombing and naval shelling of enemy airfields, supply depots and troop positions. The landings began on 10 July, with Patton's Seventh Army landing between Ragasa and Licata and Montgomery's Eighth Army between Cape Passero and Syracuse. The strategies and tactics wielded by Patton and Montgomery could not have differed more, with stunningly different results. Defending Sicily were 200,000 Italian and 35,000 German troops, including the elite Hermann Göring division. On the invasion day each Allied army outflanked the enemy on the beaches before it with an airborne division but thereafter Patton kept curling his forces around the enemy while Montgomery bludgeoned his way forward. Twenty-five thousand more German troops moved to Sicily. Patton's troops captured Palermo and San Stefano on 22 July, then advanced eastward along Sicily's north coast. Whenever the Axis troops dug in, Patton outflanked them by sea and landed troops behind them. Patton beat Montgomery into Messina on 16 August. Tragically, Montgomery's dillydallying let 60,000 Germans and 70,000 Italians escape to the mainland. Nonetheless, the Allies did inflict 27,000 German and 147,000 Italian casualties at the cost of 8,781 American and 11,843 British casualties.[110]

The Allied capture of Sicily provoked Mussolini's fall from power. Starting with the 1940 invasion of Albania, the dictator had steadily squandered his popularity with his series of disastrous campaigns. He had alienated not just the hearts and minds of most Italians but even his own Fascist Party, including senior officials. On 24 July, with Mussolini himself chairing, the Fascist Grand Council began debating a no confidence measure and finally well past midnight voted nineteen to eight against him. Late on the afternoon of 25 July, King Victor Emmanuel III summoned Mussolini and politely informed him that Marshal Pietro Badoglio would replace him as prime minister. As heavily-armed guards surrounded Mussolini, the king explained that for his protection he would be sent to a safe place where he could recover his health, ruined after years of stress. That was the king's euphemistic way of saying that Mussolini was under arrest and would be imprisoned, albeit luxuriously, at the Campo Imperatore Hotel high in the central Apennine Mountains near Gran Sasso. Badoglio formed a cabinet.

After those decisive acts, the new government dithered. Badoglio sent assurances to Hitler that Italy remained committed to the alliance. Meanwhile he and his ministers secretly debated whether to withdraw from the tripartite Fascist pact into neutrality or outright surrender to the Allies. Hitler sent massive reinforcements into Italy and ordered Field Marshal Albert Kesselring to prepare to disarm the Italian army and take over the peninsula if Badoglio broke his promise. It was not until 6 August, nearly two weeks after the coup, that Badoglio had an Italian diplomat in Tunis covertly approach his British counterpart and ask for peace negotiations.

Churchill took a hard rather than conciliatory position. His first concern and demand was for the immediate repatriation of 70,000 British prisoners in Italy, fearing that they might be shipped to Germany. He also insisted that the bombing of Rome and other Italian cities would continue until a peace treaty was signed. Negotiations shifted to Lisbon where General Giuseppe Castellano represented Italy and General Bedell Smith, Eisenhower's aide, pressed him not just to surrender but to switch sides. Castellano explained the Badoglio government's desire to avoid not just a war against Germany but a civil war with those still faithful to Fascism and Mussolini.

* * *

As Italy's fate hung in the balance, Churchill and Roosevelt met at the president's Hyde Park estate overlooking the Hudson River 90 miles north of New York from 12 to 14 August. Amidst that bucolic setting and refined hospitality, Roosevelt pressed Churchill to commit himself completely on two critical issues. The president's top priority was not Italy, which he saw as a sideshow. Instead he insisted that the prime minister accept an American commander for the cross-Channel invasion that would take place on 1 May 1944. Churchill reluctantly agreed to both demands.

The formal summit with the Combined Chiefs of Staff took place at Quebec from 17 to 23 August. There Churchill and his cohort launched a counter-attack by insisting on qualifications for the invasion that they hoped would scuttle it. The attack would be against beaches defended by no more than three divisions, with no more than twelve other enemy divisions within striking distance and no more than fifteen other divisions able to reach the front within two months, along with overwhelming Allied air superiority and mobile artificial harbours to be towed to the landing site. Roosevelt accepted those qualifications. The Combined Chiefs of Staff then began planning Overlord, a process complicated by Roosevelt's delay for several months in naming its commander.

Churchill then pressured Roosevelt and his staff to follow up Sicily with invasions of first Italy, then Rhodes and other fortified Aegean islands and finally the Balkans. However, doing so would eliminate the planned invasion of northern France in 1944. He assured the Americans that his strategy of attacking Europe's 'soft underbelly' was superior to a cross-Channel invasion. He warned against opening a front in north-western Europe because 'we might be giving the enemy the opportunity to concentrate, by reason of his excellent roads and rail communications, an overwhelming force against us and to inflict on us a military disaster greater than that of Dunkirk. Such a disaster would result in the resuscitation of Hitler and the Nazi regime.'[111]

Churchill's strategy could not have been more misguided and self-defeating. His 'soft underbelly' belief defied the mountainous geography of Italy, the Aegean Islands and the Balkans along with the scores of German divisions deployed to defend those lands. In stark contrast, the northern European plain gave the Americans and British the chance to deploy masses of tanks and mechanized infantry that would surround and destroy the German armies.

Why would such a stupid strategy obsess such an intelligent man? When it came to strategy, Churchill let his churning, complex emotions trump his reason. For nearly half a year during the First World War, he had fought in the trenches in France and feared getting sucked into another horrendous stalemate there. He had been the scapegoat for the disastrous Dardanelles campaign and sought to redeem himself in the world's eyes by a victorious campaign in that region. His love for cloak and dagger operations also partly explains his fixation. Britain's SOE dropped scores of agents behind enemy lines across the Balkans and Aegean Islands to fight with partisans against German and Italian troops and their local collaborators. Indeed, Churchill's pre-war literary assistant, William Deakin, was now a SOE captain who had parachuted into Yugoslavia to work with communist guerrilla leader Josep Broz Tito.

Tragically, Roosevelt succumbed to Churchill's insistence on an Italian campaign, which would have disastrous results for the Allies. Fortunately he held firm against Churchill's Aegean and Balkan fantasies which would have been even worse catastrophes. That rejection deeply wounded Churchill and the pain lingered even a dozen years later as he wrote his memoirs:

I remained – and remain – in my heart unconvinced that the capture of Rhodes would not have fitted in. Nevertheless, with one of the sharpest pangs I suffered in the war I submitted. If one has to submit it is wasteful not to do so with the best grace possible. When so many grave issues were pending I could not risk any jar in my personal relations with the president.[112]

The two armies that subsequently landed in Italy should have invaded the French Rivera instead and driven up the Rhône valley, followed by a landing in Normandy that drove toward Paris. The southern army's left flank and the northern army's right flank could have united somewhere in Burgundy. Although the Americans and British then had only about half the troops and supplies available that they would have on 6 June 1944, the Germans also had proportionally far fewer troops in France. Most German forces in Italy would have had to remain there to crush the rebellion against them. An Allied division could have been deployed to defend the mountain passes between south-east France and north-west Italy, thus securing that flank. That strategy's only flaw would have resided in most of the generals tapped to implement it, plodders like Montgomery and Clark, alleviated by Patton's brilliance.

* * *

After nearly five weeks of Hamlet-like indecision, Badoglio's government secretly signed an agreement with Allied envoys near Syracuse, Sicily on 3 September for Italy's unconditional surrender. Yet, having done so, the king, his prime minister and the other ministers continued to procrastinate. The Allies then began on 7 September, an invasion of Italy that was as just as indecisive and misplaced as the Italian government had been. Montgomery sailed two divisions across the Messina Straits to the city of Reggio Calabria at Italy's toe. Sixteen German divisions then occupied parts of Italy, with half under Kesselring in the south and the other half under Rommel in the north. Germany's high command interpreted the Allied landing at Reggio as a diversion before a massive invasion much further up the west coast where there were only two good landing sites with long stretches of beach and flat country beyond, one embracing Ostia just 15 miles from Rome and the other embracing Livorno. Five Italian divisions faced three German divisions in the Rome area. Had an Allied invasion force landed at Ostia, the combined forces could have routed the Germans and liberated the capital.

But Eisenhower had ruled out Ostia along with Livorno because they were then beyond the range of fighter bombers for close tactical support of the troops. Instead, he opted for the closer site of Salerno, even though it was backed by a coastal mountain range.

The Germans believed the Badoglio government's pledges until it openly resisted. On 7 September, Kesselring was relieved to hear that Italy's navy would sail from its ports at Taranto and La Spezia to attack the Allied fleet. The following day, he learned that the Italians had surrendered to the Allies. He ordered his bomber crews to scramble and pursue but they sank only a battleship while scores of other warships capitulated at Malta.

American General Mark Clark's Fifth Army landed at Salerno on 8 September. Kesselring immediately ordered his divisions to counter-attack. The result was a stalemate as the Germans pinned down Clark's army on the beach. The following day Admiral Andrew Cunningham sailed his fleet unopposed in the port of Taranto and landed a division of Eighth Army British troops to take control. On 9 September, the king, prime minister, ministers and many of their family members flew to safety to Brindisi in Italy's heel. Three days later, German commandos rescued Mussolini from the Campo Imperatore Hotel in the central Apennine Mountains and brought him to Berlin. On 1 October, the Fifth and Eighth Armies captured Naples and Foggia, respectively. Then the Allied offensive ground to a halt not far north of that line across the peninsula for the next eight months.

The stalemate on the lower Italian peninsula triggered Churchill's 'Dardanelles Syndrome'. Rather than recognize that his 'soft underbelly strategy' was a chimera, he doubled down with the same obstinacy that he had following the catastrophic defeat that he presided over in the same region in the previous war. He renewed his appeals to Roosevelt for an Aegean campaign. The president sternly rebuffed his entreaties, arguing: 'If we get to the Aegean islands, I ask myself where do we go from there and vice versa where would the Germans go if ... they retain possession of the islands.'[113] In other words, an eastern Mediterranean campaign would literally and figuratively be a massive and tragic Allied dead end. Churchill had an answer. Those islands would be stepping stones to a Balkan campaign that would encourage Turkey to join the Allies. Roosevelt stood firm and refused to divert any troops from the cross-Channel campaign for Churchill's fantasies. Indeed, Roosevelt wanted the Fifth and Eighth Armies to shift to the defensive, dig in deeply and repel German attacks rather than squander massive amounts of troops in a fruitless attempt to advance further. Here Churchill got Roosevelt grudgingly to agree to continue pouring military power into the Italian quagmire rather than divert them to the eventual campaigns in northern and southern France. Even some of Churchill's generals questioned his 'soft underbelly' strategy, including Harold Alexander, the Italian Allied commander, who bitterly quipped: 'All roads lead to Rome and they are all paved with mines.' [114]

* * *

Churchill and Roosevelt scheduled a series of summits between themselves, with Chiang Kai-shek at Cairo, Egypt, with Joseph Stalin at Tehran, and then back to Cairo for a final meeting with Chiang.[115] During the Cairo summit from 22 to 27 November 1943, Roosevelt succeeded in elevating Chiang's status to one of the four Allied powers over Churchill's objections even though the Japanese had two million troops in China. Roosevelt then convinced Churchill to back a campaign to retake the Burma Road between India and China. On 27 November, the three leaders issued the Cairo Declaration that committed them to defeating Japan and restoring all of the territory that the Japanese had conquered from China and other Asian nations beginning in 1895.

Churchill rode an emotional roller coaster during the Tehran conference that lasted from 28 November 28 to 1 December 1943. Overall it was exhilarating:

> This was a memorable occasion in my life. On my right sat the President of the United States, on my left the master of Russia. Together we controlled a large preponderance of the naval and three-quarters of the air forces in the world and could direct armies of nearly twenty millions of men, engaged in the most terrible of wars that had yet occurred in human history.[116]

Having previously repeatedly rejected Churchill's proposed Balkan campaign, Roosevelt suddenly backed it during one of the sessions. Most likely he was just trying to stir the diplomatic pot to see what surfaced. If so, he succeeded. That notion provoked a strong response from Stalin who displayed far more strategic sense than Churchill or even Roosevelt. He dismissed a Balkan campaign and hopes of enticing Turkey into the alliance as a dead end. He called for halting the offensive in Italy and instead invading southern France to link up with the invasion of northern France. Stalin's decimation of his cherished visions deflated Churchill.

Then Stalin dismissed attempts by Churchill and Roosevelt to get him to endorse the Atlantic Charter's ideals of self-determination and democracy for all nations. Churchill pressed the tyrant to accept these principles: 'The three powers should guide the future of the world. I do not want to enforce any system on other nations. I ask for freedom and for the right of all nations to develop as they like. We three must remain friends in order to ensure happy homes in all the countries.'[117] Stalin embraced the last point but was noncommittal to the preceding ones. Churchill raised the fate of Eastern Europe. Stalin insisted that those countries were entirely at the disposal of the Red Army which had 'liberated' them from the Germans. Churchill asserted that the people of each country should govern themselves through free elections within a democratic government and constitution. They split heatedly over Poland, with Churchill backing the 'London Poles' who had set up a government in exile and Stalin the 'Lublin Poles' who were a puppet communist regime controlled by the Kremlin. Roosevelt should have backed Churchill but refused to do so for another year until after the November 1944 elections during which Americans of Eastern European ancestry voted.

Churchill ended up making some huge concessions. He agreed to a massive shift in Poland's frontiers westward 110 miles to the Oder River with the eastern frontier on the 'Curzon Line', 150 miles west of its then border. In 1919, British Foreign Minister George Curzon chose the line that became named for him after carefully mapping Polish and Russian speakers across the territory. Implementing those new borders would require migrations of millions of Poles and Germans. The Soviet Union would receive Lvov and Königsberg (now Kaliningrad). Stalin also pressured Churchill to accept the Soviet takeover of the three Baltic countries, Estonia, Latvia and Lithuania.

Stalin played hard to get but Churchill and Roosevelt were elated finally to extract his pledge to declare war on Japan within three months of Germany's defeat. Actually it was Stalin who was most exultant, although he feigned reluctance. He relished the Red Army's future opportunity to overrun Manchuria, Korea and Japan's northern half after the emperor's military was devastated by years of pounding by America's air force, while he helped Mao Zedong's Communist Party destroy Chiang's regime and conquer China.

Roosevelt believed that he could handle Stalin with the same political horse-trading and charm that he deployed in America. This worried Churchill who at one point urged him to deploy a stick with his carrots, writing: 'The Soviet machine is quite convinced it can get everything by bullying and I am sure it is a matter of some importance to show that this is not necessarily always true.'[118] Roosevelt did talk Stalin into endorsing what became the United Nations, which the 'Four Policemen', America, Russia, Britain and China, would dominate. Churchill listened intently for the answer to Stalin's question about who would lead the cross-Channel invasion. Roosevelt replied that he had not yet decided but would let all concerned know as soon as he had.

Through much of the conference Churchill was hurt that Roosevelt was cool to him and occasionally provoked Stalin to laughter by making jokes about him. He was not soothed by Roosevelt's insistence that he was only trying to reassure the dictator that the Americans and British were not 'ganging up' on him. But Roosevelt's teasing encouraged Stalin to inflict his own mockery, causing Churchill to believe that they were ganging up on him. Averill Harriman later noted that among Roosevelt's personality quirks was that he 'always enjoyed other people's discomfort'.[119] Stalin soothed Churchill's hurt feelings by the birthday bash he threw for him when he turned 69 years old on 30 November. The banquet lasted hours through one dish of delicacies after another and one toast after another far beyond midnight. Churchill later recalled that 'I went to bed tired but content, feeling sure that nothing but good had been done. It certainly was a happy birthday for me.'[120]

Nonetheless, Churchill later confided that:

I realized at Tehran for the first time, what a small nation we are. There I sat with the great Russian bear on one side of me, with paws outstretched and on the other side the great American buffalo and between the two sat the poor little English donkey who was the only one ... of the three who knew the right way home.[121]

Although knowledgeable people then and since have certainly questioned Churchill's strategic direction, the prime minister's assessment of Britain's relative power among the three was unassailable. He made the greatest impression on the tyrant and his henchmen when he stated: 'In wartime truth is so precious that she should always be attended by a bodyguard of lies.'[122]

Back in Cairo, Churchill and Roosevelt resumed their debate over strategy. On 4 December , Roosevelt informed Churchill that he had chosen Eisenhower to command Overlord and the Supreme Headquarters for the Allied Expeditionary Force (SHAEF). In compensation three Britons would serve in key posts, General Arthur Tedder as Eisenhower's deputy and Admiral Bertram Ramsay and General Bernard Montgomery as the invasion's respective naval and ground force commanders.

Churchill talked Roosevelt into ending their summit with a visit to the Sphinx:

> We motored there forthwith and examined this wonder of the world from every angle. Roosevelt and I gazed for some minutes in silence as the evening shadows fell. She told us nothing and maintained her inscrutable smile. There was no use waiting longer. On December 7 I bade farewell to my great friend when he flew off from the airfield beyond the Pyramids.[123]

* * *

Eisenhower arrived in London to take command on 21 January 1944, with SHAEF's first headquarters at Norfolk House on St. James Square.[124] He was a canny diplomat. In accepting Overlord's command he extracted pledges from Roosevelt and Churchill never to meddle in his decision-making. Roosevelt got Churchill to forego his tendency to interfere with his generals by setting the example with attitudes like this: 'I am not prepared to impose from this great distance any restrictions on military action by the responsible commanders that in their opinion might mitigate against the success of Overlord or cause more Allied casualties.'[125] Eisenhower pressed Roosevelt and Churchill for an invasion of southern France ideally before or, at the very least, simultaneously or shortly after Overlord. The president was enthusiastic about the idea but the prime minister insisted on a delay while available landing craft, troops, supplies and ships completed a different landing.

Among the recent concessions that Churchill wheedled from Roosevelt was an end run around the German line that plugged Allied forces far down the Italian peninsula. Two divisions would land at a seaside resort 40 miles south-west of Rome and north of the German line called Anzio. Eisenhower was upset when he learned details about the pending operation. He warned that the invasion force was too small to be effective and that nearby German forces would most likely pin the troops on the beach and quite possibly overrun them. But that was beyond his bailiwick and Churchill insisted that the Anzio landing go ahead as planned.

An American and a British division hit the beaches near Anzio on 22 January 1944 and there they dug in as their commander, General John

Lucas, could not figure out what to do next.[126] Kesselring certainly knew what to do. He ordered rear-echelon troops to dash to Anzio while he pulled reserves from his front line and rushed them north. The German attack nearly succeeded in breaking the Allied cordon. German artillery bombarded the troops, vehicles and supplies piling up along the shore, inflicting mass death and destruction. Meanwhile, General Clark launched his Fifth Army against Kesselring's line but the Germans repulsed that attack with heavy losses as easily as they had all others that preceded it. It would be another four months of blood-soaked stalemate before Clark's army finally broke through and joined forces with the beachhead, then entered an undefended Rome on 4 June. Churchill ruefully admitted: 'I had hoped that we were hurling a wild cat on to the shore, but all we got was an old stranded whale.'[127] Anzio was Churchill's second Dardanelles, although the entire Italian campaign could be considered that. However, this time he did not resign. Instead he won a vote of confidence by 425 to 23 on 31 March 1944. On 21 April, he asserted this defiance before the House of Commons: 'I have no intention of passing my years in explaining or withdrawing anything … still less in apologizing for it.'[128]

* * *

The Allied strategy to invade France skilfully combined hard and soft power.[129] Two armies, the American First and British Second, numbering 156,000 troops, would land at five separate beaches. They would be carried, landed or protected by 6,939 vessels, including 1,213 warships and 4,126 landing craft, manned by 196,000 sailors. The landings would be preceded by a massive bombardment by naval guns and aircraft, followed by the landing of three airborne divisions behind the enemy lines. As for soft power, the Allies used a variety of means to give the impression that the invasion would come across the Channel's narrowest part at Calais, including the creation of a make-believe army with inflatable tanks and trucks commanded by Patton.

In northern France, Field Marshal Gerd von Rundstedt led the army group that included the Seventh Army in the north-west and the Fifteenth in the north.[130] Rundstedt and his deputy Rommel differed over strategy. Rommel favoured deploying armoured divisions near the beaches to immediately destroy the invaders while Rundstedt insisted on keeping them in reserve so that they could mass and counter-attack in overwhelming numbers. Along the stretch of coast where the Allies would land were around 50,000 German troops either on the beaches or within a dozen miles.

The soldiers who invaded Normandy on 6 June 1944, paid a high price to win those beaches: 10,000 casualties although they inflicted nearly as many on the Germans. Over the following days and weeks ever more troops, tanks, trucks and supplies were disgorged on those beaches and sent to the slowly expanding front. Although Normandy is mostly flat or rolling it is chequerboarded by thousands of farms surrounded by thick, high hedgerows ideal to defend. From 6 June until 25 July, the battle for Normandy was a snail-paced, blood-soaked process of Allied troops taking one enclosed farm after another. Although the Americans captured Cherbourg on 30 June, the port was so littered with sunken ships and mines that it would take weeks to clear it.[131]

Nonetheless, the unceasing Allied build-up and push forward steadily ground down the German forces. Field Marshal Wilhelm Keitel, the German army's supreme commander under Hitler, telephoned Rundstedt and rather hysterically demanded what to do. 'Make peace you fools, what else can you do!' Rundstedt snapped then slammed down the phone.[132] Hitler replaced Rundstedt with Field Marshal Gunther von Kluge on 1 July. The German army soon lost an even more brilliant commander. An Allied fighter plane strafed Rommel's car on 17 July and he was hospitalized with severe head injuries.

The war in Europe might have ended ten months sooner had a briefcase been placed on the side of a massive table leg closest to Hitler's knees. On 20 July, Colonel Claus von Stauffenberg attended Hitler's staff meeting at his Wolf's Lair headquarters in East Prussia. Stauffenberg spearheaded a plot to assassinate Hitler. At some point during the conference he excused himself and walked out the door, leaving his briefcase with a timed bomb inside behind. The explosion destroyed the room and killed four officers but only lightly bruised Hitler. Stauffenberg was soon arrested and tortured into naming names. On the long list was Rommel who was allowed to commit suicide rather than undergo a public trial.[133]

That same month, the Allies received definitive intelligence that the Nazis were mass murdering the Jews and other inmates in their concentration camps. Churchill expressed his disgust that

> this is probably the greatest and most horrible crime ever committed in the whole history of the world … It is quite clear that all concerned in this crime who may fall into our hands, including the people who only obeyed orders by carrying out the butcheries, should be put to death after their association with the murders have been proved.[134]

Other than issue public warnings to that effect, the Allies could do nothing else. The death camps were all far behind German lines and nearly all would only be liberated during the war's last few weeks and days.

The Normandy breakout occurred during Operation Cobra from 25 to 31 July. General Lawton Collins, who commanded a First Army corps, punched through the enemy line around St. Lô, then Patton raced his Third Army through that hole and into the open countryside. Patton's subsequent campaign transformed the war in France from a crawling slaughterhouse into a freewheeling liberation. He fanned out his corps in different directions, one west to overrun Brittany and besiege its ports, another south to the Loire River and then eastward and the third east to outflank the Germans. During the next month he twice tried to convince Eisenhower to let him drive a corps north into the German rear and cut off their retreat, but both times was forbidden to enter territory assigned to Montgomery. The first came at what came to be called the Falaise Gap in eastern Normandy. Patton reached his assigned objective but Montgomery was stalled a dozen miles north. Over 100,000 Germans escaped through the gap that Patton could have sealed. The second came after Patton reached the Seine River and requested permission to drive north along its east side to cut off the Germans battling Montgomery westward. Once again Eisenhower put the feelings of Montgomery and his British colleagues ahead of a strategy that would have reaped a decisive victory and shortened the war.

Eisenhower even denied Patton the opportunity to liberate Paris, diplomatically letting French General Henri Leclerc lead his armoured division into the French capital on 25 August. General Charles de Gaulle entered Paris the next day and established a provisional French government. Churchill favoured recognizing de Gaulle's government, but could only do so jointly with Roosevelt. The president despised de Gaulle and hoped that someone more congenial and cooperative would govern France. But de Gaulle's command of Free French forces was unshakeable so Roosevelt finally grudgingly agreed to endorse him on 22 October 1944.

Meanwhile, Allied forces converged against the Germans in France from a completely different direction. The American Seventh Army, commanded by General Alexander Patch, began landing along a dozen miles of beach near St. Tropez on 15 August. Against light resistance, Patch's Seventh Army drove north up the Rhone valley and eventually linked up with Patton's Third Army on 15 September.[135]

Churchill had opposed that proposed Riviera landing, codenamed first Anvil then Dragoon, for several reasons, all misguided, which he asserted to Roosevelt in a series of cables. First, he pleaded that those divisions be sent to the Italian stalemate. Then he advocated landing on the Yugoslavian coast near Split and Sibenik to linku with Tito's partisans. If the first plan annoyed Roosevelt, the second angered him because it would have spread Allied forces ever thinner to yet another mountainous front where the Germans and their allies could murderously blunt any advance. He curtly explained: 'My interest and hopes centre on defeating the Germans in front of Eisenhower and driving on into Germany, rather than on limiting this action for the purpose of staging a full major effort in Italy.' Then came an even worse blow to Churchill's visions: 'We can ... immediately withdraw five divisions (three American and two French) from Italy for "Anvil". The remaining twenty-one divisions, plus numerous separate brigades, will certainly provide Alexander with adequate ground superiority.' Then came the coup de grace: 'I cannot agree to the employment of United States troops against Istria and into the Balkans.'[136]

To that, Churchill joined General Harold Alexander in protesting the diversion of divisions from his army group. Roosevelt stood his ground here as well. So Churchill, after grudgingly accepting a second invasion of France, once again displayed a severely misplaced sense of strategy. He called for the landing to take place near Bordeaux in southwestern France, about as far from the German border as it was possible to get in that country. For that very reason German forces were slender along that stretch of coast. So the invaders would face relatively light opposition but then a very long haul to catch up to Allied forces advancing across northern France. Fortunately superior strategic minds prevailed.

It was in Italy and the eastern Mediterranean, not France, that Churchill spent seventeen days after landing in Naples on 11 August. His key meeting was with Tito, who led Yugoslavia's communist guerrilla movement. The British air force had been dropping supplies and the SOE parachuting agents to the partisans. Churchill tried and failed to get Tito to support a popular front government behind Yugoslavian King Peter II who was then living with his entourage in Cairo.

* * *

Eisenhower faced his latest critical strategic decision in late August. Patton's Third Army spearheaded Bradley's Twelfth Army Group into eastern France while Montgomery's Twenty-First Army Group ground its way across northern France. The Allies suffered a worsening fuel shortage. The pipelines across the Channel to the Normandy beaches and the subsequent long lines of fuel trucks could not keep up with the demand and widening distance of the troops at the front. Although the Allies had captured the ports of Cherbourg, Le Havre, Boulogne and Calais, it was taking engineers weeks to remove the sunken vessels and mines that prevented supply and transport ships from anchoring there. The capture of Antwerp would eventually alleviate that fuel shortage. But for now fuel would have to be rationed among the armies and that would allow the Germans to rally and dig in.

Patton and Montgomery each pressured Eisenhower to give him the lion's share of the fuel, promising in return a decisive victory. Patton explained that with enough fuel his troops could breach the undermanned Siegfried Line in western Germany before massive reinforcements filled it and then drive into Germany's industrial Saarland. Montgomery presented a plan for three airborne divisions to be landed in a row along a road leading to the Rhine; as each captured key bridges along the way, Montgomery's main army would race up that road and split Germany's forces in two.

Once again, Eisenhower put placating the British before sound strategy. He dismissed those who argued that Montgomery should concentrate on capturing Antwerp and the surrounding Scheldt estuary while Patton sliced through the Siegfried Line. He then dismissed those who worried that an offensive along a single road was a disastrous idea. Montgomery subsequently proved that the sceptics were correct. The Germans rallied and defeated his offensive, inflicting 17,200 casualties, knocking out 88 tanks and shooting down 144 aircraft while suffering 13,300 casualties, 30 destroyed tanks and 159 downed aircraft. Far worse, the Germans would hold the Scheldt Estuary around Antwerp until 8 November and the Allies would not overrun the Siegfried Line until early 1945. Once again Montgomery failed to encircle and destroy a vulnerable German army. Over 60,000 Germans escaped from the Scheldt Estuary to fight and kill for many more months.[137] Nonetheless Churchill was grateful that Eisenhower bent over backwards to indulge the British generals: 'No man has never laboured more skilfully or intensively for the unification and goodwill of the great forces under his command than General Eisenhower. He has a genius for bringing all the Allies together and is proud to consider himself an Allied as well as a United States commander.'[138]

Among Montgomery's objectives was to overrun the clusters of V-1 cruise missile and V-2 rocket sites inland from the Channel and North Sea coasts. The V-1 flew around 400 miles per hour in a trajectory that arched to 3,000ft for 160 miles. On 13 June 1944, the first of 9,251 V-1s was fired that would kill 6,184 people and wound 17,981. The far more powerful V-2 rocket flew around 3,580 miles per hour 55 miles high to land 200 miles away. On 8 September 1944, the first of 1,112 V-2s was launched that would kill 2,754 people and wound 6,523. Pilots could shoot down the slower V-1s which made a buzzing sound but there was no defence against the supersonic V-2s. The Germans justified their rocket campaign as retaliation for the carpet bombing of German cities by the British and American air forces which killed hundreds of thousands of people and wounded many times that number.[139]

* * *

Despite or perhaps because of the dazzling advances by Allied forces across France, Churchill remained obsessed with the Balkans. There his worst worry was the fate of Greece, where a three-way war raged among communist Greeks, non-communist Greeks and the Germans and their Greek puppet government.[140] Churchill struggled to ensure that the non-communists defeated both the Nazis and the Communists. As in other countries, the Communist Party (KKE) led the resistance there because it was the best led organized and motivated with parallel political and military organizations called the National Liberation Front (ELAM) and the Greek People's Army (ELAS), respectively, that infiltrated and struggled to win the hearts and minds of people across the country. Non-communists were split among royalists and republicans who turned their guns against each other nearly as much as against the communists. Churchill reviled the communists and the Byzantine maze of Greek politics: 'The Greeks rival the Jews in being the most politically minded race in the world. No matter how forlorn their circumstances or how grave the peril to their country, they are always divided into many parties, with many leaders who fight among themselves with desperate vigour.'[141]

Upon learning that the Germans had evacuated southern Greece, Churchill ordered British troops to land by ship or parachute and secure that region in early October. General Ronald Scobie and 5,000 British troops occupied Athens. That proved to be the easy part. The conflict began shortly after Prime Minister Georgios Papandreou and his entourage from the Greek government-in-exile flew from Cairo to Athens on 16 October. Brawls between communist and non-communists turned deadly until a civil war ensured. Scobie made full use of these instructions from Churchill:

You are responsible for maintaining order in Athens and for neutralising or destroying all ELAM-ELAS bands approaching the city ... Do not ... hesitate to act as if you were in a conquered city where a local rebellion is in progress ... We have to hold and dominate Athens. It would be a great thing for you to succeed in this without bloodshed if possible, but also with bloodshed if necessary.[142]

In the House of Commons the Opposition criticized Churchill's heavy-handed tactics in restoring order to Greece. On 8 December, Churchill vigorously defended his Greek policy, adamantly rejecting the charge that the British were repressing democratic forces there. Instead, they were trying to repress the communist guerrillas that threatened the development of democracy in Greece. He urged his colleagues to make these distinctions:

One must have some respect for democracy and not use the word too lightly. The last thing which resembles democracy is mob law, with bands of gangsters, armed with deadly weapons ... endeavouring to introduce a totalitarian regime with an iron hand ... Democracy is not based on violence or terrorism, but on reason, on fair play, on freedom, on respecting the rights of other people ... I trust the people, the mass of people in almost any country, but I like to make sure that it is the people and not a gang of bandits who rule.[143]

Churchill then called for a vote of confidence, which he won easily by 281 to 32 on 9 December 1944.

The fighting in Athens and beyond worsened. Churchill flew to Athens on 25 December. For security he established his headquarters aboard the cruiser HMS *Ajax* in Piraeus, Athens' port. Firing between British troops and communist guerrillas echoed across the bay. A communist gun opened fire on the *Ajax* and shells straddled the warship with waterspouts until British warplanes knocked it out. Churchill's sleep was disturbed during his nights aboard the *Ajax* as the crew periodically dropped depth charges to deter any frogmen with mines. Danger followed him ashore. On 27 December, as he was visiting the British embassy a distant communist machine gun opened fire and chewed the wall 30ft above his head and a ricochet killed a woman in the street. Between dodging shells and bullets he managed to conduct several intense rounds of diplomatic negotiations.

Churchill invited non-communist and communist representatives to a peace conference presided over by Archbishop Damaskinos Papandreou at the Hotel Grande Bretagne in Athens. He opened the first session by castigating all parties for fighting with each other rather than against the Germans. He finally browbeat all sides into forming a coalition government with republicans holding a slight majority. Churchill flew back to London on 29 December. That evening he met with exiled King George II to get his approval of Archbishop Damaskinos to act as his regent while he remained in exile. The angry king finally conceded at four o'clock the following morning. Churchill got word that the communists had broken the deal and now wanted a majority of ministries in the government. As punishment for their perfidy, Churchill authorized General Nikolaos Plastiras to replace Papandreou as prime minister and exclude all communists from his Cabinet on 3 January 1945. The civil war resumed and the fighting would persist for years.

*   *   *

Churchill and Roosevelt clashed over a critical element of strategy in the Far East. Roosevelt wanted to reopen the Burma Road that ran from India across north Burma to China. Keeping Chiang Kai-shek and his army in the fight tied down two million or so Japanese troops and drained enormous resources that Tokyo could have deployed elsewhere. China was to the war against Japan in Asia as Russia was to the war against Germany in Europe, a cancer on the enemy's military and economic power. Churchill at once paid lip service to and dismissed the China front's importance:

> Certainly we favoured keeping China in the war and operating air forces from her territory. But ... I disliked intensely the prospect of a large-scale campaign in Northern Burma ... We of course wanted to recapture Burma but we did not want to do it by land advances from slender communications and across the most forbidding fighting country imaginable ... I wished ... to contain the Japanese in Burma.[144]

Although Churchill was a master of irony, it evaded him in his discussion of Burma. The Americans opposed his beloved 'soft underbelly' Italian and Balkan strategy with the same argument he made against operations in Burma. The key difference was that securing the Burma Road was crucial to keeping China in the war. The sensible Allied strategy was to secure that road and then dig in and let the Japanese batter themselves to death trying to retake it. That should have been the strategy in Italy as well after Roosevelt reluctantly agreed to Churchill's insistence on invading the foot of the peninsula. Instead the Allies squandered countless lives and supplies trying to grind their way up that mountainous terrain against the Germans dug in with seas protecting each flank. To compound the irony, Churchill favoured a campaign to retake all of Burma after the Allies reopened the Burma Road.

* * *

Meanwhile Stalin revealed his intentions for Poland and his genocidal determination to achieve them during the Warsaw uprising. On 1 August 1944, 40,000 fighters led by General Tadeusz Komorowski rebelled against Germany's occupying army. The London Polish government had authorized the uprising in order to liberate Warsaw in conjunction with the Red Army's arrival just across the Vistula River. Stalin exulted as two enemies decimated each other. For two months, the Red Army awaited the end of gunfire in Warsaw. Komorowski surrendered with a remnant of his men on 2 October. By that time, as many as 200,000 of Warsaw's inhabitants had died and another 700,000 had fled the city, while the Germans suffered around 30,000 casualties and over 300 destroyed tanks.[145]

During that time Stalin rejected pleas by Churchill and Roosevelt not only to break through to the Poles with his Red Army but even to let American and British planes land behind Soviet lines after dropping weapons and supplies to the beleaguered fighters, effectively preventing those operations. Churchill and Roosevelt sent their first urgent message on 20 August:

> We are thinking of world opinion if the anti-Nazis in Warsaw are abandoned. We believe that all three of us should do the utmost to save as many of the patriots there as possible. We hope that you will drop immediate supplies and munitions to the patriotic Poles in Warsaw or will you agree to help our planes in doing it very quickly?

Stalin's reply was chilling: 'Sooner or later the truth about the group of criminals who have embarked on the Warsaw advance in order to seize power will become known to everyone.' He then claimed that German resistance prevented the Red Army from liberating Warsaw from both the Nazis and 'the criminals'.[146]

* * *

Feelings of triumph exceeded anxiety during the Quebec Conference from 12 to 16 September 1944. With Allied armies in France racing toward the Rhine, the key issue now was Germany's fate after its eventual defeat. American Treasury Secretary Henry Morgenthau presented a plan to break up Germany into small states stripped of industry and relying on agriculture to survive. Churchill was stunned by the plan's severity, remarking: 'I'm all for disarming Germany, but we ought not to prevent her living decently … You cannot indict a whole nation. At any rate, what is to be done ought to be done quickly. Kill the criminals, but don't carry on the business for years.'[147] Although Roosevelt was just as disturbed, both leaders grimly approved Morgenthau's plan. As for German territory, they had already decided to give Poland its current lands in East Prussia and lands west to the Oder River. At Quebec, they agreed to split Germany into three occupation zones, with the Soviets in the north-east, the British in the north-west and the Americans in the south. Although that seemed like a sensible and fair division at the time, London and Washington would deeply regret that decision along with deindustrialization. The Soviets would stymie the subsequent American and British attempts to mitigate those decisions.[148]

Anxious for the fate of Eastern Europe, on 9 October Churchill flew to Moscow. For the next ten days, he wielded all his diplomatic skills to cut a grand deal. His effort's keystone was to convince Stalin to accept a 50–50 power sharing agreement between the London and Lublin Poles. Accompanying Churchill was Stanislaw Mikolajczyk, the leader of the London Poles, and several key associates. The London Poles insisted on two things, an equal number of seats in any governing council and Lvov included in a future Poland. They got neither. The tyrant adamantly rejected the notion, asserting that the Lublin Poles would have nothing less than 80 per cent of the governing council seats and veto power over any proposed representatives from the other parties, including the London Poles. Stalin did promise a 'free and democratic Poland', but of course meant the Orwellian communist definition of those words. All along he repeatedly insisted to Churchill, Roosevelt and their underlings that: 'The problem of Poland is inseparable from the security of the Soviet Union.'[149]

In desperation, Churchill met alone with Stalin and jotted down proportions of differing Western and Soviet influence for the other east European countries, with Russia enjoying 90 per cent in Romania and 75 per cent in Bulgaria, Britain 90 per cent of Greece and each equal shares of Hungary and Yugoslavia. This greatly amused the usually humourless Stalin. How could Churchill be so naïve as to believe the Red Army would not do everything possible to bring communist parties to power in all these countries? Containing his mirth, he drew a big tick with a blue leaded pencil across the paper, smiled and slid it back. Churchill experienced a spasm of relief followed by a new concern: 'Might it not be thought rather cynical if it seemed we had disposed of these issues, so fateful to millions of people, in such an offhand manner? Let us burn the paper.' Stalin insisted that Churchill keep the document.[150]

* * *

Hitler made a last desperate attempt to win the war in the West.[151] On 16 December 1944, he launched 406,000 troops, 1,214 tanks and 4,229 aircraft against a thin screen of American troops in the Ardennes. The objective was to punch through the forest and then most of Belgium to capture Antwerp, the key Allied supply centre. Eisenhower swiftly summoned Montgomery, Bradley and their respective army commanders to coordinate a counter-attack. Within forty-eight hours, Patton shifted most of his army northward and began caving in the German left flank, liberating the besieged strategic town of Bastogne on 27 December. Meanwhile, Hodges' First Army typically advanced slower from the north. By early January 1945, the Americans had eliminated the 'bulge' and inflicted a devastating defeat on the Germans who suffered 81,834 casualties and the destruction of 324 tanks and 320 aircraft. The Americans also endured heavy losses with 76,890 casualties, 733 destroyed tanks and 647 downed aircraft.[152] But America's losses were replaceable; Germany's were not.

The Battle of the Bulge was the largest and bloodiest American battle of the Second World War and the most decisive in Western Europe after the Normandy invasion. Had Hitler avoided that battle and instead kept on the defensive, retreating slowly toward the Rhine and then massed behind it, the war in the West would have lasted months longer, inflicted hundreds of thousands more casualties and tens of billions of dollars more expense on the Western Allies and let the Soviets advance much further west, perhaps even to the Rhine itself.

Chapter 7

The Cold Warrior

'I therefore consider that from a political standpoint we should march as far east into Germany as possible and that should Berlin be in our grasp we should certainly take it.'

'From Stettin in the Baltic to Trieste in in the Adriatic, an iron curtain has descended across the Continent.'

'It may well be that we shall, by a process of sublime irony, have reached a stage where safety will be the sturdy shield of terror and survival the twin brother of annihilation.'

'We must build a kind of United States of Europe.'

The fate of Europe and much of the rest of the world was determined by the second and final summit between Churchill, Roosevelt and Stalin that took place from 4 to 11 February 1945 at Yalta in the Crimea.[1] Stalin enjoyed critical advantages over the Western leaders. Most importantly Roosevelt and Churchill failed to present a united front on the issues to the tyrant. Atop that Roosevelt was dying and merely a shadow of his former intellect, will and confidence. The conference site itself was on Soviet turf. At least the American and British delegations had nothing to complain about where they stayed and what they ate. Roosevelt and his entourage were ensconced in the Livadia Palace, Tsar Nicholas II's summer home in Yalta, while Churchill's party got the Vorontsov Palace in the countryside about a twenty-minute drive away. Stalin wanted to keep Roosevelt and Churchill as far from each other as was reasonably possible, with himself in the Yusupov Palace between them. He did ensure that each delegation enjoyed delicious dinners and wines.

For eight days, the delegations argued vociferously during the afternoons and dined mostly cordially together during the evenings. Stalin presented his list of 'understandings'. Germany and Austria would be divided into occupation zones assigned to each of the three powers, the Soviet Union, United States and Britain. Germany would pay $20 billion in reparations to the Soviet Union. Poland would be shifted westward with its eastern border the Curzon Line and western border the Oder River; Lvov would go to the Soviet Union. The Lublin Poles would govern Poland. All Russian prisoners in German camps would be returned to the Soviet Union.

Roosevelt and Churchill accepted every understanding except who would govern Poland, insisting that the London Poles be represented in a future democratic government elected freely by the Polish people. To that, Stalin grunted an acceptance that he had no intention of keeping. Roosevelt insisted that 'the elections must be above criticism ... I want some kind of assurance to give to the world and I don't want anyone to be able to question their purity. It is a matter of good politics rather than principle.'[2] Stalin assured Roosevelt that he would be happy to provide the world all the assurances that the president desired.

As for the occupation zones, Stalin gleefully accepted the divisions that Churchill and Roosevelt had agreed upon at Quebec in September 1944. Churchill swelled Stalin's sense of triumph when he called for giving France a zone mostly along its own frontier and taken from the British and American zones. Stalin happily agreed, not explaining the obvious geopolitical reality that the more divided western Germany was, the more secure the Soviet grip would be over its share. They discussed the United Nations and agreed that at first only countries that fought the Axis powers could be members. Churchill asked that Turkey be included. Roosevelt and Stalin agreed. That generosity prompted the Turkish government to declare war against Germany on 23 February, although no Turkish troops would do any fighting. Churchill agreed to repatriate all Russian prisoners of war even if they sought freedom in the west. Stalin would imprison the several million returnees and murder 10,000 of them due to his paranoia that anti-communist agents were among them.

Any 'concessions' that Stalin made would actually expand Soviet and communist power. He pledged 'free elections' in all the countries that the Red Army had overrun. He would even let American and British officials observe the Polish elections, an empty gesture since by the time they took place the communists had purged all but a token number of opposition parties and candidates. He reiterated his promise to declare war against Japan within three months of victory over Germany. His only explicit demand for territory in the Far East was the return of Sakhalin Island's southern half and the Kurile Islands that Tokyo had taken following the Russo-Japanese

War in 1905. He would recognize Chiang Kai-shek as China's ruler. Yet, in promising not to aid Mao Zedong's Communist movement against Chiang's regime, he would receive territory and special rights in Manchuria, China's resource-rich north-eastern region. He would, of course, break his promise and covertly aid the communists to undermine and destroy Chiang's regime.

Churchill recalled that at one point, Stalin expressed his trepidation for the future, anticipating that 'though the Three Powers were Allies today and none of them would commit any of aggression, in ten years or less the three leaders would disappear and a new generation would come into power which had not experienced the war and would forget what we had gone through'.[3] Actually that alliance would be dead within two years, with President Harry Truman acknowledging a Cold War before a joint session of Congress on 12 March 1947.[4]

The Big Three issued their Declaration on Liberated Europe, also known as the Yalta Declaration, on 12 February 1945. It was a rewording of the Atlantic Charter promising self-determination, democracy, prosperity and peace to all peoples that Roosevelt sincerely, Churchill sceptically and Stalin cynically pledged. Churchill later explained his concessions at Yalta as: 'It was the best I could get.'[5]

That was certainly true. Several million Red Army boots on the ground across Eastern Europe and deep into Germany and Austria determined the fate of those nations. Yet the horrific fate of those captive peoples gnawed at Churchill's conscience. On 27 March, he issued this plea to Roosevelt: 'Surely we must not be manoeuvred into becoming parties to imposing on Poland and on much more of Eastern Europe, the Russian version of democracy? ... There seems to be only one possible alternative to confessing our total failure. That is to stand by our interpretation of the Yalta declaration.'[6] Roosevelt agreed and on 1 April cabled Stalin this warning: 'I must make it plain that any solution which would result in a thinly disguised continuance of the present Warsaw regime would be unacceptable and would cause the people of the United States to regard the Yalta agreement as having failed.'[7]

Stalin quickly found an accusation to hurl against Roosevelt and Churchill to distract them from the brutal communist takeover of Eastern Europe. Kesselring, the Italian front's commander, had General Karl Wolff fly to Berne to meet Allen Dulles, the OSS station chief, and ask for surrender terms for the forces under his command. Stalin accused Roosevelt and Churchill of trying to negotiate a separate peace with the Germans because a Soviet representative was not present at the talks. The accusation, of course, was absurd. Each Allied army had negotiated numerous surrenders of enemy troops without other Allied representatives present. But this was the only card Stalin had and he was playing it for all it was worth.

* * *

By 1 March 1945, the Western Allies had reached the Rhine while the Soviets were on the Oder River. Berlin was at least 200 miles from the closest Western Allied troops and merely 50 miles from the closest Soviet troops. On 7 March, troops of Hodges' US First Army captured at Remagen the last standing bridge across the Rhine. Within weeks, all the Allied armies landed troops on the east bank, secured bridgeheads and massed forces and supplies for breakouts.

Churchill visited the front in early March, first dropping in at Eisenhower's headquarters at Rheims, France, then Montgomery's headquarters at Eindhoven, the Netherlands and finally with the American Ninth Army's commander, General William Simpson and his staff on the Rhine River. Typically Churchill insisted on running risks and came under fire. Chief of Staff Alan Brooke was with Churchill and recalled the amusing scene when Simpson tried to restrain Churchill with these diplomatic but pointed words: 'Prime Minister, there are snipers in front of you, they are shelling both sides of the bridge and now they have started shelling the road behind you. I cannot accept responsibility for your being here and must ask you to come away.' Churchill did not want to go and wrapped his arms around one of the bridge's iron girders: 'The look on Winston's face was just like that of a small boy being called away from his sandcastles on the beach by his nurse!'[8]

The Allied armies launched their breakout in late March. Eisenhower's strategy had two key elements, one accepted, the other controversial then and ever more so with time. First, the broad front strategy would prevail east of the Rhine just as it had west of the Rhine. That sensible idea was to make the most of the overwhelming Allied advantage in manpower, tanks and supplies by advancing everywhere at once, thus stretching the Germans to breaking point. Reacting to shifting tactical circumstances, local commanders repeatedly massed their forces and punched through critical parts of that thinning enemy line to encircle and destroy the forces before them. But Eisenhower also made the critical decision not to race the armies east as swiftly as possible to liberate as many people as possible from likely enslavement under Soviet rule. In doing so, he did not consult with the Combined Chiefs of Staff let alone Roosevelt or Churchill. But on

29 March, he did send word to Stalin of his intentions, thus spurring the tyrant to push the Red Army westward. On 30 March, the Combined Chiefs protested Eisenhower's decision but did not overrule it. Churchill worried that: 'The idea of neglecting Berlin and leaving it to the Russians to take at a later stage does not appear to me correct ... The fall of Berlin might cause nearly all Germans to despair.'[9] On 2 April, he wrote Eisenhower that 'I deem it highly important that we should shake hands with the Russians as far to the East as possible'.[10]

Eisenhower justified this as a purely military decision but of course it was far more vital than that. He claimed that he wanted to cut off and destroy the Alpine German national redoubt that Radio Berlin had boasted of, only to discover that it was a propaganda myth after Allied troops vainly combed the region. But even had that redoubt existed, the Seventh Army advancing in southern Bavaria would have been enough to find and destroy it. Just why Eisenhower committed such a puzzling and ultimately tragic act has been debated ever since. His only defence was that he was simply adhering to the occupation zones drawn by Churchill, Roosevelt and Stalin at Yalta. Why advance further against a routed enemy if one would have to eventually withdraw to a preset line?[11]

The military counterargument is that a routed enemy can still rally, turn and fight. The political counterargument is that lines on maps can and should at times be redrawn according to one's national interests, with the bottom line that one should take as much as one can get away with. That certainly was Stalin's view. Unfortunately Eisenhower was not privy to these words that Stalin shared with Yugoslavian communist leader Milovan Djilas: 'This war is not as in the past; whoever occupies a territory but also imposes on it his own social system. Everyone imposes his own system as far as his army can reach. It cannot be otherwise ... If now there is not a communist government in Paris, it is because Russia has no army which can reach to Paris in 1945.'[12]

Eisenhower's shift in strategy upset Churchill. On 1 April, Churchill sent Roosevelt a plea to restore the strategy of advancing eastward across the broad front with capturing Berlin the ultimate goal:

Berlin remains of high strategic importance. Nothing will exert a psychological effect of despair upon all German forces of resistance equal to the fall of Berlin ... There is another aspect which it is proper for you and me to consider. The Russian armies will no doubt overrun all Austria and enter Vienna. If they also take Berlin will not their impression that they have been the overwhelming contributor to our common victory be unduly imprinted in their minds and may this not lead them into a mood which will raise grave and formidable difficulties in the future? I therefore consider that from a political standpoint we should march as far east into Germany as possible and that should Berlin be in our grasp we should certainly take it.[13]

Tragically, Churchill reached this conclusion too late to implement it. Years before, he and Roosevelt should have committed themselves to advancing east as far as possible, ideally overrunning Germany west of the Oder River and all of Austria. They should not have carved Germany into occupation zones at Quebec in October 1944, but instead should have let the strategies of the respective armies determine the eventual frontiers. As American and British troops advancing eastward neared Red Army troops advancing westward, their generals could have coordinated final attacks against any German troops caught between them. Churchill was ultimately responsible for the failure of the American and British armies to advance beyond central Germany. His ability to browbeat Roosevelt and his military staff into following his 'soft underbelly' strategy prolonged the war by months and possibly a year or more and led to the Red Army's conquest of tens of millions of people. American and British troops would likely have overrun Germany and Austria by late 1944 had, in September 1943, the two armies that landed in Italy instead landed in southern France.

* * *

A massive cerebral haemorrhage killed Roosevelt at his home at the spa of Warm Springs, Georgia on 12 April 1945. Upon learning of his death, Churchill 'felt as if I had been struck a physical blow. My relations with this shining personality had played so large a part in the long, terrible years we had worked together. Now they had come to an end and I was overwhelmed by a sense of deep and irreparable loss.'[14] In a speech before Parliament, he reminded his colleagues that 'in Franklin Roosevelt there died the greatest American friend we have ever known and the great champion of freedom who has ever brought help and comfort from the new world to the old'.[15] He repressed the impulse to fly over for the funeral and meet the new president, Harry Truman. Swelling opposition in the House of Commons forced him to stay in London.

Meanwhile, Stalin ordered an offensive across the Oder River, scheduled for 1 May, to begin a month earlier on 1 April. The Soviets captured Vienna on 13 April, reached the outskirts of Berlin on 21 April and entirely surrounded the city four days later. American and Russian troops met at Torgau on the Elbe River on 25 April. Hitler's number one and number two designated successors, Hermann Göring and Heinrich Himmler, wangled his permission to flee Berlin while they could in return for renouncing any claim to power. Hitler then designated Admiral Karl Dönitz his successor. Hitler shot himself in his Berlin bunker on 29 April. The Third Reich would last another nine days under Dönitz.

The day Hitler that killed himself, Churchill received word that Himmler wanted to negotiate the end of the war. Churchill called Truman to discuss just how to respond to Himmler's initiative. They agreed to ignore it and instead accept surrender only from the formal German government. This was the first time the two leaders ever spoke to each other. Churchill's thinking about Hitler and the war's pending end led him to ponder another evil tyrant and Europe's fate. Later that critical day, he sent Stalin this prophetic warning:

> There is not much comfort in looking at a future where you and the countries you dominate, plus the communist Parties in many other States, are all drawn up on one side and those who rally to the English-speaking nations and their associates or Dominions are on the other. It is quite obvious that their quarrel would tear the world to pieces and that all of us leading men on either side who had anything to do with that would be shamed before history.[16]

Like Churchill, Patton understood that the Western Allies would soon destroy one totalitarian regime only to face another. After receiving Eisenhower's strategic restraining order, he replied: 'Ike, I don't see how you figure that out. We had better take Berlin and quick – and on to the Oder!' When Eisenhower asked who would want it, Patton quipped: 'I think history will answer that question for you.'[17] Patton got word that the Czechs had revolted against the Germans in Prague on 5 May. He informed Eisenhower that he was only 60 miles from Prague and his tanks could sweep away any German resistance on that road in day or two and liberate the city. Eisenhower ordered Patton to stop his army in its tracks. The Soviets entered Prague on 9 May three days after the Czechs forced the Germans to capitulate.

Germany's unconditional surrender came at Eisenhower's headquarters at Rheims on 7 May 1945, with the signatures of Generals Alfred Jodl and Bedell Smith on the document. All fighting on the Western Front would end at midnight that night. Jodl flew to Berlin to sign a similar document with the Soviets on 9 May.

Eisenhower wanted to withdraw immediately American and British troops to the prearranged occupation zones. Churchill argued that 'the Allies not ought to retreat from their present positions to the occupation line until we are satisfied about Poland and also about the temporary character of the Russian occupation of Germany and the conditions to be established in the Russianised or Russian-controlled countries in the Danube valley, particularly in Austria and Czechoslovakia and the Balkans'. The stakes could not have been higher: 'All these matters can only be settled before the United States armies in Europe are weakened. If they are not settled before the United States armies withdraw from Europe and the Western world folds up its war machines there are no prospects of a satisfactory solution and very little of preventing a third world war.'[18]

*   *   *

Churchill spoke to the British people over the BBC on 13 May 1945, but his message was one of caution rather than elation:

> I wish I could tell you tonight that all our toils and troubles were over. Then indeed I could end my five years' service happily … I told you hard things at the beginning of these last five years; you did not shrink and I should be unworthy of your confidence and generosity if I did not still cry: Forward, unflinching, unswerving, indomitable, till the whole task is done and the whole world is safe and clean.

The daunting challenges included destroying the Japanese empire, rebuilding the war-devastated countries and ensuring that democracy prevailed. It would indeed be ironic 'if totalitarian or police governments were to take the place of the German invaders'. As for Britain and America;

> We seek nothing for ourselves. But we must make sure that those causes which we fought for find recognition at the peace table … and above all we must labour to ensure that the World Organization which the

United Nations are creating … does not become an idle name, does not become a shield for the strong and a mockery for the weak.[19]

This was not the message that most Britons wanted to hear. They had suffered and sacrificed terribly during five years of incessant war and now, with Hitler's regime destroyed, they were numb to what happened on the Continent let alone the far side of the world. In all, the United Kingdom endured the deaths of 383,700 combatants and 67,200 civilians or 450,900 altogether which was 0.94 per cent of 47,760,000 people. In comparison, the United States suffered the deaths of 407,300 combatants and 12,100 civilians or 419,400 altogether which was 0.32 per cent of 131,028,000 people. Those losses compared to the British Dominion deaths, with India's 87,000, Canada's 43,600, Australia's 40,400, South Africa's 11,900 and New Zealand's 11,700; other Allied deaths, with the Soviet Union's 27,000,000, China's 20,000,000 and France's 600,000; the Axis dead, with Germany's 7,400,000, Japan's 3,238,000 and Italy's 472,407; and total global deaths of 85,000,000.[20]

A majority of Britons had rallied around a very different message from a different party. William Beveridge was a renowned economic theorist, having served as director of the London School of Economics, director of University College at Oxford and the assistant Labour secretary. On 10 June 1941, the Cabinet approved the creation of an inter-ministry committee on socioeconomic policy and assigned Beveridge to chair it. The subsequent Beveridge Report or Social Insurance and Allied Service, released on 2 December 1942, called for a four-year plan to implement an array of reforms including a national health system and expanded welfare and retirement payments. To general astonishment, the Beveridge Report became a bestseller with over 70,000 copies sold within a week or so. Clement Attlee's Labour Party embraced the Beveridge Report as the core of its legislative agenda for the post-war years. Labour did not just promise to enrich middle and lower class Britons with an array of economic benefits, they condemned the Conservatives for their misguided economic policies during the 1920s and 1930s that contributed to the Great Depression and their appeasement policies of the 1930s that had encouraged the aggression of Japan, Italy and Germany. Thus did they clearly explain to most Britons why they should vote for Labour and against the Tories.[21]

Churchill asked Atlee to delay an election until after Japan was defeated. Atlee would do so only if Churchill pledged to support an array of social security, housing and education reforms. Churchill agreed. That was good enough for Atlee but not the Labour Party's radicals who, during the party conference at Blackpool from 21 to 25 May, demanded an immediate election. That forced Atlee to inform Churchill that the Labour Party would withdraw from the National Government. Churchill promptly asked for an audience with George VI at Buckingham Palace on 23 May, during which he tendered his resignation. The king asked him to carry on until Parliament was dissolved on 15 June, then head a caretaker Cabinet until the next Parliament convened. The election would take place on 5 July. With those announcements each party had five weeks of campaigning to woo as many voters as possible.

As the Conservative Party leader, Churchill's campaign involved 'strenuous motor tours to the greatest cities of England and Scotland, with three or four speeches a day to enormous and, it seemed, enthusiastic crowds and, above all, four laboriously prepared broadcasts' which 'consumed my time and strength. All the while I felt that much we had fought for in our long struggle in Europe was slipping away and the hopes of an early and lasting peace were receding.'[22] Unable to prevent the communist takeover of eastern and central Europe, he was determined to spare Britain any socialist version of that cruel fate. He campaigned on an anti-socialist crusade, warning one audience that:

No Socialist system can be established without a political police ... They would have to fall back on some form of Gestapo, no doubt very humanely directed in the first instance. And this would nip opinion in the bud; it would stop criticism as it reared its head and it would gather all the power to the supreme party and the party leaders, rising like stately pinnacles bovver their vast bureaucracies of civil servants, no longer servants and no longer civil.[23]

Churchill had good reason for concern. The Labour Party's constitution committed itself to class warfare and destruction of the free market system. Although Labour Party leader Ramsay MacDonald had served as prime minister from January to November 1924 and from June 1929 to August 1931, he had done so in coalitions with other parties that forced him to uphold British democracy. What would happen if the Labour Party won a majority and so had no need to share power? Recently Labour Party leaders Herbert Morrison and Stafford Cripps had publicly called for eliminating parliamentary procedures and passing bills written by the Labour Party's elite with majority resolutions. That was exactly what Hitler had done after becoming Germany's chancellor by democratic means.

In pointing out those realities, Churchill put truth-telling over political correctness. As usual most Britons rejected his Cassandra-like warnings. What they wanted was an uplifting message that promised them economic and social rewards for all their sacrifices during five years of war. That certainly was the Labour Party's message. Churchill tried to counter the Labour Party's socialist agenda, point by point, but was booed by leftist bullyboys. The heckling got so deafening during one speech that he spent as much the time throwing jabs at the socialists as he did promoting his own agenda. For instance he boasted that not only had his government the previous year rebuilt over 350,000 homes destroyed by German bombing, but: 'Look out. Hold on to your chairs. This one you will not like – two-thirds of those houses were built by private enterprise.' He then promised to complete the work of rebuilding Britain 'provided we are not thrown into foolish faction fights about idiotic ideologies and philosophical dreams of absurd Utopias'.[24]

Britons went to the polls on 5 July. Because all members of the armed services were allowed to vote no matter where in the world they were deployed, the votes would not be counted and the results announced until 26 July. Just the day before that announcement Churchill had returned to London, having spent the two previous weeks at the latest Allied summit desperately trying to ensure that a victorious peace followed the victorious war, the culmination of efforts that extended back over a year and accelerated after Germany's surrender on 8 May.

* * *

Truman had occupied the White House less than a month when, on 11 May, he received a cable from Churchill suggesting that they jointly invite Stalin to meet them 'at some unshattered town in Germany' beyond the Soviet zone. Once Stalin agreed, Truman could stop in London where the two of them would forge a consensus on the issues to present the Soviet tyrant. Truman eagerly embraced the first idea but rejected the second. Aides had explained to the neophyte president his predecessor's policy of trying to avoid appearing as if the Americans and British were 'ganging up' on the Soviets. Truman cabled back that he would travel straight to the conference venue. Indeed, Truman initially wanted to meet Stalin before Churchill but the prime minister eventually dissuaded him from doing so.

Truman's attitude severely disappointed Churchill. Like Roosevelt, Truman was putting the tyrant's feelings before the interests of Western civilization. Stalin only understood brute force. He did whatever he could to aggrandize his own power and emasculate that of his enemies. Of course, he would protest if the United States and the United Kingdom stood shoulder to shoulder against him to protect their own common interests. And then, eventually, he would back off and try to advance his goals some other way. Roosevelt and now Truman naively believed that they could win over the communist dictator with goodwill, open discussions and compromises.

This handicap was compounded by Truman's ignorance of the myriad of details and reasons behind a vast array of interconnected, critical issues. It was not his fault. Churchill was flabbergasted

> that Roosevelt had not made his deputy and potential successor thoroughly acquainted with the whole story and brought him into the decisions which were being taken. This proved of grave disadvantage to our affairs ... How could Mr. Truman know and weigh the issues at stake at the climax of the war? Everything that we have learnt about him since shows him to be a resolute and fearless man, capable of taking the greatest decisions. In these early months his position was one of great difficulty and did not enable him to bring his outstanding qualities fully into action.[25]

Potsdam was the largely unshattered German town chosen for their summit.[26] It lies 20 miles south-west of Berlin and is the site of Frederick the Great's magnificent palace called San Souci, French for 'without worries'. Churchill and Truman went to Potsdam with plenty of worries and came away with a few alleviated and most worsened. The summit actually took place in another palace, Cecilienhof, built for Wilhelm II, Germany's last emperor. Stalin had agreed to the conference but rejected Churchill's call for a mid-June opening date. He delayed the conference until 15 July to give the Red Army and communist agents another month with which to consolidate their control of Eastern Europe by eliminating as many opponents to their rule as possible.

Churchill and Truman arrived separately in Berlin on 16 July and took separate tours of the shattered city. At the Chancellery, Churchill got out and walked among the people who, when they recognized him, 'began to cheer except for an old man who shook his head disapprovingly. My hate had died with their surrender and I was much moved by the demonstrations and also by their haggard looks and threadbare clothes.' Russians guided Churchill and his entourage through the ruined Chancellery then to Hitler's bunker where he 'saw the room in which he and his wife had committed suicide', and then back above ground where the bodies were burned.[27]

Visiting those sites prompted Churchill to ruminate about the paradoxes of modern warfare. Law forbade wars of aggression while new technologies gave military forces unprecedented destructive power. The policy of unconditional surrender might deter a potential aggressor, but if not it certainly encouraged imperialistic regimes 'to fight to the bitter end ... no matter how many lives are needlessly sacrifice ... It is the masses of the people who have so little to say about the starting or ending of wars.' He compared the devastation and desperation of modern warfare to the wars of the Romans whose 'conquests were due almost as much to clemency as to their prowess'.[28]

Stunning news reached Truman on 17 July, the conference's opening day. The previous day, an atomic bomb had been detonated in the New Mexico desert. When Truman informed Churchill, he immediately understood the revolutionary strategic and political consequences: 'Here then was a speedy end to the Second World War and perhaps to much else besides.' Militarily the Japanese 'might find in the apparition of this almost supernatural weapon an excuse which would save their honour and release them from their obligation of being killed to the last fighting man'. Politically 'we should not need the Russians' to participate in the conquest of Japan, thus sparing the division of that country and the brutal imposition of communism on the Soviet occupation zone. Indeed 'we had no need to ask favours of them' and so 'the whole array of European problems could therefore be faced on their merits and according to the broad principles of the United Nations'.[29]

Churchill was prescient on the military consequences. The atomic bombings would render unnecessary a blood-soaked invasion of Japan that would devour hundreds of thousands of Allied and millions of Japanese lives. Japan would be spared that destruction along with its division into American and Soviet spheres. Truman informed Stalin of the successful test but did not ask him to halt Soviet preparations to join the war against Japan. The fear was that the atomic bombs might be duds when they were dropped from B-29s. In that case, the Americans would still need the Red Army's help in destroying the Japanese will to die fighting rather than surrender, a will shared not just by the military but by virtually every one of Emperor Hirohito's imperial subjects.

Perhaps the atomic bombs would not have to be dropped. The president and the prime minister agreed to give Japan's government a chance to capitulate before any more cities were incinerated. On 26 July, Truman, Churchill and Chiang issued the Potsdam Declaration that called for the Japanese immediately to surrender or else face 'prompt and utter destruction'. Allied forces would then occupy Japan, disarm and demobilize its military forces, limit Japan's territory to its four main islands and minor islands to be decided by the Allies, extract reparations for the countries devastated by Japanese imperialism, prosecute war criminals and guarantee democracy and human rights for the Japanese people. The occupation forces would withdraw and Japan's full sovereignty would be restored as soon as these goals were achieved. Japan's government reacted to the Potsdam Declaration with a one-word statement, 'Mokusatsu', which means to regard something with utter contempt and loathing. Truman stoically approved the standing plans for the atomic bombings.[30]

* * *

The British election results were revealed on 26 July, the same day as the Potsdam Declaration. Britain had not had an election since 1935 and there was a lot of pent-up demand for change. Churchill was devastated to learn that the Labour Party had won an overwhelming victory with 393 seats while the Conservative Party plummeted to 197 seats and the Liberal Party hovered near extinction with a mere 12 seats.[31] Labour Party chief Clement Atlee was now the prime minister. His first task was to fly to Potsdam to represent Britain for the rest of the conference.[32]

Clementine tried to sooth her husband's crushing disappointment by assuring him that the election result 'may well be a blessing in disguise'. He replied, 'At the moment it seems quite effectively disguised.'[33] He issued a statement for the BBC to announce:

> The decision of the British people has been recorded in the votes counted today … I regret that I have not been permitted to finish the work against Japan … It only remains for me to express to the British people, for whom I have acted in these perilous years, my profound gratitude for the unflinching, unswerving support which they have given me … and for the many expressions of kindness which they shave shown towards their servant.[34]

Churchill had retained his seat and the leadership of the Conservative Party.[35]

* * *

After Tokyo rejected the Potsdam Declaration on 27 July, American bombers began dropping leaflets over eleven Japanese cities warning inhabitants to evacuate or else face certain death. This warning campaign continued daily until 5 August. Then, on 6 August, an atomic bomb destroyed Hiroshima. The Soviet Red Army invaded north-eastern China on 8 August. Another atomic bomb destroyed Nagasaki on 9 August. After days of debate over whether to fight to extinction despite the atomic bombings, Emperor Hirohito ended the deadlock in his Imperial War Council by calling for peace. On 14 August, Hirohito announced over the radio that Japan would accept the Potsdam Declaration and sign a peace treaty with the Allied powers. A massive American fleet with Allied contingents sailed toward Japan and anchored within Tokyo Bay. On 2 September, representatives of Japan's government signed the surrender document aboard the battleship USS *Missouri*. Later that day Allied forces began to occupy Japan and fulfil the Potsdam Declaration.[36]

For Churchill, the defeat of Germany and Japan 'brought with it a fundamental change in the relations between Communist Russia and the Western democracies. They had lost their common enemy, which was almost their sole bond of union. Henceforward Russian imperialism and the Communist creed saw and set no bounds to their progression and ultimate dominion.'[37] The timing could not have been worse given

> the deadly hiatus which existed between the fading of President Roosevelt's strength and the growth of President Truman's grip of the vast world problem. In this melancholy void one President could not act and the other could not know. Neither the military chiefs nor the State Department received the guidance they required. The former confined themselves to their professional sphere; the latter did not comprehend the issues involved. The indispensable political direction was lacking at the moment when it was most needed. The United States stood on the scene of victory, master of world fortunes, but without a true and coherent design. Britain, although still very powerful, could not act decisively alone. I could at this stage only warn and plead.[38]

Churchill was determined to change that. Once again he assumed the role of Cassandra issuing dire warnings from the political wilderness.

In early 1946, Churchill took a much-needed and well-deserved two-month vacation in Florida and other parts of the United States. One of the numerous speaking invitations that he received came from Westminster College in Fulton, Missouri. Normally he would not have considered speaking at such a remote, small and obscure venue. However, President Truman promised to accompany him to Westminster College which was in his home state and whose president was a friend. Churchill was happy to oblige. On 4 March, after breakfasting at the White House, they and their families boarded the presidential train for the overnight journey to Fulton.

It was at Westminster College on 5 March 1946, that Churchill issued his most celebrated warning against Communist tyranny and expansion:

A shadow has fallen upon the scenes so lately lighted by the Allied victory. Nobody knows what Soviet Russia and its Communist international organization intends to do in the immediate future or what are the limits, if any, to their expansion and proselytizing ... It is my duty ... to place before you certain facts about the present position of Europe. From Stettin in the Baltic to Trieste in the Adriatic, an iron curtain has descended across the Continent. Behind that line lie all the capitals of the ancient states of Central and Eastern Europe ... and all are subject ... to a very high and ... increasing ... control from Moscow.

There was a silver lining in this: 'I do not believe that Soviet Russia desires war. What they desire is the fruits of war and the indefinite expansion of their power and doctrines.' So what, if anything, should be done about that? He called for America and Britain to rally and lead the world's democratic countries through the United Nations against the imperialism of the Soviet Union and its communist movements. What must be avoided at all costs were appeasement policies like those that fuelled Fascist aggression during the 1930s. The lessons were clear:

There never was a war in all history easier to prevent by timely action than the one that has just devastated such great areas of the globe. It could have been prevented ... without the firing of a single shot ... but no one would listen and one by one we were all sucked into that awful whirlpool.[39]

Although Churchill titled his talk 'The Sinew of Peace', the press dubbed it 'The Iron Curtain Speech'. His dark warning provoked controversy on both sides of the Atlantic and far beyond. Stalin predictably condemned Churchill for 'warmongering'. Newspapers and public opinion in America and Britain split over Churchill's message with seemingly as many opponents as supporters.[40]

Although Churchill liked and respected Truman, he never developed the deep friendship with him that he had with Roosevelt. Nonetheless, he found Truman far easier to deal with as a goodhearted, honest, straight-talking Midwesterner, with none of Roosevelt's Machiavellian wiles and insincerity. Yet Truman delivered a disappointing blow to the Anglo-American relationship when on 1 August 1946, he signed the Atomic Energy Act that, among other things, forbad the United States from sharing nuclear secrets with any other country, including Britain. That abruptly ended the partnership that Roosevelt and Churchill established three years earlier.

In autumn 1946, Churchill carried his Cassandra campaign to Europe where, on 19 September, he made his most important speech at Zurich. He lauded the Swiss for providing a model for how a multinational country could achieve democracy, prosperity and peace and called on the Europeans to emulate that model: 'The first step in the recreation of the European family must be a partnership between France and Germany ... There can be no revival of Europe without a spiritually great France and a spiritually great Germany ... We must build a kind of United States of Europe.' To propel this hopeful message he reminded his listeners of potential apocalypse:

> Time may be short. At present there is a breathing space ... The fighting has stopped; but the dangers have not stopped. If we are to form the United States of Europe ... we must begin now. In these present days we dwell strangely under the shield and protection of the atomic bomb. The atomic bomb is still only in the hands of a State and nation which we know will never use it except in the cause of right and freedom. But it may well be that in a few years this awful agency of destruction will be widespread and the catastrophic following from its use by several warring nations will not only bring to an end all that we call civilization, but may possibly disintegrate the globe itself.[41]

From Washington's point of view, the Cold War officially began on 12 March 1947, when Truman essentially declared it before a joint session of Congress:

The peoples of a number of countries ... have recently had totalitarian regimes forced upon them against their will ... At the present moment in world history nearly every nation must choose between alternative ways of life ... One way of life is based upon the will of the majority and is distinguished by free institutions, representative government, free elections, guarantees of individual liberty, freedom of speech and religion and freedom from political oppression. The second way of life is based on the will of a minority forcibly imposed upon the majority. It relies on terror and oppression, a controlled press and radio, fixed elections and the suppression of personal freedoms.

Although he never mentioned the Soviet Union or communism during his speech, all knowledgeable people knew exactly what he meant. If that was the threat, what should be done about it? Truman explained: 'I believe it must be the policy of the United States to support free peoples who are resisting attempted subjugation by armed minorities or by outside pressure. I believe that our help should be primarily through economic and financial aid which is essential to economic stability and orderly political processes.' He then asked Congress to appropriate $400 million in economic and military aid to Greece and Turkey which faced imminent peril from revolutionary forces.[42]

So what led to this? A vicious cycle among three powerful forces – ideology, geopolitics and psychology – transformed the wartime alliance between the Western Allies and Moscow into a cold war between them that persisted for 44 years until the Soviet empire collapsed on 24 December 1991.[43] Ideologically, communism is dedicated to a global revolution whereby all other political systems including democracies are destroyed and replaced with totalitarian communist regimes. In November 1917, Russia became the first country to experience a communist revolution but its leader Vladimir Lenin and his coterie failed to ignite revolutions elsewhere. After taking complete power in 1928, Joseph Stalin concentrated on completing the revolution within the Soviet Union, the new name for the Russian empire. So Moscow posed no geopolitical threat until the Red Army battled its way into central Europe and north-east Asia at the end of the Second World War. The Soviets imposed communist regimes on all the countries that they conquered. Psychology exacerbated the ideological and geopolitical antagonisms between the Western democracies and the Moscow-led communist bloc. Stalin, like Hitler, was a psychopath who had millions of people murdered to consolidate his totalitarian power.[44] Stalin projected his own vilest pathologies and ambitions on others, including his wartime allies. Paranoia, if not mass murder and tyranny, can be contagious. Although Churchill, Roosevelt and Truman bent over backwards to accommodate Stalin, his brutality, cynicism and deceit forced those democratic leaders to take an increasingly tougher stand against him. As Truman put it shortly after becoming president, 'We must stand up to the Russians. We have been too easy with them.'[45] Each side interpreted everything that the other side did in the worst possible way. For instance, Stalin condemned Truman's cancellation of America's Lend-Lease programme to Moscow on 20 September 1945 as an attempt to hurt the Soviet Union, ignoring the fact that the president had ended military aid for all Allied countries now that the war was over.

Although Truman publicly expressed America's containment policy, its author was George Kennan, who had joined America's Foreign Service in 1925 and worked his way up the ranks to become the acting ambassador in Moscow during the war. He articulated the containment policy in two key documents, one his 'long telegram' from Moscow and the other his 'Mr. X' article in *Foreign Affairs* journal. He called for the 'selective' containment of the Soviet Union and communism by economic means primarily in Western Europe and Japan. Communism festered in the mass poverty, death, destruction and despair that prevailed in the war-devastated countries. By rebuilding Western Europe and Japan and reintegrating them into the global economy, prosperity would return and communism's appeal would wither. Communist revolutions elsewhere as in China were probably inevitable and could not be prevented. Indeed, trying to prop up corrupt, inept, brutal regimes like Chiang Kai-shek's only exacerbated and prolonged the civil war. Sooner or later two forces would soften those communist regimes and make them amenable to cutting deals, nationalism and poverty, which would drive them to break with Moscow and join the global economy.

Kennan's policy of selective containment lasted from Truman's speech of 12 March 1947 until communist North Korea invaded non-communist South Korea on 25 June 1950. During that brief time, Washington was able to rebuild Western Europe and Japan through $14 billion and $2.2 billion, respectively, of humanitarian aid that provided immediate food, medicine, shelter and fuel to millions of desperately needy people and developmental aid that restored infrastructure and industries. These efforts actually built upon previous ones. Washington began to rebuild the global economy during the Second World War. During the Bretton Woods conference in New Hampshire from 1 to 22 July, 730 delegates from 44 countries convened to establish two global financial institutions. The International Bank for Reconstruction and Development (IRBD or World Bank) lent money at low interest rates to governments that invested it to reconstruct and develop their economies. The International Monetary Fund (IMF) had two dimensions, a stable international currency exchange system based on gold valued at $32 an ounce and short-term loans to governments experiencing balance of payments deficits. The next major boost to the global economy came when representatives of twenty-three countries at Geneva signed a treaty establishing the General Agreement on Trade and Tariffs (GATT) Geneva on 30 October 1947. Members agreed to conduct a series of negotiations designed to lower trade and investment barriers among them and invited new members with the same commitment. Washington promoted European integration by requiring recipients of its economic aid, known as the Marshall Plan after Secretary of State George Marshall, to form the Organization for European Economic Cooperation (OEEC) with representatives from each recipient country who decided how best to distribute that largess. The most ambitious international organization of all was the United Nations, whose charter was negotiated by representatives of fifty-one countries at San Francisco from 25 April to 26 June 1945 and officially convened on 23 October 1945. Like its precursor the League of Nations, the United Nations was dedicated to peace and prosperity or collective security and economic development and had the same structure of a secretariat, council, assembly and court. The critical difference was that the United States was a key member of the United Nations, although that did not make the new international organization any more effective than the old one.

A series of events occurred that appeared to discredit Kennan's selective containment policy. On 24 June 1948, Moscow blocked the land routes from West Germany across East Germany to West Berlin, with its American, British and French zones. Kennan had predicted that the Soviets would at times test the West and the proper response was firm but nonviolent resistance. In this case, Washington began the 'Berlin Airlift' whereby planes conveyed supplies to West Berlin until the Soviets finally lifted the blockade on 11 May 1949. Washington also responded by forming the defensive alliance called the North Atlantic Treaty Organization (NATO) composed of the United States, Canada, Britain and nine European countries on 2 April 1949.

As the Leader of the Opposition, Churchill was relegated to the political sidelines during these critical events. At most he could act as a cheerleader for America's containment policies. His most fervent calls were for greater international economic and political integration: 'If, during the next five years it is found possible to build a world organization of irresistible force and authority for the purpose of securing peace, there are no limits to the blessings which all men may enjoy and share. Nothing will help forward the building of that world organization so much as unity and stability in Europe.'[46] He was perhaps the most important advocate for what became the Council of Europe, created by the Treaty of London signed by envoys from ten countries on 5 May 1949. The Council of Europe recognized his critical role by inviting him to its opening session at Strasbourg, France on 9 August 1949. He argued that reintegrating West Germany with the transatlantic world was vital for related strategic and economic reasons. In March 1949, he asserted that idea with publisher Henry Luce in New York: 'You must regard the re-entry of Germany into the family of European nations as an event which the Western World must desire and must, if possible, achieve.'[47] Nonetheless, he worried that, like the Sorcerer's Apprentice, during modern times humanity had unleashed technological and bureaucratic forces that it barely understood let alone controlled: 'On all sides we see the organizations and machinery of life and government growing stronger and more formidable. Man must, by his personality and individuality, at least keep pace with the mechanical developments; and must be sure that he uses his institutions and is not the mere expression of their workings.'[48]

Nuclear weapons poised the worst threat to humanity. He understood the paradox that the best way to prevent their use was to threaten to use them. That was his key message during an intense schedule of public speeches and private meetings in America from 18 March to 7 April 1949. He privately urged Truman to declare he would not hesitate to use the atomic bomb to defend Europe during a White House meeting and publically lauded the atomic bomb as a deterrent to Soviet aggression during a talk at the Massachusetts Institute of Technology (MIT). As he sailed home aboard the *Queen Mary*, he was pleased to hear that Truman had declared on 7 April that the United States would use the atomic bomb to defend itself and other democracies around the world. Nonetheless, that dependence as much disturbed as relieved him: 'It is indeed a melancholy thought that nothing preserves Europe from an overwhelming military attack except the devastating resources of the United States in this awful weapon. That is at the present time the sole deterrent against an aggressive Communist invasion. No wonder the Communists would like to ban it in the name of peace.'[49] Or get their own.

America's monopoly on nuclear power ended on 29 August 1949, when the Soviets detonated their first atomic bomb. That diminished but did not end America's nuclear deterrent. The Americans had scores of atomic bombs with the capacity to fly them from bases in Britain, Norway, Italy, Turkey and Japan to targets in the Soviet Union. The Soviets did not have the capacity to bomb a target in the United States unless it was a one-way suicide mission. Nonetheless, Churchill argued that Moscow's possession of a growing nuclear arsenal made the American threat of massive retaliation against a Soviet invasion of Western Europe even more compelling:

> The argument is now put forward that we must never use the atomic bomb until or unless, it has been used against us first. In other words, you must never fire until you have been shot dead. This seems to me undoubtedly a silly thing to say and a still more imprudent position to adopt. Moreover, such a resolve would certainly bring war nearer. The deterrent effect of the atomic bomb is at the present time almost our only defence. Its potential use is the only lever by which we can hope to obtain ... a peaceful settlement with Soviet Russia.[50]

More succinctly, he captured nuclear deterrence's psychological essence with this insight: 'then it may well be that we shall by a process of sublime irony have reached a stage in this story where safety will be the sturdy child of terror and survival the twin brother of annihilation.'[51] He wondered whether humanity could maintain that tenuous equilibrium given that: 'The power of man has grown in every sphere except over himself ... The fearful question confronts us: Have our problems got beyond our control? Undoubtedly we are passing through a phase where this may be so.'[52] All along he insisted that the only way to deal with the Soviet Union and Communists anywhere 'is by having superior force on your side ... and they must also be convinced that you will use – and you will not hesitate to use – these forces, if necessary in the most ruthless manner.'[53] That might lead to peace: 'Disarmament will come, if it comes at all, only when the two leviathans have in fact achieved a rough balance of power, which they realize that they do not mean to attack each other and when this balance and this realization can at last lead to written agreement.'[54]

The possibility for peaceful relations meant that the West should never sever its diplomatic relations with communist states: 'Ambassadors are not sent as compliments but as necessities for ordinary daily use. The more difficult relations are with any country in question, the more necessary it is to have the very highest form of representation on the spot.'[55] Nonetheless, he made a critical distinction in just what form such relations should be pursued. The communist takeover of China on 1 October 1949, after twenty-two years of civil war, required a vital diplomatic nuance: 'In November 1949, I was in favour of the recognition of Communist China, provided that it was de facto and not de jure … and provided that it could be brought about as a joint policy with the United States and the Dominions.' He blasted Atlee's Labour government for issuing de jure recognition of China's communist regime without getting anything of substance in return: 'The response of the Chinese Communists was very surly. They took all they could get from our recognition and gave nothing in return … The United States were very offended by our isolated action.'[56]

*   *   *

As the threat of nuclear extinction darkened humanity, Churchill's personal life brightened steadily. He transformed his beloved Chartwell from a bank property into a non-profit private trust in 1947. He did so because he was not just broke but in debt. He had never properly managed his money and lost far more than he made. Under the deal, the trust took title to his property and papers. He and his family lived at Chartwell free of tax and interest payments. That same year, he scored publishing deals that garnered him great wealth, a £50,000 advance for what became his four-volume *History of the English Speaking Peoples*, a £12,000 advance for the rights to his wartime secret-session speeches before Parliament, a £25,000 advance for the British rights what would be his six-volume Second World War memoirs and an unprecedented $1.15 million for the American rights to those memoirs. A sliver of that went to funding his Syndicate, a dozen or so short-hand secretaries, typists and researchers that enabled him to fulfil all his contracts. His vacations became longer and more extravagant at the finest hotels in places like Monte Carlo, Biarritz, Madeira, Marrakesh and the shores of the Riviera, Lake Garda and Lake Geneva.

His sybaritic lifestyle hardly softened his hatred of socialism. During the six years that he led the opposition in the House of Commons he blasted the Labour Party for bringing not prosperity but more misery to the British people with broadsides like this:

The queues are longer, the shelves are barer, the shops are emptier. The interference of Government Departments with daily life is more severe and more galling, more forms have to be filled up, more officials have to be consulted. Whole spheres of potential activity are frozen, rigid and number, because this Government has to prove its Socialist sincerity instead of showing how they can get the country alive and on the move again.[57]

Britain was deeply in debt, with outstanding bills of $4.5 billion to the United States and $1.2 billion to Canada alone. Churchill castigated Atlee's government for devaluing the pound from £4.08 to £2.80 to ease monthly interest payments on its foreign debts, then squandering $3.75 billion borrowed from the United States in 1946: 'Owing to their follies and wrongful action, a great part of all the loans and gifts we have received from abroad has been spent not upon the re-equipment of our industry, nor upon the import of basic foodstuffs; instead much of this precious aid was lavishly frittered away.' Atop that, the socialists had raised 'taxation until it is the highest in the world'. The Labour Party was guilty not just of 'incompetence and maladministration ... and ... wild extravagance, but even more by the spirit of class hatred which they have spread throughout the land and by the costly and wasteful nationalization of a fifth part of our industries'.[58] He warned that: 'If you destroy a free market you create a black market.'[59]

Churchill was not exaggerating. Socialist Britain was beset by a vicious cycle of strikes, shortages, crime, malnutrition, bankruptcies, high joblessness, low productivity, low savings and soaring trade deficits and national debt. In 1948, he issued this dire warning: 'We are oppressed by a deadly fallacy. Socialism is the philosophy of failure, the creed of ignorance and the gospel of envy. Unless we free our country while time remains from the perverse doctrines of Socialism, there can be no hope for recovery.'[60]

To save Britain from that vicious cycle, he propounded a partnership between the public and private sectors, a dynamic golden mean between the extremes of anarchy and totalitarianism. The state's role was critical in managing markets to bring out their best and stymy their worst. He sought

to benefit private enterprise with the knowledge and guiding drive of modern Governments, without sacrificing the initiative and drive of individual effort under free, competitive conditions. Our policy is based on the two main principles of fair play and adequate opportunity. We seek to establish a minimum standard of life and labour, below which no one who is prepared to meet the obligations of good citizenship should be allowed to fall. Above that minimum standard we wish to give the fullest possible play for competitive individual enterprise.[61]

Meanwhile, Churchill finally reconciled himself to the British Empire's inevitable breakup, especially the loss of India, 'the Jewel in the Crown'.[62] The Indian Independence Act split the subcontinent into two sovereign states, largely Hindu India and Muslim Pakistan on 15 August 1947. Churchill voted for the bill on 5 July. King George VI gave his royal assent on 18 July 1947. Tragically, his fear that a bloodbath would accompany independence and partition was prescient when more than a million people died as Muslims, Sikhs and Hindus slaughtered each other, mostly in West Pakistan, as tens of millions of refugees fled to the country where their faith mostly prevailed.[63] Nonetheless he later expressed these conciliatory sentiments to the new states:

> Our imperial mission in India is at an end ... It is our duty ... to hope
> and pray for the well-being and happiness of all the peoples of India,
> of whatever race, religion, social condition or historic character they
> may be ... Sorrow may lie in our hearts but bitterness and malice must
> be purged from them and ... we must ... not allow our vision to be
> clouded by memories of glories that are gone forever.[64]

Britain finally shed the burden of Palestine by transferring it to the United Nations on 29 November 1947. In the General Assembly, the Truman administration got a majority to approve a resolution to split Palestine between predominately Arab and Jewish halves. During the debate before the vote some governments protested that the land should not be divided; others criticized the division as unfair in giving the Jews 55 per cent of the land although they had only 40 per cent of the population. Yet, when the votes were counted, thirty-three delegations voted for the two-state plan, thirteen voted against it, ten abstained and one was absent. The Arab countries refused to accept that division. As soon as Israel's government declared independence on 18 May 1948, the armies of Egypt, Jordan, Syria and Lebanon attacked the new country but were eventually driven back. That would not stop the Arab states from repeatedly warring against Israel over the coming decades.[65]

*   *   *

Churchill's Conservative Party made a comeback in the general election of 23 February 1950, boosting their seats to 298, while the Labour Party fell to 315 and the Liberal Party to nine. The Tories finally inched ahead in the election of 25 October 1951, taking 321 seats, a slender majority of six seats, while Labour fell to 295 and the Liberals to six seats. Steadily worsening economic conditions under Labour Party rule explains those two election results little more than a year and a half apart.[66]

Churchill convened his Cabinet on 30 October 1951. Anthony Eden was his Foreign Secretary and right-hand man. Churchill's first policy was to terminate plans to nationalize the iron and steel industry, thus fulfilling a core campaign pledge. He followed that by sharply cutting government spending as he and his ministers set the example with reduced salaries. Yet nothing that his administration did over the next four years broke a persistent vicious economic cycle of worsening inflation, joblessness, capital flight, productivity, taxes, trade deficits and debt.

Churchill grounded British national security in three overlapping circles of relationships:

First, the British Empire and the Commonwealth of Nations growing in moral and physical strength. Secondly, the irrevocable association of the English-speaking world around the great republic of the United States. Thirdly, the safety and revival of Europe in her ancient fame and long sought unity. In all these circles we in this hard-pressed but unvanquished island have a vital part to play and if we can bear the weight we may win the crown of honour.[67]

His first foreign trip was to the United States for which he and his entourage sailed aboard the *Queen Mary* on New Year's Eve 1951. He stayed at the White House for prolonged talks with President Truman and addressed Congress. He would make three more trips to the United States during his second stint as prime minister.

Among his most important goals was to champion a united Europe with Britain a key participant. The timing could not have been better. On 9 May 1950, French Foreign Minister Robert Schuman had proposed that France, Germany and other western European coal and steel producers unite their markets for both economic and strategic interests. Eliminating trade barriers would promote efficiency, economies of scale and a growing web of cross-investments. The greater the economic interdependence among the members, the less likely any of them would consider wielding military force to settle differences to the point where that became unthinkable. And this would be merely the first step in a series leading eventually to a United States of Europe.

The logic for joining what became the European Coal and Steel Community (ECSC) could not be clearer, at least to Churchill. The national economic and strategic interests of individual European countries converged and so were enhanced in a united Europe. Once again Britain would play the role of the continent's balancer, but within an institutional framework that promoted economic integration, prosperity and peace:

> I am all for reconciliation between France and Germany and for receiving Germany back into the European family, but this implies, as I have always insisted, that Britain and France should in the main act together so as to be able to deal on even terms with Germany, which is so much stronger than France alone. Without Britain the coal and steel pool in western Europe must naturally tend to be dominated by Germany, who will be the most powerful member.[68]

But Britain was not among the signatories of the Treaty of Paris on 18 April 1951, that established the ECSC among France, Germany, Italy, the Netherlands, Belgium and Luxembourg. Churchill wanted Britain belatedly to join but could not garner enough support within his own party, let alone across the floor. Most MPs were leery of entangling Britain's economy with West Europe's. They preferred that Britain lead the Commonwealth of its former colonies as well as benefit from easy access to America's vast dynamic market. Britain did remain in the Council of Europe but that body was mostly a debating chamber void of the power actually to resolve issues. Churchill himself had ambiguous feelings about his nation's ties with the continent, once explaining: 'We are with Europe, but not of it. We are linked, but not comprised. We are interested and associated, but not absorbed.'[69]

Churchill also sought to reverse what he considered acts of appeasement toward the communists committed by his predecessor. Atlee had abolished the Combined Chiefs of Staff committee between the United States and Britain, and recognized Mao Zedong's Communist Party that finally won what had been a 22-year civil war with Chiang Kai-shek's Nationalist Party and officially took over China on 1 October 1949. Try as he might, political opposition prevented Churchill from reviving the former or reversing the latter.

He was pleased that several thousand British and some other Commonwealth forces were fighting in the Korean War, launched on 25 June 1950, when communist North Korea under Kim Il Sung had invaded non-communist South Korea under Syngman Ree. In July 1951, Churchill expanded his nation's role by establishing the First Commonwealth Division, although nearly all the troops were British, Canadian and Australia. He was unable to get significant numbers of troops from other Commonwealth countries.

A dozen years after initiating the programme on 9 April 1940, Britain finally detonated its first atomic bomb on 3 October 1952. In doing so, Britain joined an exclusive club whose only other members then were its ally the United States and its enemy the Soviet Union. Now, theoretically, NATO's deterrent power against a Soviet attack on Western Europe was enhanced.

A series of health problems including a minor stroke and a hernia operation undercut Churchill's political efforts. Fortunately those afflictions did not yet noticeably affect his wit. During a December 1951 summit with Konrad Adenauer, the German Chancellor remarked: 'If I were recreating the world I would suggest that this time we not put a limit on man's intelligence without putting a limit on man's stupidity.' Churchill replied: 'That would not at all do because it would deprive me of many of my Cabinet ministers.'[70] As if his duties as prime minister were not onerous enough, he was under increasing pressure from within his own party to give them up. The first effort came on 16 June 1952, when four of his ministers asked him to set a retirement date. This he refused to do. Then Antony Eden asked the same of him on 7 December 1952. Again Churchill refused to commit himself. He was determined to achieve one last triumph as prime minister by ending the Cold War with a settlement of differences between the Western and Soviet blocs. But for that he needed the full cooperation of the United States.

Dwight Eisenhower had won the presidential election held on 4 November 1952. Churchill was thrilled that the man with whom he had worked so closely during the Second World War was now in the White House and he was eager to exchange views with him as soon as possible. He sailed to the United States aboard the *Queen Mary*, stepping ashore at New York on 5 January 1953. He met Eisenhower that same day and urged him to join him in a summit with Stalin in Moscow. Eisenhower did not want to meet the tyrant on his own turf but would agree to meet him at a neutral site like Stockholm in Sweden. However, he did encourage Churchill to fly to Moscow for preliminary talks. Churchill then travelled to Washington to meet with lame-duck President Truman at the White House before flying to Jamaica for an extended beach vacation.

Stunning news emitted from Radio Moscow around the world on 5 March 1953: Joseph Stalin was dead. Churchill rejoiced not just because that genocidal tyrant had perished but because his death presented an opportunity to break the stalemate between the American and Soviet blocs on an array of issues. He cabled Eisenhower the suggestion that they jointly send the Kremlin a letter of condolence along with the hope that they could resolve their outstanding differences in a summit. Eisenhower might have embraced the idea had he not chosen as his Secretary of State John Foster Dulles, an extreme hard-line anti-communist who condemned even talking about talking with the Soviets as appeasement. Instead, Eisenhower once again encouraged Churchill to meet separately with the new leaders, whoever they turned out to be. A struggle for power was ongoing within the Kremlin. Eventually Georgy Malenkov and Nikita Khrushchev took over and had Lavrentiy Beria, Stalin's most ruthless henchman, arrested. After a short trial, Beria was executed on 23 December 1953.

Churchill's fragile health made a summit all the more uncertain. He suffered his latest stroke on 15 June 1953. Nonetheless he showed up to chair a Cabinet meeting the next day even though his voice was slurred, his mouth drooped and his left arm was partly paralyzed. A worse stroke hit him on 26 June, immobilizing his entire left side. Anthony Eden was also in bad shape, having undergone a botched gall blander operation on 12 April.

All these problems delayed the official summit between Churchill and Eisenhower until 4 to 10 December 1953, when they met along with French Prime Minister Joseph Lanuil at Bermuda. The number one issue on the prime minister's agenda was to talk the president into meeting the new Soviet leaders. Here again, Dulles zealously insisted that Eisenhower not do so. Churchill bitterly remarked that 'I am bewildered. It seems that everything is left to Dulles. It appears that the president is no more than a ventriloquist's doll.'[71] Churchill would have been better off going to Stockholm to receive the Nobel Prize for Literature that he was awarded that year; his wife Clementine accepted it on his behalf on 10 December 1953.

Unable to convince the Eisenhower White House of the benefits of at least discussing problems with the Soviets, Churchill shared his vision for ending the Cold War and nuclear arms race in the House of Commons:

If Russia, the British Commonwealth and the United States were gathered round the table talking about the commercial application of atomic energy and the diversion of some of their uranium stockpile, it would not seem odd if the question of the hydrogen bomb, which might blow all these pretty plans sky-high, cropped up and what I have hoped for, namely a talk on supreme issues between the Heads of States and Governments, might not seem so impossible ... One is to lose no opportunity of convincing the Soviet leaders and, if we can reach them, the Russian people, that the democracies of the West have no aggressive design on them. The other is to ensure that until that purpose has been achieved we have the strength necessary to deter any aggression by them and to ward it off if it should come.[72]

Churchill flew to Washington on 24 June 1954 for what would be his last face-to-face attempt to convince Eisenhower that only constructive talks could pull the world back from the brink of Armageddon brink. To the prime minister's relief, the president finally agreed. They chose tentatively neutral Stockholm for their meeting with Malenkov. They also agreed that they should enhance their power before they issued any invitation to the Kremlin. They ended their five days of talk on 29 June, with a joint announcement that the Federal Republic of West Germany would join NATO.

During the voyage aboard the *Queen Elizabeth* back to Britain, Eden marred the satisfaction that Churchill was savouring from his successful summit with Eisenhower by again pressing him for a firm date to resign. That prompted Churchill to cable a request to Malenkov for an August meeting between the two of them. He was determined to end the Cold War while he still had time. He ran into a barrage of criticism in the Cabinet on 8 July, when he explained his initiative. Most were upset that he had not consulted them before his message to Malenkov and they opposed any summit for now.

Churchill turned 80 years old on 30 November 1954 and he certainly looked his age. He was haggard and sluggish. His thoughts, once rapid-fire, emerged laboriously. He was nearly deaf so others had to shout to be heard, not that he paid much attention. And the pressure mounted for him to step aside and let Anthony Eden, who was himself afflicted with a cocktail of ills, replace him as prime minister. On 21 December, he finally yielded to Eden's badgering and promised to go on 5 April 1955.

He made a last eloquent speech as prime minister in the House of Commons, with the fate of humanity his appropriate swan song:

Which way shall we turn to save our lives and the future of the world? It does not matter so much to old people; they are going to die soon anyway; but I find it poignant to look at youth in all its activity and ardour and, most of all, to watch little children playing their merry games and wonder what would lie before them if God wearied of mankind.

But it was not God that humanity had most to fear: 'It may well be that we shall, by a process of sublime irony, have reached a stage where safety will be the sturdy shield of terror and survival the twin brother of annihilation.'[73]

A cable from the White House on 8 March prompted him to renege on his retirement promise. Eisenhower called for the American, British, French and German heads of government to meet in Paris on 8 May 1955, the tenth anniversary of 'Victory in Europe' day and sign the agreement that brought West Germany into NATO. Churchill had no intention of missing that exhilarating event. Naturally Eden, among many others, was enraged when Churchill informed the Cabinet of his decision. A howl of protests also arose against him in the House of Commons from both sides of the house. That finally convinced Churchill to keep his previous promise. Queen Elizabeth II accepted Churchill's resignation at Buckingham Palace on 5 April 1955. At her request, he suggested Eden as his replacement. He and Clementine then embarked to vacation a couple of weeks at Syracuse in Sicily.

After Churchill left, Eden called a general election. The Conservatives bolstered their already formidable majority with 23 more seats, bringing their total to 345. The Labour Party dropped to 277 and the Liberal Party clung to their measly six seats. Churchill easily won re-election. Without a Cabinet post he had lots of free time on his hands, which he spent dictating books at Chartwell or vacationing on the Riviera where he passed hours each day before his easel with his paintbrush in one hand and palette in the other. He devoted most of his reading to novels. Each evening he presided over multi-course meals of fine foods, wines and spirits of all kinds. Winston and Clementine celebrated their fiftieth wedding anniversary on 12 September 1958.

During the last decade of his life, he devoted considerable time to one final great project. He had first conceived the idea when he gave a talk at the Massachusetts Institute of Technology (MIT) in March 1949. He returned to Britain determined to establish a similar university dedicated to developing cutting-edge engineers, scientists and technicians. To that end, he set up a trust with his own initial contribution of £25,000 that other donors eventually swelled to £3.5 million. On 17 October 1959, he turned the first spade of dirt at the site of what would be called Churchill College at Cambridge University. Churchill College received a royal charter in 1960 and its first students in 1964. Among the donors was Aristotle Onassis, the multimillionaire Greek shipping magnate. Churchill and Onassis became close friends and Churchill was a frequent guest on Onassis's yacht, the *Cristina*.

During his last dozen or so years he received honours of all kinds. Among the highlights were his receipt of the Nobel Prize for Literature and being named a Knight of the Garter in 1953, six honorary doctorates from universities and a score or so military medals from various countries. French President Charles de Gaulle presented him with the Croix de la Liberation in Paris on 6 November 1958. He deeply cherished the gift he received at the White House on 9 April 1963, when President John F. Kennedy named him the first honorary American citizen, bestowed as an act of Congress.

The Black Dog at times reappeared to haunt his last years. He confessed that 'I have worked very hard and achieved a great deal, only to achieve nothing at all'.[74] A family tragedy marred his last years when chronic depression drove his daughter Diana to commit suicide on 20 October 1963. He battled these dark times with this attitude: 'The span of mortality is short, the end universal and the tinge of melancholy which accompanies decline and retirement is itself an anodyne. It is foolish to waste lamentations upon the closing phase of human life. Noble spirits yield themselves willingly to the successively falling shades which carry them to a better world or to oblivion.'[75]

He was long prepared for death, having had so many near misses over the decades. When he turned 75 on 30 November 1949, he quipped: 'I am ready to meet my Maker. Whether my Maker is prepared for the ordeal of meeting me is another matter.'[76] He suffered a massive stroke on 10 January 1965 and died of a cerebral haemorrhage on 24 January 1965. Whether he met his maker or not remains a mystery. What is certain that he had predicted the date of his death exactly a dozen years earlier, remarking: 'Today is the 24th of January. It's the day my father died. It's the day I will die.'[77] The funeral ceremony was held at St Paul's cathedral and he was buried at St. Martin's church in the village of Bladon, within view of Blenheim Palace.

Winston Churchill wrote his last will and testament at far back as July 1915, shortly before going to the front in the First World War. In it he left these words for Clementine:

Death is only an incident, & not the most important which happens to us in this state of being. On the whole, especially since I met you my darling one, I have been happy and you have taught me how noble a woman's heart can be. If there is anywhere else I shall be on the lookout for you. Meanwhile, look forward, feel free, rejoice in life, cherish the children, guard my memory.[78]

Notes

Abbreviations

Churchill by Himself	Richard Langworth, ed., *Churchill by Himself*, New York: Public Affairs, 2008.
Churchill Documents	Winston S. Churchill and Randolph S. Churchill, eds, *The Churchill Documents*, vols 1–5, Hillsdale College: Hillsdale College Press, 2006–07.
	Winston S. Churchill and Martin Gilbert, eds, *The Churchill Documents*, vols 6–17, Hillsdale College: Hillsdale College Press, 2008–13.
	Martin Gilbert and Larry Arnn, eds, *The Churchill Documents*, vol. 18, Hillsdale, Mich.: Hillsdale College, 2015.
Churchill Official Biography	Randolph S. Churchill, *Winston S. Churchill: The Official Biography*, vols 1–2, Hillsdale College: Hillsdale College Press, 2007–13.
	Martin Gilbert, *Winston S. Churchill: The Official Biography*, vols 3–8, Hillsdale College: Hillsdale College Press, 2007–13.
Churchill Power of Words	Martin Gilbert, ed., *Churchill: The Power of Words*, New York: Da Capo, 2012.
Churchill Speeches	Robert Rhodes James, ed., *Winston S. Churchill: His Complete Speeches*, 8 vols, London: Chelsea House Publishers, 1974.
Parliamentary Debates	*Record of Parliamentary Debates*, www.parliament/uk/business/Hansard.

Introduction

1. Winston Churchill, *Memoirs of the Second World War* (Boston: Houghton Mifflin, 1987), 227.
2. *Churchill Documents*, 2:610.
3. *Churchill by Himself*, 80.
4. Ibid., 99.
5. *Parliamentary Debates*, 28 October 1943.
6. Peter Stansky, ed., *Churchill: A Profile* (New York: Macmillan, 1973), 197.
7. *Parliamentary Debates*, 9 May 1938.
8. Leonard Wilbberley, *The Life of Winston Churchill* (New York: Farrar, Straus, Giroux , 1965), 237.
9. Winston Churchill, *History of the English Speaking Peoples*, 4 vols (New York: Dodd, Mead and Company, 1958).
10. Charles Eade, ed., *Onwards to Victory: War Speeches by the Right Hon. Winston S. Churchill* (London: Cassell, 1948), 183–4.
11. *The Times*, 10 November 1951.
12. *Parliamentary Debates*, 12 November 1940.
13. William Manchester, *The Last Lion: Winston Spencer Churchill, 1874–1922* (New York: Delta Books, 1983), 44.
14. *Churchill by Himself*, 18.

15. Winston Churchill, *Great Contemporaries: Churchill Reflects on FDR, Hitler, Kipling, Chaplin, Balfour and Other Giants of His Age* (Wilmington, Del.: Intercollegiate Studies Institute, 2012), 137.

16. *Churchill by Himself*, 23.

17. Violet Bonham Carter, *Winston Churchill: An Intimate Portrait* (New York: Harcourt, Brace and World, 1965), 4.

18. Winston Churchill, *Great Contemporaries*, 231.

19. Winston Churchill, *My Early Life, 1874–1904* (New York: Touchstone Books, 1996), 27.

20. Ibid., 28.

21. Ibid., 102.

22. Ibid., 114–17.

23. Charles Watson, Lord Moran, *Churchill: The Struggle for Survival, 1945–1965* (New York: Basic Books, 2006), 179.

24. Wilfred Attenborough, *Churchill and the 'Black Dog' of Depression* (London: Palgrave Macmillan, 2014), 72.

25. *Churchill by Himself*, 529.

26. Richard Holmes, *In the Footsteps of Churchill: A Study in Character* (New York: Perseus, 2006), 50.

27. Geoffrey Best, *Churchill: A Study in Greatness* (London: Hambledon Continuum, 2006), 77.

28. Winston Churchill, *Early Life*, 79–80.

29. Winston Churchill, *The Story of the Malakand Field Force* (London: Dover Publications, 2010), 117.

30. Winston Churchill, *Early Life*, 65.

31. Ibid., 180.

32. Winston Churchill, *Amid These Storms: Thoughts and Adventures* (New York: Charles Scribner's Sons, 1931), 183–4.

33. Manchester, *Last Lion 1874–1922*, 18.

34. Ibid., 309.

35. John Wheeler-Bennett, ed., *Action This Day: Working with Churchill* (New York: St. Martin's Press, 1969), 183.

36. Winston Churchill, *Early Life*, 124.

37. *Churchill by Himself*, 579.

38. William Manchester, *The Last Lion: Winston Spencer Churchill, 1922–1940* (New York: Delta Books, 1988), 26.

39. For insights from some of his assistants and servants, see: Wheeler-Bennett, *Action This Day*.

40. Manchester, *Last Lion 1874–1922*, 431.

41. Stansky, *Churchill*, 198.

42. Bonham Carter, *Churchill*, 5.

43. *Churchill Documents*, 4/1:471.

44. Winston Churchill, *Amid These Storms*, 300.

45. Mary Soames, ed., *Winston and Clemmie: The Personal Letters of the Churchills* (Boston: Houghton Mifflin, 1998), 69.

46. Ibid., 81.

47. Manchester, *Last Lion 1874–1922*, 367.

48. Manchester, *Last Lion 1922–1940*, 15.

49. Ibid.

50. John B. Severance, *Winston Churchill: Soldier, Statesman, Artist* (New York: Clarion Books, 1996), 123.

51. *Churchill by Himself*, 486.

52. Winston Churchill, *The Unwritten Alliance* (London: Cassell, 1961), 202.

53. *Churchill by Himself*, 49.
54. *Parliamentary Debates*, 23 January 1948.
55. *Churchill Power of Words*, vii–viii.
56. Winston Churchill, *Early Life*, 206–07.
57. *Parliamentary Debates*, 28 April 1927.
58. Kay Halle, *The Irrepressible Churchill: Stories, Sayings and Impressions of Sir Winston Churchill* (New York: Robson Books, 1987), 103.
59. Manchester, *Last Lion 1874–1922*, 34–5.
60. David Combes and Minnie S. Churchill, *Sir Winston Churchill: His Life and His Paintings* (London: Running Press, 2004); Winston Churchill, *Painting as a Pastime: Essays and Other Works* (London: Rosetta Books, 2014).
61. Winston Churchill, 'Painting as a Pastime', *Strand Magazine*, January 1922.
62. Michael Dobbs, *Six Months in 1945: FDR, Stalin, Churchill and Truman from World War to Cold War* (New York: Random House, 2013), 11.
63. William Manchester and Paul Reid, *The Last Lion: Winston Spencer Churchill, 1940–1965* (New York: Bantam Books, 2012), 17.
64. *Churchill Documents*, 3:320–1.
65. *Churchill by Himself*, 16.
66. Winston Churchill, *Parliamentary Debates* (Wilmington, Del.: ISI Books, 2012).
67. *Churchill by Himself*, 492–3.
68. Winston Churchill, *The World Crisis, 1911–1918* (New York: Free Press, 2005), 493–4.
69. *Parliamentary Debates*, November 17, 1949.
70. *Churchill by Himself*, 195.
71. Ibid., 79.
72. Ibid., 186.
73. Ibid.
74. *Parliamentary Debates*, 11 December 1941.
75. *Parliamentary Debates*, 21 February 1917.
76. Alex Danchev and Daniel Todman, eds, *Field Marshal Alanbrooke, War Diaries* (Berkeley: University of California Press, 2003), 451, 532–4.
77. Winston Churchill, *World Crisis, 1911–1918*, 293.
78. Winston Churchill, *Parliamentary Debates*, 10.
79. *Churchill by Himself*, 15.
80. *Parliamentary Debates*, 4 April 1944, 27 September 1926, 11 November 1947.
81. *Parliamentary Debates*, 25 June 1947.
82. *Churchill Documents*, 1/1:933.
83. Winston Churchill, *Memoirs of the Second World War*, 139.
84. *Churchill by Himself*, 18.
85. *Parliamentary Debates*, 22 September 1943.
86. Henry Pelling, *Churchill* (London: Wordsworth Military Library, 1999), 73.
87. *Churchill Speeches*, 6:760.
88. *Bath Daily Chronicle*, 27 July 1897.
89. *Churchill by Himself*, 23.
90. Ibid., 20.
91. Randolph S. Churchill, ed., *Stemming the Tide: Speeches 1951 and 1952 by Winston S. Churchill* (London: Cassell, 1953), 187.
92. *Churchill Speeches*, 6:164.
93. *Churchill Documents*, 5/1:306–07.
94. *News of the World*, 28 April 1938.
95. *Collier's*, 14 January 1939.
96. Winston Churchill, *Amid These Storms*, 247–51.
97. *Churchill Official Biography*, 5:837–8.

98. *News of the World*, 29 May 1938.

99. *The Times*, 12 October 1950.

100. Winston Churchill, *Parliamentary Debates*, 63.

101. *Churchill by Himself*, 28.

Chapter 1: The Child

1. *Churchill by Himself*, 572.

2. Winston Churchill, *Early Life*, 5.

3. Ibid., 31–2.

4. Ibid., 8–9, 12–13.

5. *Churchill by Himself*, 525.

6. Winston Churchill, *Early Life*, 11–12.

7. Ibid., 13.

8. Ibid., 15.

9. Ibid., 38.

10. Ibid., 37.

11. Michael Paterson, *A Brief History of Life in Victorian Britain: A Social Life of Queen Victoria* (London: Robinson, 2008); A.N. Wilson, *Victoria: A Life* (New York: Penguin, 2015).

12. Winston Churchill, *Early Life*, xxi.

13. Ibid., 34.

14. Ibid., 89.

15. Ibid., 19.

16. *Churchill Documents*, 1/1:390–1.

17. Martin Gilbert, *Churchill: A Life* (New York: Henry Holt, 1992), 39.

18. Winston Churchill, *Early Life*, 45–6.

19. Ibid., 49.

20. Ibid., 62.

21. Ibid., 73.

22. Ibid., 62.

Chapter 2: The Adventurer

1. *Churchill Documents*, 1/1:625.

2. Manchester, *Last Lion 1874–1922*, 212.

3. Winston Churchill, *Early Life*, 66.

4. Ibid., 66, 44, 65.

5. *Churchill Documents*, 1/159.

6. *Churchill Documents*, 1:268.

7. Winston Churchill, *Early Life*, 83–4, 85.

8. Ibid., 86.

9. Gilbert, *Churchill: A Life*, 60.

10. Winston Churchill, *Early Life*, 82.

11. Ibid., 89, 99.

12. Ibid., 93.

13. Ibid., 93–4.

14. Ibid., 102.

15. Byron Farwell, *The Armies of the Raj: From the Great Indian Mutiny to Independence, 1856–1947* (New York: W.W. Norton, 1991), Lawrence James, *The Raj: The Making and Unmaking of British India* (New York: St. Martin's Griffin, 2000).

16. Brian Farwell, *Queen Victoria's Little Wars* (New York: W.W. Norton, 1985); Mike Snook, *Into the Jaws of Death: British Military Blunders, 1879–1900* (Annapolis, Maryland: Naval Institute Press, 2007); Saul David, *Victoria's Wars: The Rise of Empire* (New York: Penguin, 2009).

17. Winston Churchill, *Savrola: A Tale of the Revolution in Laurania* (New York: Longmans, Green and company, 1900).
18. Brian Robson, *The Road to Kabul: The Second Afghan War 1878–1881* (London: Arms and Armour, 1986); D.S. Richard, *The Savage Frontier: A History of the Anglo-Afghan Wars* (New York: Pan Books, 2002); Michael Barthorp, *Afghan Wars and the Northwest Frontier, 1839–1947* (London: Cassell, 2002): Jules Stewart, *On Afghanistan's Plains: The Story of Britain's Afghan Wars* (London: I.B. Tauris, 2011); William Dalrymple, *Return of a King: The Battle for Afghanistan, 1839–42* (New York: Vintage, 2014).
19. Peter Hopkirk, *The Great Game: The Struggle for Empire in Central Asia* (New York: Kondasha Press, 1992); Karl Ernest Meyer and Shareen Blair Brysac, *The Tournament of Shadows: The Great Game and the Race for Empire in Central Asia* (New York: Basic Books, 2006); Karl Meyer, *The Dust of Empire: The Race for Mastery of the Asian Heartland* (New York: Public Affairs, 2004).
20. Winston Churchill, *Early Life*, 134–5.
21. Ibid., 137.
22. *Churchill Documents*, 1/1:793.
23. Winston Churchill, *Early Life*, 139–42.
24. Ibid., 146.
25. Ibid., 147.
26. Winston Churchill, *The River War: An Historical Account of the Reconquest of the Soudan* (London: Longmans, Green, 1899), 248–50.
27. Gilbert, *Churchill*, 85–96.
28. Winston Churchill, *The Story of the Malakand Field Force* (London: Dover Publications, 2010).
29. Winston Churchill, *Early Life*, 154–5.
30. Although many historians call the Mahdi's followers Dervishes, that is incorrect. Dervishes are Sufi mystics and pacifists. Jihadists are warriors committed to Islamic Holy War against infidels.
31. Edward M. Spiers, ed., *Sudan: The Reconquest Reappraised* (London: Frank Cass, 1999); Michael Asher, *Khartoum: The Ultimate Imperial Adventure* (New York: Penguin, 2006); Dominic Green, *Three Empires on the Nile: The Victorian Jihad, 1869–1899* (New York: Free Press, 2007); Robin Neillands, *The Dervish Wars: Gordon and Kitchener in the Sudan, 1880–98* (London: John Murray, 1996); David Allen Butler, *The First Jihad: Khartoum and the Dawn of Militant Islam* (London: Casemate, 2007); Mike Snook, *Beyond the Reach of Empire: Wolseley's Failed Campaign to Save Gordon and Khartoum* (London: Frontline Books, 2014).
32. Philip Montefiore Magnus, *Kitchener: Portrait of an Imperialist* (New York: Dutton, 1959); John Pollack, *Kitchener* (London: Constable, 2001).
33. Winston Churchill, *Early Life*, 161.
34. Richard Shannon, *The Age of Salisbury, 1881–1902: Unionism and Empire* (London: Longman, 1996).
35. Winston Churchill, *Early Life*, 164.
36. Ibid., 174–7.
37. Ibid., 183–5.
38. Ibid., 189–93.
39. Gilbert, *Churchill: A Life*, 99–100.
40. Winston Churchill, *The River War: An Historical Account of the Reconquest of the Soudan* (London: Longmans, Green, 1899).
41. Winston Churchill, *Early Life*, 224.
42. Gilbert, *Churchill: A Life*, 105.
43. Winston Churchill, *Early Life*, 226.
44. *Churchill Documents*, 1/1:1038.

45. Thomas Pakenham, *The Boer War* (New York: W.W. Norton, 1979); Martin Meredith, *Diamonds, Gold and War: The British, the Boers and the Making of South Africa* (New York: Public Affairs, 2009); Byron Farwell, *The Great Boer War* (London: Pen and Sword, 2009); Rodney Atwood, *Roberts and Kitchener in South Africa, 1900–1902* (London: Pen and Sword, 2012); Dennis Judd and Keith Surridge, *The Boer War: A History* (London: I.B. Tauris, 2013).
46. Winston Churchill, *London to Ladysmith via Pretoria* (London: Longmans, Green, 1900), 95, 97.
47. Winston Churchill, *Early Life*, 259.
48. Ibid., 282.
49. Ibid., 297.
50. Ibid., 318.
51. Gilbert, *Churchill: A Life*, 125.
52. Winston Churchill, *Parliamentary Debates*, 80.
53. Winston Churchill, *London to Ladysmith via Pretoria* (London: Longmans, Green, 1900).
54. Winston Churchill, *Early Life*, 353.

Chapter 3: The Reformer

1. Gilbert, *Churchill: A Life*, 134.
2. Ibid., 135.
3. Ibid., 136.
4. Winston Churchill, *Early Life*, 362.
5. *Churchill by Himself*, 368.
6. For the Conservative Party during this era, see: Frans Coetzee, *For Party or Country: Nationalism and the Dilemmas of Popular Conservatism in Edwardian England* (New York: Oxford University Press, 1990); Rhondri Williams, *Defending the Empire: The Conservative Party and British Defense Policy, 1899–1915* (New Haven, Conn.: Yale University Press, 1991); E.E.H. Green, *The Crisis of Conservatism: The Politics, Economics and Ideology of the Conservative Party, 1880–1914* (London: Routledge, 1996).
7. Winston Churchill, *Early Life*, 369.
8. John Strawson, *Churchill and Hitler: In Victory and Defeat* (New York: Fromm International, 1998), 47.
9. *Churchill by Himself*, 387.
10. Ibid., 390.
11. Anthony Howe, *Free Trade and Liberal England, 1846–1946* (Oxford: Clarendon Press, 1998),
12. B. Seebohm Rowntree, *Poverty: A Study of Town Life* (London: Macmillan, 1902).
13. *Parliamentary Debates*, 13 May 1901.
14. For the Liberal Party during this era, see: George Dangerfield, *The Strange Death of Liberal England, 1910–1914* (London: Perigee Trade Publishers, 1961); Jonathan Parry, *The Rise and Fall of Liberal Government in Victorian Britain* (New Haven, Conn.: Yale University Press, 1996); Ian Packer, *Liberal Government and Politics, 1905–15* (London: Palgrave Macmillan, 2006).
15. A.K. Russell, *The Liberal Landslide: The General Election of 1906* (London: David and Charles, 1973).
16. Winston Churchill, 'The Untrodden Field in Politics', *Finest Hour: The Journal of Winston Churchill*, No. 137, Winter 2007–08.
17. Robert Lloyd George, *David & Winston: How a Friendship Changed History* (New York: Overlook Press, 2008).
18. Winston Churchill, *Parliamentary Debates*, 96.

19. Gilbert, *Churchill: A Life*, 196.
20. For a succinct overview of these and other reforms, see: James Roy Hay, ed., *The Origins of the Liberal Welfare Reforms, 1906–14* (London: Palgrave Macmillan, 1983).
21. *Churchill Speeches*, 1:449.
22. Winston Churchill, *The World Crisis, 1911–1918* (New York: Free Press, 2005), 23.
23. Robert K. Massie, *Dreadnought: Britain, Germany and the Coming of the Great War* (New York: Ballantine Books, 1992).
24. Winston Churchill, *Parliamentary Debates*, 35, 41.
25. Gilbert, *Churchill: A Life*, 200.
26. *Churchill Power of Words*, 65–6.
27. Gilbert, *Churchill: A Life*, 210.
28. Laura E. Nym Mayhall, *The Militant Suffrage Movement: Citizenship and Resistance in Britain, 1860–1930* (New York: Oxford University Press, 2003); Shirley Harrison, *Sylvia Pankhurst: A Crusading Life, 1882–1960* (London: Aurum Press, 2004), Sylvia Pankhurst, *The Suffragette: The History of the Women's Militant Suffrage Movement* (London: Dover Publications, 2015).
29. Harrison, *Pankhurst*, 53.
30. *Churchill Speeches*, 5:44.
31. Ted Morgan, *Churchill: Young Man in a Hurry, 1874–1915* (New York: Simon and Schuster, 1982), 280.
32. Manchester, *Last Lion 1922–1940*, 415.
33. *Parliamentary Speeches*, 31 March 1910.
34. Winston Churchill, *World Crisis, 1911–1918*, 38–43.

Chapter 4: The Scapegoat
1. Robert K. Massie, *Dreadnought: Britain, Germany and the Coming of the Great War* (New York: Ballantine Books, 1992); Nicholas A. Lambert, *Sir John Fisher's Naval Revolution* (Columbia: University of South Carolina Press, 2001).
2. Winston Churchill, *World Crisis, 1911–1918* , 10.
3. *Churchill Speeches*, 2:251.
4. *Churchill Documents*, 1/1:1922
5. Winston Churchill, *World Crisis 1911–1918*, 69.
6. Gilbert, *Churchill: A Life*, 242.
7. *Churchill Documents*, 3/1:1390.
8. Manchester, *Last Lion 1874–1922*, 449.
9. For the best overviews of reasons for the war, see: Barbara W. Tuchman, *The Proud Tower: A Portrait of the World before the War, 1890–1914* (New York: Random House, 1996); Barbara Tuchman, *The Guns of August* (New York: Ballantine Books, 2004); David Fromkin, *Europe's Last Summer: Who Started the Great War in 1914?* (New York: Vintage, 2005); Margaret Macmillan, *The War That Ended Peace: the Road to 1914* (New York: Random House, 2014); Sean McMeekin, *July 1914: Countdown to War* (New York: Basic Books, 2014); Christopher Clark, *The Sleepwalkers: How Europe Went to War in 1914* (New York: Harper Perennial, 2014). For arguments that inept British diplomacy was a leading cause of the First World War, see: Niall Ferguson, *The Pity of War: Explaining World War I* (New York: Basic Books, 2000); Douglas Newton, *The Darkest Days: The Truth behind Britain's Rush to War* (London: Verso Books, 2014).
10. Ian Nish, *The Anglo-Japanese Alliance: The Diplomacy of Two Island Empires, 1894–1907* (London: Athlone Press, 1966); Philips O'Brien, *The Anglo-Japanese Alliance, 1902–1922* (London: Routledge, 2003).
11. Winston Churchill, *World Crisis 1911–1918*, 32.
12. Ibid., 33.
13. Ibid., 95.

14. Ibid., 96–7.
15. Ibid., 99.
16. Ferguson, *Pity of War*, 155.
17. Ibid., 152.
18. Geoffrey Best, *Churchill and War* (London: Hambledon, 2005), 185.
19. Frances Stevenson, *Lloyd George: A Diary by Frances Stevenson*, edited by A.J.P. Taylor (New York: Harper and Row, 1971), 38.
20. Michael and Eleanor Brock, eds, *Margot Asquith's Great War Diary* (New York: Oxford University Press, 2014), 68.
21. Ferguson, *Pity of War*, xxxvi.
22. A.J.P. Taylor, *War by Timetable: How the First World War Began* (New York: Endeavor Press, 2013).
23. R.A. Burt, *British Battleships of World War One* (Annapolis: Naval Institute Press, 2012); Lawrence Soundhaus, *The Great War at Sea: A Naval History of the First World War* (New York: Cambridge University Press, 2014); Nicholas Wolz, *From Imperial Splendor to Internment: The German Navy in the First World War* (Annapolis: Naval Institute Press, 2015); James Goldrick, *Before Jutland: The Naval War in Northern European Waters, August 1914–Febraury 1915* (Annapolis: Naval Institute Press, 2015); Marcus Faulker, *The Great War at Sea: A Naval Atlas, 1914–1919* (Annapolis: Naval Institute Press, 2015); Michele Cosentino and Ruggero Stanglini, *British and German Battlecruisers: Their Development and Operations* (Annapolis: Naval Institute Press, 2016).
24. Ted Morgan, *Churchill: Young Man in a Hurry* (New York: Simon and Schuster, 1982), 451.
25. Ian Senior, *Invasion 1914: The Schlieffen Plan to the Battle of the Marne* (London: Osprey, 2007); Terence Zuber, *Inventing the Schlieffen Plan: German War Planning, 1871–1914* (New York: Oxford University Press, 2015).
26. Ian Nish, *Alliance in Decline: A Study of Anglo-Japanese Relations, 1908–1923* (London: Bloomsbury Academic, 2013).
27. Prit Buttar, *Collision of Empires: The War on the Eastern Front in 1914* (London: Osprey, 2014); David R. Stone, *The Russian Army in the Great War: The Eastern Front, 1914–1917* (Topeka: University Press of Kansas, 2015).
28. Sewell Tyng, *The Campaign of the Marne* (London: Westholme, 2007); Holger H. Herwig, *The Marne 1914: The Opening of World War I and the Battle that Changed It* (New York: Random House, 2011).
29. Ferguson, *Pity of War*; John Keegan, *The First World War* (New York: Vintage, 2000); G.J. Meyer, *A World Undone: The Story of the Great War, 1914–1918* (New York: Delacorte Press, 2007); Peter Hart, *The Great War: A Combat History of the First World War* (New York: Oxford University Press, 2013).
30. Gilbert, *Churchill: A Life*, 287.
31. Jan Morris, *Fisher's Face: Getting to Know the Admiral* (New York: Random House, 1995).
32. Winston Churchill, *Parliamentary Debates*, 325–6.
33. Norman Friedman, *Fighting the Great War at Sea: Strategy, Tactics and Technology* (Annapolis: Naval Institute Press, 2014).
34. Robert K. Massie, *Castles of Steel: Britain, Germany and the Winning of the Great War at Sea* (New York: Ballantine Books, 2004); Peter Hart and Nigel Steel, *Jutland 1916: Death in the Grey Waters* (London: Cassell, 2007); Geoffrey Bennet, *The Battle of Jutland* (London: Pen and Sword, 2015).
35. Gilbert, *Churchill: A Life*, 289.
36. Leon Wolff, *The Flanders Campaign, Passchendaele 1917* (New York: Penguin, 2001), 190.
37. Winston Churchill, *World Crisis 1911–1918*, 292–3.

38. Ibid., 306.
39. Winston Churchill, *Parliamentary Debates*, 397.
40. Alan Moorehead, *Gallipoli* (New York: Harper, 2002); Les Carylon, *Gallipoli* (New York: Macmillan 2003); Edward J. Erickson, *Gallipoli: Command Under Fire* (London: Osprey, 2015); Edward J. Erickson, *Gallipoli: The Ottoman Campaign* (London: Pen and Sword, 2015).
41. *Churchill Documents*, 3/1:677–88.
42. Winston Churchill, *World Crisis 1911–1918*, 477.
43. Winston Churchill, *Parliamentary Debates*, 400.
44. Winston Churchill, *World Crisis 1911–1918*, 457.
45. Christopher M. Bell, *Churchill and Sea Power* (New York: Oxford University Press, 2013), 75.
46. Gilbert, *Churchill: A Life*, 342.
47. *Churchill Official Biography*, 3:473.
48. Winston Churchill, *Parliamentary Debates*, 84.
49. Gilbert, *Churchill: A Life*, 358.
50. Winston Churchill, *World Crisis 1911–1918*, 446.
51. Ibid., 315.
52. Peter Hart, *The Somme: The Darkest Hour on the Western Front* (London: Pegasus, 2016); Alexander Axelrod, *The Battle of the Somme* (London: Lyon's Press, 2016).
53. John Turner, *British Politics and the Great War: Coalition and Conflict, 1915–1918* (New Haven, Conn.: Yale University Press, 1992).
54. *Parliamentary Debates*, March 5, 1917.
55. Robert H. Zieger, *America's Great War: World War I and the American Experience* (New York: Rowan and Littlefield, 2001); Thomas Fleming, *The Illusion of Victory: America in World War I* (New York: Basic Books, 2004); H.W. Croker, *The Yanks Are Coming: A Military History of the United States in World War I* (New York: Regnery Books, 2014); Richard Striner, *A Burden Too Great to Bear: Woodrow Wilson and World War I* (New York: Rowan and Littlefield, 2014).
56. Robert Lloyd George, *David & Winston: How a Friendship Changed History* (New York: Overlook Press, 2008).
57. Manchester, *Last Lion 1874–1922*, 645.
58. *Churchill Official Biography*, 4:48.
59. Chris McCarthy, *Passchendaele: The Day by Day Account* (London: Arms and Armour, 1996); Philip Warner, *Passchendaele* (London: Pen and Sword, 2005).
60. Chris McNab, *Battle Story: Cambrai, 1917* (London: History Press, 2012), A.J. Smithers, *Cambrai: The First Great Tank Battle* (London: Pen and Sword, 2014).
61. James McWilliams and R. James Steel, *Amiens: Dawn of Victory* (London: Dundum, 2001).
62. *Churchill Documents*, 4/1:370.
63. *Churchill Official Biography*, 4:122.
64. Winston Churchill, *World Crisis 1911–1918*, 839–40.

Chapter 5: The Cassandra

1. *Commonwealth War Graves Commission*, Annual Report, 2014–15, www.cwgc.org.
2. Ferguson, *Pity of War*, xxiv, 295, 299.
3. Ibid., xxiv–v, 322–3, 325, 328, 331.
4. Margaret Macmillan, *Paris 1919: Six Months that Changed the World* (New York: Random House, 2003); Manfred F. Boeneke, Gerald Feldman and Elizabeth, eds, *The Treaty of Versailles: A Reassessment after 75 Years* (New York: Cambridge University Press, 2006); Norman A. Graebner and Edward Bennett, *The Versailles Treaty and the Legacy: The Failure of the Wilsonian Vision* (New York: Cambridge University Press,

2014): David A. Adelman, *A Shattered Peace: Versailles 1919 and the Price We Pay Today* (New York: Wiley, 2014); David Reynolds, *The Long Shadow: The Legacies of the Great War in the Twentieth Century* (New York: W.W. Norton, 2015).

5. Thomas J. Knock, *To End All Wars: Woodrow Wilson and the Quest for a New World Order* (Princeton, N.J.: Princeton University Press, 1995); John Milton Cooper, *Woodrow Wilson: A Biography* (New York: Vintage, 2011); A. Scott Berg, *Wilson* (New York: Berkley, 2014).

6. Macmillan, *Paris 1919*, 11.

7. Karl E. Meyer, *The Dust of Empire: The Race for Mastery in the Asian Heartland* (New York: Public Affairs, 2004), 6.

8. *Churchill by Himself*, 378.

9. *Parliamentary Debates*, 26 March 1936.

10. Macmillan, *Paris 1919*, 466.

11. Ibid., 489.

12. William Shirer, *The Rise and Fall of the Third Reich: A History of Nazi Germany* (New York: Simon and Shuster, 2011), 51–2.

13. John Turner, *British Politics and the Great War: Coalition and Conflict, 1915–1918* (New Haven, Conn.: Yale University Press, 1992).

14. Gilbert, *Churchill: A Life*, 407.

15. For Russia's revolution, see: Richard Pipes, *The Russian Revolution* (New York: Vintage, 1991); Orlando Figes, *A People's Tragedy: The Russian Revolution: 1891–1924* (New York: Penguin, 1998); Dominic Lieven, *The End of Tsarist Russia: The March to World War I and Revolution* (New York: Viking, 2015). For Russia's Civil War, see: W. Bruce Lincoln, *Red Victory: A History of the Russian Civil War* (New York: Simon and Schuster, 1989); Jonathan Smele, *The 'Russian' Civil Wars, 1916–1926: Ten Years That Shook the World* (New York: Oxford University Press, 2016).

16. Richard H. Ullman, *Britain and the Russian Civil War: November 1918–February 1920* (Princeton, N.J.: Princeton University Press, 1968); David S. Fogelsong, *America's Secret War against Bolshevism: U.S. Intervention in the Russian Civil War, 1917–1920* (Chapel Hill: University of North Carolina Press, 1995); Betty Miller Unterberger, *The United States, Revolutionary Russia and the Rise of Revolutionary Russia* (College Station: Texas A and M University Press, 2000).

17. *The Times*, 12 April 1919.

18. *Weekly Review*, 22 June 1919.

19. *Churchill by Himself*, 145.

20. *Evening News*, 28 July 1920.

21. Robert Rhodes James, ed., *Churchill Speaks: Winston S. Churchill in Peace and War: Collected Speeches, 1897–1963* (London: Athenaeum, 1981), 386.

22. *Churchill by Himself*, 381.

23. *Parliamentary Debates*, 26 January 1949.

24. George Scott, *The Rise and Fall of the League of Nations* (New York: Macmillan, 1974); Susan Pedersen, *The Guardians: The League of Nations and the Crisis of Empire* (New York: Oxford University Press, 2015); Patricia Clavin, *Securing the World Economy: The Reinvention of the League of Nations, 1920–1946* (New York: Oxford University Press, 2016).

25. Arnold Toynbee, *Acquaintances* (Oxford: Oxford University Press, 1967), 211–12.

26. Macmillan, *Paris 1919*, 437.

27. Bruce Clark, *Twice a Stranger: How Mass Expulsion Forged Modern Greece and Turkey* (Cambridge, Mass.: Harvard University Press, 2006); David Fromkin, *A Peace to End all Peace: The Fall of the Ottoman Empire and the Creation of the Modern Middle East* (New York: Henry Holt, 2009); Isiah Friedman, *British Miscalculations: The Rise of Muslim Nationalism, 1918–1925* (New York: Transaction Publishers, 2012); Sean McMeekin,

The Ottoman Endgame: War, Revolution and the Making of the Modern Middle East, 1908–1923 (New York: Penguin, 2015).

28. Ronald Sanders, *The High Walls of Jerusalem: A History of the Balfour Declaration and the Birth of the British Mandate for Palestine* (New York: Holt, Rinehart and Winston, 1984); Jonathan Schneer, *The Balfour Declaration: The Origins of the Arab-Israeli Conflict* (New York: Random House, 2010); Eugene Rogan, *The Fall of the Ottomans: The Great War in the Middle East* (New York: Basic Books, 2015).

29. Bernard Wasserstein, *The British in Palestine: The Mandatory Government and Arab-Jewish Conflict, 1917–1929* (London: Blackwell, 1991); Tom Segev, *One Palestine, Complete: Jews and Arabs under the British Mandate* (New York: Picador, 2001).

30. *Churchill by Himself*, 175.

31. Gilbert, *Churchill: A Life*, 435–6.

32. Manchester, *Last Lion 1874–1922*, 704–05.

33. Gilbert, *Churchill: A Life*, 449.

34. *Churchill by Himself*, 165.

35. For the Irish struggle for freedom, see: Marie Coleman, *The Irish Revolution, 1916–1923* (London: Routledge, 2013); Donald P. Corcoran, *Freedom to Achieve Freedom: The Irish Free State, 1922–1932* (London: Gill and Macmillan, 2014); Ivan Gibbons, *The British Labour Party and the Establishment of the Irish Free State, 1918–1924* (New York: Palgrave Macmillan, 2015). For Michael Collins, see: Ulick O'Connor, *Michael Collins and the Troubles: The Struggle for Irish Freedom, 1912–1922* (New York: W.W. Norton, 1996); T. Ryle Dwyer, *Big Fellow, Long Fellow: A Joint Biography of Collins and De Valera* (New York: St. Martin's Press, 2006); J.B.E. Hittle, *Michael Collins and the Anglo-Irish War: Britain's Counterinsurgency Failure* (Washington D.C.: Potomac Books, 2011).

36. Anthony J. Jordan, *Churchill: A Founder of Modern Ireland* (London: Westport Books, 1995).

37. Manchester, *Last Lion 1874–1922*, 723.

38. *Churchill by Himself*, 168.

39. Winston Churchill, *Parliamentary Debates*, 178.

40. Gilbert, *Churchill: A Life*, 444–5.

41. For the treaties and subsequent naval power, see: Richard Fanning, *Peace and Disarmament: Naval Rivalry and Arms Control, 1922–1933* (Lexington: University Press of Kentucky, 1994); Emily O. Goldman, *Sunken Treaties: Naval Arms Control between the Wars* (University Park: Pennsylvania State University, 1994); Erik Goldstein and John Maurer, eds, *The Washington Conference, 1921–1922: Naval Rivalry, East Asian Stability and the Road to Pearl Harbor* (London: Routledge, 1995); John Mauer and Christopher Bell, eds, *At the Crossroads between Peace and War: The London Naval Conference of 1930* (Annapolis: Naval Institute Press, 2014); John Jordan, *Warships after Washington: The Development of the Five Major Fleets, 1922–1930* (Annapolis: Naval Institute Press, 2015).

42. *Churchill by Himself*, 332.

43. Manchester, *Last Lion 1874–1922*, 760.

44. Philip Williamson, *Stanley Baldwin: Conservative Leadership and National Values* (New York: Cambridge University Press, 2007).

45. Chris Cook, *The Age of Alignment: Electoral Politics in Britain, 1922–1929* (London: Palgrave Macmillan, 2015).

46. David Marquand, *Ramsay MacDonald: A Biography* (London: Metro Books, 1997); Kevin Morgan, *Ramsay MacDonald* (London: Haus Publishing, 2006).

47. For an overview, see: Ivor Bulmer-Thomas, *The Growth of the British Party System, 1924–1964*, 2 vols (London: Humanities Press, 1966). For the Labour Party's ascendency, see: Maurice Cowling, *The Impact of Labour, 1920–1924: The Beginning*

of Modern British Politics (New York: Cambridge University Press, 1971); Ben Pimlott, *Labour and the Left in the 1930s* (New York: Cambridge University Press, 1977); Paul Adelman, *The Rise of the Labour Party, 1880–1945* (London: Routledge, 1996); Rhiannon Vickers, *The Labour Party and the World: The Evolution of Labour's Foreign Policy, 1900–51* (Manchester: Manchester University Press, 2013); Andrew Thorpe, *A History of the British Labour Party* (New York: Palgrave Macmillan, 2015). For the Liberal Party's near death, see: Paul Adelman, *The Decline of the Liberal Party, 1910–1931* (London: Routledge, 1995); G.R. Seale, *The Liberal Party: Triumph and Disintegration, 1886–1929* (London: Palgrave Macmillan, 2001); Lord Roy Jenkins, *The British Liberal Tradition: From Gladstone through to Young Churchill, Asquith and Lloyd George* (Toronto: University of Toronto Press, 2001); David Dutton, *A History of the Liberal Party since 1900* (London: Palgrave Macmillan, 2013). For the Conservative Party's political roller-coaster, see: Stuart Ball, *The Conservative Party and British Politics, 1902–1951* (New York: Routledge, 1995); Alan Clark, *The Tories: Conservatives and the Nation State, 1922–97* (London: Phoenix Books, 1999); Stuart Ball, *Portrait of a Party: The Conservative Party in Britain, 1918–1945* (New York: Oxford University Press, 2013).

48. Winston Churchill, *Great Contemporaries*, 282.
49. Mary S. Lovell, *The Churchills in Love and War* (New York: W.W. Norton, 2012), 344.
50. Winston Churchill, *Memoirs of the Second World War*, 14.
51. *Churchill by Himself*, 518.
52. *Parliamentary Debates*, 28 April 1925.
53. For Britain, see: Martin Dauntin, *Wealth and Welfare: An Economic and Social History of Britain, 1851–1951* (New York: Oxford University Press, 2007); Richard Overy, *The Twilight Years: The Paradox of Britain Between the Wars* (New York: Penguin, 2010). For Keynes, see: John Maynard Keynes, *The General Theory of Employment, Interest and Money* (New York: Harcourt, Brace and the World, 1965); Robert Skidelsky, ed., *The Essential Keynes* (New York: Penguin, 2016).
54. Peter Clark, 'Churchill's Economic Ideas, 1900–1930', in Robert Blake and William Roger Louis, eds, *Churchill: A Major New Assessment of his Life in Peace and War* (New York: W.W. Norton, 1993), 81.
55. *Churchill Documents*, 5/2:399.
56. Manchester, *Last Lion 1874–1922*, 814.
57. Nathan Miller, *New World Coming: The 1920s and the Making of Modern America* (New York: Da Capo Press, 2004); David E. Kyvig, *Daily Life in the United States, 1920–1940: How Americans Lived Through the Roaring Twenties and Great Depression* (New York: Ivan R. Dee, 2004); Lucy Moore, *Anything Goes: A Biography of the Roaring Twenties* (New York: Overlook Press, 2010); David Reynolds, *The Long Shadow: The Legacies of the Great War in the Twentieth Century* (New York: W.W. Norton, 2014); Adam Tooze, *The Deluge: The Great War, America and the Remaking of the Global Order, 1916–1931* (New York: Penguin, 2015).
58. Macmillan, *Paris 1919*, 480.
59. *Churchill by Himself*, 17.
60. *The Times*, 21 January 1927.
61. Stuart Ball, *Baldwin and the Conservative Party: The Crisis of 1929–1931* (New Haven, Conn.: Yale University Press, 1988); Neil Riddell, *Labour In Crisis: The Second Labour Government, 1929–31* (Manchester: Manchester University Press, 1999).
62. Winston Churchill, *Memoirs of the Second World War*, 20.
63. *Churchill Official Biography*, 5:350.
64. Manchester, *Last Lion 1874–1922*, 827.
65. Deitmar Rothermund, *The Global Impact of the Great Depression, 1929–1939* (London: Routledge, 1996); Robert Boyce, *The Great Interwar Crisis and the Collapse*

of Globalization (New York: Palgrave Macmillan, 2009); Charles P. Kindleberger, *The World in Depression, 1929–1939* (Berkeley: University of California Press, 2013); John E. Moser, *The Global Great Depression and the Coming of World War II* (London: Routledge, 2015).

66. Andrew Thorpe, *The British General Election of 1931* (New York: Oxford University Press, 1991).
67. *Daily Mail*, 4 January 1932.
68. Winston Churchill, *Memoirs of the Second World War*, 39.
69. Stanley G. Payne, *A History of Fascism, 1914–1945* (Madison: University of Wisconsin Press, 1995); Robert O. Paxton, *The Anatomy of Fascism* (New York: Vintage, 2005).
70. Jaspar Ridley, *Mussolini: A Biography* (New York: Cooper Square Press, 2000); R.J.B. Bosworth, *Mussolini* (London: Arnold, 2002); Christopher Hibbert, *Mussolini: The Rise and Fall of Il Duce* (New York: St. Martin's Griffin, 2008).
71. Bosworth, *Mussolini*, 216.
72. Ibid., 222–3.
73. John Toland, *Adolf Hitler: The Definitive Biography* (New York: Anchor Books, 1992); Ian Kershaw, *Hitler: A Biography* (New York: W.W. Norton, 2010).
74. Richard Evans, *The Coming of the Third Reich* (New York: Penguin, 2005); Eric Weitz, *The Weimar Republic: Promise and Tragedy* (Princeton University Press, 2012); Frederick Taylor, *The Downfall of Money: Germany's Hyperinflation and the Destruction of the Middle Class* (London: Bloomsbury Press, 2015).
75. For Japanese fascism, see: Alan Tansman, ed., *The Culture of Japanese Fascism* (Durham, N.C.: Duke University Press, 2009); Yoshimi Yoshiaki, *Grassroots Fascism: The War Experience of the Japanese People* (New York: Columbia University Press, 2015). For Japanese imperialism, see: Ramon H. Myers and Mark R. Peattie, eds, *The Japanese Colonial Empire* (Princeton, N.J.: Princeton University Press, 1987); W.G. Beasley, *Japanese Imperialism, 1884–1945* (London: Clarendon, 1991); Aaron Moore, *Constructing East Asia: Technology, Ideology and Empire in Japan's Wartime Era, 1931–1945* (Palo Alto, Calif.: Stanford University Press, 2015).
76. Louise Young, *Japan's Total Empire: Manchuria and the Culture of Wartime Imperialism* (Berkeley: University of California Press, 1999); Sandra Wilson, *The Manchurian Crisis and Japanese Society, 1931–1933* (London: Routledge, 2001).
77. Peijian Shen, *The Age of Appeasement: The Evolution of British Foreign Policy in the 1930s* (London: Alan Sutton, 2000).
78. Ronald McCullum, *Public Opinion and the Last Peace* (Oxford: Oxford University Press, 1944).
79. Gilbert, *Churchill: A Life*, 513.
80. Winston Churchill, *Memoirs of the Second World War*, 12.
81. Carolyn J. Kitching, *Britain and the Geneva Disarmament Conference* (New York: Palgrave Macmillan, 2013). See also Joseph Maiolo, *Cry Havoc: How the Arms Race Drove the World to War, 1931–1941* (New York: Basic Books, 2012).
82. Ronald E. Powaski, *Toward an Entangling Alliance: American Isolationism, Internationalism and Europe, 1901–1950* (Westport, Conn.: Greenwood Press, 1991), 61.
83. *Parliamentary Debates*, 13 July 1934.
84. *Parliamentary Debates*, 13 May 1932.
85. *Parliamentary Debates*, 23 November 1932.
86. *Parliamentary Debates*, 24 October 1935.
87. *Churchill by Himself*, 438.
88. For the classic account, see: Shirer, *Third Reich*. For Germany's military, see: Nicolas Stargardt, *The German War: A Nation Under Arms, 1939–45* (New York: Basic Books, 2015).
89. *Parliamentary Debates*, 28 November 1934.

90. Winston Churchill, *Memoirs of the Second World War*, 58.

91. Shirer, *Third Reich*, 296.

92. Winston Churchill, *The Second World War: The Gathering Storm* (Boston: Houghton Mifflin, 1948), 200.

93. *Churchill by Himself*, 251, 322.

94. Nick Lloyd, *The Amritsar Massacre: The Untold Story of One Fateful Day* (London: I.B. Tauris, 2011).

95. *Churchill by Himself*, 163.

96. Winston Churchill, *India: Speeches* (London: Thornton Butterworth, 1931), 87–97.

97. Winston Churchill, *Memoirs of the Second World War*, 74.

98. Ibid., 81.

99. Robert Mallett, *Mussolini and the Origins of the Second World War, 1933–1940* (New York: Palgrave Macmillan, 2003).

100. Winston Churchill, *Gathering Storm*, 196.

101. Winston Churchill, *Memoirs of the Second World War*, 94.

102. Shirer, *Third Reich*, 294.

103. *Churchill Documents*, 5/3:348.

104. Winston Churchill, *Memoirs of the Second World War*, 99.

105. *Parliamentary Debates*, 12 November 1936.

106. Winston Churchill, *Memoirs of the Second World War*, 104–05.

107. For the best biographies of each man, see: Philip Williamson, *Stanley Baldwin: Conservative Leadership and National Values* (New York: Cambridge University Press, 2007); Robert Self, *Neville Chamberlain: A Biography* (London: Routledge, 2009). For books on Chamberlain's overall appeasement policies, see: Andrew David Stedman, *Alternative to Appeasement: Neville Chamberlain and Hitler's Germany* (London: I.B. Tauris, 2015); John Ruggiero, *Hitler's Enabler: Neville Chamberlain and the Origins of the Second World War* (New York: Praeger, 2015).

108. *Churchill by Himself*, 322.

109. Winston Churchill, *Memoirs of the Second World War*, 105–06.

110. *Parliamentary Debates*, 14 April 1937.

111. For the Sino-Japanese war, see: Dick Wilson, *When Tigers Fight: The Story of the Sino-Japanese War, 1937–1945* (New York: Penguin, 1983); John Toland, *The Rising Sun: The Rise and Fall of the Japanese Empire, 1936–1945* (New York: Modern Library 2003); Rana Mitter, *China's War with Japan, 1937–1945* (New York: Penguin, 2014); Hakan Gustavsson, *The Sino-Japanese War, 1937–1945: The Longest Struggle* (New York: Fonthill Media, 2016). For Japanese war crimes, see: Yuki Tanaka, *Hidden Horrors: Japanese War Crimes in World War II* (Boulder, Colo.: Westview Press, 1996); Laurence Rees, *Horror in the Far East: Japan and the Atrocities of World War II* (New York: Da Capo, 2002); Peter Li, *Japanese War Crimes* (New York: Transaction Books, 2003); Iris Chang, *The Rape of Nanjing: The Forgotten Holocaust of World War II* (New York: Basic Books, 2012).

112. For China's civil war and leaders, see: E.R. Hootan, *The Great Tumult: The Chinese Civil War, 1936–1949* (Washington D.C.: Brassey's, 1991); Jonathan Spence, *Mao Zedong: A Life* (New York: Penguin, 2006); Jonathan Fenby, *Chiang Kai-Shek: China's Generalissimo and the Nation He Lost* (New York: Da Capo, 2005); Jay Taylor, *The Generalissmo: Chiang Kai-shek and the Struggle for Modern China* (New York: Belknap Press, 2011).

113. Shirer, *Third Reich*, 328.

114. Edward M. Bennett, *Separated by a Common Language: Franklin Delano Roosevelt and Anglo-American Relations, 1933–1939* (New York: Writer's Club Press, 2002).

115. Winston Churchill, *Memoirs of the Second World War*, 113.

116. *Parliamentary Debates*, 14 March 1938.

117. *Parliamentary Debates*, 24 March 1938.

118. Telford Taylor, *Munich: The Price of Peace* (New York: Doubleday, 1979), Erik Goldstein and Igor Luks, *The Munich Crisis: Prelude to World War II* (London: Routledge, 1999); David Faber, *Munich 1938: Appeasement and World War II* (New York: Simon and Schuster, 2010).

119. Winston Churchill, *Gathering Storm*, 304.

120. Shirer, *Third Reich*, 380.

121. Ibid., 403.

122. Winston Churchill, *Memoirs of the Second World War*, 138.

123. Bonham Carter, *Churchill*, 287.

124. *Parliamentary Debates*, 4 October 1938.

125. *Churchill Official Biography*, 5:1016.

126. Galeazzo Ciano, *The Ciano Diaries, 1939–1943: The Complete, Unabridged Diaries of Count Galeazzo Ciano, Italian Minister of Foreign Affairs, 1936–1943*, edited by Hugh Wilson (New York: Simon, 1945), 9.

127. *Churchill by Himself*, 140.

128. Alan Bullock, *Hitler and Stalin: Parallel Lives* (New York: Vintage, 1993).

129. *Parliamentary Debates*, 31 March 1939.

130. Winston Churchill, *Memoirs of the Second World War*, 148–9.

131. *Churchill by Himself*, 101.

132. *Churchill Documents*, 5:1519–20.

133. *Churchill by Himself*, 172.

134. *Parliamentary Debates*, 19 May 1939.

135. Shirer, *Third Reich*, 469–75.

136. Richard Hargreaves, *Blitzkrieg Unleashed: The German Invasion of Poland, 1939* (Mechanicsburg, Penn.: Stackpole Books, 2009); David G. Williamson, *Poland Betrayed: the Nazi-Soviet Invasion of 1939* (Mechanicsburg, Penn.: Stackpole Books, 2011).

137. Allen Paul, *Katyn: Stalin's Massacre and the Triumph of Truth* (Chicago: Northern Illinois University Press, 2010).

138. Winston Churchill, *Memoirs of the Second World War*, 166–7.

Chapter 6: The Commander

1. Virginia Cowles, *Winston Churchill: The Era and the Man* (New York: Grosset and Dunlap, 1956), 313.

2. Warren F. Kimball, ed., *Churchill and Roosevelt: The Complete Correspondence*, 3 vols (Princeton, N.J.: Princeton University Press), 1:24.

3. Joseph P. Lash, *Roosevelt and Churchill, 1939–1945: The Relations that Saved the West* (New York: W.W. Norton, 1976); Jon Meacham, *Franklin and Winston: An Intimate Portrait of an Epic Friendship* (New York: Random House, 2004); David Stafford, *Roosevelt and Churchill: Men of Secrets* (New York: Overlook Press, 2011).

4. *Churchill by Himself*, 145.

5. Edward Louis Spears, *Assignment to Catastrophe: Prelude to Dunkirk*, 2 vols (London: A.A. Wyn, 1955), 1:7.

6. Winston Churchill, *Memoirs of the Second World War*, 195.

7. Francois Kersaudy, *Norway 1940* (Lincoln, Neb.: Bison Books, 1998); Henrik O. Lunde, *Hitler's Preemptive War: The Battle for Norway, 1940* (London: Casemate, 2009); Geirr H. Haar, *The German Invasion of Norway: April 1940* (Annapolis, Maryland: Naval Institute Press, 2012).

8. Manchester, *Last Lion 1922–1940*, 645.

9. *Parliamentary Debates*, 8 May 1940.

10. Winston Churchill, *Memoirs of the Second World War*, 225.

11. Charles Watson, Lord Moran, *Churchill: The Struggle for Survival, 1945–1965* (New York: Basic Books, 2006), 827.

12. Winston Churchill, *Memoirs of the Second World War*, 227.
13. Julian Jackson, *The Fall of France: The Nazi Invasion of 1940* (New York: Oxford University Press, 2004); Alistair Horne, *To Lose a Battle: France 1940* (New York: Penguin, 2007); Karl Heinz Frieser, *The Blitzkrieg Legend: The 1940 Campaign in the West* (Annapolis: Naval Institute Press, 2013).
14. Christopher Chant, *Warfare and the Third Reich* (New York: Barnes and Noble, 1998), 151.
15. *Parliamentary Debates*, 13 May 1940.
16. Winston Churchill, *Memoirs of the Second World War*, 304–05.
17. Maxwell Philip Schoenfeld, *The War Ministry of Winston Churchill* (Ames: Iowa State University Press, 1972); Max Hastings, *Winston's War: Churchill, 1940–1945* (New York: Vintage, 2011).
18. *Churchill by Himself*, 530.
19. Mary Soames, *Clementine Churchill: The Biography of a Marriage* (New York: Mariner Books, 2003), 383.
20. Jonathan Schneer, *Ministers at War: Winston Churchill and His War Cabinet* (New York: Basic Books, 2014), 110.
21. David Fraser, *Allanbrooke* (London: Arrow Books, 1983), 202.
22. Winston Churchill, *Memoirs of the Second World War*, 190.
23. For an excellent account of these crucial days of late May 1940, see: John Lukacs, *Five Days in London: May 1940* (New Haven, Conn.: Yale University Press, 1999).
24. Winston Churchill, *Memoirs of the Second World War*, 281.
25. Julian Thompson, *Dunkirk: Retreat to Victory* (London: Arcade Publishing, 2011); Walter Lord, *The Miracle of Dunkirk* (New York: Viking, 2012).
26. *Parliamentary Debates*, 4 June 1940.
27. Gilbert, *Churchill: A Life*, 646.
28. Milton Viorst, *Hostile Allies: FDR and de Gaulle* (New York: Macmillan, 1965), 22.
29. *Parliamentary Debates*, 8 June 1940.
30. *Churchill by Himself*, 5.
31. Robert O. Paxton, *Vichy France: Old Guard and New Order, 1940–1944* (New York: Columbia University Press, 2001); Julian Jackson, *France: The Dark Years, 1940–1944* (New York: Oxford University Press, 2003).
32. David Brown, *The Road to Oran: Anglo-French Naval Relations, September 1939–July 1940* (London: Routledge, 2004).
33. Hugh Dalton, *Memoirs, 1931–1945: The Fateful Years* (London: Frederick Muller, 1957), 365–7.
34. For the Battle of Britain, see: James Holland, *The Battle of Britain: Five Months That Changed History, May–October 1940* (New York: St. Martin's Griffin, 2012); Christer Bergstrom, *The Battle of Britain: An Epic Conflict Revisited* (London: Casemate, 2015); Stephen Bungay, *The Most Dangerous Enemy: A History of the Battle of Britain* (London: Aurum Press, 2015). For the Battle of the Atlantic, see: Tony Hughes and John Costello, *The Battle of the Atlantic* (New York: Dial Press, 1972); Nathan Miller, *The War at Sea: A Naval History of World War II* (New York: Scribner's, 1995); Bernard Ireland, *The Battle of the Atlantic* (Annapolis, Maryland: Naval Institute Press, 2003); Jak P. Mallman Showell, *Hitler's Navy: A Reference Guide to the Kriegsmarine, 1935–1945* (Annapolis: Naval Institute Press, 2009); Marc Milner, *The Battle of the Atlantic* (London: History Press, 2011); Jonathan Dimbleby, *The Battle of the Atlantic: How the Allies Won the War* (New York: Viking, 2015).
35. *Parliamentary Debates*, 20 August 1940.
36. Randolph Churchill, ed., *Into Battle: Speeches by the Right Hon. Winston S. Churchill* (London: Cassell, 1941), 275.
37. Schoenfeld, *The War Ministry of Winston Churchill*, 93.

38. Winston Churchill, *The End of the Beginning* (London: Cassell, 1943), 103–04.
39. Winston Churchill, *Memoirs of the Second World War*, 410, 700.
40. Shirer, *Third Reich*, 635–6.
41. Battle of the Atlantic Statistics, *American Merchant Marine at War*, www.usmm.org; Showell, *Hitler's Navy*.
42. John Grafton, ed., *Franklin Delano Roosevelt: Great Speeches* (Mineola, N.Y.: Dover Thrift Editions, 1999), 70.
43. Waldo Henrichs, *Threshold of War: Franklin D. Roosevelt and America's Entry into World War II* (New York: Oxford University Press, 1990); Eric Hammell, *How America Saved the World: The Untold Story of U.S. Preparedness between the World Wars* (New York: Zenith Press, 2009); David Kaiser, *No End Save Victory: how FDR Led the Nation into War* (New York: Basic Books, 2014); Nicholas Wapshott, *The Sphinx: Franklin Roosevelt, the Isolationists and the Road to World War II* (New York: W.W. Norton, 2014).
44. Robert E. Sherwood, *Roosevelt and Hopkins* (New York: Enigma Books, 2008).
45. Meacham, *Franklin and Churchill*, 76.
46. William D. Pederson, *The FDR Years* (New York: Facts on File, 2006), 395.
47. Hammell, *How America Saved the World*, 235.
48. Warren F. Kimball, *The Most Unsordid Act: Lend-Lease, 1939–1941* (Baltimore: University of Johns Hopkins Press, 1969); George C. Herring, *Aid to Russia, 1941–1946: Strategy, Diplomacy and the Origins of the Cold War* (New York: Columbia University Press, 1973); Alan P. Dobson, *U.S. Wartime Aid to Britain, 1940–1946* (London: Croom Helm, 1986); Albert L. Weeks, *Russia's Life-Saver: Lend-Lease Aid to the U.S.S.R. in World War II* (Boston: Lexington Books, 2010).
49. *Churchill by Himself*, 131.
50. Winston Churchill, *Memoirs of the Second World War*, 718.
51. Roberta Wohlstetter, *Pearl Harbor: Warning and Decisions* (Palo Alto, Calif.: Stanford University Press, 1962); John Winton, *Ultra at Sea: How Breaking the Nazi Code Affected Allied Naval Strategy during World War II* (New York: Quill, 1990); David Kahn, *Seizing the Enigma: The Race to Break the U-Boat Codes, 1939–1943* (New York: Houghton Mifflin, 1991); F.H. Hinsley and Alan Stripp, eds, *Codebreakers: The Inside Story of Bletchley Park* (New York: Oxford University Press, 2001); Sinclair McKay, *The Secret Life of Bletchley Park* (London: Aurum Press, 2011); John Jackson, *Solving Enigma's Secrets: The Official History of Bletchley Park's Hut 6* (London: Book Tower Publishing, 2014).
52. Kahn, *Seizing the Enigma*, 185.
53. Ronald William Clark, *The Man Who Broke Purple: the life of Colonel William F. Friedman, Who Deciphered the Japanese Code in World War II* (Boston: Little, Brown, 1977); Ronald Lewin, *The American Magic: Codes, Ciphers and the Defeat of Japan* (New York: Farrar, Straus and Giroux, 1982); John Winton, *Ultra in the Pacific: How Breaking Japanese Codes & Cyphers Affected Naval Operations against Japan 1941–45* (Annapolis, Maryland: Naval Institute Press, 1994).
54. McGregor Knox, *Hitler's Italian Allies: Royal Armed Forces, Fascist Regime and the War of 1940–1943* (New York: Cambridge University Press, 2000); John Gooch, *Mussolini and His Generals: The Armed Forces and Fascist Foreign Policy, 1922–1940* (New York: Cambridge Military Histories, 2007); H. James Burgwyn, *Mussolini Warlord: Failed Dreams of Empire, 1940–1943* (New York: Enigma Books, 2012).
55. John Baynes, *The Forgotten Victory: General Sir Richard O'Connor* (Washington D.C.: Brassey's 1989).
56. Peter Ewer, *Forgotten Anzacs: The Campaign in Greece, 1941* (London: Scribe Publications, 2010); John Carr, *The Defense and Fall of Greece, 1940–1941* (London: Pen and Sword, 2013); Antony Beevor, *Crete 1941: The Battle and the Resistance* (New York: Penguin, 2014).

57. *Churchill Documents*, 3:445.
58. David Silverfarb, *The Twilight of British Ascendancy in the Middle East: A Case Study of Iraq, 1941–1950* (New York: St. Martin's Press, 1994): Reeva Spector Simon, *Iraq between the Two World Wars* (New York: Columbia University Press, 2004); Robert Lyman, *Iraq 1941: The Battles for Basra, Habbaniya, Falluja and Baghdad* (London: Osprey Books, 2006).
59. Peter Jacobs, *Fortress Island Malta: Defense and Re-Supply During the Siege* (London: Pen and Sword, 2016).
60. John Colville, *The Fringes of Power: 10 Downing Street Diaries, 1939–1955* (New York: W.W. Norton, 1989), 195.
61. Simon Sebag Montfiore, *Stalin: The Court of the Red Tsar* (New York: Vintage, 2005); Donald Rayfield, *Stalin and his Henchmen: The Tyrant and Those Who Killed for Him* (New York: Random House, 2005); Oleg V. Khlevniuk and Nora Seligman Favorov, *Stalin: A New Biography of a Dictator* (New Haven, Conn.: Yale University Press, 2015).
62. David Stahel, *Operation Barbarossa and Germany's Defeat in the East* (New York: Cambridge University Press, 1991); Frank Ellis, *Barbarossa 1941: Reframing Hitler's Invasion of Stalin's Soviet Empire* (Topeka: University of Kansas Press, 2015).
63. Shirer, *Third Reich*, 940.
64. Winston Churchill, *Memoirs of the Second World War*, 469–70.
65. Toland, *The Rising Sun*.
66. Joseph P. Lash, *Roosevelt and Churchill: The Partnership that Saved the West, 1939–1941* (New York: W.W. Norton, 1976); Warren F. Kimball, *Forged in War: Roosevelt, Churchill and the Second World War* (New York: William Morrow, 1997); Stafford, *Roosevelt and Churchill: Men of Secrets*; Jon Meacham, *Franklin and Winston*. For their letters, see: Warren Kimball, ed., *Churchill & Roosevelt: The Complete Correspondence*, 3 vols (Princeton, N.J.: Princeton University Press, 1987).
67. *Churchill by Himself*, 371.
68. Theodore A. Wilson, *The First Summit: Roosevelt and Churchill at Placentia Bay, 1941* (Topeka: University Press of Kansas, 1991).
69. Winston Churchill, *The Unrelenting Struggle* (Boston: Little, Brown, 1942), 231.
70. For the best mainstream historical accounts, see: Gordon W. Prange and Donald M. Goldstein, *At Dawn We Slept: The Untold Story of Pearl Harbor* (New York: Penguin, 1982); Walter Lord, *Day of Infamy: The Classic Account of the Bombing of Pearl Harbor* (New York: Henry Holt, 2001); Steven M. Gillon, *Pearl Harbor: FDR Leads the Nation into War* (New York: Basic Books, 2012). For two highly controversial revisionist views based on flimsy circumstantial evidence that either Churchill or Roosevelt knew about the pending Pearl Harbor attack and deliberately let it happen to bring America into the war, see: James Rusbridger, *Betrayal at Pearl Harbor: How Churchill Lured Roosevelt into World War II* (New York: Summit Books, 1991); and Robert Stinnett, *Day of Deceit: The Truth about FDR and Pearl Harbor* (New York: Free Press, 2001).
71. Winston Churchill, *Memoirs of the Second World War*, 506–08.
72. James Mikel Wilson, *Churchill and Roosevelt: The Big Sleepover at the White House, Christmas 1941–New Year 1942* (New York: Gatekeeper Press, 2015).
73. Winston Churchill, *The Unrelenting Struggle*, Schoenfeld, 231.
74. Eric Larrabee, *Commander in Chief: Franklin D. Roosevelt, His Lieutenants and Their War* (New York: HarperCollins, 1982); Nigel Hamilton, *The Mantle of Command: FDR at War, 1941–1942* (New York: Houghton Mifflin, 2014); Jonathan W. Jordan, *American Warlords: How Roosevelt's High Command Led America to Victory in World War II* (New York: Penguin, 2015).
75. David Irving, *The War between the Generals: Inside the Allied High Command* (London: Congdon and Lattes, 1981); Mark A. Stoler, *Allies and Adversaries: The Joint Chiefs of*

Staff, the Grand Alliance and U.S. Strategy in World War II (Chapel Hill: University of North Carolina Press, 2002).

76. *Churchill by Himself*, 118.

77. Richard Connaughton, *MacArthur and Defeat in the Philippines* (New York: Overlook Books, 2001); John Gordon, *Fighting for MacArthur: The Navy and Marine Corps' Desperate Defense of the Philippines* (Annapolis: Naval Institute Press, 2011).

78. W.H. Thompson, *Assignment: Churchill* (New York: Farrar, Straus and Young, 1955), 245–6.

79. Tony Banham, *Not The Slightest Chance: The Defense of Hong Kong, 1941* (Hong Kong: Hong Kong University Press, 2005); Kevin Blackburn and Karl Hack, *Did Singapore Have to Fall?: Churchill and the Impregnable Fortress* (London: Francis and Taylor, 2004); Brian P. Farrell, *The Defense and Fall of Singapore, 1942* (London: Tempus, 2006); Noel Barber, *Sinister Twilight: The Fall of Singapore* (London: Cassell, 2007).

80. Charles Eade, ed., *The End of the Beginning: War Speeches by the Right Hon. Winston S. Churchill* (London: Cassell, 1942), 55–6.

81. Louis Allen, *Burma: The Longest War, 1941–1945* (London: Cassell, 2000); Tom Womack, *The Dutch Naval Air Force against Japan: The Defense of the Netherlands East Indies, 1941–1942* (New York: McFarland and Company, 2006); Frank McLynn, *The Burma Campaign: Disaster into Triumph, 1942–1945* (New Haven, Conn.: Yale University Press, 2011).

82. Ronald H. Spector, *Eagle Against the Sun: The American War with Japan* (New York: Vintage Books, 1985); Paul S. Dull, *A Battle History of the Japanese Navy, 1941–1945* (Annapolis: Naval Institute Press, 2007); W.P. Hopkins, *The Pacific War: The Strategy, Politics and Players that Won the War* (London: Zenith Press, 2009); John Costello, *The Pacific War: 1941–1945* (New York: Harper Perennial, 2009); Ian W. Toll, *Pacific Crucible: War at Sea in the Pacific, 1941–42* (New York: W.W. Norton, 2011); Mark Stille, *The Japanese Imperial Navy in the Pacific War* (London: Osprey, 2014): Ian W. Toll, *The Conquering Tide: War in the Pacific, 1942–1944* (New York: W.W. Norton, 2015).

83. William Manchester, *American Caesar: Douglas MacArthur, 1880–1962* (New York: Back Bay Press, 2008); Brayton Harris, *Admiral Nimitz: The Commander of the Pacific Ocean Theater* (New York: St. Martin's Press, 2012); Walter R. Borneman, *The Admirals: Nimitz, Hasley, Leahy and King: The Five Starred Admirals Who won the War at Sea* (New York: Little, Brown, 2012).

84. Richard B. Frank, *Guadalcanal: The Definitive Account of the Landmark Battle* (New York: Penguin, 1992); Jonathan Parshalls and Anthony Tully, *Shattered Sword: The Untold Story of the Battle of Midway* (Washington D.C.: Potomac Books, 2007); Robert Leckie, *Challenge for the Pacific: Guadalcanal, The Turning Point for the War* (New York: Bantam, 2010); Craig L. Symonds, *The Battle of Midway* (New York: Oxford University Press, 2013); J.E. Harrod and John Rodgaard, *Turning the Tide: The Battles of Coral Sea and Midway* (Plymouth: Plymouth University Press, 2016).

85. Christopher Alan Bagley and Tim Harper, *Forgotten Armies: Britain's Asian Empire and the War with Japan* (London: Penguin, 2005).

86. Louis Allen, *Burma: The Longest War, 1941–1945* (London: Cassell, 2000); McLynn, *The Burma Campaign.*

87. *Churchill by Himself*, 93.

88. Peter Clarke, *The Last Thousand Days of the British Empire: Churchill, Roosevelt and the Birth of Pax Americana* (London: Bloomsbury Press, 2010).

89. Hamilton, *Mantle of Command*, 247.

90. Winston Churchill, *Second World War: The Hinge of Fate* (Boston: Houghton Mifflin, 1985), 194.

91. *Churchill by Himself*, 553.

92. Samuel Mitcham, *Rommel's Greatest Victory: The Desert Fox and the Fall of Tobruk, Spring 1942* (San Francisco: Presidio Press, 2001).

93. Norman Rose, *Churchill: An Unruly Life* (London: I.B. Tauris, 2009), 317.

94. Terry Brighton, *Patton, Montgomery and Rommel: Masters of War* (New York: Broadway Books, 2010); Nigel Hamilton, *Monty*, 3 vols (New York: McGraw-Hill, 1981, 1984, 1986).

95. Winston Churchill, *Memoirs of the Second World War*, 619, 623, 624, 631.

96. Manchester and Reid, *Last Lion 1940–1965*, 566.

97. Robin Neillands, *The Dieppe Raid: The Story of the Disastrous 1942 Expedition* (Bloomington: University of Indian Press, 2005); Mark Zeuhlke, *The Tragedy at Dieppe: Operation Jubilee, August 19, 1942* (London: Douglas and McIntyre, 2014).

98. John Beirman and Colin Smith, *The Battle of Alamein, The Battle of Alamein: Turning Point of World War II* (New York: Viking, 2002); Niall Barr, *The Pendulum of War: The Three Battles of El Alamein* (London: Overlook Press, 2006); Bryn Hammond, *El Alamein: The Battle that Turned the Tide of the Second World War* (London: Osprey, 2012).

99. For Eisenhower as commander, see: Dwight Eisenhower, *Crusade in Europe* (Baltimore: Johns Hopkins, 1997); Carlo D'Este, *Eisenhower: Allied Supreme Commander* (London: Cassell, 2004); Stephen Ambrose, *The Supreme Commander: The War Years of Dwight Eisenhower* (New York: Anchor, 2012); Niall Barr, *Eisenhower's Armies: The American-British Alliance during World War II* (New York: Pegasus, 2015). For the North African campaign, see: Rick Atkinson, *An Army at Dawn: The War in North Africa, 1942–43* (New York: Henry Holt, 2007); Vincent O'Hara, *Torch: North Africa and the Allied Path to Victory* (Annapolis, Maryland: Naval Institute Press, 2015).

100. Sherwood, *Roosevelt and Hopkins*, 648.

101. Danchev and Todman, eds, *Alanbrooke, War Diaries*, 333.

102. George Patton, *War as I Knew It* (New York: Houghton Mifflin, 1995); Carlo D'Este, *Patton: A Genius for War* (New York: Harper Perennial, 1996); Ladislas Farago, *Patton: Ordeal and Triumph* (New York: Westholme, 2005).

103. *Churchill by Himself*, 8.

104. Anne Armstrong, *Unconditional Surrender: The Impact of the Casablanca Policy upon World War II* (New Brunswick, N.J.: Rutgers University Press, 1961); Nigel Hamilton, *Commander in Chief: Franklin D. Roosevelt's Battle with Churchill, 1943* (New York: Houghton Mifflin, 2016).

105. Jean Lacouture, *De Gaulle* (New York: Hutchinson, 1970), 100.

106. Winston Churchill, *Memoirs of the Second World War*, 670–2.

107. Ibid., 672–3.

108. Ferenc Morton Szasz, *British Scientists and the Manhattan Project* (London: Palgrave Macmillan, 1992); Cynthia C. Kelly, ed., *The Manhattan Project: The Birth of the Atomic Bomb in the Words of Its Creators, Eyewitnesses and Historians* (New York: Black Dog and Leventhal, 2009); Richard Rhodes, *The Making of the Atomic Bomb* (New York: Simon and Schuster, 2012).

109. Winston Churchill, *Memoirs of the Second World War*, 696.

110. Rick Atkinson, *The Day of Battle: The War in Sicily and Italy, 1943–1944* (New York: Henry Holt, 2007); Samuel W. Mitcham and Friedrich von Stauffenberg, *The Battle of Sicily: How the Allies Lost Their Chance for Total Victory* (Mechanicsburg, Penn.: Stackpole Books, 2007); Carlo D'Este, *Bitter Victors: The Battle for Sicily* (London: Arun Press, 2008).

111. Gilbert, *Churchill: A Life*, 756.

112. Winston Churchill, *Memoirs of the Second World War*, 736.

113. Manchester and Reid, *Last Lion 1940–1965*, 736.

114. Ibid., 748.

115. Herbert Feis, *Churchill-Roosevelt-Stalin: The War They Waged and the Pace They Sought* (Princeton, N.J.: Princeton University Press, 1966); Keith Sainsbury, *The Turning Point: Roosevelt, Churchill, Stalin and Chiang Kai-Shek, 1943: The Moscow, Cairo and Teheran Conferences* (New York: Oxford University Press, 1986); Ronald Heiferman, *The Cairo Conference of 1943: Roosevelt, Churchill, Chiang Kai-Shek and Madame Chiang* (New York: McFarland, 2011); L. Douglas Keeney, *The Eleventh Hour: How Great Britain, the Soviet Union and the U.S. Brokered the Unlikely Deal That Won the War* (New York: Wiley, 2015).

116. Winston Churchill, *Memoirs of the Second World War*, 768.

117. Ibid., 759.

118. Ibid., 747.

119. W. Averell Harriman and Ellie Abel, *Special Envoy to Churchill and Stalin, 1941–1946* (New York: Random House, 1975), 191.

120. Manchester and Reid, *Last Lion 1940–1965*, 768.

121. Terry Reardon, *Winston Churchill and Mackenzie King: So Similar, So Different* (Toronto: Dundern Press, 2012), 263.

122. Winston Churchill, *Memoirs of the Second World War*, 767.

123. Ibid., 778–9.

124. Russell F. Weigley, *Eisenhower's Lieutenants: The Campaign of France and Germany, 1944–1945* (Bloomington: University of Indiana Press, 1981).

125. Anthony Eden, *The Reckoning: The Memoirs of Anthony Eden, Earl of Avon* (New York: Houghton Mifflin, 1965), 524–5.

126. Lloyd Clark, *Anzio: Italy and the Battle for Rome, 1944* (New York: Grove Press, 2007); Carlo d'Este, *Fatal Decision: Anzio and the Battle for Rome* (New York: Harper Perennial, 2008).

127. *Churchill by Himself*, 283.

128. *Parliamentary Debates*, 21 April 1944.

129. Cornelius Ryan, *The Longest Day: The Classic Epic of D-Day* (New York: Simon and Schuster, 1994); Stephen Ambrose, *D-Day, June 6, 1944: The Battle for the Normandy Beaches* (New York: Pocket Books, 2002); Samuel W. Morrison, *Defenders of Fortress Europe: the Untold Story of the German Officers during the Allied Invasion* (Washington D.C.: Potomac Books, 2009), Antony Beevor, *D-Day: The Battle for Normandy* (New York: Wiley, 2010).

130. Morrison, *Defenders of Fortress Europe*.

131. John Keegan, *Six Armies in Normandy: From D-Day to the Liberation of Paris* (New York: Penguin, 1994); Max Hastings, *Overlord: D-Day and the Battle for Normandy* (New York: Vintage, 2006); Stephen Napler, *The Armored Campaign in Normandy, June–August 1944* (London: Casemate, 2015).

132. Morrison, *Defenders of Fortress Europe*, 89.

133. Nigel Jones, *Countdown to Valkyrie: The July Plot to Assassinate Hitler* (London: Frontline Books, 2008).

134. Michael J. Cohen, *Churchill and the Jews* (New York: Frank Cass, 1985), 291.

135. William Breuer, *Operation Dragoon: The Allied Invasion of the South of France* (New York: Presidio Press, 1996); Henry Yeide, *First to the Rhine: The Sixth Army Group in World War II* (London: Zenith Press, 2009); Jean Loup Gassend, *Anatomy of a Battle: The Allied Liberation of the French Riviera* (Atglen, Penn.: Schiffer Publishing, 2014).

136. Winston Churchill, *Memoirs of the Second World War*, 830.

137. Cornelius Ryan, *A Bridge Too Far: The Classic History of the Greatest Battle of World War II* (New York: Simon and Schuster, 1995).

138. *Parliamentary Debates*, 340.

139. Dieter Hosken, *V-Missiles of the Third Reich: The V-1 and V-2* (London: Monogram Aviation Publications, 1994); Benjamin King and Timothy Kutta, *Impact: The History of Germany's V-Weapons in World War II* (New York: Da Capo Press, 2009).

140. Heinz Richter, *British Intervention in Greece: From Varkiza to Civil War* (London: Merlin Press, 1985); E.C.F. Myers, *Greek Entanglement* (London: Sutton Publishing, 1985); Andre Gerolymatos, *Red Acropolis, Black Terror: The Greek Civil War and the Origins of the Soviet-American Rivalry, 1943–1949* (New York: Basic Books, 2004); John Carr, *The Defense and Fall of Greece, 1941* (London: Pen and Sword, 2013).
141. Winston Churchill, *Memoirs of the Second World War*, 900.
142. Ibid., 903.
143. *Parliamentary Debates*, 8 December 1944.
144. Winston Churchill, *Memoirs of the Second World War*, 854–85.
145. Wlodzimierz Borodziej, *The Warsaw Uprising of 1944* (Madison: University of Wisconsin Press, 2006); Alexander Richie, *Warsaw 1944: Hitler, Himmler and the Warsaw Rising* (New York: Farrar, Straus and Giroux, 2013).
146. Winston Churchill, *Memoirs of the Second World War*, 848–50.
147. *Churchill by Himself*, 286.
148. John Dietrich, *The Morgenthau Plan: Soviet Influence on American Postwar Policy* (New York: Algora Publishing, 2003); David Irving, *The Morgenthau Plan, 1944–45* (London: Focal Point Publications, 2010).
149. Manchester and Reid, *Last Lion 1940–1965*, 889–90.
150. Winston Churchill, *Memoirs of the Second World War*, 884–6.
151. Peter Caddick-Adams, *Snow and Steel: The Battle of the Bulge* (New York: Oxford University Press, 2014); Antony Beevor, *Ardennes 1944: The Battle of the Bulge* (New York: Viking, 2015).
152. Chant, *Warfare and the Third Reich*, 175.

Chapter 7: The Cold Warrior

1. Fraser J. Harbutt, *Yalta 1945: Europe and America at the Crossroads* (New York: Cambridge University Press, 2010); S.M. Pokhy, *Yalta: The Price of Peace* (New York: Penguin, 2011).
2. Winston Churchill, *Memoirs of the Second World War*, 926.
3. Ibid., 915–16.
4. Daniel Yergin, *Shattered Peace: The Origins of the Cold War* (New York: Penguin, 1990), John Lewis Gaddis, *The United States and the Origins of the Cold War, 1941–1947* (New York: Columbia University Press, 2000); Melvyn P. Leffler and David S. Painter, eds, *The Origins of the Cold War: An International History* (London: Routledge, 2005); Michael Dobbs, *Six Months in 1945: FDR, Stalin, Churchill and Truman from World War to Cold War* (New York: Random House, 2013).
5. Manchester and Reid, *Last Lion 1940–1965*, 901.
6. Kimball, ed., *Churchill and Roosevelt: The Complete Correspondence*, 3:588.
7. Marc Trachtenberg, *The Cold War and After: History, Theory and the Logic of International Relations* (Princeton, N.J.: Princeton University Press, 2012), 73.
8. Danchev and Todman, eds, *Alanbrooke, War Diaries*, 333.
9. Winston Churchill, *The Second World War: Vol 6 Triumph and Tragedy* (Boston: Houghton Mifflin 1953), 403.
10. Robert Blake and William Roger Louis, eds, *Churchill: A Major New Assessment of his Life in Peace and War* (New York: Oxford University Press, 2002), 404.
11. Dwight Eisenhower, *Crusade in Europe* (Baltimore: Johns Hopkins, 1997); Carlo D'Este, *Eisenhower: Allied Supreme Commander* (London: Cassell, 2004); Stephen Ambrose, *The Supreme Commander: The War Years of Dwight Eisenhower* (New York: Anchor, 2012).
12. Milovan Djilas, *Conversations with Stalin* (New York: Harcourt Brace, 1963), 114.
13. Winston Churchill, *Memoirs of the Second World War*, 936.
14. Ibid., 945.
15. *Parliamentary Debates*, 17 April 1945.

16. Herbert Feis, *Churchill-Roosevelt-Stalin: The War They Waged and the Peace They Sought* (Princeton, N.J.: Princeton University Press, 1966), 579.

17. D'Este, *Patton*, 721.

18. Winston Churchill, *Memoirs of the Second World War*, 952.

19. Ibid., 967–8.

20. The highest figures for these countries were culled from the following sources: John Ellis, *World War II: The Essential Facts and Figures for all the Combatants* (New York: Facts on File, 1993); Peter Howlett, *Fighting with Figures: Statistical Digest of the Second World War* (London: Stationary Office, 1995).

21. Stephen Brooke, *Labour's War: The Labour Party and the Second World War* (New York: Oxford University Press, 1992); Paul Addison, *The Road to 1945: British Politics and the Second World War* (London: Pimlico, 1994); Sonya O. Rose, *Which People's War?: National Identity and Citizenship in Wartime Britain, 1939–1945* (New York: Oxford University Press, 2004).

22. Winston Churchill, *Memoirs of the Second World War*, 977.

23. *Churchill Speeches*, 7:172–3.

24. Ibid., 7:200–04.

25. Winston Churchill, *Memoirs of the Second World War*, 946.

26. Michael Neiberg, *Potsdam: The End of World War II and the Remaking of Europe* (New York: Basic Books, 2015).

27. Winston Churchill, *Memoirs of the Second World War*, 979.

28. Ibid., 979–80.

29. Ibid., 980.

30. Gar Alperovitz, *The Decision to Use the Atomic Bomb* (New York: Vintage, 1996); Wilson D. Miscamble, *The Most Controversial Decision: Truman, the Atomic Bomb and the Defeat of Japan* (New York: Cambridge University Press, 2011).

31. R.B. McCallum and Alison Readman, *The British General Election of 1945* (London: Frank Cass, 1964).

32. Nicklaus Thomas Symonds, *Atlee: A Life in Politics* (London: I.B. Tauris, 2012).

33. Winston Churchill, *Memoirs of the Second World War*, 990.

34. *Churchill Speeches*, 7:204.

35. Frank A. Mayer, *The Opposition Years: Winston S. Churchill and the Conservative Party, 1945–1951* (Washington D.C.: American University Studies, 1992); Kevin Hickson, *The Political Thought of the Conservative Party since 1945* (New York: Palgrave Macmillan, 2005); Timothy Heppell, *The Tories: From Winston Churchill to David Cameron.* (London: Bloomsbury Academic, 2014).

36. For the best accounts of the year leading to Japan's defeat, see: Richard B. Frank, *Downfall: The End of the Imperial Japanese Empire* (New York: Penguin, 2001); Max Hastings, *Retribution: The Battle for Japan, 1944–45* (New York: Vintage, 2009).

37. Winston Churchill, *Memoirs of the Second World War*, 938.

38. Ibid., 937–8.

39. *Churchill Speeches*, 7:286.

40. James W. Muller, ed., *Churchill's 'Iron Curtain' Speech Fifty Years Later* (Columbia: University of Missouri Press, 1999).

41. *Churchill Speeches*, 7:380–2.

42. Akis Kalaitzikis and Gregory W. Streich, eds, *United States Foreign Policy: A Documentary and Reference Guide* (Westport, Conn.: Greenwood Press, 2013), 148.

43. Walter LaFeber, *America, Russia and the Cold War, 1945–1990* (Ithaca, N.Y.: Cornell University Press, 1991); John Lewis Gaddis, *The United States and the Origins of the Cold War, 1941–1947* (New York: Columbia University Press, 2000); John Lewis Gaddis, *The Cold War: A New History* (New York: Penguin, 2006); Carole K. Fink, The Cold War: An International History (Boulder, Colo.: Westview Press, 2013).

44. Allan Bullock, *Hitler and Stalin: Parallel Lives* (New York: Vintage, 1993).
45. LaFeber, *America, Russia and the Cold War*, 16.
46. *New York Times*, 15 May 1947.
47. Kenneth Thompson, *Winston Churchill's World View: Statesmanship and Power* (Baton Rouge: Louisiana State University Press, 1983), 97.
48. *The Times*, 17 July 1948.
49. *The Times*, 11 October 1948.
50. *Parliamentary Debates*, 14 December 1950.
51. Randolph S. Churchill, ed., *The Unwritten Alliance: Speeches 1953–1959 by Winston S. Churchill* (London: Cassell, 1961), 250.
52. *Churchill by Himself*, 20.
53. Ibid., 147.
54. *The Times*, 1 December 1951.
55. *Parliamentary Debates*, 10 December 1948.
56. *Parliamentary Debates*, 10 May 1951.
57. *Churchill Speeches*, 7:505.
58. Ibid., 8:909.
59. *Churchill by Himself*, 17.
60. *Churchill Speeches*, 7:653.
61. *Churchill by Himself*, 390.
62. Colin Cross, *The Fall of the British Empire, 1918–1968* (London: Putnam Publishers, 1968); W. David McIntyre, *British Decolonization, 1946–1997: Why and How did the British Empire Fall?* (London: Palgrave, 1998); John Darwin, *The End of the British Empire: The Historical Debate* (London: Wiley Blackwell, 2006).
63. Alex von Tunzelmann, *Indian Summer: The Secret History of the End of an Empire* (New York: Picador, 2008); Yasmin Khan, *The Great Partition: The Making of India and Pakistan* (New Haven, Conn.: Yale University Press, 2008); Stanley Wolpert, *Shameful Flight: The Last Years of the British Empire in India* (New York: Oxford University Press, 2009); Nisid Hajari, *Midnight's Furies: The Deadly Legacy of India's Partition* (New York: Houghton and Mifflin, 2015).
64. *Parliamentary Debates*, 28 October 1948.
65. Benny Morris, *1948: A History of the First Arab-Israeli War* (New Haven, Conn.: Yale University Press, 2009); Frank W. Brecher, *American Diplomacy and the Israeli War of Independence* (New York: McFarland, 2013).
66. H.G. Nichols, *The British General Election of 1950* (London: Macmillan, 1951); David E. Butler, *The British General Election of 1951* (London: Macmillan, 1999).
67. *Churchill by Himself*, 80.
68. *Parliamentary Debates*, 27 June 1950.
69. *News of the World*, 9 May 1938.
70. *Churchill by Himself*, 557.
71. Charles Moran, *Churchill: Taken from the Diaries of Lord Moran: The Struggle for Survival, 1940–1965* (Boston: Houghton Mifflin, 1966), 540.
72. *Parliamentary Debates*, 5 April 1954.
73. Gilbert, *Churchill: A Life*, 935–6.
74. *Churchill by Himself*, 530.
75. Ibid., 564.
76. Ibid., 463.
77. Ibid., 501.
78. *Churchill Documents*, 3/2:1098.

Bibliography

Primary Sources

Arnn, Larry P., *The Churchill Documents*, vol. 18, Hillsdale College: Hillsdale College Press, 2015.

Bonham Carter, Violet, *Winston Churchill: An Intimate Portrait*, New York: Harcourt, Brace and World, 1965.

Brock, Michael and Eleanor, eds, *Margot Asquith's Great War Diary*, New York: Oxford University Press, 2014.

Churchill, Randolph S., ed., *Into Battle: Speeches by the Right Hon. Winston S. Churchill*, London: Cassell, 1941.

Churchill, Randolph S., ed., *Stemming the Tide: Speeches 1951 and 1952 by Winston S. Churchill*, London: Cassell, 1953.

Churchill, Randolph S., ed., *The Unwritten Alliance: Speeches 1953–1959 by Winston S. Churchill*, London: Cassell, 1961.

Churchill, Winston, *The River War: An Historical Account of the Reconquest of the Soudan*, London: Longmans, Green, 1899.

Churchill, Winston, *London to Ladysmith via Pretoria*, London: Longmans, Green, 1900.

Churchill, Winston, *Savrola: A Tale of the Revolution in Laurania*, New York: Longmans, Green and Company, 1900.

Churchill, Winston, *Amid These Storms: Thoughts and Adventures*, New York: Charles Scribner's Sons, 1931.

Churchill, Winston, *India: Speeches*, London: Thornton Butterworth, 1931.

Churchill, Winston, *The Unrelenting Struggle*, Boston: Little, Brown, 1942.

Churchill, Winston, *The End of the Beginning*, London: Cassell, 1943.

Churchill, Winston, *The Second World War: The Gathering Storm*, Boston: Houghton Mifflin, 1948

Churchill, Winston, *The Unwritten Alliance*, London: Cassell, 1961.

Churchill, Winston, *History of the English Speaking Peoples*, 4 vols, New York: Dodd, Mead and Company, 1958.

Churchill, Winston, *The Second World War: The Hinge of Fate*, Boston: Houghton Mifflin, 1985.

Churchill, Winston, *The Second World War: Triumph and Tragedy*, Boston: Houghton Mifflin, 1953.

Churchill, Winston, *Memoirs of the Second World War* (abridged version), Boston: Houghton Mifflin, 1987.

Churchill, Winston, *My Early Life, 1874–1904*, New York: Touchstone Books, 1996.

Churchill, Winston, *The World Crisis, 1911–1918*, New York: Free Press, 2005.

Churchill, Winston, *The Story of the Malakand Field Force*, London: Dover Publications, 2010.

Churchill, Winston, *Great Contemporaries: Churchill Reflects on FDR, Hitler, Kipling, Chaplin, Balfour and Other Giants of His Age*, Wilmington, Del.: Intercollegiate Studies Institute, 2012.

Churchill, Winston, *Painting as a Pastime: Essays and Other Works*, London: Rosetta Books, 2014.

Churchill, Winston, *The World Crisis: The Aftermath, 1918–28*, London: Bloomsbury Academic, 2015.

Churchill, Winston S. and Randolph S. Churchill, eds, *The Churchill Documents*, vols 1–5, Hillsdale College: Hillsdale College Press, 2006–07.

Churchill, Winston S. and Martin Gilbert, eds, *The Churchill Documents*, vols 6–17, Hillsdale College: Hillsdale College Press, 2008–13.

Ciano, Galeazzo, *The Ciano Diaries, 1939–1943: The Complete, Unabridged Diaries of Count Galeazzo Ciano, Italian Minister of Foreign Affairs, 1936–1943*, edited by Hugh Wilson, New York: Simon, 1945.

Colville, John, *The Fringes of Power: 10 Downing Street Diaries, 1939–1955*, New York: W.W. Norton, 1989.

Dalton, Hugh, *Memoirs, 1931–1945: The Fateful Years*, London: Frederick Muller, 1957.

Danchev, Alex and Daniel Todman, eds, *Field Marshall Alanbrooke, War Diaries*, Berkeley: University of California Press, 2003.

Dietrich, John, *The Morgenthau Plan: Soviet Influence on American Postwar Policy*, New York: Algora Publishing, 2002.

Djilas, Milovan, *Conversations with Stalin*, New York: Harcourt Brace, 1963.

Eade, Charles, ed., *The End of the Beginning: War Speeches by the Right Hon. Winston S. Churchill*, London: Cassell, 1942.

Eade, Charles, ed., *Onwards to Victory: War Speeches by the Right Hon. Winston S. Churchill*, London: Cassell, 1948.

Eden, Anthony, *The Reckoning: The Memoirs of Anthony Eden, Earl of Avon*, New York: Houghton Mifflin, 1965.

Eisenhower, Dwight, *Crusade in Europe*, Baltimore: Johns Hopkins, 1997.

Erickson, Edward J., *Gallipoli: Command Under Fire*, London: Osprey, 2015.

Erickson, Edward J., *Gallipoli: The Ottoman Campaign*, London: Pen and Sword, 2015.

Gilbert, Martin, ed., *Churchill: The Power of Words: His Remarkable Life Recounted through his Writings and Speeches*, New York: Da Capo, 2012.

Gilbert, Martin and Larry Arnn, eds, *The Churchill Documents*, vol. 18, Hillsdale, Mich.: Hillsdale College, 2014.

Grafton, John, ed., *Franklin Delano Roosevelt: Great Speeches*, Mineola, N.Y.: Dover Thrift Editions, 1999.

Halle, Kay, *The Irrepressible Churchill: Stories, Sayings and Impressions of Sir Winston Churchill*, New York: Robson Books, 1987.

Harriman, W. Averell and Ellie Abel, *Special Envoy to Churchill and Stalin, 1941–1946*, New York: Random House, 1975.

James, Robert Rhodes, ed., *Winston S. Churchill: His Complete Speeches*, 8 vols, London: Chelsea House Publishers, 1974.

Kalaitzikis, Akis and Gregory W. Streich, eds, *United States Foreign Policy: A Documentary and Reference Guide*, Westport, Conn.: Greenwood Press, 2013.

Kimball, Warren F., *Churchill and Roosevelt: The Complete Correspondence*, 3 vols, Princeton, N.J.: Princeton University Press, 1987.

Langworth, Richard, ed., *Churchill by Himself*, New York: Public Affairs, 2008.

Moran, Charles Watson, Lord, *Churchill: The Struggle for Survival, 1945–1965*, New York: Basic Books, 2006.

Muller, James W., ed., *Churchill's 'Iron Curtain' Speech Fifty Years Later*, Columbia: University of Missouri Press, 1999.

Pankhurst, Sylvia, *The Suffragette: The History of the Women's Militant Suffrage Movement*, London: Dover Publications, 2015.

Patton, George, *War as I Knew It*, New York: Houghton Mifflin, 1995.

Skidelsky, Robert, ed., *The Essential Keynes*, New York: Penguin, 2016.

Soames, Mary, ed., *Winston and Clemmie: The Personal Letters of the Churchills*, Boston: Houghton Mifflin, 1998.

Spears, Edward Louis, *Assignment to Catastrophe: Prelude to Dunkirk*, vol. 1, London: A.A. Wyn, 1955.

Spears, Edward Louis, *Assignment to Catastrophe: The Fall of France*, vol. 2, London: A.A. Wyn, 1955.

Stansky, Peter, ed., *Churchill: A Profile*, New York: Macmillan, 1973.

Stevenson, Frances, *Lloyd George: A Diary by Frances Stevenson*, edited by A.J.P. Taylor, New York: Harper and Row, 1971.

Wheeler-Bennett, John, ed., *Action This Day: Working with Churchill*, New York: St. Martin's Press, 1969.

Secondary Sources

Addison, Paul, *The Road to 1945: British Politics and the Second World War*, London: Pimlico, 1994.

Addison, Paul, *Churchill on the Home Front, 1900–1955*, New York: Faber and Faber, 2013.

Adelman, Paul, *The Decline of the Liberal Party, 1910–1931*, London: Routledge, 1995.

Adelman, Paul, *The Rise of the Labour Party, 1880–1945*, London: Routledge, 1996.

Allen, Louis, *Burma: The Longest War, 1941–1945*, London: Cassell, 2000.

Alperovitz, Gar, *The Decision to Use the Atomic Bomb*, New York: Vintage, 1996.

Ambrose, Stephen, *D-Day, June 6, 1944: The Battle for the Normandy Beaches*, New York: Pocket Books, 2002.

Ambrose, Stephen, *The Supreme Commander: The War Years of Dwight Eisenhower*, New York: Anchor, 2012.

Andelman, David A., *A Shattered Peace: Versailles 1919 and the Price We Pay Today*, New York: Wiley, 2014.

Armstrong, Anne, *Unconditional Surrender: The Impact of the Casablanca Policy upon World War II*, New Brunswick, N.J.: Rutgers University Press, 1961.

Asher, Michael, *Khartoum: The Ultimate Imperial Adventure*, New York: Penguin, 2006.

Atkinson, Rick, *An Army at Dawn: The War in North Africa, 1942–43*, New York: Henry Holt, 2007.

Atkinson, Rick, *The Day of Battle: The War in Sicily and Italy, 1943–1944*, New York: Henry Holt, 2007.

Attenborough, Wilfred, *Churchill and the 'Black Dog' of Depression*, London: Palgrave Macmillan, 2014.

Atwood, Rodney, *Roberts and Kitchener in South Africa, 1900–1902*, London: Pen and Sword, 2012.

Axelrod, Alexander, *The Battle of the Somme*, London: Lyon's Press, 2016.

Bagley, Christopher Alan and Tim Harper, *Forgotten Armies: Britain's Asian Empire and the War with Japan*, London: Penguin, 2005.

Ball, Stuart, *Baldwin and the Conservative Party: The Crisis of 1929–1931*, New Haven, Conn.: Yale University Press, 1988.

Ball, Stuart, *The Conservative Party and British Politics, 1902–1951*, New York: Routledge, 1995.

Ball, Stuart, *Portrait of a Party: The Conservative Party in Britain, 1918–1945*, New York: Oxford University Press, 2013.

Banham, Tony, *Not the Slightest Chance: The Defense of Hong Kong, 1941*, Hong Kong: Hong Kong University Press, 2005.

Barber, Noel, *Sinister Twilight: The Fall of Singapore*, London: Cassell, 2007.

Barr, Niall, *The Pendulum of War: The Three Battles of El Alamein*, London: Overlook Press, 2006.

Barr, Niall, *Eisenhower's Armies: The American-British Alliance during World War II*, New York: Pegasus, 2015.

Barthorp, Michael, *Afghan Wars and the Northwest Frontier, 1839–1947*, London: Cassell, 2002.

Baynes, John, *The Forgotten Victory: General Sir Richard O'Connor*, Washington D.C.: Brassey's 1989.

Beasley, W.G., *Japanese Imperialism, 1884–1945*, London: Clarendon, 1991.

Beevor, Antony, *D-Day: The Battle for Normandy*, New York: Wiley, 2010.

Beevor, Antony, *Crete 1941: The Battle and the Resistance*, New York: Penguin, 2014.

Beevor, Antony, *Ardennes 1944: The Battle of the Bulge*, New York: Viking, 2015.

Beirman, John and Colin Smith, *The Battle of Alamein: Turning Point of World War II*, New York: Viking, 2002.

Bell, Christopher M., *Churchill and Sea Power*, New York: Oxford University Press, 2013.

Bennett, Edward M., *Separate by a Common Language: Franklin Delano Roosevelt and Anglo-American Relations, 1933–1939*, New York: Writer's Club Press, 2002.

Bennett, Geoffrey, *The Battle of Jutland*, London: Pen and Sword, 2015.

Berg, A. Scott, *Wilson*, New York: Berkley, 2014.

Bergstrom, Christer, *The Battle of Britain: An Epic Conflict Revisited*, London: Casemate, 2015.

Best, Geoffrey, *Churchill and War*, London: Hambledon, 2005.

Best, Geoffrey, *Churchill: A Study in Greatness*, London: Hambledon, 2006.

Blackburn, Kevin and Karl Hack, *Did Singapore Have to Fall?: Churchill and the Impregnable Fortress*, London: Francis and Taylor, 2004.

Blake, Robert and William Roger Louis, eds, *Churchill: A Major New Assessment of his Life in Peace and War*, New York: Oxford University Press, 2002.

Boeneke, Manfred F., Gerald Feldman and Elizabeth Glaser, eds, *The Treaty of Versailles: A Reassessment after 75 Years*, New York: Cambridge University Press, 2006.

Borneman, Walter R., *The Admirals: Nimitz, Hasley, Leahy and King: The Five Starred Admirals Who won the War at Sea*, New York: Little, Brown, 2012.

Borodziej, Wlodzimierz, *The Warsaw Uprising of 1944*, Madison: University of Wisconsin Press, 2006.

Bosworth, R.J.B., *Mussolini*, London: Arnold, 2002.

Boyce, Robert, *The Great Interwar Crisis and the Collapse of Globalization*, New York: Palgrave Macmillan, 2009.

Brecher, Frank W., *American Diplomacy and the Israeli War of Independence*, New York: McFarland, 2013.

Breuer, William, *Operation Dragoon: The Allied Invasion of the South of France*, New York: Presidio Press, 1996.

Brighton, Terry, *Patton, Montgomery and Rommel: Masters of War*, New York: Broadway Books, 2010.

Brooke, Stephen, *Labour's War: The Labour Party and the Second World War*, New York: Oxford University Press, 1992.

Brown, David, *The Road to Oran: Anglo-French Naval Relations, September 1939–July 1940*, London: Routledge, 2004.

Bullock, Alan, *Hitler and Stalin: Parallel Lives*, New York: Vintage, 1993.

Bungay, Stephen, *The Most Dangerous Enemy: A history of the Battle of Britain*, London: Aurum Press, 2015.

Burgwyn, H. James, *Mussolini Warlord: Failed Dreams of Empire, 1940–1943*, New York: Enigma Books, 2012.

Burt, R.A., *British Battleships of World War One*, Annapolis: Naval Institute Press, 2012.

Butler, David Allen Butler, *The First Jihad: Khartoum and the Dawn of Militant Islam*, London: Casemate, 2007.

Butler, David E., *The British General Election of 1951*, London: Macmillan, 1999.

Buttar, Prit, *Collision of Empires: The War on the Eastern Front in 1914*, London: Osprey, 2014.

Caddick-Adams, Peter, *Snow and Steel: The Battle of the Bulge*, New York: Oxford University Press, 2014.

Carr, John, *The Defense and Fall of Greece, 1940–1941*, London: Pen and Sword, 2013.

Carylon, Les, *Gallipoli*, New York: Macmillan, 2003.

Chang, Iris, *The Rape of Nanjing: The Forgotten Holocaust of World War II*, New York: Basic Books, 2012.

Churchill, Randolph, *Winston S. Churchill: The Official Biography*, vol. 1, Hillsdale, Mich.: Hillsdale College Press, 2006.

Clark, Alan, *The Tories: Conservatives and the Nation State, 1922–97*, London: Phoenix Books, 1999.

Clark, Bruce, *Twice a Stranger: How Mass Expulsion Forged Modern Greece and Turkey*, Cambridge, Mass.: Harvard University Press, 2006.

Clark, Christopher, *The Sleepwalkers: How Europe Went to War in 1914*, New York: Harper Perennial, 2014.

Clark, Lloyd, *Anzio: Italy and the Battle for Rome, 1944*, New York: Grove Press, 2007.

Clark, Ronald William, *The Man Who Broke Purple: the life of Colonel William F. Friedman, Who Deciphered the Japanese Code in World War II*, Boston: Little, Brown, 1977.

Clarke, Peter, *The Last Thousand Days of the British Empire: Churchill, Roosevelt and the Birth of Pax Americana*, London: Bloomsbury Press, 2010.

Clavin, Patricia, *Securing the World Economy: The Reinvention of the League of Nations, 1920–1946*, New York: Oxford University Press, 2016.

Coetzee, Frans, *For Party or Country: Nationalism and the Dilemmas of Popular Conservatism in Edwardian England*, New York: Oxford University Press, 1990.

Cohen, Michael J., *Churchill and the Jews*, New York: Frank Cass, 1985.

Coleman, Marie, *The Irish Revolution, 1916–1923*, London: Routledge, 2013.

Combes David and Minnie S. Churchill, *Sir Winston Churchill: His Life and His Paintings*, London: Running Press, 2004.

Connaughton, Richard, *MacArthur and Defeat in the Philippines*, New York: Overlook Books, 2001.

Cook, Chris, *The Age of Alignment: Electoral Politics in Britain, 1922–1929*, London: Palgrave Macmillan, 2015.

Cooper, John Milton, *Woodrow Wilson: A Biography*, New York: Vintage, 2011.

Corcoran, Donald P., *Freedom to Achieve Freedom: The Irish Free State, 1922–1932*, London: Gill and Macmillan, 2014.

Cosentino, Michele and Ruggero Stanglini, *British and German Battlecruisers: Their Development and Operations*, Annapolis: Naval Institute Press, 2016.

Costello, John, *The Pacific War: 1941–1945*, New York: Harper Perennial, 2009.

Cowles, Virginia, *Winston Churchill: The Era and the Man*, New York: Grosset and Dunlap, 1956.

Cowling, Maurice, *The Impact of Labour, 1920–1924: The Beginning of Modern British Politics*, New York: Cambridge University Press, 1971.

Croker, H.W., *The Yanks Are Coming: A Military History of the United States in World War I*, New York: Regnery Books, 2014.

Cross, Colin, *The Fall of the British Empire, 1918–1968*, London: Putnam Publishers, 1968.

Dalrymple, William, *Return of a King: The Battle for Afghanistan, 1939–42*, New York: Vintage, 2014.

Dangerfield, George, *The Strange Death of Liberal England, 1910–1914*, London: Perigee Trade Publishers, 1961.

Darwin, John, *The End of the British Empire: The Historical Debate*, London: Wiley Blackwell, 2006.

Dauntin, Martin, *Wealth and Welfare: An Economic and Social History of Britain, 1851–1951*, New York: Oxford University Press, 2007.

David, Saul, *Victoria's Wars: The Rise of Empire*, New York: Penguin, 2009.

D'Este, Carlo, *Patton: A Genius for War*, New York: Harper Perennial, 1996.

D'Este, Carlo, *Eisenhower: Allied Supreme Commander*, London: Cassell, 2004.

D'Este, Carlo, *Bitter Victors: The Battle for Sicily*, London: Arun Press, 2008.

D'Este, Carlo, *Fatal Decision: Anzio and the Battle for Rome*, New York: Harper Perennial, 2008.

Dietrich, John, *The Morgenthau Plan: Soviet Influence on American Postwar Policy*, New York: Algora Publishing, 2003.

Dimbleby, Jonathan, *The Battle of the Atlantic: How the Allies Won the War*, New York: Viking, 2015.

Dobbs, Michael, *Six Months in 1945: FDR, Stalin, Churchill and Truman from World War to Cold War*, New York: Random House, 2013.

Dobson, Alan P., *U.S. Wartime Aid to Britain, 1940–1946*, London: Croom Helm, 1986.

Dull, Paul S., *A Battle History of the Japanese Navy, 1941–1945*, Annapolis: Naval Institute Press, 2007.

Dutton, David, *A History of the Liberal Party since 1900*, London: Palgrave Macmillan, 2013.

Dwyer, T. Ryler, *Big Fellow, Long Fellow: A Joint Biography of Collins and De Valera*, New York: St. Martin's Press, 2006.

Ellis, Frank, *Barbarossa 1941: Reframing Hitler's Invasion of Stalin's Soviet Empire*, Topeka: University of Kansas Press, 2015.

Ellis, John, *World War II: The Essential Facts and Figures for all the Combatants*, New York: Facts on File, 1993.

Evans, Richard, *The Coming of the Third Reich*, New York: Penguin, 2005.

Ewer, Peter, *Forgotten Anzacs: The Campaign in Greece, 1941*, London: Scribe Publications, 2010.

Faber, David, *Munich 1938: Appeasement and World War II*, New York: Simon and Schuster, 2010.

Fanning, Richard, *Peace and Disarmament: Naval Rivalry and Arms Control, 1922–1933*, Lexington: University Press of Kentucky, 1994.

Farago, Ladislas, *Patton: Ordeal and Triumph*, New York: Westholme, 2005.

Farrell, Brian P., *The Defense and Fall of Singapore, 1942*, London: Tempus, 2006.

Farwell, Byron, *Queen Victoria's Little Wars*, New York: W.W. Norton, 1985.

Farwell, Byron, *The Armies of the Raj: From the Great Indian Mutiny to Independence, 1856–1947*, New York: W.W. Norton, 1991.

Farwell, Byron, *The Great Boer War*, London: Pen and Sword, 2009.

Faulker, Marcus, *The Great War at Sea: A Naval Atlas, 1914–1919*, Annapolis: Naval Institute Press, 2015.

Feis, Herbert, *Churchill-Roosevelt-Stalin: The War They Waged and the Peace They Sought*, Princeton, N.J.: Princeton University Press, 1966.

Fenby, Jonathan, *Chiang Kai-Shek: China's Generalissimo and the Nation He Lost*, New York: Da Capo, 2005.

Ferguson, Niall, *The Pity of War: Explaining World War I*, New York: Basic Books, 2000.

Field, Frank, ed., *Attlee's Great Contemporaries: The Politics of Character*, New York: Continuum, 2009.

Figes, Orlando, *A People's Tragedy: The Russian Revolution: 1891–1924*, New York: Penguin, 1998.

Fink, Carole K., *The Cold War: An International History*, Boulder, Colo.: Westview Press, 2013.

Fleming, Thomas, *The Illusion of Victory: America in World War I*, New York: Basic Books, 2004.

Fogelsong, David S., *America's Secret War against Bolshevism: U.S. Intervention in the Russian Civil War, 1917–1920*, Chapel Hill: University of North Carolina Press, 1995.

Frank, Richard B., *Guadalcanal: The Definitive Account of the Landmark Battle*, New York: Penguin, 1992.

Frank, Richard B., *Downfall: The End of the Imperial Japanese Empire*, New York: Penguin, 2001.

Fraser, David, *Allanbrooke*, London: Arrow Books, 1983.

Friedman, Isiah, *British Miscalculations: The Rise of Muslim Nationalism, 1918–1925*, New York: Transaction Publishers, 2012.

Friedman, Norman, *Fighting the Great War at Sea: Strategy, Tactics and Technology*, Annapolis: Naval Institute Press, 2014.

Frieser, Karl Heinz, *The Blitzkrieg Legend: The 1940 Campaign in the West*, Annapolis: Naval Institute Press, 2013.

Fromkin, David, *Europe's Last Summer: Who Started the Great War in 1914?*, New York: Vintage, 2005.

Fromkin, David, *A Peace to End all Peace: The Fall of the Ottoman Empire and the Creation of the Modern Middle East*, New York: Henry Holt, 2009.

Gaddis, John Lewis, *The United States and the Origins of the Cold War, 1941–1947*, New York: Columbia University Press, 2000.

Gaddis, John Lewis, *The Cold War: A New History*, New York: Penguin, 2006.

Gassend, Jean Loup, *Anatomy of a Battle: The Allied Liberation of the French Riviera*, Atglen, Penn.: Schiffer Publishing, 2014.

Gerolymatos, Andre, *Red Acropolis, Black Terror: The Greek Civil War and the Origins of the Soviet-American Rivalry, 1943–1949*, New York: Basic Books, 2004.

Gibbons, Ivan, *The British Labour Party and the Establishment of the Irish Free State, 1918–1924*, New York: Palgrave Macmillan, 2015.

Gilbert, Martin, *Churchill: A Life*, New York: Henry Holt, 1992.

Gilbert, Martin, *Churchill and America*, New York: Free Press, 2005.

Gilbert, Martin, *Winston S. Churchill: The Official Biography*, vols 2–8, Hillsdale, Mich.: Hillsdale College Press, 2007–13.

Gillon, Steven M., *Pearl Harbor: FDR Leads the Nation into War*, New York: Basic Books, 2012.

Goldman, Emily O., *Sunken Treaties: Naval Arms Control between the Wars*, University Park: Pennsylvania State University, 1994.

Goldrick, James, *Before Jutland: The Naval War in Northern European Waters, August 1914–Febraury 1915*, Annapolis: Naval Institute Press, 2015.

Goldstein, Erik and John Maurer, eds, *The Washington Conference, 1921–1922: Naval Rivalry, East Asian Stability and the Road to Pearl Harbor*, London: Routledge, 1995.

Goldstein, Erik and Igor Luks, *The Munich Crisis: Prelude to World War II*, London: Routledge, 1999.

Gooch, John, *Mussolini and His Generals: The Armed Forces and Fascist Foreign Policy, 1922–1940*, New York: Cambridge Military Histories, 2007.

Gordon, John, *Fighting for MacArthur: The Navy and Marine Corps' Desperate Defense of the Philippines*, Annapolis: Naval Institute Press, 2011.

Graebner, Norman A. and Edward Bennett, *The Versailles Treaty and the Legacy: The Failure of the Wilsonian Vision*, New York: Cambridge University Press, 2014.

Green, Dominic, *Three Empires on the Nile: The Victorian Jihad, 1869–1899*, New York: Free Press, 2007.

Green, E.E.H., *The Crisis of Conservatism: The Politics, Economics and Ideology of the Conservative Party, 1880–1914*, London: Routledge, 1996.

Gustavsson, Hakan, *The Sino-Japanese War, 1937–1945: The Longest Struggle*, New York: Fonthill Media, 2016.

Haar, Geirr H., *The German Invasion of Norway: April 1940*, Annapolis, Maryland: Naval Institute Press, 2012.

Hajari, Nisid, *Midnight's Furies: The Deadly Legacy of India's Partition*, New York: Houghton and Mifflin, 2015.

Hamilton, Nigel, *Monty*, 3 vols, New York: McGraw-Hill, 1981, 1981, 1984, 1986.

Hamilton, Nigel, *The Mantle of Command: FDR at War, 1941–1942*, New York: Houghton Mifflin, 2014.

Hamilton, Nigel, *Commander in Chief: Franklin D. Roosevelt's Battle with Churchill, 1943*, New York: Houghton Mifflin, 2016.

Hammell, Eric, *How America Saved the World: The Untold Story of U.S. Preparedness between the World Wars*, New York: Zenith Press, 2009.

Hammond, Byrn, *El Alamein: The Battle that Turned the Tide of the Second World War*, London: Osprey, 2012.

Harbutt, Fraser J., *Yalta 1945: Europe and America at the Crossroads*, New York: Cambridge University Press, 2010.

Hargreaves, Richard, *Blitzkrieg Unleashed: The German Invasion of Poland, 1939*, Mechanicsburg, Penn.: Stackpole Books, 2009.

Harris, Brayton, *Admiral Nimitz: The Commander of the Pacific Ocean Theater*, New York: St. Martin's Press, 2012.

Harrison, Shirley, *Sylvia Pankhurst: A Crusading Life, 1882–1960*, London: Aurum Press, 2004.

Harrod, J.E. and John Rodgaard, *Turning the Tide: The Battles of Coral Sea and Midway*, Plymouth: Plymouth University Press, 2016.

Hart, Peter, *The Great War: A Combat History of the First World War*, New York: Oxford University Press, 2013.

Hart, Peter, *The Somme: The Darkest Hour on the Western Front*, London: Pegasus, 2016.

Hart, Peter and Nigel Steel, *Jutland 1916: Death in the Grey Waters*, London: Cassell, 2007.

Hastings, Max, *Overlord: D-Day and the Battle for Normandy*, New York: Vintage, 2006.

Hastings, Max, *Retribution: The Battle for Japan, 1944–45*, New York: Vintage, 2009.

Hastings, Max, *Winston's War: Churchill, 1940–1945*, New York: Vintage, 2011.

Hay, James Roy, ed., *The Origins of the Liberal Welfare Reforms, 1906–14*, London: Palgrave Macmillan, 1983.

Heiferman, Ronald, *The Cairo Conference of 1943: Roosevelt, Churchill, Chiang Kai-Shek and Madame Chiang*, New York: McFarland, 2011.

Heppell, Timothy, *The Tories: From Winston Churchill to David Cameron*, London: Bloomsbury Academic, 2014.

Herring, George C., *Aid to Russia, 1941–1946: Strategy, Diplomacy and the Origins of the Cold War*, New York: Columbia University Press, 1973.

Herwig, Holger H., *The Marne 1914: The Opening of World War I and the Battle that Changed It*, New York: Random House, 2011.

Hibbert, Christopher, *Mussolini: The Rise and Fall of Il Duce*, New York: St. Martin's Griffin, 2008.

Hickson, Kevin, *The Political Thought of the Conservative Party since 1945*, New York: Palgrave Macmillan, 2005.

Hinsley, F.H. and Alan Stripp, eds, *Codebreakers: The Inside Story of Bletchley Park*, New York: Oxford University Press, 2001.

Hittle, J.B.E., *Michael Collins and the Anglo-Irish War: Britain's Counterinsurgency Failure*, Washington D.C.: Potomac Books, 2011.

Holland, James, *The Battle of Britain: Five Months That Changed History, May–October 1940*, New York: St. Martin's Griffin, 2012.

Holmes, Richard, *In the Footsteps of Churchill: A Study in Character*, New York: Perseus, 2006.

Hootan, E.R., *The Great Tumult: The Chinese Civil War, 1936–1949*, Washington D.C.: Brassey's, 1991.

Hopkins, W.P., *The Pacific War: The Strategy, Politics and Players that Won the War*, London: Zenith Press, 2009.

Hopkirk, Peter, *The Great Game: The Struggle for Empire in Central Asia*, New York: Kondasha Press, 1992.

Horne, Alistair, *To Lose a Battle: France 1940*, New York: Penguin, 2007.

Hosken, Dieter, *V-Missiles of the Third Reich: The V-1 and V-2*, London: Monogram Aviation Publications, 1994.

Howe, Anthony, *Free Trade and Liberal England, 1846–1946*, Oxford: Clarendon Press, 1998.

Howlett, Peter, *Fighting with Figures: Statistical Digest of the Second World War*, London: Stationery Office, 1995.

Hughes, Tony and John Costello, *The Battle of the Atlantic*, New York: Dial Press, 1972.

Ireland, Bernard, *The Battle of the Atlantic*, Annapolis, Maryland: Naval Institute Press, 2003.

Irving, David, *The War between the Generals: Inside the Allied High Command*, London: Congdon and Lattes, 1981.

Irving, David, *The Morgenthau Plan, 1944–45*, London: Focal Point Publications, 2010.

Jackson, John, *Solving Enigma's Secrets: The Official History of Bletchley Park's Hut 6*, London: Book Tower Publishing, 2014.

Jackson, Julian, *France: The Dark Years, 1940–1944*, New York: Oxford University Press, 2003.

Jackson, Julian, *The Fall of France: The Nazi Invasion of 1940*, New York: Oxford University Press, 2004.

Jacobs, Peter, *Fortress Island Malta: Defense and Re-Supply During the Siege*, London: Pen and Sword, 2016.

James, Lawrence, *The Raj: The Making and Unmaking of British India*, New York: St. Martin's Griffin, 2000.

Jenkins, Roy, *The British Liberal Tradition: From Gladstone through to Young Churchill, Asquith and Lloyd George*, Toronto: University of Toronto Press, 2001.

Jones, Nigel, *Countdown to Valkyrie: The July Plot to Assassinate Hitler*, London: Frontline Books, 2008.

Jordan, Anthony J., *Churchill: A Founder of Modern Ireland*, London: Westport Books, 1995.

Jordan, John, *Warships after Washington: The Development of the Five Major Fleets, 1922–1930*, Annapolis: Naval Institute Press, 2015.

Jordan, Jonathan W., *American Warlords: How Roosevelt's High Command Led America to Victory in World War II*, New York: Penguin, 2015.

Judd, Dennis and Keith Surridge, *The Boer War: A History*, London: I.B. Tauris, 2013.

Kaiser, David, *No End Save Victory: how FDR Led the Nation into War*, New York: Basic Books, 2014.

Keegan, John, *Six Armies in Normandy: From D-Day to the Liberation of Paris*, New York: Penguin, 1994.

Keegan, John, *The First World War*, New York: Vintage, 2000.

Keeney, L. Douglas, *The Eleventh Hour: How Great Britain, the Soviet Union and the U.S. Brokered the Unlikely Deal That Won the War*, New York: Wiley, 2015.

Kelly, Cynthia C., ed., *The Manhattan Project: The Birth of the Atomic Bomb in the Words of Its Creators, Eyewitnesses and Historians*, New York: Black Dog and Leventhal, 2009.

Kersaudy, François, *Norway 1940*, Lincoln, Neb.: Bison Books, 1998.

Kershaw, Ian, *Hitler: A Biography*, New York: W.W. Norton, 2010.

Keynes, John Maynard, *The General Theory of Employment, Interest and Money*, New York: Harcourt, Brace and the World, 1965.

Khan, Yasmin, *The Great Partition: The Making of India and Pakistan*, New Haven, Conn.: Yale University Press, 2008.

Khlevniuk, Oleg V. and Nora Seligman Favorov, *Stalin: A New Biography of a Dictator*, New Haven, Conn.: Yale University Press, 2015.

Kimball, Warren F., *The Most Unsordid Act: Lend-Lease, 1939–1946*, Baltimore: University of Johns Hopkins Press, 1969.

Kimball, Warren F., *Forged in War: Roosevelt, Churchill and the Second World War*, New York: William Morrow, 1997.

Kindleberger, Charles P., *The World in Depression, 1929–1939*, Berkeley: University of California Press, 2013.

King, Benjamin and Timothy Kutta, *Impact: The History of Germany's V-Weapons in World War II*, New York: Da Capo Press, 2009.

Kitching, Carolyn J., *Britain and the Geneva Disarmament Conference*, New York: Palgrave Macmillan, 2013.

Knock, Thomas J., *To End All Wars: Woodrow Wilson and the Quest for a New World Order*, Princeton, N.J.: Princeton University Press, 1995.

Knox, McGregor, *Hitler's Italian Allies: Royal Armed Forces, Fascist Regime and the War of 1940–1943*, New York: Cambridge University Press, 2000.

Kyvig, David E., *Daily Life in the United States, 1920–1940: How Americans Lived Through the Roaring Twenties and Great Depression*, New York: Ivan R. Dee, 2004.

Lacouture, Jean, *De Gaulle*, New York: Hutchinson, 1970.

LaFeber, Walter, *America, Russia and the Cold War, 1945–1990*, Ithaca, N.Y.: Cornell University Press, 1991.

Lambert, Nicholas A., *Sir John Fisher's Naval Revolution*, Columbia: University of South Carolina Press, 2001.

Larrabee, Eric, *Commander in Chief: Franklin D. Roosevelt, His Lieutenants and Their War*, New York: HarperCollins, 1982.

Lash, Joseph P., *Roosevelt and Churchill, 1939–1945: The Relations that Saved the West*, New York: W.W. Norton, 1976.

Leckie, Robert, *Challenge for the Pacific: Guadalcanal, The Turning Point for the War*, New York: Bantam, 2010.

Leffler, Melvyn P. and David S. Painter, eds, *The Origins of the Cold War: An International History*, London: Routledge, 2005.

Lewin, Ronald, *The American Magic: Codes, Ciphers and the Defeat of Japan*, New York: Farrar, Straus and Giroux, 1982.

Li, Peter, *Japanese War Crimes*, New York: Transaction Books, 2003.

Lieven, Dominic, *The End of Tsarist Russia: The March to World War I and Revolution*, New York: Viking, 2015.

Lincoln, W. Bruce, *Red Victory: A History of the Russian Civil War*, New York: Simon and Schuster, 1989.

Lloyd, Nick, *The Amritsar Massacre: The Untold Story of One Fateful Day*, London: I.B. Tauris, 2011.

Lord, Walter, *Day of Infamy: The Classic Account of the Bombing of Pearl Harbor*, New York: Henry Holt, 2001.

Lord, Walter, *The Miracle of Dunkirk*, New York: Viking, 2012.

Lovell, Mary S., *The Churchills in Love and War*, New York: W.W. Norton, 2012.

Lukacs, John, *Five Days in London: May 1940*, New Haven, Conn.: Yale University Press, 1999.

Lunde, Henrik O., *Hitler's Preemptive War: The Battle for Norway, 1940*, London: Casemate, 2009.

Lyman, Robert, *Iraq 1941: The Battles for Basra, Habbaniya, Falluja and Baghdad*, London: Osprey Books, 2006.

Macmillan, Margaret, *Paris 1919: Six Months that Changed the World*, New York: Random House, 2003.

Macmillan, Margaret, *The War That Ended Peace: the Road to 1914*, New York: Random House, 2014.

Magnus, Philip Montefiore, *Kitchener: Portrait of an Imperialist*, New York: Dutton, 1959.

Maiolo, Joseph, *Cry Havoc: How the Arms Race Drove the World to War, 1931–1941*, New York: Basic Books, 2012.

Mallett, Robert, *Mussolini and the Origins of the Second World War, 1933–1940*, New York: Palgrave Macmillan, 2003.

Manchester, William, *The Last Lion: Winston Spencer Churchill, 1874–1922*, New York: Delta Books, 1983.

Manchester, William, *The Last Lion: Winston Spencer Churchill, 1922–1940*, New York: Delta Books, 1988.

Manchester, William, *American Caesar: Douglas MacArthur, 1880–1962*, New York: Back Bay Press, 2008.

Manchester, William and Paul Reid, *The Last Lion: Winston Spencer Churchill, 1940–1965*, New York: Bantam Books, 2012.

Marquand, David, *Ramsay MacDonald: A Biography*, London: Metro Books, 1997.

Massie, Robert K., *Dreadnought: Britain, Germany and the Coming of the Great War*, New York: Ballantine Books, 1992.

Massie, Robert K., *Castles of Steel: Britain, Germany and the Winning of the Great War at Sea*, New York: Ballantine Books, 2004.

Mauer, John and Christopher Bell, eds, *At the Crossroads between Peace and War: The London Naval Conference of 1930*, Annapolis: Naval Institute Press, 2014.

Mayer, Frank A., *The Opposition Years: Winston S. Churchill and the Conservative Party, 1945–1951*, Washington D.C.: American University Studies, 1992.

Mayhall, Laura E. Nym, *The Militant Suffrage Movement: Citizenship and Resistance in Britain, 1860–1930*, New York: Oxford University Press, 2003.

McCallum, Ronald, *Public Opinion and the Last Peace*, Oxford: Oxford University Press, 1944.

McCallum, Ronald and Alison Readman, *The British General Election of 1945*, London: Cass, 1964.

McCarthy, Chris, *Passchendaele: The Day by Day Account*, London: Arms and Armour, 1996.

McIntyre, W. David, *British Decolonization, 1946–1997: Why and How did the British Empire Fall?* London: Palgrave, 1998.

McKay, Sinclair, *The Secret Life of Bletchley Park*, London: Aurum Press, 2011.

McLynn, Frank, *The Burma Campaign: Disaster into Triumph, 1942–1945*, New Haven, Conn.: Yale University Press, 2011.

McMeekin, Sean, *July 1914: Countdown to War*, New York: Basic Books, 2014.

McMeekin, Sean, *The Ottoman Endgame: War, Revolution and the Making of the Modern Middle East, 1908–1923*, New York: Penguin, 2015.

McNab, Chris, *Battle Story: Cambrai, 1917*, London: History Press, 2012.

McWilliams, James and R. James Steel, *Amiens: Dawn of Victory*, London: Dundum, 2001.

Meacham, Jon, *Franklin and Winston: An Intimate Portrait of an Epic Friendship*, New York: Random House, 2004.

Meredith, Martin, *Diamonds, Gold and War: The British, the Boers and the Making of South Africa*, New York: Public Affairs, 2009.

Meyer, G.J., *A World Undone: The Story of the Great War, 1914–1918*, New York: Delacorte Press, 2007.

Meyer, Karl Ernest, *The Dust of Empire: The Race for Mastery of the Asian Heartland*, New York: Public Affairs, 2004.

Meyer, Karl Ernest and Shareen Blair Brysac, *The Tournament of Shadows: The Great Game and the Race for Empire in Central Asia*, New York: Basic Books, 2006.

Miller, Nathan, *The War at Sea: A Naval History of World War II*, New York: Scribner's, 1995.

Miller, Nathan, *New World Coming: The 1920s and the Making of Modern America*, New York: Da Capo Press, 2004.

Milner, Marc, *The Battle of the Atlantic*, London: History Press, 2011.

Miscamble, Wilson D., *The Most Controversial Decision: Truman, the Atomic Bomb and the Defeat of Japan*, New York: Cambridge University Press, 2011.

Mitcham, Samuel, *Rommel's Greatest Victory: The Desert Fox and the Fall of Tobruk, Spring 1942*, San Francisco: Presidio Press, 2001.

Mitcham, Samuel W. and Friedrich von Stauffenberg, *The Battle of Sicily: How the Allies Lost Their Chance for Total Victory*, Mechanicsburg, Penn.: Stackpole Books, 2007.

Mitter, Rana, *China's War with Japan, 1937–1945*, New York: Penguin, 2014.

Montfiore, Simon Sebag, *Stalin: The Court of the Red Tsar*, New York: Vintage, 2005.

Moore, Aaron, *Constructing East Asia: Technology, Ideology and Empire in Japan's Wartime Era, 1931–1945*, Palo Alto, Calif.: Stanford University Press, 2015.

Moore, Lucy, *Anything Goes: A Biography of the Roaring Twenties*, New York: Overlook Press, 2010.

Moorehead, Alan, *Gallipoli*, New York: Harper, 2002.

Morgan, Kevin, *Ramsay MacDonald*, London: Haus Publishing, 2006.

Morgan, Ted, *Churchill: Young Man in a Hurry, 1874–1915*, New York: Simon and Schuster, 1982.

Morris, Benny, *1948: A History of the First Arab-Israeli War*, New Haven, Conn.: Yale University Press, 2009.

Morris, Jan, *Fisher's Face: Getting to Know the Admiral*, New York: Random House, 1995.

Morrison, Samuel W., *Defenders of Fortress Europe: the Untold Story of the German Officers during the Allied Invasion*, Washington D.C.: Potomac Books, 2009.

Moser, John E., *The Global Great Depression and the Coming of World War II*, London: Routledge, 2015.

Myers, E.C.F., *Greek Entanglement*, London: Sutton Publishing, 1985.

Myers, Ramon H. and Mark R. Peattie, eds, *The Japanese Colonial Empire*, Princeton, N.J.: Princeton University Press, 1987.

Napler, Stephen, *The Armoured Campaign in Normandy, June–August 1944*, London: Casemate, 2015.

Neiberg, Michael, *Potsdam: The End of World War II and the Remaking of Europe*, New York: Basic Books, 2015.

Neillands, Robin, *The Dervish Wars: Gordon and Kitchener in the Sudan, 1880–98*, London: John Murray, 1996.

Neillands, Robin, *The Dieppe Raid: The Story of the Disastrous 1942 Expedition*, Bloomington: University of Indian Press, 2005.

Newton, Douglas, *The Darkest Days: The Truth behind Britain's Rush to War*, London: Verso Books, 2014.

Nichols, H.G., *The British General Election of 1950*, London: Macmillan, 1951.

Nish, Ian, *The Anglo-Japanese Alliance: The Diplomacy of Two Island Empires, 1894–1907*, London: Athlone Press, 1966.

Nish, Ian, *Alliance in Decline: A Study of Anglo-Japanese Relations, 1908–1923*, London: Bloomsbury Academic, 2013.

O'Brien, Phillips, *The Anglo-Japanese Alliance, 1902–1922*, London: Routledge, 2003.

O'Connor, Ulick, *Michael Collins and the Troubles: The Struggle for Irish Freedom, 1912–1922*, New York: W.W. Norton, 1996.

O'Hara, Vincent, *Torch: North Africa and the Allied Path to Victory*, Annapolis, Maryland: Naval Institute Press, 2015.

Overy, Richard, *The Twilight Years: The Paradox of Britain Between the Wars*, New York: Penguin, 2010.

Packer, Ian, *Liberal Government and Politics, 1905–15*, London: Palgrave Macmillan, 2006.

Pakenham, Thomas, *The Boer War*, New York: W.W. Norton, 1979.

Parry, Jonathan, *The Rise and Fall of Liberal Government in Victorian Britain*, New Haven, Conn.: Yale University Press, 1996.

Parshalls, Jonathan and Anthony Tully, *Shattered Sword: The Untold Story of the Battle of Midway*, Washington D.C.: Potomac Books, 2007.

Paterson, Michael, *A Brief History of Life in Victorian Britain: A Social Life of Queen Victoria*, London: Robinson, 2008.

Paul, Allen, *Katyn: Stalin's Massacre and the Triumph of Truth*, Chicago: Northern Illinois University Press, 2010.

Paxton, Robert O., *Vichy France: Old Guard and New Order, 1940–1944*, New York: Columbia University Press, 2001.

Paxton, Robert O., *The Anatomy of Fascism*, New York: Vintage, 2005.

Payne, Stanley G., *A History of Fascism, 1914–1945*, Madison: University of Wisconsin Press, 1995.

Pedersen, Susan, *The Guardians: The League of Nations and the Crisis of Empire*, New York: Oxford University Press, 2015.

Pederson, William D., *The FDR Years*, New York: Facts on File, 2006.

Pipes, Richard, *The Russian Revolution*, New York: Vintage, 1991.

Pokhy, S.M., *Yalta: The Price of Peace*, New York: Penguin, 2011.

Pollack, John, *Kitchener*, London: Constable, 2001.

Powaski, Ronald E., *Toward an Entangling Alliance: American Isolationism, Internationalism and Europe, 1901–1950*, Westport, Conn.: Greenwood Press, 1991.

Prange, Gordon W. and Donald M. Goldstein, *At Dawn We Slept: The Untold Story of Pearl Harbor*, New York: Penguin, 1982.

Pulling, Henry, *Churchill*, London: Wordsworth Military Library, 1999.

Purnell, Sonia, *Clementine*, New York: Viking, 2015.

Rayfield, Donald, *Stalin and his Henchmen: The Tyrant and Those Who Killed for Him*, New York: Random House, 2005.

Reardon, Terry, *Winston Churchill and Mackenzie King: So Similar, So Different*, Toronto: Dundern Press, 2012.

Rees, Laurence, *Horror in the Far East: Japan and the Atrocities of World War II*, New York: Da Capo, 2002.

Reynolds, David, *The Long Shadow: The Legacies of the Great War in the Twentieth Century*, New York: W.W. Norton, 2015.

Rhodes, Richard, *The Making of the Atomic Bomb*, New York: Simon and Schuster, 2012.

Richard, D.S., *The Savage Frontier: A History of the Anglo-Afghan Wars*, New York: Pan Books, 2002.

Richie, Alexander, *Warsaw 1944: Hitler, Himmler and the Warsaw Rising*, New York: Farrar, Straus and Giroux, 2013.

Richter, Heinz, *British Intervention in Greece: From Varkiza to Civil War*, London: Merlin Press, 1985.

Riddell, Neil, *Labour In Crisis: The Second Labour Government, 1929–31*, Manchester: Manchester University Press, 1999.

Ridley, Jasper, *Mussolini: A Biography*, New York: Cooper Square Press, 2000.

Robson, Brian, *The Road to Kabul: The Second Afghan War 1878–1881*, London: Arms and Armour, 1986.

Rose, Norman, *Churchill: An Unruly Life*, London: I.B. Tauris, 2009.

Rose, Sonya O., *Which People's War?: National Identity and Citizenship in Wartime Britain, 1939–1945*, New York: Oxford University Press, 2004.

Rothermund, Deitmar, *The Global Impact of the Great Depression, 1929–1939*, London: Routledge, 1996.

Rowntree, B. Sebum, *Poverty: A Study of Town Life*, London: Macmillan, 1902.

Ruggiero, John, *Hitler's Enabler: Neville Chamberlain and the Origins of the Second World War*, New York: Praeger, 2015.

Rusbridger, James, *Betrayal at Pearl Harbor: How Churchill Lured Roosevelt into World War II*, New York: Summit Books, 1991.

Russell, A.K., *The Liberal Landslide: The General Election of 1906*, London: David and Charles, 1973.

Ryan, Cornelius, *The Longest Day: The Classic Epic of D-Day*, New York: Simon and Schuster, 1994.

Ryan, Cornelius, *A Bridge Too Far: The Classic History of the Greatest Battle of World War II*, New York: Simon and Schuster, 1995.

Sainsbury, Keith, *The Turning Point: Roosevelt, Churchill, Stalin and Chiang Kai-Shek, 1943: The Moscow, Cairo and Teheran Conferences*, New York: Oxford University Press, 1986.

Sanders, Ronald, *The High Walls of Jerusalem: A History of the Balfour Declaration and the Birth of the British Mandate for Palestine*, New York: Holt, Rinehart and Winston, 1984.

Schneer, Jonathan, *The Balfour Declaration: The Origins of the Arab-Israeli Conflict*, New York: Random House, 2010.

Schneer, Jonathan, *Ministers at War: Winston Churchill and His War Cabinet*, New York: Basic Books, 2014.

Schoenfeld, Maxwell Philip, *The War Ministry of Winston Churchill*, Ames: Iowa State University Press, 1972.

Scott, George, *The Rise and Fall of the League of Nations*, New York: Macmillan, 1974.

Seale, G.R., *The Liberal Party: Triumph and Disintegration, 1886–1929*, London: Palgrave Macmillan, 2001.

Segev, Tom, *One Palestine, Complete: Jews and Arabs under the British Mandate*, New York: Picador, 2001.

Self, Robert, *Neville Chamberlain: A Biography*, London: Routledge, 2009.

Senior, Ian, *Invasion 1914: The Schlieffen Plan to the Battle of the Marne*, London: Osprey, 2007.

Severance, John B., *Winston Churchill: Soldier, Statesman, Artist*, New York: Clarion Books, 1996.

Shannon, Richard, *The Age of Salisbury, 1881–1902: Unionism and Empire*, London: Longman, 1996.

Shen, Peijian, *The Age of Appeasement: The Evolution of British Foreign Policy in the 1930s*, London: Alan Sutton, 2000.

Shirer, William, *The Rise and Fall of the Third Reich: A History of Nazi Germany*, New York: Simon and Shuster, 2011.

Showell, Jak P. Mallman, *Hitler's Navy: A Reference Guide to the Kriegsmarine, 1935–1945*, Annapolis: Naval Institute Press, 2009.

Silverfarb, David, *The Twilight of British Ascendancy in the Middle East: A Case Study of Iraq, 1941–1950*, New York: St. Martin's Press, 1994.

Simon, Reeva Spector, *Iraq between the Two World Wars*, New York: Columbia University Press, 2004.

Smithers, A.J., *Cambrai: The First Great Tank Battle*, London: Pen and Sword, 2014.

Smele, Jonathan, *The 'Russian' Civil Wars, 1916–1926: Ten Years That Shook the World*, New York: Oxford University Press, 2016.

Snook, Mike, *Into the Jaws of Death: British Military Blunders, 1879–1900*, Annapolis, Maryland: Naval Institute Press, 2007.

Snook, Mike, *Beyond the Reach of Empire: Wolseley's Failed Campaign to Save Gordon and Khartoum*, London: Frontline Books, 2014.

Soames, Mary, *Clementine Churchill: The Biography of a Marriage*, New York: Mariner Books, 2003.

Soundhaus, Lawrence, *The Great War at Sea: A Naval History of the First World War*, New York: Cambridge University Press, 2014.

Spector, Ronald H., *Eagle Against the Sun: The American War with Japan*, New York: Vintage Books, 1985.

Spence, Jonathan, *Mao Zedong: A Life*, New York: Penguin, 2006.

Spiers, Edward M., ed., *Sudan: The Reconquest Reappraised*, London: Frank Cass, 1999.

Stafford, David, *Roosevelt and Churchill: Men of Secrets*, New York: Overlook Press, 2011.

Stahel, David, *Operation Barbarossa and Germany's Defeat in the East*, New York: Cambridge University Press, 1991.

Stargardt, Nicolas, *The German War: A Nation Under Arms, 1939–45*, New York: Basic Books, 2015.

Stedman, Andrew David, *Alternative to Appeasement: Neville Chamberlain and Hitler's Germany*, London: I.B. Tauris, 2015.

Stewart, Jules, *On Afghanistan's Plains: The Story of Britain's Afghan Wars*, London: I.B. Tauris, 2011.

Stille, Mark, *The Japanese Imperial Navy in the Pacific War*, London: Osprey, 2014.

Stinnett, Robert, *Day of Deceit: The Truth about FDR and Pearl Harbor*, New York: Free Press, 2001.

Stoler, Mark A., *Allies and Adversaries: The Joint Chiefs of Staff, the Grand Alliance and U.S. Strategy in World War II*, Chapel Hill: University of North Carolina Press, 2002.

Stone, David R., *The Russian Army in the Great War: The Eastern Front, 1914–1917*, Topeka: University Press of Kansas, 2015.

Striner, Richard, *A Burden Too Great to Bear: Woodrow Wilson and World War I*, New York: Rowan and Littlefield, 2014.

Symonds, Craig L., *The Battle of Midway*, New York: Oxford University Press, 2013.

Symonds, Nicklaus Thomas, *Atlee: A Life in Politics*, London: I.B. Tauris, 2012.

Szasz, Ferenc Morton, *British Scientists and the Manhattan Project*, London: Palgrave Macmillan, 1992.

Tanaka, Yuki, *Hidden Horrors: Japanese War Crimes in World War II*, Boulder, Colo.: Westview Press, 1996.

Tansman, Alan, ed., *The Culture of Japanese Fascism*, Durham, N.C.: Duke University Press, 2009.

Taylor, A.J.P., *War by Timetable: How the First World War Began*, New York: Endeavor Press, 2013.

Taylor, Frederick, *The Downfall of Money: Germany's Hyperinflation and the Destruction of the Middle Class*, London: Bloomsbury Press, 2015.

Taylor, Jay, *The Generalissmo: Chiang Kai-shek and the Struggle for Modern China*, New York: Belknap Press, 2011.

Taylor, Telford, *Munich: The Price of Peace*, New York: Doubleday, 1979.

Thompson, Julian, *Dunkirk: Retreat to Victory*, London: Arcade Publishing, 2011.

Thompson, Kenneth, *Winston Churchill's World View: Statesmanship and Power*, Baton Rouge: Louisiana State University Press, 1983.

Thompson, W.H., *Assignment: Churchill*, New York: Farrar, Straus and Young, 1955.

Thorpe, Andrew, *The British General Election of 1931*, New York: Oxford University Press, 1991.

Thorpe, Andrew, *A History of the British Labour Party*, New York: Palgrave Macmillan, 2015.

Toll, Ian W., *Pacific Crucible: War at Sea in the Pacific, 1941–42*, New York: W.W. Norton, 2011.

Toll, Ian W., *The Conquering Tide: War in the Pacific, 1942–1944*, New York: W.W. Norton, 2015.

Toland, John, *Adolf Hitler: The Definitive Biography*, New York: Anchor Books, 1992.

Toland, John, *The Rising Sun: The Rise and Fall of the Japanese Empire, 1936–1945*, New York: Modern Library 2003.

Tooze, Adam, *The Deluge: The Great War, America and the Remaking of the Global Order, 1916–1931*, New York: Penguin, 2015.

Toynbee, Arnold, *Acquaintances*, Oxford: Oxford University Press, 1967.

Trachtenberg, Marc, *The Cold War and After: History, Theory and the Logic of International Relations*, Princeton, N.J.: Princeton University Press, 2012.

Tuchman, Barbara, *The Proud Tower: A Portrait of the World before the War, 1890–1914*, New York: Random House, 1996.

Tuchman, Barbara, *The Guns of August*, New York: Ballantine Books, 2004.

Tunzelmann, Alex von, *Indian Summer: The Secret History of the End of an Empire*, New York: Picador, 2008.

Turner, John, *British Politics and the Great War: Coalition and Conflict, 1915–1918*, New Haven, Conn.: Yale University Press, 1992.

Tyng, Sewell, *The Campaign of the Marne*, London: Westholme, 2007.

Ullman, Richard H., *Britain and the Russian Civil War: November 1918–February 1920*, Princeton, N.J.: Princeton University Press, 1968.

Unterberger, Betty Miller, *The United States, Revolutionary Russia and the Rise of Revolutionary Russia*, College Station: Texas A and M University Press, 2000.

Viorst, Milton, *Hostile Allies: FDR and de Gaulle*, New York: Macmillan, 1965.

Warner, Philip, *Passchendaele*, London: Pen and Sword, 2005.

Wasserstein, Bernard, *The British in Palestine: The Mandatory Government and Arab-Jewish Conflict, 1917–1929*, London: Blackwell, 1991.

Weeks, Albert L., *Russia's Life-Saver: Lend-Lease Aid to the U.S.S.R. in World War II*, Boston: Lexington Books, 2010.

Weigley, Russell F., *Eisenhower's Lieutenants: The Campaign of France and Germany, 1944–1945*, Bloomington: University of Indiana Press, 1981.

Weitz, Eric, *The Weimar Republic: Promise and Tragedy*, Princeton University Press, 2012.

Wilbberley, Leonard, *The Life of Winston Churchill*, New York: Farrar, Straus, Giroux, 1965.

Williams, Rhondri, *Defending the Empire: The Conservative Party and British Defense Policy, 1899–1915*, New Haven, Conn.: Yale University Press, 1991.

Williamson, David G., *Poland Betrayed: the Nazi-Soviet Invasion of 1939*, Mechanicsburg, Penn.: Stackpole Books, 2011.

Williamson, Philip, *Stanley Baldwin: Conservative Leadership and National Values*, New York: Cambridge University Press, 2007.

Wilson, A.N., *Victoria: A Life*, New York: Penguin, 2015.

Wilson, Dick, *When Tigers Fight: The Story of the Sino-Japanese War, 1937–1945*, New York: Penguin, 1983.

Wilson, James Mikel, *Churchill and Roosevelt: The Big Sleepover at the White House, Christmas 1941–New Year 1942*, New York: Gatekeeper Press, 2015.

Wilson, Sandra, *The Manchurian Crisis and Japanese Society, 1931–1933*, London: Routledge, 2001.

Wilson, Theodore A., *The First Summit: Roosevelt and Churchill at Placentia Bay, 1941*, Topeka: University Press of Kansas, 1991.

Winton, John, *Ultra at Sea: How Breaking the Nazi Code Affected Allied Naval Strategy during World War II*, New York: Quill, 1990.

Winton, John, *Ultra in the Pacific: How Breaking Japanese Codes & Cyphers Affected Naval Operations against Japan 1941–45*, Annapolis, Maryland: Naval Institute Press, 1994.

Wohlstetter, Roberta, *Pearl Harbor: Warning and Decisions*, Palo Alto, Calif.: Stanford University Press, 1962.

Wolff, Leon, *The Flanders Campaign, Passchendaele 1917*, New York: Penguin, 2001.

Wolpert, Stanley, *Shameful Flight: The Last Years of the British Empire in India*, New York: Oxford University Press, 2009.

Wolz, Nicholas, *From Imperial Splendor to Internment: The German Navy in the First World War*, Annapolis: Naval Institute Press, 2015.

Womack, Tom, *The Dutch Naval Air Force against Japan: The Defense of the Netherlands East Indies, 1941–1942*, New York: McFarland and Company, 2006.

Yeide, Henry, *First to the Rhine: The Sixth Army Group in World War II*, London: Zenith Press, 2009.

Yergin, Daniel, *Shattered Peace: The Origins of the Cold War*, New York: Penguin, 1990.

Yoshiaki, Yoshimi, *Grassroots Fascism: The War Experience of the Japanese People*, New York: Columbia University Press, 2015.

Young, Louise, *Japan's Total Empire: Manchuria and the Culture of Wartime Imperialism*, Berkeley: University of California Press, 1999.

Zeuhlke, Mark, *The Tragedy at Dieppe: Operation Jubilee, August 19, 1942*, London: Douglas and McIntyre, 2014.

Zieger, Robert H., *America's Great War: World War I and the American Experience*, New York: Rowan and Littlefield, 2001.

Zuber, Terence, *Inventing the Schlieffen Plan: German War Planning, 1871–1914*, New York: Oxford University Press, 2015.

Index